There Women in

There We'll Meet Again

A young German girl's diary of the First World War.

By Piete Kuhr, later known as Jo Mihaly

With an introduction and postscript by the
translator, Walter Wright.

First published in Germany 1982
© 1982 F.H. Kerle Verlag GmbH., Freiburg/Br
First published in Great Britain by Walter Wright 1998
© English language translation Walter Wright 1998

ISBN 0 9532633 0 4

Produced by Action Typesetting Limited, Gloucester
Printed in Great Britain.

Contents

	Pages
Acknowledgements	viii
Introduction	ix

1914 *August–December*
Description of family and town. Excitement at outbreak of
war, soon tempered by growing disillusionment. Longing for
peace by Christmas — 1–97

1915 *January–March*
Growth of longing for peace. Sympathy for sufferings of all
nations intensified by experiences with grandmother at
railway station Red Cross Centre. — 99–130

April–June
Celebration of thirteenth birthday. Increasing love of music.
Effects of brother Willi contracting scarlet fever. Blockade
of England. — 130–141

July–September
Visiting wounded soldiers in hospital. Criticism of churches.
Arguments about war. Emotional night after death of friends
dog. Fire at military hospital. — 141–161

October–December
French abandon offensive in the Champagne; beginning of
the end of the war? Uncle Bruno leaves unwanted army boots
and sword, which Piete vows to use later in anti-war dances. — 161–168

1916 *January–March*
Rising cost of living and growing scarcities. First sense
that a soldier likes her because she is a girl. — 169–175

April–June
Fourteenth birthday and feeling of growing up. Battle of
Jutland. Dismay at mother having to give up Berlin music
school. Continuing German victories but at great cost.
Growth of left wing opposition. Despair at seeing no end
to the slaughter. — 175–182

July–September
Enjoyment of nature. Pessimism about never-ending war.
Reluctance to carry on with diary. Grandmother's Red
Cross award. Distress at mother's criticism of Piete's
piano-playing for suspect entertainment of soldiers. Visit
to best friend's new home near Bromberg.   182–198

October–December
More distress at vain battles. Receives from Uncle Bruno a
dead Belgian soldier's helmet. Meets Lieutenant Waldecker.
Becomes interested in courting. Depression at deaths of many
gifted people leads to attempted suicide as sacrifice for peace.
Ballad-singing and story-telling encouraged by school friends. 198–213

1917 *January–March*
Mother attempts to delay brother Willi's call-up by getting
him into high-class Cadet College. Piete meets Waldecker
while skating. Revolution begins in Russia.   215–229

April–June
America declares war on Germany. Piete's fifteenth birthday.
In top class at school with many new friends. Devotion to
new woman teacher.   230–234

July–September
Brother Willi rejected by Cadet College. Visits to new
friends in school holidays. Discussions with mother about
the diary. Talk of mutinies inspired by the Reds. Long walk
with Waldecker and friends.   234–247

October–December
Completion of Revolution in Russia. Discussions with
brother's friend Androwski. More thoughts about Waldecker.
Waldecker killed in air crash. Shattering effect on Piete and
her schoolwork. Peace negotiations with Russia. Piete starts
dancing-lessons.   247–254

1918 *January–March*
President Wilson's Fourteen Points. Brother Willi called up.
Progress with dancing lessons. Spread of strikes against the
war. Piete's confirmation on Palm Sunday.   255–265

April–June
Failed school-leaving certificate. Reluctantly agrees to stay
another year with younger classmates. Talk with Grandma
leading to random selection of Bible text that will be binding
on Piete. Her acceptance of the challenge to work for good
of mankind and for peace. Sudden end to school life.   265–283

July–November
Starts work in home for sick children. Murder of Tsar of
Russia and family. Satisfaction in work with sick children.

Feeling that Germany is finished. Thoughts on what the
outcome will be. Grandmother ill, but determined to
maintain Red Cross Centre. Closing events of the war.
Final visit to prisoner-of-war cemetery.   283–319

Postscript   320

Translator's Notes   324

Acknowledgements

My thanks are due to Anja Ott for her ready agreement to publication of an English translation of her mother's book, to Dr. Margit Wagner, another writer, for her painstaking examination of the translation, and to Stephen Tunnicliffe for help with proof-reading.

For several of the photographs I am indebted again to Anja Ott and for some others to the Schneidemühler Heimatkreis in Cuxhaven. Specific acknowledgements are due to Messrs Cassell for the *Karlsruhe and Bowes Castle* illustration, to the Imperial War Museum for the hospital train and medical dogs illustrations and the cover scene, and to Alfons Kutz for drawings taken from his remarkable hand-written book 'Ein Händedruck Mit Schneidemühl', viz. the map, the street plan and the advertisments for Kleinschmidt's dancing school and Fliegner's café.

I am also grateful to my near neighbours Dr. Malcolm Lambert and his wife Joyce, and to my one-time German teacher Hilary Olszewska, for their continual encouragement and occasional help with translation. Finally, I cannot fail to mention Miles Bailey, Managing Director of Action Typesetting Limited, for his patient attention to detail.

Walter Wright

Introduction

For the last three years or more I have been in love – captivated by a girl who was born in the year 1902, who died in 1989, and whom I first encountered in the summer of 1993.

It all began when, in preparation for a visit to friends in Germany, I was looking for a German book to read in order to 'brush up' the language. What I found (for 10p on a charity book stall) was this diary, which had not been published until 1982, the authoress having found it among her brother's papers after his death. I was very soon gripped by the 12–16 year old girl's account of the events going on around her, their effect on her school and family life, and the rapid change from her initial excited reaction to the war to a deep longing for an end to the suffering of all the nations involved. As early as 10th Sept. 1914 she writes that she no longer regards the war as fine.

She developed two strong ambitions for the future – to become a dancer and a writer – and vowed to use her talents in each of these spheres in the cause of peace and in support for all victims of oppression.

My interest in the diary has been even further increased following the course of her later life, in which she fulfilled both of her ambitions and pursued her expressed aims. Upon Hitler's acquisition of power in 1933 it was necessary, in view of her open opposition to Nazism and the fact that she had married a Jew, to leave Berlin in haste for Switzerland with her husband and a five month old daughter; it is through this daughter, now living in Bavaria, that I have had access to accounts of 'Jo Mihaly's' later life. I suspect that readers of the diary will be as interested as I was to know something of that life, so I have attempted an outline of it in a Postscript, which I may develop further as a sequel to this book.

ix

The young diarist's home town was Schneidemühl, only about 80 miles from what was then the German–Russian frontier, Poland having no existence as a separate state. At the end of the First World War the town narrowly escaped being taken into the Polish Corridor, and after the Second War, when it suffered heavy damage on the final approach of the Russians, it became a part of the newly-constituted Poland under its ancient name of PILA.

This story vividly illustrates the suffering and distress brought upon individuals and families by events beyond their control, and it is my hope that it may contribute, if only in a small way, to international understanding and goodwill. That would be the wish of my friend Piete, who learned early in life not to judge people by the colour of their flag.

Walter Wright October 1997

My mother Jo Mihaly began the writing of a diary on 1st August 1914 on the advice of her mother. She was then 12 years old. It became a war diary; a genuine and moving firsthand report of the first catastrophic war which shook our century, and changed world history with consequences to this day.

Not until sixty years later did my mother find her diary when she was clearing up my late uncle's effects. The simple sketches, the accurate reports and thoughts, have become a moving document of humanity. Unfortunately it has lost none of its topicality...

W.G. Wright's very good, literal translation into English has managed to retain the spontaneity and originality of the young person's lively language.

Anja Ott, daughter of Jo Mihaly, October 1997

1914

'The little woodland birds
Sang such a wonderful refrain;
In the homeland, in the homeland,
There we'll meet again!'

I am called Piete.

I shan't say what my real name is, it is so stupid. Yes I will, though; it is Elfriede, Frieda. (Frieda is the giddy limit!) My brother's name is Willi-Gunther, he is fifteen years old. I am twelve. We live with my grandmother in Schneidemühl in the province of Posen. My mother has a music school in Berlin, the 'Leading School of Music and Drama'. She often visits us. Those are great times.

Today is the 1st of August, 1914. It is very hot. They started to harvest the rye on 25th July, it is almost white. When I came past a field this evening I plucked three ears and fixed them over my bed with a drawing pin.

From today Germany is at war. My mother has advised me to write a diary about the war; she thinks it will be of interest to me when I am older. This is true. When I am fifty or sixty, what I have written as a child will seem strange. But it will be true, because you must not tell lies in a diary.

The Serbs began it. On 28th June, they shot the Austrian Crown Prince Franz Ferdinand and his wife Sophie. The royal couple were travelling by car through the town of Sarajevo, and as they were driving along in fine state and waving, shots were fired from an ambush. No one knows who did it. It says in the newspaper that the whole of Austro-Hungary is in indescribable uproar. In Vienna an ultimatum was drawn up and sent to Serbia but the Serbs have rejected it. Everyone says the Serbs want war in order to maintain their independence and Russia will support them. I once got to know a Russian student in Kolberg, Nikolai Kedrin; my brother Willi-Gunther was very fond of him. Now he too will be involved in the

1

shooting. I asked Willi whether he could imagine this. Willi thought for a moment and said, 'no.'

Austro-Hungary, Germany, Serbia, Russia and France have mobilised. We have no idea what war will be like. There are flags on all the houses in the town, just as if we were engaged in a festival. They are black, white and red.[1]

2nd August 1914

I must now describe the town of Schneidemühl. It has 25,000 inhabitants, three Evangelical Churches, one Lutheran, one Catholic and one Jewish Church and several bridges. There are also a large number of squares with old trees in them. The biggest square is the Neue Markt, a smaller one is called Wilhelmsplatz, another is Alte Markt. Our river is the Küddow; where it is at its narrowest it is called the Zgordalina. That is a Polish name. So you see indeed that Poles live here too – many Poles in fact. The seasonal workers, who come to work on the land, are nearly all Poles.

The Küddow is a little river with many whirlpools and rapids, shallow and covered in vegetation that looks like blue-green hair. It is not navigable. It is most beautiful when the sun goes down, and also in moonlight. I am definitely going to write poems about it – at any rate I will try to.

My mother is visiting us at present. She had wanted to spend her holiday in Sweden, but as the situation was critical she came here. My mother is quite tall and slim, she has bronze-coloured hair and wears unusual clothes. She has high-heeled shoes. She is the most beautiful lady that my brother and I know. We glow with pride when we walk through the streets with her.

It is Sunday today. There is no school. When I woke up I heard Mama and Grandma talking excitedly together on the veranda. I wanted to understand what they were saying, but Marie, our maid, was making so much noise that I couldn't hear. She was scrubbing the floor hard because she had spilt some milk. I ran on to the veranda in my nightie and called out 'What has happened?' Mama, who was drinking coffee and eating a ham roll, said 'In Berlin two Russians have fired on our Crown Prince. He is said to be seriously wounded.' I was flabbergasted. Grandma said, 'People talk so much, you can't believe all they say.' Why shouldn't you believe it? If the Russians declare war on us, they'll fire on the Crown Prince. It's obvious.

When Grandma and I were on our way to church we stopped by the window of the newspaper office where many people were crowding around. There was a paper hanging behind the glass with a statement written in blue pencil –

'The report of the attempt on the life of the German Crown Prince is not true. The Crown Prince is in the best of health.'

'You see!' said Grandma.

Countless people sat and stood in church. The air was hot and stuffy. The minister preached a very fervent sermon, speaking of Germany's exaltation and the fight for justice. I was very cross because I was only just twelve years old and was not a man. What's the use of being a child when there is a war? A child is of no use at all in wartime. You have to be a soldier. Most men enrol of their own free will.

We sang 'A mighty fortress is our God'. Grandma sang in her thin voice which sometimes quavers a bit. I am terribly fond of Grandma. The minister said the Lord's Prayer and ended with 'God give victory to our brave troops'.

'I have lived through this twice before,' said Grandma on the way home. 'It was just the same when the Danish war broke out, and again in 1870. Why can't people live in peace!'

'Will the war last long?' I asked.

Grandma answered that she didn't know and that no one could really tell. But it would certainly be over by Christmas.

'Will we win the war?' I asked.

'We haven't yet lost a war in my lifetime,' said Grandma, 'and we shan't lose this one.'

The street was full of reservists – that is, civilians who want to become soldiers. In front of the old arsenal stood military vehicles packed high with kitbags, underwear, trousers, jackets, caps, boots, ties and overcoats. They were grey. The uniforms used to be blue – at any rate those of our infantry were.

We watched for a while, as more and more uniforms were brought out through the open door. An old man pointed with his stick to a grey military overcoat with grey buttons and said, 'If only I could still wear that!'

Tears came into my eyes, and I drew Grandma away.

In the evening a section of the newly-formed Home Guard came past our house. The window-panes rattled with the tread of the heavy boots and the singing. After supper we all went into the town. The streets were again full of people. Special news-sheets were being handed out and eagerly read by the light of street lamps. They cost five pfennigs. Mama bought one and exclaimed, 'Russia has begun hostilities!' What had happened? The Russians had made an attack on the railway bridge at Eichenried on the railway line between Wreschen and Jarotschin, but had been repulsed. But stronger Russian forces had advanced on Johannisburg.

I can't realise that the war must have started and yet we haven't seen anything of it. I had thought that everything would have changed. But it is quite otherwise. We eat white bread and good meat and go for walks as if nothing had happened.

I feel sad. I would like to be there where the war is, so that I know what it is like. It is not yet a proper war, I think. Or is it? A man said out loud on the street, 'It is all lies that a French airman has dropped bombs on Nürnberg. Berlin is just seeking an excuse to make war on France.' The man was fiercely scolded. A woman shouted in his face, 'You ought to be ashamed of yourself, you're not fit to be a German!'

I'm sitting now by the open window and while I'm gazing at the moon Russian forces are marching on Johannisburg. We live in an old military town; I know just how it is; Russian infantry columns with their rear covered by light artillery.

3rd August 1914

At school the teachers say it is our patriotic duty to stop using foreign words. I didn't know what they meant by this at first, but now I see it – you must no longer say 'adieu' because that is French. It is in order to say 'lebwohl' or 'auf wiedersehen', or 'Grüss Gott' if you like. I must now call Mama 'Mother', but 'Mother' isn't tender enough. I'll say 'Mummy'. We have bought a little tin box in which we'll put five pfennigs every time we slip up. The contents of the war savings box will go towards buying knitting wool. We must now knit woollen things for the soldiers.

I said to our Nature Study teacher to-day, 'Am I to write the history of the Buzzard in my journal (Diarium)?' Herr Schiffman answered, 'We have decided to speak in our lovely German language. The word for "journal" is "Kladde" (daybook).'

I thought Herr Schiffman was joking, and began to laugh. Then he got cross. I can't help it but it seems comic to me when any one says 'Kladde'. I find it just as funny when Vera Heck in Religious Knowledge says, in the Beatitudes, 'Blessed is he who

4

forgets what can't be altered'. Vera got away with it scot free, but I got a black mark in the class-book because I laughed. It's always like that with me.

At school (I go to the Empress Augusta Victoria School) they talk of nothing but the war now. The girls are pleased that Germany is entering the field against its old enemy France. The most pleased of all are the teachers. We have to learn new songs that glorify war. We have tried out this song today, and we sing it in four-part harmony. (I sing the fourth part):

> O Germany high in honour
> O holy land of the true,
> High gleams the splendour of your fame
> In East and West anew.
> You stand as do your mountains firm
> 'Gainst hostile treacherous force
> And as the eagle flies to its nest
> Your spirit flies its course.
>
> Stand firm! Stand firm!
> And hold the banner high
> And show to all the world,
> When roused by the battle cry,
> That true to each other in the fray,
> We all our former strength display.
> Hold fast, hold fast, throughout the storm,
> Hold fast, hold fast, throughout the storm!
>
> Raise to the Lord your heart and hand,
> God save our precious Fatherland.
> Our ancient swords serve as of yore,
> Lasting as long as iron ore.
> To save us from another's yoke,
> Preserving the heart of the German folk.

Then comes the refrain again.

Our headmaster (we call him 'the Head') held an assembly in the hall today in which he exhorted us to be true Germans and to pray to God for the victory of our forces. At one point emotion prevented him from speaking. Our headmaster is tall and has a white pointed beard; he usually wears a black frock-coat, but sometimes a shiny grey alpaca suit as well. We are afraid of him, he is very strict. He has a strange manner of speech too. (Foreign word: 'strange!' five pfennigs!) I have made up a sentence in which all the words that he often uses appear. The sentence runs

5

like this; 'Look here, you naughty child. I thought you were a good little girl, but now I see you are a wicked little thing! Shame on you, think about it, you should be ashamed of yourself, you must mend your ways!'

Today he told us the following: In Berlin a crowd of a thousand people was waiting in front of the Imperial Palace. Then the Emperor sent a policeman out to inform them that a state of war had been declared. The deeply moved crowd sang 'Now thank we all our God!'

So then we all had to sing 'Now thank we all our God!' Many teachers, both men and women, cried, as did several girls too. The headmaster wiped his nose and took his pince-nez off to dry his eyes. He closed the assembly with the words, 'With God for King and Fatherland!'

We all hope that England will fight on our side. The faithful Italians, our third ally, will also soon join the fight. Japan, Turkey and Rumania will also in all probability be for us.

The enthusiasm in our town increases hourly. People wander through the streets in flocks, shouting 'Down with Serbia! Long live Germany!' Everyone wears black, white and red pompons in their button holes or black white and red bows. In our school people wear bows. Many girls have broad black white and red shoelaces, too, made of a kind of silk, and German hair-ribbons. I had one too but I've lost it. My Auntie Emma, who with her sisters Minna and Lisa has a little milliners and fancy goods shop in Friedrichstrasse, says she just can't get enough black, white and red ribbon to meet the demand. I spoke about it to my brother Willi. He said – 'I think all this fuss about German shoelaces and hair-ribbons is tommy-rot. Professor Philipp thinks so too.'

Professor Philipp is his geography and history master. Willi worships him because he is all for justice in Mexico. My brother is mad on Mexico and the Indians; he is even learning Spanish all on his own, and can already converse quite well in Spanish with Professor Philipp. I know a bit of Spanish too; it is a Mexican freedom song that I often sing:

> Yo soy puro Mexicano
> Viva Mexico!
> Viva la libertad
> y viva la unidad!

In the course of this day three spies, two Russian and one

6

French, were sentenced to death by shooting by the Schneidemühl military court. One of the Russians had intended to blow up the Albatros aircraft factory. The other sought to infect the water in the municipal water tower with cholera germs. What the third intended I don't know for certain, but it is said that he was after the Küddow bridges. He is said to have been a French officer. The Küddow bridges divide the town into two sections; in the Northern half are the infantry barracks, which my grandfather built; In the Eastern is the railway station. If the officer had blown up the bridges it would have been difficult to bring the soldiers to the station. But it turned out otherwise. A Schneidemühl townswoman had noticed him on one of the bridges and thought his behaviour suspicious. She ran up to him and shouted 'Hey! What are you doing there?', caught hold of him and boxed his ears. Two soldiers with fixed bayonets took him away, while he kept calling out – 'What's the matter with you, I'm no spy!'

Fräulein Ella Gumprecht, whom I met afterwards and to whom I told this, said laughing, 'That should have been put in the newspapers – "French officer gets drubbing from German woman!"'

An order came from the town council to boil all drinking water – as a precaution. Boiled water is insipid. I would rather not drink water at all. Gipsies also drink hardly any water. I am always playing at being a gipsy, and a soldier of course. A gipsy who is a soldier. Sentries with loaded rifles stand in front of the railway station. They sometimes fire shots off. I have passed close to them and seen the fixed bayonets. They are long – and much thinner and sharper than I had thought. The blade is smeared with oil. The authorities expect the Russians will blow the station up, for Schneidemühl is one of the most important junctions in the East. All troop transports for Russia and from East to West are routed through our town. It would be good tactics for the enemy to destroy the station. As we live close to the station we think this is dangerous for us. I asked the sentries to guard the place well. They laughed and said, 'We certainly intend to, little girl.' They kept laughing a long time behind my back, which I didn't think particularly polite.

In the evening we sat on the veranda and ate semolina pudding with raspberry juice which had been left over from lunch time. The light in the rose-coloured lamp was on and Willi smiled and said he thought the light looked like raspberry sauce. We spoke of the danger that threatened us from the East.

'If the Russians penetrate as far as Schneidemühl,' said Mummy, 'then you must flee and come to me in Berlin.'

I thought it wonderful to be allowed to go to Berlin, but Grandma answered, 'I'm not leaving Schneidemühl.' 'Then I shall stay with you,' I said.

We decided that if there was a bombardment we would shut ourselves up in the family vault. We would take with us below ground foodstuff, drinking water, beds and a spirit stove with a sufficient supply of spirit and matches. I thought for a long time what it would be like to have to live in the narrow gloomy passages between the coffins. My great-grandparents Haber are buried there, Grandma's sister Wally who was burned to death when she tried to light a stove with spirit, and Grandfather Golz with his two little children. Grandma still wears on her breast a locket containing the blond hair of her little children; I once asked to be allowed to stroke the hair, it is as soft as silk.

Willi, who kept playing the fool, said he would rather stay above ground, and kicked my shin under the table. I kicked him back and declared that we would be safer with the dead than with the living.

While we were still talking a shot rang out. A streak of light flashed past the tall glass screens of the veranda. It was an artillery shell. We could distinctly follow its flight. 'God in heaven!' said Grandma. We were all struck dumb and went quite pale.

4th August 1914

'It's certainly going to be interesting again today,' I said, as I was getting up and dressing. 'Foreign word!' cried Willi. 'You mean – fascinating'. 'OK, then it will be a fascinating day,' I said as I buttoned up my bodice. We ran to the window and fought for the best place, because a crowd of reservists was passing our house, singing loudly.

My brother Willi-Gunther is in the upper third form. We are both thin and quite tall and look alike, except that Willi's eyes are brownish, while mine are rather green. My friend Gretel insists that I have cat's eyes. (Really!) When my brother and I were smaller and sillier we decided that we would marry each other. We wanted to adopt and bring up an Indian child to be called Harry and a Negro child called Muck, because we believed that all the world's children were adopted. Now, of course, I know all the facts of life, but it doesn't seem quite nice. At school they call Willi and me 'Mr and Mrs Kuhr' because we are always walking arm in arm and in spite of our fights are quite inseparable. I find Willi interesting. Only I have to laugh about his long bony feet that are as white as roots. Willi would never, never make a soldier. I would make a good soldier.

I have forgotten to say that we have two other brothers. They are called Ernst and Hans Kuhr and are older than we are. At one time we didn't know them at all. They lived in Danzig with Papa, whom also we didn't know; later on he boarded them out with a pastor. I can still well remember how Ernst and Hans came to Schneidemühl. It was four years ago. Willi and I were sitting on Grandpa's tool bench, so-called because his building workers used to keep their tools there. Grandpa was a master mason; he died in 1912. Willi and I were discussing a new circus programme that we wanted to rehearse; Willi was to be Circus Director and I was to be the leopard 'Lassa'. Then two young lads in long blue sailor suits came along the boundary fence and called out 'Hi, you there, are you Willi and Piete Kuhr?' 'Yes, we are!' we replied. 'Well then, we are your brothers.' But we didn't want to fall into a trap and answered that our brothers were boarding with Pastor Wurlitzer in Danzig.

'Quite right,' said the taller one, brother Ernst, laughing. 'But now that is over. We are to come and stay in Schneidemühl.'

'Why so?'

'Papa can no longer pay for our board. So Grandpa is to look after us.'

'But Grandpa is already looking after us!'

'He'll cope with us as well.'

We were doubtful. But our brothers stayed with us until after our grandfather's death. Willi liked Hans and was always going for walks with him; that was an awful time for me. Ernst was already nearly grown up and I didn't like his games. I used to creep away behind a chimney on the roof of our house and read some book or other or did school work. But then if I saw Ernst wandering around the yard, I would feel sorry for him and would come down from my hiding-place. Ernst has a long, narrow face and looks like an English ship's officer.

In the summer of 1913 our brothers went into the Navy. Ernst became a sailor on the 'Lucie Vinnen' and Hans on the 'Magdalena Vinnen'. These are sister ships, four-masters of the Merchant Navy. We were told that they are the largest German

9

merchant ships. Hans went to South America and Ernst to Australia. Hans wrote that in a typhoon he had seen a sea-serpent. Ernst had a dispute with his superiors and jumped ship at Melbourne. He is now a kind of overseer on an Australian cattle ranch and can spend the whole day riding. Mummy says she worries day and night about the future of both of them.[2]

Despatches came in to-day from the theatre of war, saying that not only Russians in the East but also the French in the West had invaded German territory. So it is really war. From now on we have a 'West Front' and an 'East Front'. Towards evening came news that our forces have occupied the Russian towns Kalisch and Alexandrowo and have set fire to the naval base Libau. Now we know at last who murdered the Austrian Crown Prince and Princess. It was a Serbian student named Princip. Every one says he is a criminal who ought to be lynched. I keep wondering why he did it. His face in the newspaper picture looks handsome but horror-struck. Was he perhaps insane?

Night time. In bed, I must write some more.

The 149th regiment of infantry is stationed in Schneidemühl. It is going to be sent to the Western Front. This evening we heard the faint sound of drums, bass drums and kettle-drums. 'A Military band!', I shouted. We strained our ears to listen to it. The music kept getting louder and clearer. Now it was the Hohesfriedberger March that was being played. We couldn't bear to stay any longer in the room and ran out into the street. 'To the station!', cried Willi. We ran through Grandpa's subway (which he had built) and pushed our way through the crowd of people on to the Droschkenplatz. The arc-lamps were alight, and the foliage of the chestnut trees in the white light looked just like paper. I climbed on to the iron fence; from there I could see everything: on the left the yellow station building on whose four turrets stood sentries with shouldered rifles, in front of me the railway platforms and behind me the Square with crowds standing shoulder to shoulder. At Platform Three there stood a goods train, full of reservists. They leaned against the open doors of the wagons, waving and laughing.

I heard Willi exclaim 'They're coming! The 149th!' Our regiment marched down the street to the station. The soldiers wore the new grey field uniform and grey spiked helmets. Their boots were of untanned leather and shorter than the black waxed boots of peace-time! Their packs were so full that the soldiers half disappeared beneath them. In front came the regimental band in

10

full blast. I strained my eyes to see whether the big white poodle which always carried a kettle-drum was with them, but he was not there. The drummer was beating time with the staff with the red and silver tassel. The band played 'There's a call like a clap of thunder'. Then we heard the soldiers singing '... firm and true stands the watch on the Rhine', and everyone joined in the singing, with shouts of 'Hip, Hip, Hurray!'

So came the 149th shoulder to shoulder, flowing over the platform like a surge of grey water. All the soldiers had long garlands of summer flowers round their necks and on their chests. Bunches of asters, stocks and roses were even stuck into the barrels of their rifles as if they would shoot down the enemy with flowers. The soldiers' faces were serious. I had expected that they would be laughing and rejoicing. But there was only one lieutenant rejoicing. I knew him, he was the son of Frau Schön, a member of Grandma's sisterhood. Lieutenant Schön was cheerfully bidding good-bye to all his relatives and friends and was kissed, hugged and patted all the way through the crowd. I wanted to shout 'Hello, Lieutenant Schön!', but no words would come out.

Now the band was playing, 'The laurels of victory be yours'. The people remaining in the square waved their hats and handkerchiefs. The reservists in the rear wagon mimicked the instrumentalists with their hands and mouths and caused a good deal of laughter. Some of our 149th rushed to the pump and made water spurt all over themselves and down their necks. It was very oppressive with the August heat and the crowd of people packed close together. One of the reservists at Platform 3 now climbed on to the roof of his goods wagon and shouted to our soldiers: 'You, fine sirs, are already in full battle array but we have yet to get dressed' and on the words 'have yet' he plucked so comically at his civilian gear that all around broke into laughter and clapping. Then the reservists' train began to move off, the reservists sang and cheered, and we waved for as long as we could see anything of them. The crush in the Station Square had meanwhile become so great that I jumped down from the fence; I was half suffocated. An old lady wailed loudly: 'Paul! Where is my darling Paul? Let me at least see my son!' She was pushed forward to the railings, but I couldn't make out whether she found her Paul in the crowd of soldiers. She had little red eyes, probably inflamed with crying. I made a quick prayer to God: 'Dear God, protect this Paul! Give him back to her! Please,

11

please, please, I beseech you!' I was suddenly as much taken up with this Paul as if the heavens were falling.

'Good-bye, soldier!' suddenly called out a tiny boy and stretched out his hand through the railings.

'Good-bye, little brother!' answered the soldier and shook the little boy's hand.

Everybody laughed. Now the regimental band played, 'Germany, Germany above everything'. I knew that was the end, now they were off! The 149th became agitated, only a few joined in the singing. Then came a long, decorated goods train into Platform One. A trumpet call rang out. The soldiers stormed on to the train, there was a great commotion, pushing and shoving, joking and words of command. A soldier as tall as a tree came past me. I stretched out my hand over the fence and murmured 'Farewell!' (I could only just murmur.) He smiled at me and seized my hand. 'Good-bye, lassie!' I gazed after him as he clambered through the doorway of a goods-wagon behind his companions. He turned towards me again.

Gradually the train began to move. The cheers grew into a roar, the soldiers' faces crowded into the open doorways, flowers flew through the air, and suddenly many people in the square began to cry.

'Good-bye! See you again in the homeland!'

'Don't worry! We shall soon be home again!'

'We'll celebrate Christmas with Mother!'

'Oh yes! Come back safe and sound!'

Now the soldiers began to sing a song I had never heard before, which suddenly drowned all else. I could only understand a few lines:

> The little woodland birds
> Sang such a wonderful refrain:
> In the homeland, in the homeland,
> There we'll meet again.

It wouldn't have taken much for me to burst out crying. I went home by a roundabout way. I held carefully in front of me the hand that the soldier had squeezed. As I went up our poorly lit steps I stared at the palm of the hand. Then I quickly kissed it. Daft, wasn't it?

Willi had got home before me. He was sitting on the arm of Mummy's chair with Mummy's arm around him. Mummy looked sad. She said 'How empty the town will be to-morrow!'

12

5th August 1914

In our geography lesson we were again concerned with Serbia. I myself had quite forgotten where exactly its frontiers ran and had difficulty in pointing it out on the map. We now have a great hatred for this little country and shout, 'Down with Serbia!' No one in my class can say what flag Serbia has or what its inhabitants are like, for example what religion they have. I said in school today, 'Princip is better-looking than the Archduke Franz Ferdinand.' I couldn't have done anything more to stir the hornet's nest if I had said that our Emperor Wilhelm was a traitor. 'What!' cried my friend Hertha, of whom I am normally very fond. 'How can you say such things! He's a murderer!' 'I still say he has a handsome face,' I said. 'No,' cried Hertha, 'a murderer can't have a handsome face.' 'Why ever not?' 'Because he couldn't then be a murderer. Or is murder perhaps something handsome?'

Then there was tremendous uproar, and I was nearly torn to pieces. Perhaps I would have torn myself to pieces if I had been someone else. But suddenly I felt sorry for Princip because everyone was down on him. And what do you think happened? The big girl Dalüge, who has twice failed to go up into the next class, and who has a friend in the 149th, said 'Leave Kuhr alone, for thundering heaven's sake! Kuhr at least has some breeding!'

I looked closely at Dalüge because I thought she was trying to tease me. The class immediately began to shout 'Breeding? We'd like to know what breeding Kuhr has!'

In the maths lesson, when Dalüge couldn't do her decimal fractions I copied the answers from my neighbour Käthe Brunn, who is very good at sums. I sent the folded note to Dalüge. I had written in the margin, in our secret class code, 'Thank you! Kuhr.'

It really doesn't matter to me what the girls think of me. But I was annoyed – mostly with myself because I had said so much about Princip.

Grandma is now often at the house of the Mayor's wife and with the leading women of the Red Cross. She is herself one of the leaders. She is now to be put in charge of the Red Cross depot on Schneidemühl railway station. The depot is established for the time being in a little room in the station building. All the ladies on duty wear white aprons and a white armband with a red cross like medical orderlies. Later on they are to get black and white striped nurses' uniforms.

I have helped pack into baskets at least a hundred coffee cups that have been bought by the Red Cross for eight pfennigs each. Our house in Alte Bahnhofstrasse is like a warehouse. Every moment there is a ring at the door, and messengers arrive dragging washing baskets full of rolls, sausages, cakes, wine, fruit-juice and fruit intended for the soldiers passing through. We have to make up the gift parcels and take them to the station. I have never before in my life seen so many sausages in one pile. Grandma got back from duty at the station at five o'clock in the morning, she was dog-tired. But when Willi and I went off to school at half past seven she was already on her feet again. She said that England had declared war on us as the third hostile power. We were thunderstruck. There is certainly no one in our town who would not have sworn on the help of our 'cousins'. This will be a heavy blow to our Emperor. We are now caught like a mouse in a trap.

The flags in the town have been lowered upon this declaration of war. It is quite quiet in the streets. People stand in front of our two newspaper offices and read the special news sheets. We met the old Councillor Schön, who was wearing in his button-hole the black and white ribbon of the Iron Cross from 1870/71. He was standing with a group of civilians and said, 'That's what you call cousinly behaviour!' A man who looked like a forester struck the window-pane with the crook of his stick and shouted 'The more enemies, the greater honour!' Another man said, 'You're a blockhead!', whereupon the one who looked like a forester yelled 'Social Democrats like you ought to be sent to the front right away!' It nearly came to a fight. I bought a special news sheet and ran back home with it. The Russians have been defeated near Kibarty and have retreated eastwards.

But it also said, 'Casualties on the German side are few.' Now the first German soldiers have fallen.

6th August 1914

Copenhagen: Denmark has declared its neutrality.
Constantinople: The Turks have declared their neutrality.
Bern: Switzerland has declared to the powers its neutrality.
Bucharest: Rumania has declared its neutrality.

Troops are constantly passing through the station. They come in endless trains. We once counted fifty wagons on one single goods train. The soldiers and reservists laugh and sing. They arrive cheering and leave again cheering. The Red Cross ladies distribute coffee, lemonade and sandwiches to the soldiers. When a train has left the station the baskets are empty. But there are fresh gift parcels waiting in our house and our maid Marie and I run to and fro bringing one basket after another. As it is very hot there, I had some of the soldiers' coffee too. I drank the large mug empty in one gulp. I pretended I was a soldier being well looked after and I was very happy.

The railway wagons are decorated with foliage nailed on. Nearly every door has a young birch tree on which coloured ribbons hang. You might think it was Whitsuntide: or else a May tree. The sides are covered with drawings and sentences in chalk. On one wagon was written 'To Siberia!' On another 'Off to Petersburg!' And: 'Free concert in Moscow in 14 days time!' – 'Nicholas, beware – we'll pluck your every hair!' – 'We're fighting not for Gold and Precious Stones, but for Emperor, Women and Children' (This last one was especially pleasing to the Red Cross ladies). One train came in with black Death's Head Hussars, an Elite–Regiment. I couldn't help keep looking at the horses as they stood pawing and leaning their heads over the iron bars. They too were going to the front! They were lovely horses, their hides glistened and glittered. I am terribly fond of horses. Through the kindness of a school friend I am always going into the stables and to the spacious, separate paddocks where the mares and foals graze.

On one railway wagon it said: 'Merrily to Russia! Japan is helping too!' But we haven't really got as far as that; Japan hasn't declared which power it supports and whether it is willing to take any part in the war. A few days ago we thought the whole world would stand by us. But see how things are now!

There was another slogan that I liked:–

> Every Prussian shoot a Russian,
> Every German clobber a Frog,
> The Serb's'll get what they deserve.
> Whether they're Serbs or Russian fiends
> We'll smash'em all to smithereens.

I should like to go with them! I don't want to stay behind and be a child! I am so sorry for the soldiers and the horses!

7th August 1914

There is talk of an outbreak of famine in Russia and it is said that the rebellious population are being driven into battle with whips. If famine is already prevalent in Russia the war will soon be over. Perhaps instead it would be better if it were already over. There is so much corn standing in the fields that needs to be harvested. The mobilisation has taken the farm-workers away from the harvest. But with God's help the corn will not be spoilt, so that we have enough to eat in the winter. The older children in the grammar school have offered themselves for harvest work. Eighteen members of my brother's form, the Upper Third, have already been detailed for land work. I asked Mummy to write me too a note giving me leave for harvest work. She wrote:

> 'I give permission for my daughter Elfriede ("Elfriede!") to do such harvest work as may be suited to her strength.
> Yours faithfully'

This afternoon I went to our headmaster's house and gave him the letter. I was very frightened. He read the note and said: 'But you are still much too young, Elfriede.'

'No, not at all!' I said. 'I am really much older than I look.'

'Really!' answered the head, pouting. 'And how have you come to be so much older than you look?'

I knew very well what he was getting at. He was thinking of the incident two years ago when I was nearly chucked out of the school. (I will tell you why, later on.) I looked at him coldly. But before I could make any further reply, he said: 'Go back home, you naughty, horrid-looking child! Girls like you are no use to the Fatherland!'

That is just the question, whether I can be of use to the Fatherland. I can be very useful on the railway station anyway. But the headmaster will never send me to work on the land. There are certainly 'horrid-looking' soldiers too, yet the Emperor sends them to the front. What am I to tell Mummy now?

Mummy is at this moment with Grandma at the station. I should like to know what the soldiers think when she hands them coffee. My mother has really delicate hands, piano-hands, through which bright blue veins glisten. No one in the whole town has hands like my mother.

Emperor Wilhelm has to-day renewed the Order of the Iron Cross for the war. There must be heavy fighting in the West.

16

German troops are fighting in Belgium. Willi asked Grandma, 'Nanny, is Belgium also then our enemy?' Grandma answered, 'It must be!'

No one knows for certain. We now have so many enemies. And Italy, our ally, on whose support we had firmly counted, has declared its neutrality.

This evening, while we were on the veranda eating baked potatoes and pickled herrings, a man in the street called out loudly, 'Lüttich [Liège] has fallen!' We all jumped up and Willi upset the basin of pickles. 'Children, children!' said Mummy, and tears were running from her eyes. We could hardly grasp the fact that we must have gained the first great victory. Grandma threw the window open and called out: 'Please come up here for a moment!' She ran down towards the newsman and bought a copy of the special news sheet. There it was in black and white!

We went into the street, none of us wanting any more to eat. There was a great rejoicing in the town. People were dancing on the pavements, there was singing and whistling, and people were calling out to one another, 'Lüttich has fallen!'

In the midst of all the joy I was seized by a terrible aching sadness. The 149th! When we were sitting on the veranda again I collected up the melted grease from a candle and formed it into a little cross on which I scratched with a darning-needle the words: 'Lüttich fallen, 7.8.1914.' I hung the cross on a cotton thread next to the ears of corn by my bed.

8th August 1914

A commemoration of Lüttich took place in school. We had to assemble in the hall, then the headmaster made a speech. And then, when we had sung, 'Germany, Germany above everything' the Headmaster called out 'Something more! I will now read you the latest news-sheet. "Montenegro has declared war on Austro-Hungary". I see here in brackets the two little words: "So what!"'

He laughed as he spoke. The school roared with laughter. Then we were allowed to pack our bags and go home. A victory holiday! My friend Dora called to me: 'Oh boy, that's great! We shan't be having any French!'

I met Willi on the way, going through Milchstrasse with his friend Hans Androwski. His school had a holiday too. Androwski is the head boy of the Upper Third; he is very quiet and wears glasses. I asked what they had just been talking about. About the war, they said. Androwski asked me whether I would be a soldier if I were a man. I said 'Yes!' Then Androwski wanted to know why. I said; 'It is so hard for me to live here when all the soldiers are at the Front.' Androwski asked whether I didn't like living then. Of course I like living, very much so. It is wonderful to be alive. 'Could you shoot people then?', Androwski asked me. (He used the polite 'you'.) I answered that I wouldn't shoot any one; I would always fire into the air. I had often thought about that. But Androwski said that in that case I would probably be shot, and definitely so under martial law, for refusal of military duty. 'Why would you want to go to the Front then?' asked Androwski.

I was once again cross with myself, first because I couldn't think of any answer, and second because I blushed! Willi said I was a phantasist and that you couldn't discuss any problem with me.

9th August 1914

Sunday! We slept longer than usual. I first woke when our maid Marie was already getting breakfast ready. Willi was drinking coffee in his shirtsleeves on the veranda. It was hot – 29° in the shade. He said 'Marie is so silly, she wants to get away'.

I rushed into the kitchen. Dear Marie was chopping carrots into thin slices and saying that the Russians had murdered women and children in East Prussia. 'But we have thrown the Russians back over the frontier,' I said indignantly. 'But yesterday and to-day whole train-loads of refugees have arrived,' said Marie. 'Your Grandma has said that they moan terribly. The Russians have nailed a woman to a barn door – like this ... ' Marie placed herself by the kitchen door with outstretched arms and legs, looking like one of those owls that our superstitious farmers nail on their barn doors as a safeguard against lightning. When Marie relates horror stories, however true they may be, you can't help laughing at them. She has a broad, bony, red face and quite thin, straw-coloured hair. Also she lisps.

I stifled my laughter and said: 'Don't you worry, Marie dear. The Russians won't do anything to you. When they see you, they'll say, "Duschinka moj", that means: "My little dove".' 'They may well duschinken me!' cried Marie. 'And they'll do something else to me too.'

I heard Willi laughing behind the open door.

'Young Master Willi's laughing!' said Marie, upset. 'But Miss Piete will understand me! Dear Miss Piete always understands me, poor soul that I am!'

I was honestly taken aback by this remark. It was the last thing I had expected to hear. I put on Grandpa's old, broad-brimmed panama hat and went into the garden.

The garden belongs to me alone and is no bigger than a large room, but the soil is fertile because I manure it with goats' and rabbits' droppings. Flowers, cooking herbs and an old apple tree grow in my garden. Next to this little piece of ground is my Aunt Louise Otter's garden, which is at least twenty-five times as big as mine. In the furthest corner next to a plum tree there is a brown summer-house with green painted benches, window-shutters and a table. The summer-house is used exclusively by Mummy, Willi, my friend Gretel from the back premises, and myself. We take possession of it by turn, Mummy and Willi for work, Gretel and me for playing.

Mummy was at this moment sitting in the summer-house writing; her white-flowered dress of Turkish towelling shone through the long stems of wild vine. Mummy is writing a novel; it is called 'The Whirling Self'. The self is the 'ego', Mummy says; that is the individual personality that revolves around itself, or something like that.

I fetched the watering-can from the summer-house and with twelve strokes of the pump filled it to the brim in order to water my flower-beds. The earth soaked up one can of water after another, then the sun dried out the ground again. It was pure wasted effort. Then I had to go to the station. Immediately there came in a long train with soldiers in field grey. They were famished and at least as thirsty as my earth. 'You can give out postcards,' said Frau Annchen to me; she lives in our house and I am very fond of her. 'We have obtained a hundred from Wiek's the paper firm.'

The soldiers receive the postcards free of charge and they can send them without stamps if they just write on them the words 'Forces Mail'. I was soon surrounded by a crowd of soldiers. They were very polite. 'Give me a picture card, please!' 'Give me one too, please, Missy!' 'Me, too, please. Is that a picture of the town we're now passing through?'

'Yes,' I said, 'that is Schneidemühl!'

When I had no more cards left, I washed up the cups at the buffet. Granny, Frau Annchen and two more Red Cross helpers

19

served white coffee, lemonade, bread and rolls spread with dripping or butter. But we also served bread with thick slices of bacon. The soldiers were mad on the bacon sandwiches. Many asked whether we hadn't a bowl of soup. Grandma said: 'That's a great idea, folk! We ought to have a cauldron and make soup every day!' She decided to raise the matter at the next Red Cross committee meeting. 'But,' said Frau Annchen, 'we would then need to have a larger room. We certainly couldn't set up a stove in this little room.'

That's true. There's only just enough room here for the table on which the bread is set out and for the gas-cooker on which the water for coffee and tea is heated. Grandma suggested asking for a disused goods wagon to be used as a Red Cross canteen. 'Or a fourth class carriage,' said Frau Annchen. 'Then we should have seats for the soldiers as well.' Everyone was enthusiastic about this suggestion.

Then I had to go and get soap, and Grandma fastened on my upper arm an armlet stamped with the Red Cross. I was proud, as I was able to pass the sentry at the barrier unhindered. My friend Gretel was sitting with a doll on the steps in front of our house.

'What's that on your arm?' she asked.

'I'm pretending to be an officer. I can pass all sentries. Great, isn't it?'

'What sort of officer are you, then?' asked Gretel. I thought for a moment and said: 'Lieutenant in the First Uhlan Guards Regiment. My name is von Yellenic.' I had seen that name at some time in a book. 'Oh, I say,' said Gretel. 'Fancy that – Von!' 'It's just a game,' I cried. Then I took the packet of soap from the kitchen cupboard and ran back to the station.

'When are you coming back?' called Gretel after me. 'I don't know,' I called back. 'To-morrow morning probably. It will certainly go on through the night.'

At the station Grandma chopped up the soap into little pieces to distribute to the reservists, who were dirty with dust and sweat from the mucky goods wagons. A hole was made in the last piece of soap, a piece of string was threaded through it, and we hung it on the pump on the platform. A great feast of washing began at once. When the reservists were all back in the train and about to depart another train came into the next platform. This too was full of reservists. They called out after those departing: 'Good shooting, lads! But leave something for us to do! Hurra! Hurra! Hurra!'

The departing reservists cheered likewise. So came and went every train, and from each one men roared 'Hurra'. One particular train brought two thousand infantrymen. They swallowed up all our provisions in a flash. Grandma climbed on to a table; despite the fact that she is an old lady, who no longer enjoys climbing. 'My dear lads,' she cried as loudly as she could, 'listen to me a moment! If you upset the coffee-urn I can't give you any more to drink! Have a bit of sense!'

Many of the soldiers kissed Grandma's hand in gratitude.

I think to-day was the seventh day of mobilisation.

11th August 1914

I can't write in the war diary every day, I know that very well now. Mummy wants me to keep it up whatever happens. 'So long as our soldiers give up their lives for us, you can at least write a few lines for them,' she said. She is cross with me, which hurts me. I want to write everything I know about the war.

In the larger towns no more volunteers for war service can be taken on before 1st September, because as a result of the many advertisements all the reserve units have more than their full complement. The two eldest sons of Councillor Schön have already been rejected; the third went off with the 149th, the fourth has the rank of Acting First Lieutenant in the Dragoons. My uncle, Dr. Bruno Golz, Grandma's only son, has offered himself at the town hall in Halle as a volunteer in the Field Artillery Regiment. He has been accepted.

When Grandma had read Uncle Bruno's letter, she put it in the drawer without a word. Later on she was lying on the sofa to get an hour's sleep, while I was playing with our old paper Indians. After a while I saw that Grandma's face was wet.

'Are you perspiring, Granny?' I asked.

She didn't answer.

I got frightened and asked again; 'are you perspiring?'

Grandma opened her eyes. 'There are tears in your eyes, Grandma,' I said. 'Your face is all wet. Shall I get you a handkerchief?'

There are some fools about, and I am one of them. Grandma was of course crying because her son had joined up.

Towards evening the Rector's wife, Frau Lakoschus, came to bring fifty sausage-rolls and three bottles of raspberry juice for the soldiers. She said that three of her sons were with their

21

regiment; the fourth was in China and couldn't get back to Germany. 'Be thankful for that, dear Frau Lakoschus,' said Grandma. 'You have him at least in safety.' 'But pardon me!' answered Frau Lakoschus. 'That would make me a bad soldiers' mother! Is it not an honour to have our sons wearing the Emperor's uniform?' 'Mine has joined the Field artillery in Halle,' said Grandma quietly.

I ran into the garden, where Mummy was walking up and down between the flower-beds with a book in her hand. She wore a fiery red Pelargonium in her white collar and she looked very lovely.

'Darling,' I said, putting my arms round her, 'Frau Lakoschus is upstairs and is upsetting Granny.'

Mummy immediately stood still and looked at me startled. 'What is she doing?' she asked.

'Oh, she's going on about the Emperor's uniform and so forth,' I answered. 'While Uncle Bruno is Grandma's only son ....'

Mummy said nothing, but looked up at the sky, where a bi-plane was just then flying over. From the station you could hear the songs of the soldiers who were passing through.

12th August 1914

It says in the newspaper that the Austrians are advancing strongly on the Russian frontier. But the railwaymen who take the troop trains close to the front, say: 'The Austrians are not born soldiers.' Mummy said, 'That is why they have produced a Mozart!'

Rifle shots were heard in our town. They rang out as short and sharp as when fire-crackers are thrown on to the pavements on the Emperor's birthday. When four or five shots had gone off after one another, Fräulein Ella Gumprecht, who had come to visit us, said: 'Thank God, that's one less of the gang!'

'What gang?' said Willi interested. 'Russian spies,' answered Fräulein Gumprecht. 'Are there so many spies then?' I asked. Fräulein Gumprecht said, 'Yes!'

Now I can't help thinking all the time that somewhere on our streets lies a dead person. Mummy talks a great deal about a 'Women's Home Guard'. I'm not quite sure what she means by it. But if it means that women too go to the Front, I am all for it. For I've got to see for myself all that I hear about the war. If I get married later on I shall be able to say to my children: 'That is what the war was like!'

13th August 1914

Troop train after troop train. I went with Gretel a little while ago to a railway-crossing in the woods, when a goods train with eighty-three wagons thundered past. (We were counting the wagons for ever.) It was loaded with cannons and field-grey machine-guns. Soldiers leaned against the cannons and looked out over the country-side. Perhaps they thought the East was near here. When the train was out of sight we knelt down and placed our faces against the rails. They were quite hot.

'Let's make the sign of the Cross over the rails,' I said to Gretel, and we did so, although we are not Catholics, but Evangelicals.

'Now the soldiers will all stay alive,' I said.

'That would be lovely,' said Gretel. She didn't seem altogether to believe it.

In the evening paper there was a poem about Lüttich and General Emmich who had stormed the Belgian stronghold which, in its modernised state, was almost impregnable. It was in the Posen Evening News and it goes as follows:–

The Story of Lüttich [Liège]

Our boys were on their way to France,
A trek from the Rhine right through to Paris,
But Lüttich threatened their advance
And, blocking their way, did them embarrass.
Then heartily swore our General Emmich,
'By God, I'll seize it from the Flemish!'[3]

By heaven, how can a man in his senses
Hope to conquer such mighty defences!
'Look here, lads', said the General, 'we just drive a hole
Through the lot and, hey presto, we've gotten our goal'.
So, vexed at the hindrance, he quickly began an
Assault on the numerous forts and their cannon.

'But, General Emmich, do me a favour,
That's 'gainst all the rules of normal behaviour.
You should settle your troops down, not acting so brutish
And patiently wait as you lay siege to Lüttich'.
'Stuff and nonsense,' said he, 'that's just idle talk,
For the rules I don't care one blind bit of chalk'.

23

And so the lads stormed and forced their way through,
'Spite of all that the fortress's cannons could do.
And now they continue their way towards France,
To Paris right through from the Rhine they advance.
And what were the words of our General Emmich?
'By God, I'll seize it from the Flemish!'

I still don't know when Belgium declared war on us. What a
muddle it is! Willi says, it's 'all against all'.

14th August 1914

Oh, at last!
'The powers involved in the European War have so far made
eleven declarations of war and in the following exact order:

1.   Austro-Hungary v Serbia
2.   Germany v Russia
3.   Germany v France
4.   England v Germany
5.   Belgium v Germany
6.   Austro-Hungary v Russia
7.   Montenegro v Austro-Hungary
8.   Serbia v Germany
9.   France v Austro-Hungary
10. Montenegro v Germany
11. England v Austro-Hungary'

There are whispers in the streets that preparations are being
made for a great battle both in France and in Russia. In France
we are drawing up our troops around the stronghold of Belfort.
In Russia we are pushing on towards St. Petersburg. The Russian
government has to try and win over the Poles for the Russian
cause. German and Austrian columns of cyclists are now sticking notices on the walls in Polish towns and villages which say,
in the Polish language, 'Poles, rise up and bring yourselves under
the orderly German régime.'
Our railway station bridges are now barricaded too. You come
up against sentries everywhere. Notices are hung on the bridges,
saying 'Drive slowly!' Every driver is questioned and every
vehicle searched. No one crossing the bridges is allowed to
loiter. Military trains rumble through under the bridges. You
suddenly have the feeling that the enemy is quite near.

People are becoming uneasy. We heard that some families have left the town. Our Marie is not the only one who wants to escape. Fresh refugees have arrived from East Prussia. This time I have seen them myself, mothers, children, old women and old men. Some well-dressed, others badly. They all carry bundles and cases, bedding, coats and cloaks all tied together. The refugees are looked after at our Red Cross depot on the station. One woman with noisy children kept crying out, 'Just where can we go? Where can we go?' I wished her good luck and said, 'Don't worry, the Emperor will look after us all!' 'Dear child,' said the woman (pronouncing it in her funny way) 'a child like you can have no idea what it's like, can you?' And tears ran all over her chubby red face.

15th August 1914

Now I'll tell you why the teachers at school have not been nice to me for the last two years. I will tell you the whole truth, nothing more and nothing less.

In the summer of 1911 my grandfather was still alive and he went with grandma to a gall-stone treatment centre at Karlsbad. Meanwhile Willi went to a boarding-house for boys and I went to Fräulein Gumprecht, who is a teacher at the elementary school. Every morning I missed the first lesson at school through over-sleeping because Fräulein Gumprecht forgot to wake me. Sometimes it happened that she woke me in time, but I would go to sleep again because I had been awake so late the night before on account of all the people in the house. By the time I awoke with an awful fright, Fräulein Gumprecht had long since gone off to her school. Then I would run without breakfast and without washing to my own school, the Empress Augusta Victoria School. I asked Fräulein Gumprecht not to let me oversleep. She promised, but three days later I was late again. At that time our form-mistress was Fräulein Finsch. She was the most fearsome teacher in the whole school. She said to me: 'If you are ever late again, I will send you to the headmaster.' The next day I was again ten minutes late. My heart was in my boots, I didn't know what to do. I hated the school and I hated all the world. I couldn't possibly face Fräulein Finsch. I imagined she would explode or do some other terrible thing. So I went back, took a sheet of Fräulein Gumprecht's notepaper and wrote (I shall never forget the words!):

Dear Fräulein Vinsch! Piete Kuhr could not attend the first lesson, because she was violently sick.

I used the wrong gender for the word 'Dear', and spelled Finsch with a V instead of an F. And my hand-writing was also very bad. In any case it wasn't Teacher Gumprecht's writing. Now the matter was reported to the headmaster. 'Why have you done this?' he said. 'You have lied and deceived and forged a signature. Do you know you could go to prison for that?' I didn't answer. But I would rather have gone to prison than be told every day by the teachers what a wicked child I was.

I could have stood up for myself. But I thought I mustn't tell tales against Fräulein Gumprecht because she was a teacher herself. Every teacher would have sided with Fräulein Gumprecht – you bet! So I kept quiet through all their rebukes, and I got the reputation of being sulky and stubborn. When nearly three weeks had gone by, the headmaster sent for me to go to the conference room in the middle of a maths lesson. I felt quite sick. The headmaster said to me: 'Elfriede Kuhr, look me in the eyes!'

It was difficult to look him in the eyes, but I tried all the same. 'Elfriede Kuhr,' he began, 'tell me now whether you have thought about your disgraceful behaviour.'

'Yes,' I said. What else could I have said?

'And tell me also whether you have cried about it.'

I said yes again, but that wasn't true; I had never cried about it.

'When have you cried?' asked the headmaster.

'At night,' I lied.

'Have you cried for long?'

'Yes.'

The headmaster looked at me, and then scowled.

I looked at the ground because I could no longer look at him.

'Are you sorry for the offence then?'

'Yes,' I said, feeling stone cold. During the whole questioning I could have gone to sleep on the spot.

The headmaster then said he had thought the matter over and had decided that for three months the class would not be allowed to have anything to do with me or speak to me.

That's fine, thought I. In the headmaster's sight I clenched my fists and looked at him wildly; I should have liked to scratch and bite him. I thought, 'He will see what the class says about it. The class will stand by me.' But the class did not stand by me. They truly shunned me for three months, indeed even longer, as the headmaster had directed. I slunk along the walls like a mangy tom-cat. When on one occasion a girl said to me, 'I feel sorry for you, Piete!', I said, 'Don't fret yourself for me!'

Since that time I know what little love I can expect. Luckily I could at least make an exception of Gretel; she knew nothing of the affair, because she goes to the elementary school. When Grandma moved to this house after Grandpa's death, I saw Gretel sitting on the doorstep of the back quarters playing with a doll. The doll had a hard head and was ugly.

'What's your doll's name?' I said, for the sake of something to say. 'Ingelborg,' answered Gretel.

'I have a baby doll – a boy whose name is Harry. You can play with him if you like.'

I have never played with dolls, but always just with animals. But as Gretel loves little Harry so much, I play the part of either aunt or father. I like playing father and soldier best.

One day Gretel accidentally dropped the baby doll. The china immediately broke into a thousand pieces. I was a bit cross, but only a little bit. Really because Mummy had given me the baby for Christmas.

Gretel has yellow hair like straw. Her mother plaits it into two pigtails. There are two more sisters there, Anni and Hede, and a brother called Fritz. He is a bit taller than I am.

17th August 1914

Food has become a few pfennigs dearer. It is said that we are facing a famine and may even be eating dogs and cats. 'Why not horses!' said Grandma. She is angry because housewives are beginning to buy up non-perishables. The shopkeepers are delighted with the increased takings and sell all their stocks. There are articles in the papers against 'hoarding'. Hoarding is forbidden.

I was at the station until 6 o'clock in the evening. A troop train arrived nearly every half hour. Often we couldn't carry the coffee-urn quickly enough from one platform to another. The railway guards helped us. My coat and skirt got wet with coffee slopped over. The town is swarming with strange officers. I met Greta Dalüge and went with her to the market-place down Posener Strasse. She was greeted by many officers.

'How do you come to know these officers?' I said. Greta said, 'From the casino. We supply the food from our hotel.'
'Do you know them personally? Do you talk with them?'
'Of course. Here comes the young Count, shall I introduce you to him?'
'No,' I said. 'Don't bother, I've no wish to be introduced, and besides I've got geography to swot up.' I left Greta just as the Count greeted her. He was a First Lieutenant in the Fusilier Guards. When I turned into the quiet Uscher Strasse I began to run. I ran and ran until I reached home. Then I looked out of the open window. It was such a lovely day. The swallows were flying in all directions over the garden and the sun was setting. I sang, at the top of my voice;

> The little woodland birds
> Sang such a wonderful refrain;
> In the homeland, in the homeland ....

Gretel was helping her mother hang out washing in the yard ....
'Piete,' she called up to me, 'are you singing?' 'Yes,' I replied. 'I'm singing The little woodland birds.'
Suddenly I heard Mummy laughing out loud in the summer-house. Gretel's mother was laughing too. And now everybody was laughing. Mummy came out of the summer-house and waved to me; she was quite red with laughing.
'My treasure!' she called out, and I hugged the window-bars for joy. I was terribly happy because I am still a child and officers mean nothing to me. I should like to stay young, not a single year older. I wonder whether Greta Dalüge is happy. She is so much older than I am and puts make-up on her face. She does it very carefully so that the teachers don't notice. Our classmate Trudi told me this. Trudi puts make-up on too, but not so well. Nearly all the big girls at the High School wear make-up.

20th August 1914

The news sheets giving the names of dead soldiers are called 'Casualty Lists'. A black Iron Cross is printed at the top, and below this are the words 'Fallen on the field of honour ....' Then follow the ranks and names of the dead, the army unit, the battle and the date of death. After the killed, the wounded are listed, and again after these the missing. Above the missing it says, 'Reported missing.'

Every soldier carries an identity card. The soldiers call it the 'death ticket'. The medical orderlies who search the battlefield for the dead establish the names of the fallen by means of the identity cards. We are afraid every time we see a casualty list. We always expect to find sons, brothers or husbands of people we know among the fallen. The war had better be ended.

Yesterday it said in the paper that the Emperor has been to the Western Front. Some one had written a poem, the last verse of which ran like this:

> O Emperor, proceed with joy
> To the battlefield;
> By you the whole world's destiny will be sealed.
> Above your brazen armies there arise
> Golden clouds of glory filling the skies.

How can the Emperor proceed 'with joy' to the battle-field? If he walks over the battlefield and hears a dying man at his feet calling 'Mother!' – what then?

Willi laughed when I said this to him. 'Do you really believe that the Emperor goes walkabout on the battlefield?', he asked.

'It says so there though!' I cried, and pointed with my finger to the newspaper.

22nd August 1914

Japan has given an ultimatum to Germany. They want to have our Chinese Protectorate Kiaochow. A map of the world hangs in our classroom on which the enemy countries are marked with red flags. Now we have the island nation of Japan also flagged with red. The areas that are for Germany bear black, white and red flags. When we have won a battle a flag is moved forward. In the West we can certainly advance the front line. Lüttich, Mulhausen, Lagarde, Weiler .... The day before yesterday Brussels surrendered. Yesterday we had a victory behind Metz. The French are in disorderly retreat. It says in all the papers: 'Flags out in honour of the victors!' Every one is now hanging flags from their attics, windows and balconies as they do on the Emperor's birthday.

23rd August 1914

Mummy goes back to Berlin the day after to-morrow. Then we

shall feel like a dog who has lost his master. The war will seem even sadder. There will be no one to talk to about it.

Willi and I are always running about after Mummy and if it doesn't bother her we like to watch her closely. At all events we don't want to forget what she looks like when we think of her during the winter.

In the evening, when Mummy and Willi were sitting in the summer-house working on Willi's own poetical composition, 'In the land of the Ringing Stone', my sadness became so great that I ran out. In the Güterbahnhof Strasse I encountered three lorries that were slowly turning the corner. The lorries were carrying stretchers on which wounded soldiers lay. They groaned when the wheels rattled over rough stones. Women in the street stood watching and one working-class woman called out: 'There go our boys now!', pointing to the bandaged soldiers. The material was covered with encrusted blood. One soldier was sitting up on the edge of the second lorry. His left arm was missing from the shoulder. His chest was like a four-cornered box of dried bandages. His lips were drawn up so that you could see the teeth behind them. His head kept drooping to one side. The woman suddenly grasped me by the arm, tugged me this way and that, and shouted: 'It's your fault that they're all dying! Your fault!'

I tore myself free and struck the woman's hand. Then I ran down the street, while the woman went on scolding behind me, shouting 'You toffee nosed little snob!' When I reached our yard I sat down on the sandheap under the cherry tree and began to cry. Gretel came out of the door and asked: 'Why are you crying?'

'A woman said it's my fault that the soldiers are dying.'

'She's absolutely mad,' said Gretel indignantly. 'Think nothing of it! She's quite mad!' She sat down by me and prodded the sand. Then she asked: 'What about the soldiers then?'

'Oh, the wounded. They were badly wounded, coming from the East. On lorries.'

'Did you see them?'

'Yes.'

'Were they bad?'

'Very bad. Some looked almost dead.'

'And are you to blame for that?' Gretel began to laugh. I poked a finger in the sand and said, 'Perhaps I am partly to blame. Perhaps I have committed some sin. You never know.'

During the night, while Grandma was asleep, I got up quietly and stood by the open veranda window. The stars were shining brightly; I had to keep looking at them. If every dead soldier were to become a star in the sky, it would be so bright that we would no longer need the sun and the moon. Then it struck me, what rubbish that was, because the stars get their light from the great constellations. In any case a dead body can't become a star. Then I thought of the working-class woman's words and became furious. I considered for a long time whether I shouldn't creep secretly to the station and smuggle myself into a troop train. It would be best for me to die with the others. I dreamed how our headmaster would make a speech in the school hall: 'Our comrade Elfriede Kuhr has given her life on the field of honour. Honour the young girl who truly became a brave girl at the end of her days!' At the thought of how difficult it would be for him to utter these words, I had a job not to explode. I would have shamed the Head.

25th August 1914

Mummy has gone back to Berlin to-day. As the station is closed to passers-by because of the spy-danger, Willi and I had to stay at home. From the veranda window we watched the train stop at the platform. When the engine began to puff clouds of black smoke into the air and the train began to move we waved with long white towels so long as it was still in sight. A hand in a white sleeve waved back with a bunch of flowers. That was Mummy.

When we were smaller we were always rushing into Mummy's bedroom and scrambling for her pillow. Whoever snatched it was blissfully happy because he could bury his face in it at night and breathe Mummy's scent. It kept her scent for days, until Marie put it in the wash.

At six o'clock in the evening some troop trains arrived with the first Russian prisoners. People thronged both sides of the street to see the enemy. The Russians are tall, fair and bronzed, with curly fair beards. Their uniforms are an ugly grey brown and ragged. Instead of helmets they wear peaked caps or fur hats worn at an angle. Many of them had woollen rags wrapped round their feet instead of boots. But there were also officers with wonderful long sheepskin boots; they smoked self-rolled cigarettes. The Russian soldiers searched the ground for discarded bits of tobacco. They picked up crumpled pieces of paper and rummaged in rubbish bins. Willi and I would have liked to throw food or cigarettes to them but we hadn't any. The Russians crowded on to the platform and waited for the departure train.

Then a train with lightly wounded German soldiers came in. They were allowed to leave the train and walk up and down the platform quite cheerfully, while the Russians stood by. The Schneidemühl lookers-on immediately began to throw to the German soldiers apples and pears, rolls, cigars, cigarettes and packets of tobacco. One man actually pulled a pocket-knife out of his jacket, it had a hartshorn covering; he threw that over the railings too. A soldier with a bandage round his head bent down and called out with delight 'Thank you very much!' The rest of the lightly wounded also shouted 'Thank you!' and caught the shower of gifts in their helmets and caps. The Russians looked on quietly as the others shared the gifts.

Suddenly a company of soldiers marched down the street. They were armed and took the Russian prisoners away. We were very excited. Our first Schneidemühl prisoners! Where were they being taken? We followed them for a while, and then met Willi's friend Androwski and went with him across the fields in which women were working. The rye has been cut long since.

28th August 1914

Victories all the time! Five forts in the Namur stronghold and the barrier fort Manonviller have been taken by us. The Belgian newspapers appear from to-day on in German. The English army has been defeated north of St. Quentin. Several thousand prisoners, seven field batteries and one heavy battery are in our possession. But the best has happened on the Eastern front. There General Paul von Hindenburg after three days of battle has brought about the complete defeat of the Russians who had pushed forward in strength with five army corps and three cavalry divisions against the East Prussian towns of Gilgenburg and Ortelsburg. There were an enormous number of prisoners.

The Emperor ordered that after so many victories the schools should take a holiday. Unfortunately the news came so late that we still had mathematics and geography before we assembled in the school courtyard. The headmaster made a speech from the window of his room, ending with the words: 'A cheer for our beloved German Fatherland! ("Hurrah"). And now you can pack up your bags and quietly and, ah, decorously, make your way home.'

As I fastened my satchel on my back in the lobby, my school-mate Sibylla Löwenthal began to cry near me. I asked why she was crying. She said that a boy in the street kept shouting 'Jewess' after her and that she was afraid of him. 'You mustn't take that to heart,' I answered. 'A woman shouted "toffee-nosed little snob!" after me.'

At that moment a girl called from the open class-room door, 'Piete, help me please.'

I told Sibylla to wait and ran back into the class-room, where the girl was rolling up the big map of Austro-Hungary. While I was helping her put the map in its sheath, she whispered, 'You're not going with Bylla, are you?'

'Why on earth not?' I asked.

'But you can't do that any more. It's the Jews that have caused all this.'

I was curious as to what the Jews had done.

My classmate said, 'The war, of course. The Jews just want to make money, and so they have caused the war.'

I was quite dumbfounded and asked, 'Who has said that?'

My friend answered, 'Every one knows that to-day. Because of this no German girl may associate with a Jew or shop in a Jewish concern.'

'Not even at Warschauer's or Schachian's?' I asked. Schachian's is the only large toy shop in Schneidemühl. For a long time I have wanted a grey and white plush cat with a green collar that is in there.

'Of course not!' said my friend. She told me also that according to the latest newspaper reports the nine richest Jews in the world had got together in Poland and concocted the war plan.

'Then is it all lies about the assassination of the Archduke Franz Ferdinand et cetera?' I asked in amazement.

'Oh no, the Jews indeed contrived that.'

'You're just crazy!' I cried. 'You mean the shooting of the Crown Prince and Princess by the student Princip! And in any case, what has Sibylla to do with it?' I was livid and ran back to Sibylla. She told me a lot on the way about the wickedness of people. In earlier times they attacked Jews who hadn't done them the slightest harm and killed them by cutting their throats or simply stringing them up on a tree. They have also done other things to the women. And then they have set fire to Jews' houses. I was greatly aroused by all that I heard, but I couldn't believe it.

33

At home Willi said Bylla was right and that these persecutions of the Jews were still going on to-day in Poland and Russia.

I ran to our Marie and told her about it. She said 'Well, these Jews killed our Lord Jesus on the Cross! It just serves them right!'

'But listen!' I cried, 'didn't Jesus expressly say: "And forgive us our trespasses, as we forgive those who trespass against us?" Where is religion in all this?'

'Miss Piete mustn't ask me about things I don't understand.'

I can't and won't believe it at all. What's the use of all religion, if we do the opposite of what Jesus taught? In our next Religious Knowledge lesson we have to learn the following sentence by heart: 'A new commandment I give you, that you love one another; as I have loved you, so you must love one another.'

Although I can indeed repeat this sentence by heart, I'm not going to. What's the use? I don't learn false propositions in mathematics. Fortunately Androwski came in the evening to swot Latin with Willi. I told Androwski about my conversation with my school friend. And what did the head boy of the Upper Third say? 'There are some fools who won't be cured of their folly till they die!'

30th August 1914

Now suddenly the members of Grannie's sisterhood are complaining about the Jews and are not going to shop at Jewish people's businesses any more. It has become obvious to me that that working-class woman recently took me for a Jewish girl. I was just going to tell this story to Grannie's sisterhood ladies when a messenger brought a gigantic basket full of wine, fruit, bread and sausages. It just happened to have been sent by a Jewish shopkeeper's wife for the soldiers. Her name is Frau Edel and she lives in our Alte Bahnhof Strasse. We do a lot of shopping at Edels.

Fighting is raging all the time on the Eastern Front. Along the whole line of nearly 400 kilometres there is furious fighting. If you stand quite still and pay attention you can feel the ground slightly quivering beneath your feet. It is an uncanny feeling.

Whole columns of East Prussian refugees came through our town. Many are crying. But some are quite quiet. There are mothers with quite tiny children. They put their infants under their shawls and let them drink. The little ones' behinds are bloody because the mothers haven't enough nappies to lay them out to dry. We have torn up old sheets and shirts and given them the pieces to wrap the babies in. Gretel and I now play a game in the yard in which her old celluloid doll is a refugee child that has no more nappies. She has painted its behind red, indicating soreness.

The girls of the Schneidemühl schools come together in the afternoons in their particular classes in order to knit stockings, scarves, head-warmers, knee-covers, mittens, gloves and ear-muffs for the soldiers. Field-grey wool is bought by the pound out of various collections of money. A scarf is not difficult to knit – always right-hand stitches and left at the back. But you have to be a wizard to knit the foot of a stocking. When I have with great difficulty finished both legs Grandma takes the stockings with her to the station and between making soup and pouring coffee she knits the feet on.

1st September 1914

The battle is won! This is really true, so it says in the special news sheet; General Paul von Hindenburg has defeated the Russians at Tannenberg. More than 60,000 prisoners have been taken, including two commanding generals; many guns and standards were also captured. The retreating Russians were forced back into the Masurian lakes and swamps. The Emperor has in gratitude appointed General von Hindenburg as senior general and has conferred on him the Iron Cross First Class.

The excitement of victory prevails in the town. The military band is playing all soldiers' songs and marches in the Neue Markt. People are walking around as thick as flies in the streets, laughing, wishing each other good luck and joining in singing the National Anthem. The officers' faces are beaming.

At the street corner we met the wife of Councillor Schön (a Government adviser). She looked sad. 'Oh God. Oh God,' she said, 'the good God will indeed watch over and protect my son; he is at Tannenberg.' Her eyes were full of tears. We comforted her as well as we could. We love the old lady; she is Grannie's oldest friend. She also has such a sweet little dog; his name is Bello.

Two steps further on we met Fräulein Ella Gumprecht. 'Have you written to your mother yet?', she cried. 'Such good news! The Russians all stuck in the swamp!'

35

Willi thought that Mummy would read the army reports in Berlin before we could, back here in Schneidemühl. Hardly had Fräulein Gumprecht left us when I asked Willi: 'Are the Russians really stuck in the swamps?'

'It is certainly Hindenburg's very great victory,' he declared.

'Will no one help them out? Must they be drowned?' I asked. Willi said, 'How do you imagine they could be helped out? We would certainly be shot if we approached without cover.'

The war is one month old to-day.

2nd September 1914

Sedan Remembrance Day! Another holiday from school. We assembled at 9 o'clock in the school courtyard in order to march in procession to the church where a service was held to celebrate the day. The girls of our school wore black, white and red rosettes with long tails on the left breast. Our old Aunt Emma, who has the little fancy goods shop in Friedrichstrasse, made my rosette. As she was pinning it on me, she said, 'Ask your Grandma, child, whether she is going to leave. Lieschen and Minna (they are Aunt Emma's twin sisters) are definitely going to Berlin, but I can't really leave the shop empty!'

'Grandma won't run away,' I cried. 'She has to look after things at the station!'

'The ground trembles!' said Aunt Emma. 'The Russians can't be far away.'

'But Hindenburg has defeated the Russians!' I said proudly.

A long column of soldiers was marching past up the street; they were the newly kitted-out 149th who had been ordered on church parade. Aunt Emma said she felt life no longer had any joy in it and she would like to die. I had to promise to put a red rose in her hand as she lay in her coffin. Aunt Emma is very old, seventy-one. She has grey hair and a big hooked nose with little blue and red veins; she also wears gold-rimmed spectacles. She is the nicest of my aunts.

'I will put into your hand the most beautiful rose that there is,' I cried. 'I hope it will not be in the depth of winter.'

Then I ran after the soldiers. They were marching to another church. They certainly ought not to be together with us girls in the same church, because that would disturb their devotions.

St. John's Church was full of schoolgirls. A man or woman teacher sat at the end of every fourth pew to see that there was no fooling about. I sat between my friends Dora Haensch and Trude Jakobi. Then the minister gave an address. He spoke of the battle of Sedan in the year 1871 and compared it with the battle of Tannenberg. He praised the battle of Tannenberg, saying that it was greater than the battle of Sedan and that there were many men captured and killed. God had stood by our gallant soldiers and blessed their weapons. Countless Russians had perished in the Masurian swamps. 'With men and steeds and chariots has the Lord conquered!', he cried out from the chancel. Then the organ started up, and we sang 'We praise thee, O God'. Then every one put two pfennigs in the collection bag; the amount is to be devoted on this occasion to the widows and orphans of those on War Service. It is customary always to put two pfennigs in the collection. I think it is very little. While the steward was going round with the red velvet bag I couldn't help thinking again of the Russians in the swamps and imagined how they would go under – first the chest, then the shoulders, then the chin, then the mouth and all. I whispered to my friend Dora: 'We have to praise and thank God that we have killed so many Russians!'

Dora didn't answer, for our class-teacher was watching us closely; she raised her eyebrows high. I didn't join in the Lord's Prayer, because I wouldn't say, 'as we forgive those who trespass against us!'

Then we went home. On the way we met four soldiers who were leading away a woman and a man. The crowd of people accompanying them were shouting 'Shame on them! Put them up against the wall!' We ran with them as far as the Küddow Bridge before we discovered what it was all about. They were Belgian spies, husband and wife, who had been arrested on a train. The woman wore a slim black costume and a little hat with a veil, the man a black overcoat and a hard hat and carried a brief-case. Both were silent, but were very pale.

Dora and I ran home. I listened all day at the open window for rifle-shots. Towards five o'clock in the afternoon there was the distant crackle of a salvo. I pressed my fists against my temples and rushed madly around the room.

What a Sedan-day!

4th September 1914

Eastern Front: The Russians are fighting around the town of Lamberg, but it is still in our possession, although the Russians

37

are in greater strength. Western Front: Heavy fighting between Rheims and Verdun. French attacks from the fortress of Verdun were repelled at the cost of much bloodshed.

More and more people are fleeing from Schneidemühl. Whole blocks of flats are empty. Household furniture is taken by van to the goods station and put on a train. 'They're fleeing just now,' says Grandma. 'They'll be back soon enough.'

But those fleeing from East Prussia will not be back so soon. I saw this to-day. A goods train comes in from the Allenstein region. The platform is immediately swarming with wailing refugees. A young mother with a black headband is crying loudly because she has lost her children. An old, refined-looking man grabs Grandma's sleeve and asks, 'Have you not seen my daughter? She is wearing a blue coat. I am nearly blind and cannot recognise anything properly!' A hundred women on the platform are wearing blue coats. We set the old man on a seat, where he whimpers quietly to himself. It is in vain that I run around calling 'What woman is looking for her blind father?'

In the train a woman is detained who suspects every person of being an enemy who is going to shoot her dead. She is shrieking, raving and praying. There are five children with her, also shrieking. Medical orderlies carry out a fourteen year old boy from the same train. During the journey he kept trying to jump out of the train. Now he is put in a cab and taken to the municipal hospital.

'Has he no parents then?' Frau Annchen asked the refugees. They don't know either; the boy was all on his own in the train.

'Where we were living there is not a single stone left on another,' said one countrywoman. 'Everything is burning. Not a single head of cattle is still alive. Some bedding and clothing and a little money is all that we could bring with us.'

We ran around, serving bread, coffee and soup. On average 400 kilos of bread, ½ hundredweight of coffee, 100 litres of milk and 1 hundredweight of fat are consumed each day at the station. Sometimes three or four troop trains, with 1500 men each, arrive in a single hour. In between these come trainloads of refugees and passenger trains that have been converted into hospital trains. Yesterday evening a soldier burst out of a hospital train screaming at the top of his voice. All he was wearing was a grey woollen shirt, his identity disc around his neck and tattered military trousers. He ran up and down in front of the Red Cross depot, tearing his hair, and struck his forehead at least ten times

38

against one of the iron lamp-posts, yelling: 'I heard them shrieking! You've never heard anything like it! I heard them shrieking, heard them shrieking!' Then he himself, with wide open mouth, roared 'Aaaah .... aaaah .... aaaah', until some orderlies came running up and held his arms firmly behind his back. He had thoroughly battered his face against the lamp-post and blood was trickling from his forehead. We ran up to them too and Grandma asked in horror, 'What is the matter with the lad?' 'He's gone mad,' said one of the orderlies. 'He was present at the fighting in Masuria and went crackers. There's nowt else wrong with him.'

'Don't squeeze his arms so much,' ordered Grandma, and she went up to the bleeding soldier and just stroked his cheek. The soldier cried 'Oh Mummy, I actually heard them shrieking!' and looked at Grandma with wild eyes. Grandma said 'No, my lad, you're dreaming. Come to your senses, my boy, and I'll give you some coffee.'

And he drained a whole pot of coffee that Grandma held to his mouth while she and Frau Annchen kept smiling at him. When he had at length been taken away I said to Grandma, 'They were really shrieking, Granny! You see, they were shrieking in the swamps. The soldier wasn't telling lies!'

But Grandma suddenly became angry and said I mustn't keep sneaking around among the soldiers but should make my way home and get my homework done. At this I also got angry, tore off my coffee-apron and swept off without saying goodbye.

7th September 1914

Something has happened. I got into a fight with a boy because he was calling after Sibylla Löwenthal, 'Jewish sow!'

'Take that remark back at once!' I cried and stood stock still. It was in Milch Strasse right in front of the Diaconate House which my grandfather had built just before he died. A deaconess with a blue hood, and a blue gown with blue shoulder-bands was walking up and down in the garden cutting asters. 'Jewish rabble!' cried the boy. 'War-hoarder!'

We immediately went for each other. The boy struck me on the face and I gave him a punch under the chin. He knocked my school hat off and I knocked his cap off. Then he seized my hair and nearly pulled my pigtails off. If the deaconess had not run out of the garden gate we would have hit each other a lot more. She said 'Now children! Aren't you ashamed of yourselves? Don't you want to behave like German children?' I pointed to Sibylla, who was pressing up against the garden fence. 'He called my friend a Jewish sow, sister.'

Then the boy ran away. I ran a few steps after him, and called out: 'You wait – we'll meet again!'

The deaconess shook her head and asked: 'Are you not the grand-daughter of the late town councillor Golz? Whatever would your grandmother say to such behaviour!' Then she went back into the flower garden. Sibylla was very unhappy about the scrap and thought that in future she would always walk home from school alone. I'm not very happy about the affair either. It is a long time since I last had a fight in the street.

It rained this afternoon and was very windy. Towards six o'clock the victors from Namur came through our station. Marie and I had taken a basket full of bread to the Red Cross and were just going back for the second one when the train came in. The soldiers were sitting in coaches decorated with flowers and with flowers in their button-holes. The guns captured at Namur stood on open flat trucks and they too were decorated with flowers and wreathed with garlands of pine leaves. Soldiers in long grey cloaks leaned against the guns and looked down proudly on us civilians. They had made a dummy out of straw to look like a Frenchman and had set it up on a cannon.

'How are things going with you in the East?' shouted the victors from Namur. We yelled back: 'Going well! And how are things in the West?'

'Very good,' replied the soldiers. 'We're winning!' The Namur victors must know – they actually come from the Front. The people who had collected behind the platform fence began to sing:– 'There burst out a shout like a thunder-clap, like the clashing of swords and the roaring of waves ...' The Namur heroes joined in the singing and waved greetings.

Special bulletins to-day gave the news that in the West two forts and their connecting defences in the stronghold of Maubeuge have fallen. The German artillery fire is directed against the town, which is burning in various places.

The army of Senior General Bülow reports the taking of 12,934 prisoners up to the end of August. The names of our commanders in the West are:–

Crown Prince William,
Crown Prince Rupert of Bavaria,
Duke Albert of Württemberg,
Senior General von Bülow,
Senior General von Kluck,
Senior General Heeringen, and
Senior General von Hausen.

The most important commander on the Eastern Front is Senior General von Hindenburg. He now reports the carrying off of 90,000 unwounded Russian prisoners, mostly from the battles of Ortelsburg and Tannenberg.

8th September 1914

The fortress of Dendermonde, which lies in front of Antwerp, has now also been taken by us. In addition we have seized the town of Maubeuge, around which the soldiers had been fighting so long. At the same time we have captured 400 guns and taken 40,000 prisoners. I often close my eyes and picture what it is like at the front. Certainly everything in pieces, holes in the ground, stumps of trees burning like torches, dead soldiers, and such as are not yet dead rolling on the ground pressing their entrails back into their stomachs with their hands. And pitch-black air and a terrible stench. And crows, lots of crows. And rats.

It says in the Schneidemühl News that Rheims has surrendered without a fight. But the French write (as it says also in our paper) that we have shot to pieces the magnificent old tower of Rheims Cathedral and that we are therefore 'swine' ('boches'). Our paper adds that the French had placed machine guns on the Cathedral tower. After all this it says 'Surrendered without a fight'. You read and read: one says this and another says that.

9th September 1914

We have another holiday from school of course. The girls danced for joy in the class-room. We missed Mathematics, German grammar, French, Physics and Religion. Trude Jakobi exclaimed: 'A victory every day, and we shan't have to come to school any more!'

I had no wish to go home, but went up the hill out of town right to the cemetery. Our family graves lie just behind the wall. ('Resting-place of the Golz and Haber families.') It was quite

41

quiet in the cemetery, and after I had said the Lord's Prayer for the great-grandparents and Grandpa, I walked and walked until I came out again at the other end of the cemetery. There was a newly-ploughed area there and a rubbish dump. I walked further up the hill. The soil here was sandy and poor; even straggling weeds could hardly grow in it. Many crows were flying around the rubbish heap, cawing. I turned left and came to a little wood of small pine trees. Here I suddenly encountered a line of barbed wire. It was the same as the strong barbed wire behind which the soldiers at the Front fortify the trenches. This time the wire served to enclose several graves. The graves were bare and had neither cross nor stone, not even an identity post with a number. Dozens of hooded crows were sitting in the pines. Everything was deathly quiet apart from their 'Caw, Caw'; no humans far and wide. I tried several times to crawl through the barbed wire. But it was too firmly fixed and wouldn't give at all. On the little wooden gate, which also had barbed wire fixed over it, hung a rusty lock. As if any one would want to steal the dead! I poked around for a long time in the sand and mould, looking for buttercups. I tried to throw them on to the graves. But they were too light and fell down in front of them. Then I broke a branch of pine. It made so loud a crack that the crows flew up in the air and around me, calling out as if they would attack me. I got so frightened that I didn't quite break the branch off. It remained hanging on the tree like a dislocated arm. Poor tree! I ran home as fast as I could.

When I asked Grandma about this cemetery, she said I must be mistaken, there is no such cemetery in Schneidemühl. I have asked a few friends, but they don't know it either.

To-day is the birthday of Uncle Bruno, Grandma's son. He is posted to the No. 54 Field Artillery Regiment and is at present stationed at the assembly room in Halle. I have put a bunch of heather on Grandma's writing-desk for Uncle Bruno.

10th September 1914

Horror stories about guerilla fighters! They say Russians tie German women who stay behind to trees, set up wooden crosses in front of them and nail their little children to them. When the kiddies have died before their mothers' eyes, the Russians mutilate the women and kill them. The Belgian guerillas are said to be no better, but they do it all more secretly. The guerillas are described as 'Hyenas of the battlefield'. Whenever they are encountered they are shot.

In peace-time there were no guerillas. They have only appeared during the war. Dear God, just bring the war to an end! I don't look on it as fine any more, in spite of 'school holidays' and victories.

11th September 1914

I have sent Mummy the first pages of my War Diary. Now she will see that I have kept my word.

I came over faint in school to-day. It was during Religious Knowledge. Fräulein Becker had asked me to recite the passage on love of one's neighbour that I had recently written down. But I had sworn not to say it, and remained silent. Fräulein Becker said, 'What's the matter, Elfriede? Is there something wrong?'

Suddenly there was a very light buzzing in my ears as if a fly was buzzing in each one. Then it seemed like the rushing of water and everything began to swim around. I was just able to say 'no'. Then it was lovely and calm and dark. Afterwards I was lying on the sofa in the Staff Room and Fräulein Becker was sitting next to me, looking at me. No other teachers were in the room. She asked me whether I slept badly at nights. I said 'yes'. She asked, 'why?' I said, 'because the soldiers passing through sing so loudly'. She asked whether I couldn't close the window. But it makes no difference whether the window is closed or not. Even in my sleep I hear the soldiers singing ... 'in the homeland, in the homeland, there we'll meet again!'

'Have you any other worry?' asked dear Fräulein Becker. Very nice of her! But how can you talk of such things to a teacher?

12th September 1914

There is an important new war medal, awarded 'Pour le mérite' (the Order of Merit). Emperor Wilhelm has conferred it on Senior General von Hindenburg, the victor of the Masurian Lakes. Paul von Hindenburg is mighty big and strong; he has a square head with a moustache and many wrinkles in his face. The people here in the East worship him. When it is reported, as it is to-day, that another 1000 men of the Russian Guards and three Caucasian army corps have been taken prisoner, they say at once: 'Ah, our Hindenburg!' But this was not Hindenburg at all, but the Silesian Yeomanry. 'Well, they are under Hindenburg's command,' people then say. But they are not under Hindenburg – that is pure imagination.

In East Prussia, Hindenburg has decisively beaten the Russian army which was advancing upon Lyck. Our troops pursuing the retreating Russians have already crossed the frontier. More than 30,000 unwounded prisoners have again been reported.

Many German towns now have prisoner-of-war camps, where the prisoners can be accommodated. Schneidemühl will have a big camp too. Bread and other food will then become dearer because the many hundred thousand prisoners eat so much.

Some big soup cauldrons have now been installed at the station, in which the Red Cross ladies have to make more and more soup for the soldiers, for the gifts of things like sausages, ham and fat become fewer now. It is now getting cold too. A plate of soup costs 5 pfennigs. But Grandma thinks it will soon cost more. One day they make lentil soup, another day pea soup and another potato soup. The soup is cooked with meat. It tastes very good. I have eaten some too. Service at the station is now regulated. Grandma no longer has to go on duty every day – only on Mondays. In her Monday group are Frau Annchen Schönfeld, the fat and jolly Frau Schimz, Fräulein Karboschewsky, Fräulein Pfennig and your humble servant. But Grandma goes every day just the same, to 'superintend' and see that all goes well. She said, 'They can make fun of me and call me "Sergeant" if they want to – I know these characters!'

13th September 1914

We have a cruiser, the 'Karlsruhe', that sinks enemy ships like nothing on earth. Yesterday it sent the English steamer 'Cowes Castle'[4] to the bottom off Barbados (heavens! where is that?). It says in the newspaper 'A cheer for our gallant boys in blue!'

Otherwise nothing special has happened. Grandma was not at the station, because for once no military trains were expected. To break the monotony my brother Willi and I went for a ramble. We went into the woods around the Sandsee and walked all over the place. My brother was not wearing shoes or socks and hopped over pine-needles and sharp stones with his long, pale, spindly legs. He carried his shoes tied together round his neck to save them.

'I may perhaps have to go into the Army too,' said Willi. 'It's

44

certainly not out of the question.' (Willi is fifteen years old.)

'Androwski as well?' I asked.

Willi thought Androwski would be exempted from military service because of his bad eyesight.

'If you have to go to the war,' I said, 'I will go dressed as a soldier. We have always been together, and I will not leave you.'

Willi said gravely, 'They would recognise you at the first inspection, kid.'

I said I would not attend any inspections. I would know how to get hold of a uniform myself. But Willi dismissed the idea with a wave of his white fingers. I think he has the hands of a real musician.

We had come to the edge of the wood. Suddenly we were in the midst of steep, grassy slopes, foothills of the Ural–Baltic mountain range. It was at one time sea here. You still find amber in the mountains. We stood still. It was lovely and peaceful here. Far and wide there were no houses, only hills, lush grass and birch-trees. Three boys were looking after a herd of goats grazing on a slope. Suddenly a he-goat came running towards us at great speed. We knew that a he-goat can attack you. In spite of this we couldn't help laughing. But when he made straight for us with lowered horns we got moving and ran up a hill with him after us. At the top there was a long, broad field which had been mown. 'Good Lord,' shouted Willi. 'He'll get us!' We rushed across the field. We often stumbled as we went, for it was covered with deep old rabbit-holes filled with rain-water. We ran until we came to a slope, down which we slid on our behinds, and reached the bottom alright but with the goat close behind us. A friendly looking cottage suddenly appeared in front of us, with an orchard surrounded by a high wire fence. 'Home!' At last we had reached the fence. We turned round panting and saw that the goat was on the point of catching us. 'Boy, oh boy,' cried Willi, 'just like the Russians at Tannenberg!' I climbed wildly on to the fence, while Willi stood with opened umbrella. Just as the goat had caught up with us, he stopped all of a sudden, looked at us in amazement and careered (foreign word!) at full gallop into the yard of the cottage, where he belonged.

I climbed down from the fence. Then we began to laugh so heartily that the dogs in the farm buildings began to bark. We wiped the tears of laughter from our faces and exclaimed that in this instance (another foreign word!) we had been miserable (foreign word!!) soldiers.

There is a joke at the Front that goes like this: Grischka has been taken prisoner. He stands ragged and overrun with lice, but perfectly happy, in front of the Germans. They say, 'Aren't you ashamed to have been taken prisoner?' Grischka replies, 'Not a bit of it. Better five minutes a coward than a life-time dead!'

14th September 1914

The little cemetery is the burial-place for our enemies. A few Russian prisoners who have died in transit and several spies who have been shot rest there. The Belgian husband and wife are also buried there. Frau Annchen and Grandma have asked me to show them the cemetery. As they were not on duty at the station to-day we went there together. Gretel Wegner came with us too.

As we stood in front of the barbed wire fence, Grandma suddenly looked around her in a pained way and cried: 'Now that beats everything! It's our own land!' We were really amazed. The strip of sandy ground that immediately adjoined the cemetery was the last piece of land that we owned. As the ground was infertile we had never been able to sell it. Our former coachman Schulz had once tried to sow potatoes there, but it was never worth while. Frau Annchen thought Grandma ought to be pleased. She would now certainly be able to sell the land to the town, for there would be many more enemies dying and needing graves. Then the council will soon buy additional land in order to enlarge the cemetery. Besides, the fine sand is good for burials.

Gretel and I broke off pine twigs and threw them on to the nearest mounds. We secretly decided to look after the Russian cemetery. It was to belong entirely to us. Gretel would even bring a little rake, for we had found a hole in the barbed wire through which some one must already have crawled. The wire was twisted and bent down outwards, you could just manage to squeeze through. We would tie the rake up in the top of a pine so that it couldn't be stolen. Then we would rake between the graves every week and lay little bunches of wild flowers on the mounds.

Gretel hadn't known that we still owned some land. 'Shall we play at being farmers?' I said. 'You are the farmer's wife and I am your farm-hand, working for you.' Gretel agreed to this. She took the name Martha and I was 'Joan'.[5] I had read the name Joan in a book about the Hungarian plains. We cleared Grandma's land and collected the biggest stones together in a heap. We enjoyed the game very much. We didn't want to go home when Grandma and Frau Annchen went home.

On the way we learned that we had defeated the Russians at Lemberg after five days' hard struggle and had taken 10,000 prisoners. 'Will you be off school then to-morrow?' asked Gretel. 'No,' I said, 'not for anything less than fifty thousand.' 'Pity!' said Gretel.

After supper we wanted to rush off to the cemetery with the rake but it quickly grew dark and we got frightened, so we turned back and hid the rake in the summer-house. From the station there rang out, first five and then again seven sharp shots. 'Heavens, what a war!' I said.

When I went up into the house, Willi was sitting at the table by the oil lamp reading the newspaper. 'Listen to this,' he said, 'here's something good!' And he read; 'What is the best-loved and so far most frequently sung soldier's song? You can hear it in every barracks, on every parade ground and from every troop train. But as far as we know it has never been printed. It is a poetical and, so to speak, unreal creation, and yet it is not to be scoffed at, for it shows in a striking way how the nation, like children, can combine well-loved words with well-loved images, whether they are in harmony or not. It runs like this:–

> I had the very best of friends,
> Unequalled far and wide;
> The drum-beat called to battle
> And he was by my side.
> Glorious, Glorious, Happy and Victorious!
> Yes, with heart and hand
> Yes, with heart and hand
> Serving the Fatherland!
> The little woodland birds
> Sang such a wonderful refrain:
> In the homeland, in the homeland,
> There we'll meet again!'

'Stop – that's enough!' I exclaimed. I was so happy and didn't want to cry again.

15th September 1914

When we had had supper there was a ring at the door, and Frau Schön (the Councillor's wife) was standing there in tears.

47

'God in Heaven, what has happened?' said Grandma. 'Dear Frau Schön, come in and sit down on the sofa and calm yourself!' But Frau Schön couldn't speak at all and just cried louder, until we gathered that her youngest son, who was serving as First Lieutenant, had been killed at Tannenberg. Just before that he had been awarded the Iron Cross, Class II. Councillor Schön had just gone to the family of his eldest son, so Frau Schön was all alone when she received the sad news. She had just hurried to Grandma in her misery because she knew of no other earthly comfort. Grandma and Frau Schön cried together for some time. Frau Schön kept calling out 'If only I knew just how he was killed! Whether he had to suffer much .... and whether he remained whole, without losing any limbs.' It was so sad that she worried herself as to whether her boy had remained whole in all his limbs, when after all he was dead.

16th September 1914

Last night I heard Grandma crying. She was crying so much that it greatly distressed me. The young First Lieutenant Schön is the first of our friends to be killed. I buried my head in my pillow so that Grandma would not hear me crying.

This morning there was a letter from Mummy. 'Now my dear pupil Siegfried Dahlke has been killed at Maubeuge,' she wrote. 'The best pupil in my singing class, a singer, a heroic tenor, who could have become a second Caruso! You can't imagine my grief, I go around as if I had a stone in my chest and another in my throat.' That is the second friend! Mummy then goes on – 'Thank you, dear Piete, for the first pages of your diary! How busy you have been! It is already almost a book! But you ought to see the war in a more heroic light – not so much of the "down" side. It clouds the view of the greatness of an event. Don't let yourself be overwhelmed with sloppy sentimentality. Our enemies want to rob us of our country and our honour. Our men are defending both. And Siegfried Dahlke died the death of a hero! Never forget that!'

I certainly will not forget it. Indeed I cry, not because our soldiers are dying the deaths of heroes, for there is something great about the death of a hero. I cry simply because they have died – just died. No more morning, no more evening – dead. When a mother's son is killed, she will cry her eyes out, not because he had died a hero, but because he has gone away and is buried. No more will he sit at the table, no longer can she cut a slice of bread for him or darn his socks. So she cannot say 'Thank you' that he has died like a hero. (Please, please, Mummy, don't be angry!)

17th September 1914

I had nearly forgotten that our troops are fighting in the Balkans. There are so many theatres of war. It was in the newspaper. 'The Serbian forces that had broken through over the Sava have everywhere been thrown back. Syrmien and Barat are completely free of the enemy.'

On the Western theatre of war it says: 'The fighting taking place on the right flank of the Western forces extends, through the adjacent armies on their Eastern flank, as far as Verdun.'

In the East Hindenburg's armies are re-grouping after completing the pursuit of the Russians. It says that there is no foundation for the widespread rumours of impending danger in Upper Silesia.

But it is true, nevertheless, that the earth trembles. So the danger must be near. We have heard that defensive earthworks have been constructed a few kilometres behind our town. The furniture vans with refugees' goods and chattels pass through the streets all day long. One family after another is leaving. We think Aunt Emma Haber's two twin sisters, Lieschen and Minna, will leave too. Grandma said to-day to her sister Luise Otter: 'I tell you, Luise dear, if the old girls run away, ten horses wouldn't drag me back to them. Old Schneidemühlians don't turn their backs. We must preserve our respect at least.'

I haven't yet properly described Aunt Luise Otter, although she lives in our house at 17 Alte Bahnhofstrasse and we use her garden. We call her our 'Cavalier' Aunt because she wears such old-fashioned clothes that people in the streets laugh behind her back. She always has most peculiar bonnets and ribbons on her head. They have probably come down from Great Grandmother Karoline Haber. And she is very small too. Grandma, who is her younger sister, is nearly twice her height. At one time Aunt Otter could play the piano very well. She has composed many pieces of music although she couldn't reach an octave with her small hands. She doesn't play any more these days, but Grandma has learned her pieces by heart and used to play them often. Willi now takes care of the piano playing and composition. Aunt Luise

Otter is short-sighted. If she wants to read anything she holds the writing so close to her face that her nose touches the lettering.

Grandma says that Aunt Otter is very clever – 'the cleverest of us all', she declares. Aunt has in the course of time made seven inventions, all of which she registered with the Patent Office in Berlin. She constructed small-scale models of the inventions out of matchboxes. Now she is very worried about burglars on account of the patents and she carries the models in a thick black leather pouch on a girdle under her skirt. Her door is always bolted too; even Grandma is only allowed to speak through a slot in the door. Her husband, Post Secretary Georg Otter, is hardly ever to be seen. He too is now 72 years old and has snow-white hair on which a little black silk cap sits. Aunt Luise keeps him shut up in his room, because otherwise he makes the curtains reek of smoke, or so she says. But he has no wish to go out, but is quite content sitting at his table reading and puffing at a pipe or smoking a cigar. Sometimes he looks out from behind the curtain and nods quite happily to us when we are playing under his window. Once he even laughed out loud, when I called to him: 'Uncle, we're having beans and mutton to-day. Lovely, eh?' If once in a blue moon Uncle and Aunt do go out together, Uncle Otter always trots three paces behind, because he is bad on his feet. Then everybody runs to the window. Willi and I in particular make jokes. We often tease Aunt Otter and specially enjoy pulling her leg because of her fear of burglars. Once she had bought a goose for Christmas, which hung for three days on a strong nail in front of her kitchen window. For three nights Aunt kept watch behind the window because she thought burglars would steal her goose. But she is not a bit stingy – just the opposite. She gives so much to beggars that she is always short of cash. She spends very little on herself. Yet when she has the washerwoman (who is a loathsome old creature) in the house, she buys a whole basketful of cakes, and there is meat, pure coffee, whipped cream and God knows what else. She once said: 'If beggars cry at my funeral, my life will not have been in vain.'

She never goes into her garden. So we have it all to ourselves.

19th September 1914

To-day is Mother's birthday. We have sent her a parcel. It contained cakes, sausages and a side of bacon. Willi has written a lovely poem for her. I was going to write one too, but it wouldn't come right. So I scribbled in small writing on one corner of a slab of chocolate:

> As the little kitten pines
> For the mother-cat that roams,
> So my heart does beat in longing;
> Mother, Mother, do come home!

The town has asked all residents to contribute to a 'First War Loan'. Every one is to put in as much money as he can spare, for there is an urgent need to buy munitions and guns. People will be given a printed receipt for the money they hand over, the so-called 'Acknowledgement of Debt', which must be kept until the end of the war. Then you get all your money back, to the last farthing, plus five per cent interest. The interest will be paid out by the Royal Prussian Municipal Loan Sinking Fund in Berlin. (Jesus, what a mouthful!)

Everybody has contributed money to the War Loan. It is more or less a matter of honour. There are notices all over the school: 'Enlist the support of your parents, relatives and friends for the War Loan!'

Grandma put in three hundred marks and Willi and I fifty marks each from our savings bank. I have in all a hundred and fifty marks in the savings bank; it is money which I am always given on my birthday by my godparents. Aunt Otter has stumped up two hundred marks for the War Loan; she let me pay it in for her at school and I got a prize for it in the form of a cardboard brooch. The result of the first German War Loan is now out: three and a half thousand million marks Government Loan and over one thousand million marks Exchequer Bonds; that makes four and a half thousand million marks War Loan altogether.

20th September 1914

'My one and only beloved Mummy!

I must write to you again, although it was your birthday yesterday and we all wrote to you and there is really nothing more to write about. But I would like to ask your advice about something. Something I am not sure about. We have in our class a girl called Sibylla Löwenthal who is a Jewess – and there is nothing wrong with that. But the girls are so horrible to her that I can't bear it. I have always shared my

51

bread with her, but now the girls say I must not hand-feed a Jew – they are responsible for the war. But Sibylla is such a nice girl, and I know her parents too; they have a whole-sale sausageskin business and have had nothing whatsoever to do with the war. They say their prayers often and light candles every Friday evening and give a tenth of their earn-ings to the poor. And then, if the Jews have caused the war and people despise them so much for that – why then is everyone cheering and saying that the war is a matter of honour and it is glorious to die for your Fatherland?

Now I have already had one big quarrel with the girls over Sibylla and I have had a fight in Milchstrasse with a boy (forgive me) because he insulted Bylla. I met the same boy again to-day. We immediately went for each other hammer and tongs. He hit me over the head with his school atlas and I took my big drawing-board and hit him on the head. He cried and kicked out at me. Then I ran off. Now forgive me again but I should really like to know whether any one can be allowed to insult people like Bylla without blame. It was certainly right for me to fall out with the boy because he called Sibylla a Jewish sow. What I did with the drawing-board was of course not right. But what else could I have done? Please write to me as soon as possible, before I get involved in a third quarrel with the lout. Otherwise all is well with us. A million kisses! Your ever-loving daughter, Piete.'

21st September 1914

Every Saturday afternoon now we have two hours handiwork at school. We just knit things for the soldiers. While we work at stockings, mufflers, head protectors and body-belts our needle-work teacher reads little stories about events in the field or war stories from 1870/71.

There are two large wooden chests in our class-room. One contains a collection of old iron, the other serves for the storage of copper articles. We have sorted out all our cooking pots. I have already coaxed out of Grandma a great 20-litre copper boiler. It glistens like gold. We always used to make plum jam in it. 'My dear lovely old copper boiler,' sighed Grandma. Now cartridges are being made out of it.

22nd September 1914

The Red Cross canteen at the station has been transferred to a disused 4th Class railway carriage. It stands without wheels on the platform, close to a big round flower bed. There is a door in front and windows to the left and right. The door at the back is blocked. In front of this door is the stove, and so-called 'Wizard-cooker' on which soup and coffee can be made at the same time. On the left side of the carriage there are long, narrow tables on which the Red Cross ladies prepare the food for the soldiers, cut bread and wash-up and stack the crockery. On the right side there are benches. That's where the soldiers sit and rest. Grandma and Frau Annchen have made up some pretty little curtains out of one old curtain and have hung them in front of the windows. The other ladies have brought in pictures of the Imperial family and Army generals and nailed them on the wall. The outside of the carriage is painted field-grey and distinguished with the sign 'Red Cross on a white ground'. The Red Cross sign has also been painted on the roof. A great heat prevails inside and it smells of coffee, soup and uniforms. I love the Red Cross centre. The soldiers love it too. 'It is just like home,' they say, when they poke their heads through the door. They often sit for a long time on the bench, in silence or chatting with us. 'Hey, little lass, are you doing a good job too in the war?' said one militia man to me. 'A very good job,' answered Frau Schimz. 'She lugs the coffee urn about like an old-timer on the railway.' 'She's got the freckles of one, too,' said the soldier, and every one laughed.

23rd September 1914

The German submarine 'U9' under the command of Lieutenant-Commander Weddigen yesterday sank the big English pocket-battleships 'Aboukir', 'Hogue' and 'Cressy' in the North Sea.

Flags were out in the town. Everyone was rejoicing over the feat of the little submarine. Lt. Commander Weddigen is the hero of the day. At school our Nature Studies teacher, Herr Schiffman, asked if we knew what a submarine looked like. I know exactly and was able to draw one on the black-board. I was praised for this – I, the scapegoat of the school! Herr Schiffman actually said: 'Why don't you others know what such an important weapon as a submarine looks like? Follow the example of

Kuhr, who does at least kept her eyes open.'

Oh, I nearly burst with pride. Throughout the Nature Study lesson we drew warships, pocket-battleships, torpedo-boats, mine-sweepers, etc. Herr Schiffman explained to us the characteristics of battleships. Big battleships are just as important as the little dangerous submarines, because they carry heavy guns with a greater range and can cover greater distances.

Southern theatre of war: Austro-Hungarian forces have forced the Serbs back and have crossed the rivers Drina and Sava.

Western theatre of war: The fighting is taking place beyond the Oise. Heavy French attacks south of Verdun were repelled with much bloodshed. There were considerable losses on both sides.

Eastern theatre of war: Nothing fresh.

25th September 1914

The casualty lists from the fighting around Verdun become longer and longer, and more and more often are troops being transferred from East to West. All leave has been stopped.

The Schöns want their dead son to be brought home; it has been granted. The young Schön had made a war-time marriage shortly before getting his marching orders. His young widow is on a visit to the Schöns – 'absolutely devastated', they say. Many soldiers make war-time marriages.

Gretel Wegner, her brother Fritz, Dora Haensch's brother Julius, a few neighbouring children and I now play a new game of soldiers. I have bought myself a little yellow book that contains all the drill regulations for infantry officers, all the words of command and even little illustrations of the way in which the infantrymen must handle their rifles, bayonets, etc. Jule Haensch (we call him Jule rather than Julius) and Fritz Wegner have carved rifles and bayonets out of wooden boxes. Now in every spare moment we practise the 'holds' exactly according to the drill book and they are done with such a snap that it resounds right across the yard. We practise also all the body movements – 'Stand at ease!', 'Easy!', 'Quick March!', 'Get down!', and whatever they are called. All the mothers of our playmates complain about our clothes which are quite grey with dust from lying down. When playing soldiers I now only wear my gym knickers or a discarded pair of shorts from Willi's blue sailor suit. This is much more convenient.

When I asked the children who should be the Lieutenant they

54

all shouted 'You!' I would myself rather have been a private soldier so that I carry out the orders with the others, but that was not to be, for even Fritz, who is our eldest, called out 'Piete must be our officer!'

Willi doesn't play with us. He is much too big for such games and has to study. Besides, in his spare time he composes music at the piano. He has just composed a song about a rose-bud that dreams of the sunshine and then wakes up. Androwski is very critical; he wants to be an art critic one day. Willi takes no notice of Androwski's criticism and I am proud of that. Willi says: 'That's rubbish! I'm just trying it out!' And he tries and tries until just one piece, and then another, of a song is finished. Suddenly the most lovely song is completed. Then Willi plays it and I sing the words.

But we much prefer to make 'Orchestral Music'. Then Willi plays his songs on the piano, and I blow the singing part loud and clear on Grandma's comb, on which I have stretched a piece of tissue-paper. I am already so well practised in this that the comb effect sounds just like a fiddle. And what do you think happened recently? You'll never believe it! Suddenly there was clapping outside the house. We rushed to the open window. There, standing in the street, was a group of people who looked up at us, smiled and clapped their hands. One gentleman called 'Bravo! Bravo!'

Weren't we amazed!

28th September 1914

'Do you know the Zouaves?' asked Willi.

I said that I had not yet had the honour to be introduced to one.

'Stupid!' answered Willi, 'I mean, do you know what a Zouave is?'

'A Zouave is a negro of the Berber race,' I said. 'In particular he is an infantryman in the French colonial troops.'

Willi said it could certainly be thought that I was well-informed about the war. He said that a French colonial brigade of 8,000 were caught in German machine-gun fire. The news placards say that up to 1,000 were wiped out.

'Poor negroes!' I said.

People talk much of the ferocity of the French Colonial troops. The blacks are said to have sharp, curved knives which they carry between their teeth when charging. They are very tall and as strong as lions.

'They'll be sending beasts of prey against our brave boys next!' said Fräulein Gumprecht the teacher.

When I was little I wanted to have a negro baby. I didn't want to have a white baby. I should like to know now, in all fairness, do they send to a black mother too a letter of honour with the news that her son has died as a hero for the Fatherland? When I asked Willi he said that probably in the tropical forests or the African bush no letters would be sent at all.

'Listen,' I said, 'War is war, a hero's death is a hero's death, and a mother is a mother.'

I think that a black mother or a black wife cries and exclaims 'My child' or 'My darling husband', when she hears that he has been killed, just as much as a white woman. How the negresses in the book 'Uncle Tom's Cabin' cried and mourned when anything happened to their men-folk!

'Oh yes, child' said Willi, 'but there always remains a difference between the civilisations.'

But, if you please, do not our gallant Bavarian soldiers also carry knives in their leather boots?

And again, are we not told with pride that they likewise attack like lions and sometimes hold their knives between their teeth so that their hands are free to hold their rifles?

1st October 1914

Letter from Mummy in Berlin. Hurra! I'll copy it:–

'My darling Piete, what fine goings-on! The worst of it is that I must almost approve of you. [Ah, you're so sweet, Mummy!] One thing anyway I approve of – that you do not let your friend be insulted in a stupid manner. That you had, on this account, to beat a guttersnipe on the head with your drawing-board (which could have been highly dangerous) is, as you very well know, quite another matter. Above all, Piete dear, you ought to maintain a rather greater reserve towards the common folk; it has often struck me that you have a certain leaning towards them that could perhaps one day be harmful to you. But your feeling is certainly right when you reject the accusations that the Jews are responsible for the war. I have learnt to honour the Jews (with some few exceptions as is always the case), as a highly respectable and gifted race. Of course there are differences of religion and race. To see these things clearly, we both probably still have much to learn. Meanwhile we want to regard

56

the hatred of the Jews as the outcome of a war-time nervousness and trust that the healthy instincts of our nation will find the way back in the future. In Berlin, this splendid city, hardly anything is to be seen of aggression towards the Jews; there are undoubtedly excesses in some Border States.

Good-bye, my treasure. Good luck at school!

Best wishes to Grandma and dear Willi (how are his plans for land work going?) a hug and a kiss from your loyal Mother.'

I am so grateful to Mummy for this letter. What a wonderful, lovely Mama I have! Willi too was enthusiastic about the letter. The only thing I don't quite understand is what Mummy meant by the 'leaning towards the common folk'.

2nd October 1914

A cold, horrible day. The leaves on the trees are already yellow and red and in some places are falling. They will not last much longer, and then everything will be bare and empty. To follow this weather there will be a mild and dirty winter. We shall therefore be twice as busy knitting. When I have finished the second pair of mittens I want to knit knee-warmers. The soldiers at the station have said that the rain-water in some of the trenches is half a metre deep. Wet through to the skin, the soldiers paddle in water as they fire. The damp penetrates right into the dugouts. There is much bladder and kidney trouble among the soldiers.

As the weather began to brighten up towards evening I put warm clothing on and went out. Thick drops of water hung on the branches of the trees. I got a blue nose and numbed fingers. There was much activity in the town. Everyone was about, all the High School seniors and the upper classes of the juniors. Among them walked grammar-school boys, officers of the 149th and strangers who were officers of the First and Second Flying Reserve Units.

Greta Dalüge was walking arm in arm with Trude Jakobi, Greta looked like a lady; she was wearing a green costume trimmed with fur and carried a grey muff. Trude also seemed very grown-up. She called, 'Do you want to come with us, young Kuhr? Just up and down Posener Strasse?' They took me between them and we walked twice up Posener Strasse as far as the market-place. Trude said I ought to go out with them more often, she would introduce a number of officers to me. But I don't want to. We also met Greta's friend, the little Count B. He had just pulled up a soldier who had not saluted him in accordance with regulations, and he had shouted at him in the open street and made him stand to attention and salute. I can't stand that. I said to Greta that Count B. was a pompous ass and that I had no desire for his lordship's acquaintance. Greta laughed and said, 'I'll let him know!'

As we stood in front of the newspaper office window to read the latest news, some one thrust a note into Greta's hand. I saw how she read it furtively and then passed it to Trude. She read it too and laughed. I didn't know what was in the note but Trude whispered in my ear that it was a date with a First Lieutenant in the Second Flying Reserve Unit.

'A rendezvous?' I said, greatly astonished. 'With you two?'

'Come with us,' said Greta. 'You're good-looking.'

'But look here,' I said, 'I'm not yet even thirteen!'

'Quite so, that's just what they like best of all,' said Greta.

'Who?' I asked. 'The Officers,' answered Trude. 'Don't be so dim.'

I said I would think about it. In my heart I was fully decided. I am still just a child. I would much rather play soldiers and do duty at the station.

3rd October 1914

Grandma has gone to Halle to say good-bye to Uncle Bruno who returns to the Field in the next few days as Acting Sergeant-Major in the 54th Field Artillery Regiment. Grandma was so quiet when she went off; and she was wearing her black dress. Why didn't I take her to the station, why did I play ball with Gretel in the garden? Sometimes it is good to be a child, sometimes not. Grandma certainly thought that she might not see her son again. Uncle has been posted to the Western Front. There Antwerp is under attack. We have seized the forts Lierre, Waelhem, and Koningshoyckt and 30 guns. It is possible that Uncle may witness the fall of Antwerp. Perhaps even the fall of Verdun.

Will the war be over by Christmas as every one at first thought? Willi says he doubts it.

4th October 1914

The Russians have been defeated at Suwalki after bloody fighting. They have lost 3000 prisoners, 18 guns, including a heavy battery, many machine-guns, vehicles and horses.

6th October 1914

Feverish excitement reigned yesterday in Schneidemühl. Early in the morning every one who had eyes was looking up at the sky. There had been reports that two Russian aircraft had been observed heading towards Schneidemühl. They were said to have the objective of destroying the main railway station as the Army Command were planning for further troop trains. You can imagine the excitement. Willi and I prowled like cats all day long around the station building. The bridges were again barred to any one without a pass. We were sorry about that for we had hoped to watch the sky from the Karlsbergs. 'If they blow up the station, we shall go up with it,' said Willi. 'Do you want to be blown up?'

'No, and you?'

'No, I want to go to Mexico, some time in my life,' said Willi, who has a passion for Mexico. At twelve years old he gave a lecture on Mexico to an invited audience.

'And I want to see the whole world,' I cried.

We decided to annoy Aunt Luise Otter and knocked violently at her door. 'The aircraft are coming!!!' we shouted.

'Where? Where?' We heard Aunt call. 'Georg, Georg, the aircraft!'

We crouched on the steps and laughed like mad. We heard Aunt closing the wooden window-shutters and running here and there in her heel-tipped shoes. Then our maid Marie came back from shopping and we frightened her too by shouting that the aircraft would be here in half an hour. 'Quick, into bed!' ordered Marie, who was trembling from head to foot. Willi asked whether the bombers were to smash us to pieces in bed. It would be better to run to the municipal park which was at the other end of the town. The park is where girls, soldiers and grammar-school boys go walking in the evening. But Marie was not wholly taken in. We were ordered to go to bed and sleep and we slept like tops.

This morning everything was back to normal. The station was still standing and the 'planes had not come. I called for my friend Dora Haensch on the way to school. She said, 'We stayed up all night for you know we live right by the station. Something could easily have happened.'

That is true. We also live close to the station, but Dora lives even nearer. The Haensch's rent the 'Station Canteen for Railway Workers'.

'Were there guards on the station building during the night?' I asked.

'Of course,' said Dora. 'There were in all fifty men and two officers on the station. They were posted on the guard-room and on our roof.'

'Splendid!' I cried. 'And was anything else going on?'

'A lot was happening,' said Dora. 'There were machine-guns clearly visible and searchlights were set up.'

I asked whether the searchlights had lit up the sky.

'Of course,' said Dora. 'The sky lit up every hour. But only faintly.'

'And then,' I sighed, 'the 'planes didn't come!'

'No.'

'Egg and spinach!' I said sadly. 'It would have been so wonderful to die for the Fatherland!'

Dora laughed. Fräulein Gumprecht came past with a bag of books under her arm on her way to the elementary school, and we curtsied. Fräulein Gumprecht strode off like a Teuton. We fooled around until we reached our Girls' High School. The headmaster was standing at the window of his room and he scowled when he saw me. 'Take cover, girl!' whispered Dora, and we ran as if possessed through the vestibule into our class-room.

Newspaper report: The forts Kessel and Broechem by Antwerp have both been silenced. The railway forts on the Mecheln–Antwerp line have been taken.

Nothing new from Verdun.

7th October 1914

Uncle Bruno has gone off to the Front. Grandma returned to Schneidemühl by the night train. She slept for only a few hours, then put her striped nurse's dress on, donned the little white cap, tied the white apron round her waist and went to the station to help look after the soldiers. 'Madam will kill herself one day,' complained Marie.

'Let me be, Marie,' said Grandma. 'It's better for me to work than to sit around.'

She didn't return from station duty until nearly seven o'clock in the evening. There are hardly any more gift parcels now. The Red Cross itself has to buy nearly everything: bread, meat and vegetables, potatoes, coffee and whatever else is needed. The townspeople make the excuse that they have relatives and friends in the field, to whom they have to send parcels. Only on Mondays, when Grandma is on duty, they send gifts of food to the station. Thus there are often eggs, brandy and wine there on a Monday but not on the Tuesday. Grandma distributes the alcohol sparingly. Only the wounded and the weak get it to drink.

Many hospital trains stop at the station. They are painted field grey with gigantic Red Crosses on the sides and on the roofs. That means, for friend and foe, 'Take notice – wounded – don't fire!'

It is always quiet around a hospital train. Sometimes a few lightly wounded stagger out and ask for refreshments. Often the orderlies fetch coffee for the nursing staff or for those wounded who cannot walk and are thirsty. Sometimes stretchers are quickly brought out from the room where members of the station branch of the Order of Nursing Sisters are on duty, and the orderlies carry out from the train and into the nursing centre a badly wounded man who cannot travel any further or one who is dying. Later the ambulance comes and takes him to the military hospital.

While one soldier was being transferred his wound opened up; the blood soaked through the thick muslin bandage and ran on to the ground, where it formed a long line of red spots. The soldier's face was as if made of plaster, his mouth was half open and looked like a black hole.

'He is done for!' said the orderly helping to carry the stretcher as he passed by.

When I heard this I was very much afraid that the dying man might have heard it, and I called out as loud as I could, 'Not a bit of it! He is already a lot better!'

'Well, if you think so, lassie,' said the orderly in a friendly tone.

When I was still tiny, three or four years old, I escaped from Grandma one day and strayed into Karlstrasse. A hearse stood in front of a house there and many people were going through the open door. I was curious and followed them in. I was wearing – I remember it clearly – a red and white striped frock and had no shoes or stockings on, for it was a hot summer. Extraordinary dress for a funeral! Suddenly I was standing in front of the coffin

61

in which lay a dead man in black attire. Right and left of his head were lighted candles. Many people were crying. He was a workman who had fallen from scaffolding and broken his neck. Just as another man in black with a black book in his hand – the pastor – was taking his position behind the coffin, I imagined quite definitely that the dead man raised himself and smiled at everyone. I even saw that he opened his eyes. Then I cried out in my piping voice: 'He's alive! Look, all of you, he's alive!' The pastor immediately exclaimed with a fervent voice: 'That is assuredly true, our beloved friend – he is alive! A child's mouth has proclaimed everlasting truth!' As the people turned towards me I thought they would make mincemeat of me and I squeezed past the trousers and skirts as quickly as I could to get outside. There it was broad daylight and I skipped for joy.

I couldn't help thinking of that when the orderly said the soldier was on the point of dying.

8th October 1914

Heavy fighting in the province of Suwalki and in Russian Poland. The battle is going well for us. We are taking many prisoners.

The Russian, they say, is in general no good as a soldier. He doesn't have the right notion of what he's fighting for. This must be true, otherwise we wouldn't be taking such a dreadful number of prisoners. But what people keep saying about the Cossacks is quite wrong. The Cossacks, they say, are so weak that they fall from their horses from weakness. Yes, they fall from their horses – but only when their horses are shot from under them or when they *want* to fall. And they often fall on purpose in order to mislead us and avoid being a target for a bullet. They are such wonderful horsemen that they and their horses are as it were one being. They can lower themselves in the stirrup, clutching the saddle-girth or the mane tightly with their hands and hang down on the other side of the horse so that you don't see them from the front. Then people think, 'Riderless horses!' But the Cossacks shoot under the horse's belly or past his neck and their bullets find their mark. Oftentimes they charge on their little wild horses and over-run our advance guard or isolated patrols. If a Cossack's horse dies, it is for him as if his bride has died. He cries and cries and will never more be happy. It is a mistake to say that the Cossacks are weak from hunger. Of all the Russian regiments they are the best provisioned. They are nearly all sons of farmers and their horses are their property for life. Until now they lived comfortably well-off in their villages. The Cossacks are the most feared regiments in the East. That is what soldiers coming from the Eastern Front have told us. Professor Philipp has confirmed this to Willi. Professor Philipp has a wide knowledge of all the peoples of the earth.

Once when some Russian prisoners were asked what German troops they feared the most, one of them answered: 'Prussians with boards and Prussians with potatoes.' There was at first general astonishment. Then came the explanation: 'Prussians with boards' means the Uhlans (because of the rectangular-shaped helmet) and 'Prussians with potatoes' means artillery-men.

Uncle Bruno is also a 'Prussian with potatoes'. He has a nice brown horse. It once threw him on the parade ground in Halle. He fell with his back against the stable wall but suffered no damage. You can't imagine Uncle Bruno, an independent scholar and a book-worm, sitting and riding a nag.

Frau Annchen's eldest brother Paul, who is a railwayman, has also been with the forces for a few days. He is an infantryman, or a 'foot-slogger' as the soldiers call it. Frau Annchen's husband, Yard-master Schönfeld, is being sent to the East on troop transport work. He has to take troop trains up close to the Front. Frau Annchen is very anxious about her husband, for the troop trains are attacked by the enemy with bombs.

9th October 1914

The Rector's wife, Frau Lakoschus, has four sons. Three are serving as soldiers in the German army, the fourth lives in Tsingtau in China. It was not long ago that Frau Lakoschus said to Grandma that her son in China was, so to speak, in a lost posting. Grandma then answered that she should thank God that she knew at least one of her children was safe.

Now this son has just been killed! Up to now we have read only a brief German Army announcement:-

In an attack on Tsingtau the Japanese and English were driven back with the loss of 2,500 men. The effect of the German mines, cannons and machine-guns was devastating. The enemy's right flank was effectively bombarded by the Austro-Hungarian cruiser 'Empress Elizabeth' and the German gunboat 'Jaguar'.

We had often thought that war was now going on in the Far East, so very distant from us, and that we didn't know what soldiers were being killed. Frau Lakoschus's son was not a soldier. He was probably killed in the bombardment of the town. He was an engineer.

10th October 1914

It's cold, very cold! If you go into the country, you see and hear women working in the fields instead of men. Thickly muffled up, they dig turnips and clear the ground in long rows. The schools have sent many pupils on to the land to help the women with the harvest work, but the school children have soon returned home. Willi was not allowed to work with them, for he has a weak heart as a consequence of growing too quickly. It must have been the same with the other boys. They all said that they could not stand up to the work. Most of them complain bitterly. They claim, too, that they never had enough to eat. I can understand this with the small farmers for they themselves have nothing. But the boys didn't work for the small farmers, but for the big ones or on the big estates. I think it's shockingly mean that the boys were not given enough to eat. For our big farmers and land-owners are well-off, they have plenty of fat, meat, eggs and milk in their cold stores and curing-rooms. I have often looked around them and I know that. One of Willi's classmates, Andreas Zorn, said that at the big farm where he worked the grammar-school boys were awakened at 4 o'clock in the morning. Then they had a poor breakfast and had to go straight off to the fields in thick darkness. They stooped for hours picking potatoes or digging turnips. Sometimes it was still so dark that they could hardly see a thing. The boys' fingers went dead with cold and they got quite bent with backache, but they were forced to go on working. Many couldn't help being sick or falling down with sheer exhaustion. But no consideration was shown. It was always: 'Get on with your work, you Mother's darlings!'

At first the boys enjoyed working on the land. Now it is as Andreas Zorn says: 'Ten horses wouldn't drag us back on to the land!'

Perhaps it's a good thing the Head wouldn't let me go to do land work. I would soon have got nose-bleeds from bending.

11th October 1914

We have won the battle in the province of Suwalki. The Russians again lost 27,000 prisoners. To the West of Iwangorod we took another 5,800 prisoners.

Just what are we to do with all these prisoners! We now see so many train-loads of prisoners coming through our station that the long brown coats and tattered trousers are no longer a novelty. Fräulein Gumprecht, who came for coffee to-day, thought the prisoners would only bring us famine and disease into the country. 'Why not simply shoot the beggars dead?' she cried. But we thought it awful to go so far as to shoot the prisoners. Fräulein Gumprecht told us war stories the whole afternoon. I remember one of them: The Cossacks had captured a German of the cyclists' corps, shut him up in an empty farmhouse and set fire to its four corners. But the German soldier found some old woman's clothing in a wardrobe and put them all on over one another. As the flames flared upwards through the house he climbed out of the cellar window. The Cossacks broke into fits of laughter at the old woman they had smoked out. But they soon stopped laughing, for hardly had the old woman got three hundred metres from the house when she mounted a hidden bicycle and rode quickly off. They followed the soldier on horse-back, but he had already reached the lagoon, flung the bicycle into the water and swum away. The Cossacks fired at him but didn't score a hit.

Willi asked: 'Where then did the German who swam into the lagoon land?' Fräulein Gumprecht thought he would eventually have landed somewhere.

Mummy recently sent us a printed war story which is much nicer. This is it:-

A German lance-corporal in the Reserve, in civil life a profes-sor of Romance languages at Göttingen, had to escort a troop of French prisoners from Maubeuge into Germany. The cannons are thundering in the distance. All at once the duty Lieutenant sees that his lance-corporal is involved in an argu-ment with a Frenchman. The Frenchman is gesticulating excitedly with his hands, and the lance-corporal's eyes are blazing angrily behind his glasses. The lieutenant rides up to them as he fears violence. He gets between them and curses them. Then the lance-corporal explains to him in great agitation that the French prisoner, who had repaired his torn boots with

65

string, was a professor at the Sorbonne. The two gentlemen were involved in argument with each other because they differed over the frequency of use of the subjunctive in the old provençal Minnelieder!

Fräulein Gumprecht laughed so much at this story that she nearly choked on a piece of nut chocolate. Willi said he would have sworn that the lance-corporal was Uncle Bruno if he had not known for sure that Uncle was not yet at the Front. Grandma smiled too. Then she said: 'Tell me, children, is it not a wicked, scandalous thing that two professors have to shoot at each other? The soldiers ought to throw away their rifles and say "We'll have nothing more to do with it" and go home!'

Then she was really for it with Fräulein Gumprecht. 'And you in charge of the Red Cross?' she cried. 'What about our Emperor? And our honour as Germans? And the good name of the German soldiers?'

Willi grinned from ear to ear at the row. But Grandma was quite angry. 'If you saw as much misery at the station as Piete and I do,' she said, 'you would wish the war was over too. You will talk differently if only you lose your brothers!'

Fräulein Gumprecht has two brothers in the Field. The third brother, who is an upper sixth form boy, will also perhaps be called up. Fräulein Gumprecht's old mother, who has been ailing for a year, and whom we all like very much, has become worse through anxiety for her sons. 'All mothers should go to the Emperor and say: 'Now we want peace!'' exclaimed Grandma. We were quite amazed. We had never heard Grandma talk like this before. If all women thought like Grandma the war would soon be over. But I couldn't say this at school, every one is so much in favour of the war. What a hullabaloo there was at school to-day when the teacher read out the news report! When it was announced that Fort Breendonck near Antwerp had been taken and that the bombardment of the part of the town behind it had begun, you could hardly make out the actual words because of the screams of joy. Sometimes I think the girls keep rejoicing so much just because they hope there will be a holiday from school. It is for this very reason that they scream. If the headmaster sees what a patriotic school he has, perhaps they will be let off the last lesson. I do scream, but not because of victory. Nor because I think we shall be let out. I scream just for the fun of it. I think it's marvellous to shout at the top of my voice in a place where

I usually have to keep my mouth shut. I can't stand school very much because so much injustice has been done to me there.

12th October 1914

Yesterday it was reported at about 12 noon; Antwerp is just about to be taken. Then in the evening came the bulletin; Antwerp has been taken by the Germans!

A large amount of booty fell into our hands; 5000 prisoners, 500 guns, countless motor vehicles, an armoured car, many loco-motives and trucks, several supply vehicles, 4,000 kilos of corn, 10,000 marks' worth of wool and copper, 500,000 marks' worth of silver, a mass of ammunition, innumerable saddles and other war material. In spite of the good news the rejoicing in the town was not so great as at other victories. A good many people stood in front of the newspaper office but they were fairly quiet. Perhaps it was too cold out-of-doors for them to celebrate with dancing. Perhaps, too, they have become too much accustomed to victories.

16th October 1914

I don't feel like writing to-day.

In the West Bruges was occupied by our troops on the 14th and Ostende on the 15th.

At sea: Our pocket battleship the 'Emden' has sunk a Japanese liner in the Malay Archipelago.

18th October 1914

A girl refugee from Goldap, East Prussia, has come into our class. She has black eyes and long, thick, black pig-tails. 'Like a genuine Pole!' declared my friend Dora Haensch. 'Shall you like her, Piete?' 'No,' I said, 'because she was horrible to Bylla!'

This girl, who had been placed at the empty desk next to Sibylla Löwenthal, asked our class teacher if she could sit some-where else. She said she couldn't see properly from that seat; but what she really meant was that she didn't want to sit next to a Jewess. She was then actually given another seat. I was furious. I immediately asked our class teacher if I could sit next to Sibylla.

'But why all of a sudden?' asked our teacher in astonishment.

67

'Because I can't see properly from my seat either!' I cried, so loudly, that everybody knew what I meant, and I went straight over to the empty place next to Sibylla.

'Stupid thing, get back to your own seat!' ordered our class-teacher, Fräulein Finsch. I went back to my place as slowly as if I had a hundredweight block on each foot. All the girls laughed. Our teacher smiled too. I had to laugh myself, too, in the main, but acted as if I was offended. Fräulein Finsch calmed down eventually and entered a black mark against me in the class book for unseemly behaviour.

To-day we have lost the torpedo-boats S115, S117 and S118 not far from the Dutch coast. They were involved in a fight with the English cruiser 'Undaunted' and four English destroyers. Only 31 crew members were rescued.

19th October 1914

The Russian losses in the latest attack on Przemysl were esti-mated at 40,000 dead and wounded. 40,000 in a single battle!

Gretel and I went to-day to the little Russian cemetery to rake it and clear the graves of weeds. When we stood in front of the barbed-wire fence we couldn't believe our eyes. There were suddenly three times as many graves. I was so amazed that I grasped Gretel's arm. Gretel shrieked 'Ow!' and I cried, 'Say, what's all this? How come all these graves to be here?'

The remarkable thing was that the graves had black wooden crosses but of a quite unusual shape, for under the cross-piece a second somewhat smaller bar had been placed. Willi said later that that was the cross of the Greek Orthodox religion. On the wooden cross in white lettering was the date of death. In one case the name was also shown in foreign letters.

There was again a deathly stillness all around. Gretel kept cave while I crawled through the damaged place in the barbed wire. Then I quickly raked the paths and cleaned up the mounds. At length a whole heap of dead twigs had been gathered together. Gretel was anxious.

'And what if we're punished for what we are doing?' she asked. 'You're not doing anything at all!' I said. 'It's I who am doing it! If any one comes I shall say you had nothing to do with the whole affair.'

Finally we hung the rake up in the tree. Then we pulled off some fir twigs and laid two crossed twigs on each grave. Now everything

68

looked in good order. Lastly we played 'Helmets off for prayer'. We stood to attention, gave a military salute, and I prayed: 'Our Father, which art in Heaven, hallowed be thy name. Take these dead enemies into your care. For ever and ever, Amen.'

Then we raced over Grandma's own piece of field and shouted for joy because nothing had happened to us. When we reached home Grandma asked where we had been hanging around. 'We were in the churchyard,' we said quite innocently, and that was not a lie.

'Well, I never!' exclaimed Grandma in astonishment.

23rd October 1914

To-day we met Frau Lakoschus, the Rector's wife. She was all in black, and wore a black mourning veil over her face. And she walked bent like an old woman. Willi whispered to me: 'Do you remember her saying that every mother must be proud if her son dies as a hero?' I was scared to death that Frau Lakoschus could hear us. 'Come on,' I said, 'You see what rubbish it was.' Willi and I had been upset to hear her speak like that. But now all was well. We had great respect for her distress.

On the corner of Güterbahnhofstrasse we met Lotte Voss. Lotte is the only girl in the town whom Willi is keen on. He greeted Lotte like a Mexican Hidalgo. Lotte Voss is very beautiful; she is as pale as a marble statue and has large blue almond-shaped eyes. While thanking Willi for the greeting, she looked straight in front of her.

Willi has written a song for her and set it to music. It goes like this:–

> The other day the roses in bloom
> Spoke so gently and sweetly to me.
> 'We are indeed beautiful,' they said,
> 'But better the flower that blooms in thee.'
>
> 'We give forth both our scent and blossom
> And then are carelessly cast away,
> But love does never wither or die,
> It blooms unceasing for many a day.'
>
> My Queen, my most beloved Charlotte,
> As the flowers truly speak their parts,
> Tear not apart the golden threads
> That closely bind together our hearts.

I don't know whether there are really golden threads round Lotte's heart, but we sing this song every day. Hans Androwski says the words of the song are trash, but the composition is excellent. He declares that I am the real poet in the family. Willi on the other hand is a composer, and you can pin great hopes on him. I love Willi's compositions; they are sad and yet not too sad, jolly but not too jolly. Mummy once sang one of his songs in a house concert.

24th October 1914

Writing this War Diary helps me at school. The teachers say my style has improved. I used to find writing essays atrocious, now I can write for hours and I often get an A for it. Fräulein Finsch recently said to me: 'What has happened to you, Kuhr? The spirit of enlightenment has certainly got into you!' When I quite deferentially said 'Yes!' I immediately got another black mark in the class book for impertinence. Dora Haensch then wrote me a note, which said 'Don't take it too much to heart!' Half the class had written silly comments underneath, such as 'Heartfelt sympathy', 'Sometimes God inspires you in your sleep', 'Not all good things come from above', 'To-morrow will bring gold', and other such nonsense.

Fräulein Finsch does not like to admit that I do well in German. She tries to correct my grammar, especially in the matter of the subjunctive. She can never forget that I once wrote a faked note of absence. No one at school knows that I am keeping a war diary. I am writing it just for the soldiers and for later on. There are a thousand more things that should be said about the war, but I don't know how. Before my pen has got to the end of a sentence I have forgotten what else there was to say. Grandma doesn't like me doing a lot of writing. 'Sitting down all bent up again!' she says. 'Your mother should have found something better for you to do!'

She doesn't think any good thing will come out of the writing. But I shall persevere with it all the same. Probably not many children will write a war diary, and it will perhaps be important later on to learn how children in particular came through this war.

25th October 1914

There is more heavy fighting around Przemysl. The fighting must be almost as dreadful as the Battle of the Masurian Lakes.

In the West there is also a fresh and bloody sector of fighting; the Yser–Ypres Canal. The soldiers are always saying; 'The war in the East is terrible enough, but in the West it is even more frightful; especially at Verdun,' they say. 'Anyone in the trenches at Verdun is there for good,' said a tall artilleryman the other day in the Red Cross depot. Frau Annchen wouldn't listen; she said we would very soon take Verdun. The soldier laughed at this and said 'We shall *never* take Verdun!'

The ladies became downright angry. 'You should be ashamed of yourself,' cried Frau Annchen. 'What must your comrades think when you talk like that?' The artilleryman replied quite affably: 'Oh, they think the same as I do, dear Sister. Actually, we have all come from Verdun!' We at once asked whether he had met the people from our regiment. He told us that he had encountered the 149th but the regiment had in general been as good as wiped out. We were speechless, although we should have realised this from the long list of casualties.

'Now, eat as much as you can, lads,' said Grandma and distributed soup to all the soldiers. And to us as well. We ate potato soup with garlic sausage and gulped down our tears.

There is war everywhere. In Africa too. In the Orange Free State and the Transvaal a rebellion has broken out, headed by Colonel Maritz, General Dewet, General Beyers and General Hertzog. Colonel Maritz has attacked the English at Keimus, and they have suffered many casualties. There is nothing in the papers about our losses.

The war has indeed spread through the whole world!

30th October 1914

Now I don't know; Is Turkey also in the war then? In any case she is fighting on our side. We had read nothing about it in the newspapers. Suddenly we hear that a Turkish cruiser has bombarded the town of Feodosiya and destroyed the cathedral, the Greek church, the harbour warehouse and the mole. The Turkish cruiser 'Hamidije' arrived at Novorossijsk, secured the surrender of the town and arrested the Russian consul and the officials.

Grandma didn't know anything about the entry of the Turks into the war either. So we suddenly have an ally that we never expected. There are hardly any more to be found among the many war powers.

It's beginning to get wintry. The first snow fell yesterday. What advantage will it give to our troops? None at all. They will be frozen. The Zouaves, the Indians and the other colonial troops in the enemy's Western army will freeze even more. They will get cramp in their arms holding their rifles, their teeth will chatter, and they will shiver all over and be incapable of moving their limbs. Christmas will come and if the nations do not make peace there will be red pools of blood in the snow.

Mummy wrote yesterday:–

Such great, noble, and uplifting times have never before been experienced by any nation. So many enemies .... and so many victories!

Why can I not myself write such words as Mummy does? It all strikes me quite differently. I agree that we live in great times but I wish it were all as it was before.

Perhaps it is because Mummy sees the war from a greater distance, not so close to the frontier?

1st November 1914

So this is how it is: While the Turks were peacefully carrying out manoeuvres in the Black Sea the Russian Black Sea fleet attacked the Turkish ships. The Turkish ships on manoeuvres thereupon sank the mine-layer 'Prut', damaged a Russian torpedo-boat, sent a Russian destroyer to the bottom and captured a coaling-vessel.

The people who were reading the report outside the newspaper office rejoiced over the fact that we had an ally. Then a gentleman who had also studied the special announcement said: 'Ships on manoeuvres have no ammunition on board with which they could sink Russian warships! It's lies! Lies!' 'Then kindly give us your opinion of the affair!' shouted a man who had turned crimson with anger. 'Obvious!' yelled the man in reply. 'There was no question of any manoeuvres!'

'Indeed?' cried the gentleman and came up close to the man. 'And what was the truth of the matter then?' 'It was a trap!' cried the man. 'The Russians knew it. Attack is the best means of defence!'

There was a great outcry. The gentleman raised his stick and struck the other on the head, shouting 'Lieb Knechthund'. The man tried to turn the stick aside but fell over, whereupon the gentleman struck him again. I would have cried out in fear, but

72

produced only a small sound. When I went to help the man up I was pulled aside. He recovered himself on his own and ran off. Many people raced after him, shouting 'Lieb Knechthund!' I had never heard that word before. I felt terribly ill, so I ran into a gateway and sat down under a carpet-beater hook. I got such a stomach-ache. When I got home I asked Grandma what a 'lieber Knechthund' was. Grandma didn't know. Then I asked my brother Willi who was doing geometry exercises with Androwski. 'Don't you know who Liebknecht is?'

'Don't tell her, don't tell her!' cried Willi jumping for joy on grandfather's old office chair. 'Leave the people in darkness! This goose has nothing but silly soldier games in her head!'

'I'll explain it to you some other time,' said Androwski in a friendly way.

I went into the drawing-room quite doubled up with stomach-ache and practised on the piano some chromatic scales that our piano teacher, Frau Übe, had set for me. Then I slammed the piano lid down.

2nd November 1914

There is no chance of peace by Christmas. Otherwise they wouldn't be hustling us so much at school about Christmas. Every day they say: 'Every pfennig for the soldiers.' Grandma says we are making her bankrupt with the school collections. We now have a big Iron Cross made of wood hung on the wall at school in which we have to knock 1,000 iron nails. When all the nails have been knocked in it will really be an 'iron' cross. Every girl can hammer in as many nails as she likes. The black nails cost 5 Pfennigs each, the silver ones 10 Pfennigs. I have so far knocked in two black nails and one silver. It makes a bit of fun. The proceeds are devoted to war purposes.

The snow has gone again. It is raining. In the West all operations are ruled out by floods. In other battle areas too the trenches are under water. Perhaps they will be unable to shoot at Verdun because of the dampness.

A soldier has written the following poem:–

> Our hair grows like a mane
> And we are strangers to soap
> Our teeth uncleaned remain;
> A change of shirts? No hope!

Our clothes are sopping wet,
Our stomachs often empty.
No wine or beer we get.
Gone are the days of plenty.

We've really got mud in the eye,
Our shoes and our socks are afloat,
We've nothing left that is dry
Except for our humour and throats.

And yet this heroism
Does earn its special coin;
We display our patriotism
Through rheumatics in the groin.

The soldier has certainly not exaggerated, although there is one thing I can't imagine – that their stomachs are often empty. For the best meat, best preserves and all the best foodstuff go to the army supplies. But in the turmoil of battle it must often be the case that the field-kitchens cannot come forward. Then the soldiers' stomachs rumble. Ours too will soon be rumbling, for many provisions in the home country have become still dearer and there is no longer as much meat. Everyone talks of scarcity.

Most people are buying in such massive stocks that their cellars are nearly bursting. Grandma refrains from doing this. She says she doesn't want to deprive the Fatherland of anything. We are not hoarders. The Fatherland is not likely to let us starve.

But when the soldier speaks of his clothing, he is certainly quite right. To those who see the troops who are being trans-ferred from one theatre of war to another it is frightening to see how uncivilised the soldiers look. Dirty, ragged and with stubbly beards. Nearly all those who come from Russia have lice. There are indeed military de-lousing centres but there is often no time at all for the soldiers to be de-loused, so they sit in our Red Cross depot and secretly scratch themselves. We have instructions to refuse admittance to soldiers with lice. But Grandma says, you cannot very well say to a soldier who is scratching, 'Please do your scratching outside!' When we return home after station duty we have to search our clothing thoroughly for lice. 'Lice are carriers of disease,' it is said.

There is now a remarkable illness around, a kind of influenza. It begins with giddiness, headache and aching limbs and then inflammation of the lungs usually follows. On the Eastern front many soldiers are suffering from this influenza and there have already been cases of it in the towns. Perhaps I shall fall ill too. For some time I have been feeling unwell.

5th November 1914

England has declared war on Turkey. The Turks are in conflict with the Russians on the Caucasian frontier. Up to now they have beaten the Russians.

It is reported from Peking that German artillery fire has destroyed all Japanese defences. The country behind Tsingtau has been planted with electrified mines. In the news sheet it says, 'Three cheers for the brave lads of Tsingtau!'

Grandma had a coffee party to-day. The ladies talked a lot about the heroes of Tsingtau and the son of Frau Lakoschus, the Rector's wife. It was only a small party, for Frau Lakoschus and Frau Schön were absent because they were in mourning. The Schöns are daily expecting their son's coffin; it must already be on the way. But because of the risky train connections in the East it hasn't yet arrived.

Granny's youngest sisterhood member, Fräulein Dreier, sighed and said, 'We have had no news of my young cousin Paul for three weeks. He is serving in Ypres.'

Paul Dreier[6] is a merchant's son and is serving in the 149th. We said nothing. Every one knows how bad it is with the 149th. Paul Dreier went to the Front as a volunteer. He had only passed his school-leaving exam at Easter. His sister Käthe is in my class. She is one of the nicest girls. 'God protect Paul!' said Grandma.

I ran to Gretel in the yard and because of the rain we sat under the roof of the drying-room. There I told Gretel that Paul Dreier had not written for three weeks. I said: 'Grandma prayed to God to protect Paul. If God granted all our prayers no soldier need die. But he hardly hears them at all. He has probably become stone deaf – through the thunder of the guns!'

Gretel begged me not to commit sin. 'Something will happen to you afterwards, you will become ill and might have to die,' she said.

'Believe it or not,' I said, 'It wouldn't matter to me at all. Before, when there was yet no war, it did matter. But now it doesn't. And then I'm going to tell you something else .... I can no longer play with dolls. Such small dolls, you know – they have no place in war.'

Gretel asked me what I would like to play then. I said,

'Soldiers'. Gretel was sad because she loves her dolls so much. But I can in fact no longer play with dolls. I cannot help listening all the time to the songs of the soldiers passing through, the bugle-calls from the station or the shots of the sentries and all the other war-time sounds. And also to the aircraft of the 1st and 2nd FEA, that take off over our heads. Sometimes the engine cuts out, then there is a dreadful popping, spluttering and crackling. Then the 'plane crashes. Many 'planes crash in Schneidemühl. I have seen two crashes. It is due to the fact that we train young airmen here. When they make their first solo flight they are often nervous and then an accident happens. But a flying instructor once said to Greta Dalüge, we use inferior materials in the construction of aeroplanes. A flying instructor crashed recently. It is said that he committed suicide. No one knows why.

7th November 1914

Half a million prisoners-of-war in Germany, and that's a fact:-

	Officers	men
French	3,138	188,618
Russian	3,121	186,779
Belgian	537	34,907
English	417	15,730
Totals	7,213	426,034

Schneidemühl now has a prisoner-of-war camp. It is near to the infantry barracks that grandpa built. To the right is the starch factory, which stinks horribly. My friend Dora Haensch has been to see the camp twice. We have not yet been there. The camp is called the 'Russian Camp' because they are nearly all Russians in it. Grandma has strongly forbidden us to go to the Russian camp, because influenza is prevalent there. In the last eight days six of the town's inhabitants have died of influenza. It's an epidemic of some kind of lung infection.

8th November 1914

I write little about the war at sea. But there is so much to write that every theatre of war gets short shrift. However, we achieved a great sea victory off the coast of Chile on 1st November. We sank the English cruiser 'Monmouth' and severely damaged the pocket battleships 'Good Hope' and 'Glasgow'.

On 23rd October our ship 'Karlsruhe' sank 13 British steamers.[7] But the best of all is our cruiser 'Emden'. On 22nd October it sank 4 British steamers and a dredger bound for Tasmania as well as capturing a steamer. On 27th October it again sank a ship, namely the Japanese steamer 'Kanaratu Maru', which was on its way to Singapore.

On 30th October it sent to the bottom off Pulo Pinang the Russian cruiser 'Schemtschug' and a French destroyer. It had disguised itself by the addition of a dummy funnel.

The 'Emden' is the darling of the Germans. They laugh at its deeds like those of a mischievous schoolboy. I don't know how many enemy ships she has sunk already. Sometimes I have nightmares and dream that I am standing on a ship that is underway. Slowly it heels over, the waves rise quite high and then giant black fish appear. These are frightful dreams. But it must be just like that and even more terrible for the sailors who go down after a sea-fight. No ship in sight to help them. At the time when the 'Titanic' hit an ice-berg and all the people were drowned, the whole world cried in horror. Now ships go down every day and no one asks afterwards what happened to the sailors.

My brother Hans, who at the outbreak of the war was on the way to South America with his ship 'Magdalena Vinnen', has at last written again. The 'Magdalena Vinnen' has been interned in the Chilean port Talcahuano. Hans writes that one day an enemy mine exploded in the harbour. Shortly afterwards all the water in the harbour became as black as a raven and everything was covered with horribly mutilated cuttle-fish. In the heat, too, there was soon a stink of decomposition just as in a plague, so that the crew of the ship nearly fainted. I had never thought of this before, that in sea warfare not only men but also fish are killed. We have also had news from my brother Ernst who, before war broke out, ran away from his ship 'Lucy Vinnen' and then became overseer on an Australian cattle-ranch. When my brother heard that there was war in Germany he wanted to return to Germany immediately in a Dutch ship in order to volunteer for war service. But the English detained him in the port of Sydney and put him in a prison-camp in Melbourne. Ernst writes that he is doing well. As he ranks as a 'Sea Cadet' in the Merchant Navy (there is really no such thing) he has been put in officer's barracks. The food is good too. They have a lot of curried rice.

77

10th November 1914

1st Lieutenant Schön's coffin is there. The train arrived overnight. The coffin was taken privately to the cemetery chapel. There it lies in state. The funeral is at three o'clock to-morrow afternoon. Lieutenant Schön will rest in the new 'Heroes' cemetery' that lies behind the old cemetery. There are just 12 graves there. Granny is going to the funeral too. She has been sewing for hours, attaching a long black crêpe veil to her black widow's hat. We children cannot go with her. Willi, because he doesn't want to, and I because I have had a cold for two weeks. I didn't go to school to-day either.

Grandma says that the wooden cross that the soldiers placed on Lieutenant Schön's grave in Masuria has been sent with him. A wreath of fir came with the coffin too. It was made by the men of his company.

11th November 1914

Our Marie brought in a news sheet bearing the news that S.M. Cruiser 'Emden' was set on fire by the English ship 'Sydney' on 9th November off the Cocos Islands in the Indian Ocean. The 'Emden's' crew thereon beached their own ship. The captain of the 'Emden', v. Müller, and Lieutenant z. See Prince Franz Joseph von Hohenzollern were both taken prisoner. The English Admiralty has arranged for full military honours to be granted to the survivors of the 'Emden'. The captain and the officers retain their swords. That is very decent of the English.[8]

So the German 'Fortune of the Sea' has been destroyed.

The day was made still more sad by the funeral of Lieutenant Schön. At three o'clock in the afternoon the church bells were tolled. Then the blessing was given to the dead man. In the spirit I saw the dear old parents crying by the coffin; I myself cried bitterly. I couldn't help continually picturing the dead man in his grey field uniform. No one would dare open the coffin. It is much better to leave the lid closed.

Dear Diary, we have nevertheless taken Dixmuiden by storm and taken 2,000 French prisoners west of Langemarak. At Ypres we took another 1,000 French prisoners. But it does not make me happy because a First Lieutenant named Schön has been killed and is buried, because the Schöns' jolly little dog Bello is securely shut up at home and howls and howls, and because I definitely – quite definitely – have caught the influenza lung infection.

1st December 1914

I was mighty ill. It was the influenza epidemic. Our health officer Dr. Briese said to Grandma to-day: 'Thank God, we can now rejoice that she is out of the wood!' Grandma didn't go to the station for three weeks. She looked after me continuously. I love her so much! The fever sometimes caused my temperature to rise to over 40 degrees. At 42 degrees you die. Once I reached nearly 41 degrees. Then I asked Grandma whether I was going to die. Grandma, sitting by my bed in the dark room, said: 'If you have to die, my child, then we both go together.' I shall never forget that.

Then my fever dropped to 36.2 degrees. I was certainly still ill, but no longer so seriously. The worst day was 21st November, Remembrance Day. And Gretel and I had intended to tidy up the Russian cemetery for Remembrance Day! I couldn't ask her to go up there alone, because no one except Grandma was allowed in my room for fear of infection. From the window to-day I saw my brother Willi going across the yard. I knocked madly on the window-pane and Willi waved with both hands and shouted: 'Darling! Darling!' Oh, how glad I was to see my brother again. He looked pale, but lovely and tall. My dear Willi!

I saw Gretel too, she was sliding on a little strip of ice across the yard. When I knocked the window she stood still in astonishment and looked up. I gave a military salute. Gretel jumped for joy around the yard, waved and laughed and pretended to fall down. We laughed like anything. Then Grandma came with a cup of hot milk and a honey sweet and said 'You just get back to bed, you pale little chick!'

Aren't there some good people around!

2nd December 1914

I must belatedly report that on 26th November we took 40,000 Russian prisoners. They were captured by General v. Mackensen's army at Lodz and Lowicz, together with 70 heavy guns, 30 light guns, 160 ammunition trucks and 156 machine-guns.

On this victory day Dora Haensch put a note for me through the letter-box. It read:–

Dear Piete, we have taken 40,000 Russian prisoners! Just imagine, we were even let off school! How we cheered! When are you coming back, you dear monster? It's deadly boring at school without you. You will be pleased to have missed two French dictations and 2 Mathematics tests. I got a 2nd and a 3rd plus in French and a 2nd in Maths. The fat girl from Goldap is getting on alright. She is quite nice. I think we have got her properly trained. But you are the nicest of all. Do come back soon. Yours, Dora.

3rd December 1914

Willi was allowed into my room for the first time to-day, after it had first been aired for a long time. It was great. Willi said, 'you look like August Piependeckel – so thin.' We laughed.

'You wait,' I answered. 'I shall soon look like a barrel.'

'With the shortage of meat?' cried Willi. He then related something very exciting. On 26th November when we had taken so many Russian prisoners there was suddenly great activity in the Neue Markt. There was an endless sea of field-grey motor cars between which an even more unending sea of field-grey soldiers marched. Huge lorries and suchlike that looked like grey-painted houses with windows, doors, and little rooms containing beds, wash-stands, tables, chairs and so forth. Beyond these, a multitude of gun-carriages and mobile kitchens. Soldiers and officers were running around with billeting notices. A lieutenant with a batman came to Grandma for lodging, but Grandma said she could not take any one as there was influenza in the house. Then – all of a sudden – they were all away again, vanished from the face of the earth, cars, gun-carriages, canteens and soldiers.

What had happened? Schneidemühl was to become the base for the 8th Army. The Army Pay Corps was to be based here too. Then the whole plan was betrayed to the Russians. So it is said.

4th December 1914

You can hardly believe it! What a carry-on! Aunt Emma, Aunt Lieschen and Aunt Minna Haber from Friedrichstrasse are no longer there! They have left the milliner's shop empty. Grandma went to-day to take them a jar of dripping and tell them about my illness, but found the little shop closed. The roller blinds were down and the door was locked. The house door at the back was also locked. As Grandma stood at a loss in the yard, a woman came out of the wash-house and said, 'Are you looking for the Miss Habers? They went off to Berlin yesterday evening.'

'What!' exclaimed Grandma, dumbfounded. 'Flown? And what have they done with their things?' 'Most of them are also on their way to Berlin,' said the woman. 'Only old rubbish is left inside.'

Grandma came home so stirred that she could hardly speak. She sent at once for Aunt Luise Otter, and when Aunt wouldn't come over because of the danger of burglary Grandma said angrily, Aunt Luise should not make herself a laughing-stock. When Aunt finally came over, but stood in the open doorway as a precaution, Grandma exclaimed, 'Shut the door, it's draughty! The child might catch another cold!' Then she told all of us about Aunt Emma, Lieschen and Minna's flight! 'And without saying a word to us!' She said, nearly crying. 'Such cowardly girls, and so old too! It's naught but a disgrace and a scandal!'

And Aunt Otter was quite shocked; she wrung her hands and wailed loudly 'Without saying adieu to us!'

Aunt Otter always says 'Adieu' instead of 'Good-bye'. She is so old-fashioned that she cannot get used to anything new. It is a wonder that she has got used to the war. Grandma and Aunt Otter churned it all over and concluded that the three aunts had left because of the 8th Army base. For where a base is, the enemy is not far away. The general staff and the high command certainly want to be safe, but yet near the Front, so that they can supervise the fighting soldiers. Finally Aunt Otter said, 'Now sit down, Bertha dear, and don't get so upset. I'll make you some coffee, you look quite ill.' But Grandma wouldn't be quietened. She kept repeating, 'And without taking leave of us!'

5th December 1914

His Majesty Emperor Franz Joseph of Austro-Hungary received on his birthday the following loyal telegram from the commander of the 45th Army:-

I am most happy to convey to Your Imperial and Apostolic Majesty on the day of the completion of the 66th year of Your Majesty's glorious reign the most respectful good wishes of the 5th Army, and also beg to be allowed to lay at your feet the most humble announcement that the city of Belgrade was to-day occupied by the troops of the 5th Army.

Frank, General of Infantry.

6th December 1914

A letter came to-day from Berlin from Aunt Emma, the oldest of the three Haber sisters. I will copy it, although it has at least a thousand mistakes.

My dear Bertha
    I am letting you know, on behalf of us three sisters, that because of the Russian danger we came to Berlin on 3rd December. We wanted to say good-bye to you and dear Luise Otter, but the maid was to blame. She couldn't finish the packing in time, so we had to take a cab to catch the train. We didn't mean to offend you, before God we didn't! And then young Piete was so ill; how is the child getting on? Sincere greetings to her and Willi. You can well imagine that I, like you, dear Bertha, didn't want to come to Berlin at all. But Lieschen and Minna wanted to at all costs. What could I do about it? The good God would have looked after us in Schneidemühl. Minna thought it would be safer in Berlin. She has her faith-healer there, that is really the main reason, dear Bertha, why she and Lieschen wanted to go to Berlin. For Minna's asthma is not good. Good hats are in demand in Berlin and the same with millinery. We have brought money with us, and our keepsakes too. Dear Bertha, the good God will grant that we shall all soon be together again. I can't bear to be in Berlin for a long time. You can't transplant an old tree, and when you have lived 71 years and have an expensive grave it is time to die, albeit at the hand of the Russians. So good-bye, dear Bertha, greetings to Luise and her husband and the children Piete and Willi. The dear Lord God bless and protect you all. Your old cousin Emma.

When Grandma had read the letter she cried. But she said: 'I certainly won't answer her! She must come back and get the answer in person!'

7th December 1914

I am back at school now. The girls were pleased. The teachers were not nearly so pleased, although in my heart I felt a secret pleasure when I saw some of them again, e.g. our R.E. teacher Fräulein Gertrud Becker and our drawing teacher.
    As it was fine outside, bright sunshine and quite still air, I decided in the afternoon to call for my friend Dora to go for a

walk. Dora was knitting soldiers' stockings by the stove and was complaining because she didn't finish off the heels, and holes kept coming where she picked up the stitches. 'Just the same with me!' I said. I was delighted.

Dora put her coat on and donned her red peaked cap. (I wear a green one.) We went to the station and pressed our faces up against the platform fence. Two hospital trains were standing at the platform. Grandma was there too. We recognised her by the white cap with the bow at the back and tried to wave to her. But she didn't see anything for she was just helping to get a severely wounded man out of the train. Some orderlies laid him on a field-grey stretcher and spread a brown woollen blanket, full of holes, over his body right up to his throat. Grandma slowly raised his head and gave him something to drink, then she let it sink down again. Then the orderlies carried him away.

Dora and I went into the town. 'Not to Posener Strasse!' I said. Posener Strasse is the true 'Lovers Lane'. Dora can't bear the 'flirting', as it's called in Schneidemühl, either, so we chose the lonely way across the Horse Market. It had grown half dark. The gas lamps were alight. We came past the Rohleder military hospital. Behind the windows a few lightly wounded men were singing. 'Dear Fatherland, peace be to you'. A gentleman was standing near us, listening. He said to us: 'It is certainly a good thing that the brave lads can still sing' – 'Yes,' answered Dora. The gentleman went off and a Red Cross nurse stepped out from the door of the hospital. She smiled at me and said in a friendly voice, 'Good evening, children.' I turned quite red, because this was the nurse who was cutting flowers in the garden of the Diaconate House when I hit the boy who had called Sibylla 'Jewish sow'. The nurse said, 'Listen, child, give your dear grandmother my best wishes and ask her whether she could lend us a few pillows. We are very short of pillows here. Many of the wounded have newspaper to cover them, we are so short.'

I promised to bring some pillows the very next day. We were very shocked to hear about the newspaper coverings.

8th December 1914

The Russian General Paul von Rennenkampf has been relieved of his post because he was 'two days too late in protecting his positions from the encircling movements of the Germans.'

You should see the cartoons in the newspapers: Rennenkampf, who can't 'rennen' [run]. No other news.

Oh yes. The Mannheimer Generalanzeiger published the following field post-card:–

To-day our men in the 2nd Company shook hands with the French. We were positioned only 30 metres away from the French. There were frequent shouts on both sides. Now a Frenchman called out that we ought to cease firing so that we could jointly bury three dead Germans who lay between us. We ceased fire. Eight or ten Frenchmen and one French Officer laid down their weapons and we did the same. Then we shook hands, buried the dead, exchanged cigars, cigarettes and newspapers, and the Frenchmen said we ought to do no more firing. They would stop also.

'You see,' said Willi, 'and what happens is that someone again gives the order to shoot and they start firing one after another. The men really want peace, but not the officers.'

I said he was talking utter nonsense, because one French and one German officer were there when they laid down their weapons.

'An exception!' answered Willi. 'Just ask the officers on Posener Strasse if they want peace. They want to fight for Germany! And even if two or three want peace, the higher officers don't want it at all. What do you think – a General ...'

I said the highest officer is the Emperor and he definitely wants peace; it's not for nothing that he is called the 'Emperor of Peace'.

Willi said it's easy to be called 'Emperor of Peace' when no country wants to go to war with Germany. 'But you know,' he said, 'that the Emperor has said to any Englishman, if any nation were to attack Germany then he would strike with an "iron fist"'.

I became quite bitter and asked what else the Emperor could do if a foreign nation attacked Germany. Willi answered that in spite of this he should maintain peace, otherwise he was just no 'Emperor of Peace'.

'But how! how!' I cried.

Willi put on his silliest grin and said that was the Emperor's business, not his. The Reichstag should rack their brains about that, and the Emperor should rack his brains too.

Now, enough is enough, and this was too much for me. I punched Willi in the right shoulder and he nearly fell off his chair. Then I sprang up and shook his chair so long that he did in fact fall down, but he laughed, so he didn't really defend himself. When eventually he picked himself up he took his school books under his arm and disappeared into grandpa's old office, which is now his own room. He bowed in the doorway and said, again with that stupid grin, 'I will now take leave of Your Imperial and Apostolic Majesty!'

It probably made a powerful impression on him when I read the greetings telegram to Emperor Franz Joseph that time in the kitchen. The silly part of it is that I had to laugh at it myself and forgot my fine fit of anger.

9th December 1914

It will soon be Christmas. We will certainly not have peace by Christmas Eve. Grandma wants to decorate a fir-tree at the station, so that the soldiers passing through will have some enjoyment on Christmas Eve. For this purpose we are collecting money round the houses and on the streets in a soldier's steel helmet inscribed 'Christmas for our field-greys'. A fair amount of money has been collected already. Things will be bought with it for the Holy Night.

I was with Grandma to-day at the Rohleder hospital. We took two feather pillows, chocolate and cigarettes there. Grandma asked for the sister in charge. An old nurse dressed in grey, with a friendly face, came. She led us into the large ward for the severely wounded. There lay about ninety wounded in high white beds. On each head-board a little black tablet was fixed, on which the name of the wounded man was chalked. Below the tablet was a hook with his cap. If any one had an Iron Cross, that too hung on the hook. Grandma asked after a soldier named Schneider who had asked for her. Many field-greys know her from the station. Thousands and thousands, healthy or sick, go past her each day, and she remembers all of them. The sick grenadier Schneider was the only one who was not in bed. He hobbled towards us on crutches and accepted cigarettes and chocolates with much pleasure, while asking for one of the two pillows for a comrade who had been badly shot in the head and lay, with paralysed arms and quite indifferent to all around him, on a cushion of cotton-wool. At the beginning of the war we thought that the many sick-beds in the hospital would never be filled. Now neither the bed-spaces, nor the pillows and blankets are sufficient. The wounded lie on cotton-wool and hay; the cotton-wool gets burning hot and the hay presses into them and some of the wounded are covered with newspaper stuffed between the sheets. The inhabitants of every house cart bolsters, feather-beds and cushions there. And all the time more bedding is needed. How much longer will the war last? For a few weeks people thought – till Christmas! Now it is only a little while to Christmas, the woodmen are felling the first Christmas trees. But no end to the war is in sight.

And what wounds! We saw one soldier with shattered legs; a heavy iron weight was attached to his left leg and hung over the end of the bed and stretched his foot to straighten it. That must be very painful; the soldier was groaning. One had been shot in the lung and there was continually on his lips a kind of bright red froth coming from the lung. I should have liked to wipe away the froth but I had no handkerchief with me. Many soldiers were turning over on their beds, quietly moaning. One lay quite apathetic, just staring all the time at the ceiling. What particularly struck me was that many of the wounded lay with the upper part of their bodies bare and did not cover themselves when we women approached their beds. Grandma went up to one soldier who lay amid pillows with a heavily bandaged shoulder and a chest bandage. Below this his trunk was bare. Grandma asked gently, 'Are you not cold, my lad?' The wounded man didn't answer. When Grandma repeated the question, he said slowly as if from another world, 'Hot! Hot!' Grandma took his hand; it was burning with fever. We went up to the beds of others severely wounded, to give them our little presents. Nearly all of them took no notice of what was going on around them. On one bed lay a draughts-board, the little pieces were in a heap, with the sick man's fingers rummaging among them. 'We need many more games,' whispered the nurse to us. Grandma nodded. We have a draughts set, halma and dominoes at home.

We said good-bye to Lance-corporal Schneider and went out on to the long corridor. There we heard coming through closed doors a frightful, inhuman cry, so awful that I clutched Grandma's arm in terror. The nurse said 'It is someone in the operating theatre.' I didn't know that any human could shriek like that – like an animal that was being slaughtered. Grandma squeezed the nurse's hand and said, 'We must have peace, dear Sister!'

The nurse had tears in her eyes as she answered: 'Peace – Oh yes, Frau Golz, yes! We all look for peace, those of us who see so much of the war here.'

On the way home I asked Grandma why then we didn't after all make peace. The assassination of the Austrian Crown Prince and Princess had been avenged thousands of times. 'Yes, darling,' answered Grandma (saying 'darling' with great sincerity), 'we must go right through with the wretched business, or we lose our Fatherland.'

'And when will it end?'

'When we have won.'

'And what if we don't win?'

'Then God help us. But that is impossible.'

15th December 1914

It is so cold that we can hardly play 'soldiers' in the yard. I had however arranged a drill session to harden us; after all our troops at the Front suffer much greater cold. Fritz Wegner was coughing in great form and I had to keep wiping his nose – as Officer: What a laugh!

Then I went to the station because many hospital trains were expected. Suddenly the Station Commandant (a Captain) came and announced a transport of three hundred sappers from the East. We had just placed three long tables on Platform 1 with bread and soup plates for the wounded. The steaming soup cauldron had already been wheeled up to them. The Commandant said to Grandma, 'The sappers will *not* be fed. They have to go on to Berlin, there is food for them there.' Grandma answered, 'Very good, Captain!' The captain went off with due dignity. Grandma asked a station official, 'When is the next transport train due?' 'In three minutes,' said the official. Scarcely three minutes had passed when the sappers arrived – grey, dirty workers in civvies under military escort. They immediately rushed for the tables, shouting 'We're starving! Starving! Oh, thank God, here's something to eat at last!'

Grandma covered the plates and bread with both arms and said, 'Listen, lads, the Commandant has forbidden the Red Cross to cater for you. The food is intended for the next transport of wounded.'

What disappointment there was in their faces! Everything had changed. One old bearded worker said to Grandma, 'We have had nothing for twenty-four hours except a pot of black coffee in Graudenz. Sister, we can't go on!'

I looked at Grandma; her cheeks were quite flushed. The Red Cross ladies stood around her at a loss. Grandma asked the soldiers of the escort whether they too had been twenty-four hours without food. The soldiers said 'Yes'. Then Grandma winked at her helpers and called out cheerfully, 'Gentlemen, just get into the canteen, all of you, coffee's boiling away there!' The ladies had understood immediately and sprang out of the way as if by order. Grandma looked cautiously around for the Station Commandant, and as he was nowhere to be seen she said to the sappers and soldiers 'Help yourselves. We have been forbidden to feed you. But I say: What if no one is there whom you can ask? The ladle is in the soup cauldron!'

With this she took me by the scruff of the neck and drew me too into the canteen. We were as happy as snow queens. Through the little window of the door we saw our 700 rolls vanish in a trice and the soup plates were filled and emptied. The men ate quietly and furtively and then hurried back to their train. The Station Commandant had not noticed anything. 'And if there's any trouble,' said Grandma, 'I'll take the blame!'

We found quite a pile of money on the empty tables. The workers and soldiers had left it for us without saying anything. When the train-load of wounded was announced shortly afterwards, we had prepared fresh bread. We just hadn't such good sausages left, only bread and dripping and watered-down pea soup. The wounded liked it, however.

Towards evening I bought fresh sausages with the money left by the sappers, but I had to run to two butchers before getting anything. On the way I met Gretel, who was bored. She was so muffled up against the cold that really only her nose and blue eyes peeped out. I hung the whole string of garlic sausages on her like a garland and shouted 'Help me carry them, so that you don't catch the idleness disease.'

I stayed at the station until nearly 10 o'clock with Gretel. We lugged buckets of coffee around and got sausage rolls and pea soup as a reward. They tasted first rate. We were dog-tired when at last we trudged home through the falling snow. It looked so beautiful, with the snow-flakes driven past the gas lamps. Mother Wegner had been waiting for her daughter; she was standing below the house door with her arms folded under a thick black shawl. She smiled kindly at us and said to Gretel: 'Oh, you've come at last! I thought you had got run over!'

I hadn't done any of my school homework. Never mind.

16th December 1914

Special news report: The offensive against Poland and Silesia announced by the Russians has collapsed. Attack by German warships on the East coast of England. Bombardment of the fortified positions at Scarborough and Hartlepool. The inhabitants flee inland. The situation created by the withdrawal of the special flank in the Balkans makes it seem advisable for Belgrade now to surrender again.

21st December 1914

Mummy arrives to-morrow. Willi and I are running around in great excitement. Mummy's bed is freshly made up. We have brought in from the garden a few twigs that have still got little leaves on and put them in a vase. Willi is spending the whole day practising a new composition for the poem by Eichendorff: 'Over the garden through the air I heard birds of passage on the wing'. We sing it as a duet, although Willi has composed it for only one voice. Although it is not a Christmas song but a Spring song, it is nevertheless Willi's Christmas present for Mummy. Our friend Androwski thinks it is his best composition.

Yesterday we had three ladies from the Women's Patriotic Guild with us. We were making up Christmas parcels for the soldiers until midnight. Grandma had collected a vast quantity of apples, nuts, gingerbread, tobacco, pipes, cigars and cigarettes. Whole washing-baskets full of gifts stand in our house. We have also received a lot of brightly-coloured handkerchieves. Towards evening Frau Annchen and her mother, dear old Frau Zühlke, came to help with the packing. Our little parcels look very jolly. We made up the handkerchieves into tight bundles with the corners hanging out like long ears. I fastened a fresh twig of fir to each bundle. (I pinched a few particularly good twigs on the quiet for Mummy's vase.) We also made up five washing-baskets full of knitwear, on the top of which a trifle such as cigarettes or cigars was placed. The nicest presents were thirteen little puppets. They consisted of a large pink handkerchief which was sewn on to a body with coarse stitches. The head was filled with sweets. Three bath sponges formed the hair, nose and beard; the eyes were buttons. The arms and legs were stuffed with a cigar, the body filled with a packet of tobacco. Instead of a rifle the soldier-puppet had a pipe under the arm. The knapsack was a reel of thread with a needle stuck in it. We didn't make the little soldiers ourselves: they are gifts from a school. One of the puppets is slightly broken. He sits upright on a basket of gifts and looks at me. 'Like Emil', I said and this made all the ladies laugh. How I hit upon the name Emil I don't really know.

We have other baskets full of packets. These consist of boxes of fine-cut tobacco, to which a pipe and a piece of gingerbread are tied. Then we have other tobacco pouches of soft glove-leather. It is white kid, sown with red stitches. The lady who sent the tobacco pouches to us asked for one to be sent to Uncle Bruno. She worships him. He will be very pleased. While we packed and arranged everything, the ladies told sad stories from the town. There was a lot said about Paul Dreier, the nephew of one of Grandma's club members who is serving with the hundred and forty-ninth and has lost both eyes. Frau Kaufmann Dreier is almost as unhappy as if her son had been killed in the West. She cries day and night. How will Dreiers celebrate Christmas. . . . Mother Zühlke's second eldest son, Fritz, Frau Annchen's brother, has also been called up. He is in the pioneers. Now only the youngest son, Arthur, is left at home. He and I are close friends. Frau Annchen's husband is coming home on leave for Christmas. We are glad for her.

Dear Diary, forgive me my weakness, and our heroes at the Front must forgive me too, and also the makers of the puppets, please. I have pinched the particular soldier-puppet that we had christened 'Emil'. He looked so sweet and sad. I don't play with dolls at all, but Emil is a soldier. I have hidden him on the wash-house floor under the peg-bag. Perhaps I'll play with the soldier-doll now.

22nd December 1914

Mummy arrived from Berlin at 5.42 this afternoon. She has never looked so lovely! She was wearing a black fur coat with silver collar on which a bunch of artificial violets was fixed. And a little black lacquered hat with a veil which had genuine little black spots on it; she had spread this close to her face. When I am close to my mother I feel like a country lass. I have such clumsy shoes and such a horrible grey-green dress. My hands are bony and the fingernails are bitten and, most important, my freckled face and big mouth, through which Willi said, I could eat asparagus cross-wise.

My brother and I hang around Mummy like angels around the Christmas tree. (No, the comparison doesn't hold good – we are not angels!) Incidentally, we have bought a Christmas tree to-day. It is not ceiling-high as in other years, and isn't a blue-fir, but just a pine. But we are pleased with it all the same. This year there are only a few trees and those are small ones. When I look at the thin little trees I think of 'Emil' under the peg-bag, and my heart jumps for joy.

23rd December 1914

One day before Christmas. No peace. The Pope wanted a cease-fire during the days of Christmas. But the cease-fire has been rejected by all the warring states. So the Holy Night will be a night of war. In the East the Russians have brought up rein-forcements. In the West the enemy is going on to the offensive, thinking that our armies there have been weakened by the masses of troops we have thrown into the East. He is mistaken. We have many forces in the West.

This evening we all decorated our Christmas tree. I greatly enjoyed it because I was allowed for the first time to join in the decoration. It was such fun hanging up the silver threads, the old coloured balls, stars, glass birds and chains. We only stuck a few candles in the holders. 'The day is not so bright that we cannot make it brighter,' said Grandma. She was fighting against her tears at the same time, for Uncle Bruno is at Verdun. We hung great-grandfather Haber's coloured paper horsemen and his very, very old cardboard angel in the branches and then the tree was finished. 'Now let's sit down in the dining-room and treat ourselves to a quiet hour,' suggested Mummy. Grandma brought in apples, nuts and our home-made gingerbread. Mummy placed another giant box of sweets on the table, the Christmas present from her Polish singing pupil Broszat. He adores Mummy. And we ate, cracked nuts, peeled apples and told each other all that had happened to us in the meantime. We also talked a lot about our brothers Ernst and Hans. It was lovely to sit round the table like that. We all loved each other so much. To-morrow is Christmas.

24th December 1914

It is about to strike midnight. I am writing secretly in bed by the light of Grandma's war torch.

Christmas! It is Christmas now!

We exchanged presents at six o'clock. Before that Grandma, Willi and I went to the old Town Church for Christmas Service. The Market was quite full of silent people. The bells rang and then stopped, we went through the porch and sat in our seats. Suddenly the organ began to play, first a voluntary, but the tune of 'Silent Night, Holy Night' could definitely be recognised. Everybody bowed their heads, as if an order had been given, and began to sob and cry. Then the melody was brought out clearly and we sang as well as we could. Then our Senior Minister Schammer went up to the altar, gazed for a time at the Christmas tree with its lighted candles and said: 'Peace on earth! And good-will to men!' Then everybody sobbed and cried still more.

The whole church was full of people wearing black clothes and black mourning veils. For a long time we couldn't speak as we came out of church. Our military band was playing Christmas music in the market-place. If anyone met any friends they just shook hands in silence. We went home quickly. Mummy was standing at the door; she was laughing and there was a pleasant smell of carp in beer and gingerbread sauce. Our maid Marie had gone to her sweetheart who lives in Karlstrasse. So we celebrated alone.

Grandma and Mummy couldn't join in singing carols for emotion. Mummy smiled at us all the time. Our present-giving was only a small affair – it is after all war-time. Immediately afterwards we ate the carp. Then we went to the station for the soldiers' Christmas festivities.

Our old disused fourth-class carriage stood on the platform handsomely decorated as a gingerbread house. It was brightly lit inside. The little Christmas tree stood on a long table, which was covered with a white cloth and laid out with Christmas packets. On the wall there hung a large picture of the Emperor surrounded by a garland of fir. Also hanging on the walls were our soldier-puppets, pairs of braces and thick shoe-stiffeners that the soldiers like so much.

As we walked in they all cried 'Aaaah!', as though we were the life and soul of the party. The Red Cross ladies had been expecting Grandma, as had also the soldiers. Grandma now lit the lights on the Christmas tree. Our gramophone, which we had lent them, played 'There is a rose in bloom'. Nearly all the soldiers present sat or stood in silence in front of the lighted candles, some of them crying bitterly. A lieutenant sidled up to the carriage door. He took off his cap, kissed Grandma's hand and listened thoughtfully in a corner. One of the soldiers was as lanky as a lath and as dark as a gipsy. He squinted horribly as he cried. Another, a young wounded dragoon, was ceaselessly writing postcards 'home' with lightning speed, wiping his nose and eyes with his fist all the time. A broad-shouldered Territorial Reserve with an Iron Cross on his chest expressed his great pleasure with much humour on receiving a pocket torch in the distribution of gifts. We were able to give pocket torches as well; they were our most expensive Christmas gifts.

After the giving of presents we all drank good pure coffee and ate heaps of bread and butter and cakes. Any one who wanted to drank a Schnapps as well. Everything was plentiful to-day.

Willi and I went home late. Grandma spent the night at the station, so that she could light fresh candles on the Christmas tree for all the soldiers passing through.

It was a sad end to Christmas. But we didn't let it get the better of us. Willi was still playing his latest composition shortly before midnight. Mummy rested in her armchair with her head thrown back and said, 'That is so lovely, my boy, that I will get my pupils to sing it.' Then she sat at the piano and sang the hymn to the Emperor, 'Hail to thee in the victor's laurels', newly arranged by her assistant, Max Battke. Herr Battke has sent me a special copy with the inscription 'To dear, gifted Piete with best wishes for Christmas, from the composer.' I was very proud, but I think Willi should really have received it.

Now we are all in bed. The house is dark. In the rear quarters also, where the Wegner and Zühlke families live, it is all dark and quiet. Gretel will certainly be asleep by now.

What are they doing out there .... all of them?

Please, please, dear God, do bring the war to an end!

26th December 1914

Heavy fighting on all fronts! Victorious for us, but at great sacrifice.

Frau Annchen's husband, Yardmaster Schönfeld, who is home on Christmas leave, told of the wolves that are appearing this winter in Russia and Russian Poland. The battlefields attract them. Wounded men, left at the scene of battle, have described to him how the wolves roam over the fields. How the men shriek! How they defend themselves with revolvers and bayonets and how they believe that they are bound to go mad. You keep thinking you know the worst about war, but new things that you hadn't thought of keep coming up.

The earth is covered in snow. Mummy enjoys the clean snow of the provincial town. Willi and I hang on to Mummy like chains. Every one looks at Mummy as she goes by so like a queen. She wears dainty little buttoned-up boots, trimmed with fur, that keep her feet beautifully warm. She finds the town of Schneidemühl altered. 'Listen, dear children,' she said to-day, 'there is a definite elegance with you here as on the Kurfürstendamm in Berlin. What has happened?'

Now, this is hardly to be wondered at. It is the effect of the many strange officers of the 134th Reserve Battalion and the 1st and 2nd Reserve Flying Corps. The women and girls go to great lengths making themselves up on account of these. A few days ago a thirteen year old girl, a baker's daughter, was expelled from our school because she is going to have a child by a First Lieutenant. She is a big, strapping girl with blonde pig-tails. None of us had noticed anything. The whole school was in turmoil. The Head went to each class and gave a talk about morals. When he was speaking to us, we all looked down at our desks; it was very embarrassing for us. We thought it was quite unnecessary to make a schoolmate the occasion for a talk on morals. When the headmaster went out, notes flew from hand to hand. Trude Jakobi looked over at me and said in the secret sign language of our class, 'What nonsense!' I just waved my hand. We can't stand such twaddle from our teachers. The same morning some one smeared the door-knob of the headmaster's room with charcoal and wrote on it, 'Every one mind their own business.'

29th December 1914

Grandma said at table, 'I don't know where my money goes. I have less and less in the bank. If it goes on like this, I don't know what is to happen. Everything has become so dear, and then all the taxes and collections! You give what you can, but it doesn't make you any richer!'

We comforted Granny, but were very shocked when she said she had given our Marie notice as from 1st February. Although we often laugh at Marie, she does really belong to us. Marie will then just come in the morning to do the shopping and clean the house.

Mummy and Grandma then nearly came to blows because Mummy asked her to stop sending her parcels. Grandma wouldn't agree to that. We knew very well that the war was making things worse and worse for Mummy. All the teachers in her music school, and nearly all the male pupils, had been called up and some of the foreigners who studied with her had returned to their own countries. Mummy talked of giving up the school, selling the instruments and renting a small flat, so that she could just continue giving singing-lessons. For this she would have to continue to be faultlessly dressed, so that she didn't lose her reputation in Berlin society. Mummy calls this, 'maintaining face'.

'That is the great unavoidable lie,' she said. She wore a proud look as she said it.

30th December 1914

In the evening Mummy got Willi and me to go out and visit the 'Russian cemetery'. We plodded laboriously through the snow; the crescent moon was in the sky above us.

'There it is!' I said, and pointed out to Mummy the bleak, quiet cemetery. Gretel and I had previously covered the mounds with fir twigs. Now I saw that besides our twigs yet more winter foliage lay on the graves.[9] It was all quiet, serious and solemn. I pointed out to Mummy our own piece of land that reached as far as the Belgian spies' graves. It had meanwhile become darker. The graves shimmered in the snow like linen sheets. The trees in the little wood creaked eerily. We went further on to the new German 'Heroes' cemetery'. There among many decorated graves was that of Lieutenant Schön. It was covered with flowers and wreaths. At the head of it stood a little Christmas tree with a few silver cords hanging on it. They quivered so sadly.

Mummy looked around her. 'So many soldiers!' she said. 'Oh, children, I am freezing!'

Then we kissed and caressed her. We also visited our family tomb. It is made of sandstone and polished marble. The subterranean vault containing the coffins is like a little hall with square pillars. The air down there is fresh. No spiders or other vermin because bats have for years inhabited the place. No one can explain how they got in there or how they found the little air-hole that provides ventilation. The old laurel wreaths on the coffins are dry, but green in colour. If they were taken down, they would fall to pieces. We shall all rest there one day.

We spoke about our intention at the beginning of the war to take refuge in the tomb if the Russians came. Meanwhile we have come to know that no cemetery is safe from the heavy onslaughts of shells. Many cemeteries in the East have had their ground torn up and coffins, earth, name-plates and skeletons all hurled into the air so that the old dead made it even more gruesome for the soldiers than the new dead. We decided that life was no longer beautiful and that a change must come about.

31st December 1914

New Year's Eve! The war situation is unchanged. We see the severity of the fighting by the crowds of wounded coming through our station.

To-day Mummy read the pages of my war diary that she wants to take back to Berlin with her to get them typed and bound. And she explained to me that the word which the people shouted that time at the man by the newspaper officer was not 'Lieb Knechthund' but 'Liebknecht-hund'. Karl Liebknecht and a woman named Rosa Luxemburg are so-called 'Reds', who stir up the nation against the Emperor and all orderly government. When the war broke out they voted against the war credits that were to provide the supply of war material and so forth; they wanted Germany to remain neutral. 'They are the traitors who stab Germany in the back,' said Mummy. Also she finds that my diary is not just what she had wanted it to be. She has friends in Berlin, high ranking military people, to whom she wanted to give the diary to read. But the way I have written it she couldn't show it to them. I was very sad and asked whether it was bad then. Mummy answered that she didn't consider it bad, but in some places strange. 'Strange in what way?', I asked. Then Mummy said something terrible. She said in fact: 'It might be thought that you too have a bit of a red streak in you'. I got quite heated and couldn't say anything. Then I asked whether she thought the same about me as about Karl Liebknecht and this Rosa Luxemburg.

Mummy threw her head back, put on a harsh look and, speaking into the air, said 'Yes!' Willi and I were at a loss. Mummy then went on to say 'You are too familiar with the lower classes for my liking.' Then I went off, shut myself in the lavatory and cried for ages and ages.

Why am I not with the soldiers! Why am I not dead! Why on earth am I still living this life? For a long time I have got no enjoyment out of it, first school, then the war. I just can't write otherwise. No, I can't; do you hear, Mummy? And I won't! Life with us here is like that, and if I am to describe it differently, then I've got to tell lies! I would definitely rather not write any more at all.

1915

I am quite slow to write the number of the new year – 1915. If only I knew what to do about the diary. I'll carry on scribbling for the time being. I can at least write it for my brother Willi. Perhaps his sons will enjoy it later on.

New Year's Eve was sad. We had taken at least a dozen washing-baskets full of pancakes to the station. Carrying a white-lined basket-full on each arm, I walked through the blood-spattered carriages of the hospital trains. One wounded man took a pancake out of the basket with difficulty, and said, 'Many thanks Miss. To-day, New Year, I get a piece of cake; at Christmas I got a piece of lead in the back.'

An orderly asked me urgently for a few clean shirts for severely wounded suffering from vermin. Where on earth am I to get shirts? We have no shirts on the whole station. Well into the night came train after train. At one time there were three Red Cross trains standing next to one another at the platforms. In one they were nearly all suffering from bayonet wounds. All from the East. Mostly from the Warsaw area. So that is where the fighting has reached.

Grandma doesn't allow herself a moment to pause and take a breath. She didn't come home until nearly midnight. Mummy had already poured the punch into the glass and had lit the candles on our war-time Christmas tree for the last time. Now we all drank to peace, kissed each other and wished each other a happy New Year.

'Happy New Year!' shouted some people outside who had seen our lighted windows.

'Happy New Year!' we shouted back and waved the glasses out of the window. Mummy said to us: 'The year 1914 has been a very depressing one. 1915 must bring us deliverance from the enemy – and victory!'

We emptied our glasses right to the bottom. Granny sat between us with her lovely peaceful face under her white cap, wearing her blue and white striped nurses uniform with the white apron. I was so sorry for her. She was certainly thinking of her son on the Western Front. I always know what she is thinking. I therefore said to Mummy, 'Pour us a second glass, please, and let's drink that to Uncle Bruno's happy home-coming!'

And that's what we did. Then we wished Aunt Luise Otter and Uncle Georg Otter a blessed new year. Finally I stuck my head out of the lavatory window and whistled for Gretel. She came running out of the house in the darkness at once. She was already in her night-dress.

'Cheers, Gretel!' I cried.

'Cheers, Piete!' she replied. 'Are you tipsy?'

'No. Are you?'

'A little bit.'

That was New Year 1914/15.

10th January 1915

Mummy went off on the 2nd January. A letter came from her to-day. She had written in the margin:-

'Piete, what is happening to your diary? You are still writing it, aren't you? I have already had the pages typed. It reads better in print.'

What now? I must start writing again for Mummy.

14th January 1915

The fighting around Warsaw has begun. I have received the first 'Field postcard'.

'Dear young lady' (he makes just the same mistake of gender in the word 'dear' as I did that time when I forged an absence note!) 'As I have received your valuable Christmas parcel, which gave me much pleasure, I give you my sincere thanks. Sincere greetings and a happy new year from a young soldier. The holiday will soon be over, even in the trenches. Good-bye. Best wishes and many thanks,
    From Fusilier Emil Szagun'

I was delighted and had to laugh because my soldier was called

'Emil', just like the little puppet soldier. Gretel and I often play with him; he is an infantryman serving in the field. Sometimes we fire buttons at him – they are bullets. Gretel is a nurse in the field hospital and I am a doctor – or officer.

16th January 1915

Our biggest cannon is a 42 cm howitzer that has up to now demolished every fortress. It is called 'Big Bertha'. Big Bertha's father is the manufacturer Krupp in Essen. The French are firing 'dumdum' bullets which twist after exploding in the body and cause horrific wounds.

Uncle Bruno wrote a 16 page letter to-day from Belgium, mainly describing the majestic old Belgian and Flemish towns and art treasures. And he says it is always like a dream to him that swords, rifles and pistols are hanging close to him. He has sent Grandma an expensive Brussels lace-collar that he bought with his first soldier's pay. Grandma held it a long time in her hand.

The snow has gone, there is a howling gale, and rain is pelting down in the streets and turning gardens into a quagmire. Going to school in the morning it is as dark as in the evening, and the gas lamps are alight. To-day I read in a news report on the way to school that we have again taken 1400 Russian prisoners. In the window of the newspaper office there hung a big coloured picture in a gold frame depicting the battle of Tannenberg. Countless Russian soldiers are stuck in a vast lake with distorted faces, staring eyes and open mouths, which the water is already reaching. On one you can only just see his forehead and his field cap. Others are desperately stretching their arms up in the air, while the white clouds from our gunfire float over the banks. Masuria!

I looked at this picture so long that I was almost late for school. When I entered the class-room it was as dark as in a sack. We were having Nature Study, and Herr Schiffmann came in. I put my hand up and asked 'Please, Herr Schiffmann, may we stick the lights on?'

Herr Schiffmann answered, 'What sort of German expression is that? You cannot *stick* a lamp on like fastening something with glue. You should say, "*turn*" on. Do you understand? Another thing – we do not say, "The flower smells beautifully." A flower hasn't a nose and so cannot itself smell. We say, "it smells beautiful". Again, do you understand?' We called out. 'Yes, quite.'

'Good,' said Herr Schiffmann. 'Then we can proceed.'

I couldn't stop myself asking, 'Where are we to proceed to, Herr Schiffmann?' The class broke into peals of laughter. But I got a black mark in the class book 'for being cheeky'. I think that is my sixth this month already. Six is a particularly unlucky number for me.

Then Herr Schiffmann asked whether we had brought any new poems for the lesson. Bertha Müller read one out that particularly pleased Herr Schiffmann. It is by the poet, Arno Holz. Our teacher said that Arno Holz is one of the *significant* modern German poets. I know nothing at all about him – what a disgrace!

20th January 1915

The attack of German warships on the coast of England in the Christmas month developed into a naval battle in the Falkland Isles. The German ships were defeated. We have just heard of this through a sort of casualty list. The terrible battle took place on 8th December, 1914.

S.M.S. 'Gneisenau':	17 officers rescued, 17 warrant officers, petty officers and crew.
S.M.S. 'Marnberg':	1 officer, 7 warrant officers and crew rescued.
S.M.S. 'Leipzig':	15 warrant officers and crew rescued.
S.M.S. 'Scharnhorst':	None rescued.

Of the whole ship's company of the 'Scharnhorst' none rescued! Now I should like to know how many men a large battleship carried on board! I have asked all around, but nobody could give me an answer.

When Willi and I were smaller and had whooping-cough, Grandma took mother and us to the seaside to cure the whooping-cough. We stayed at that time with an old captain. He told us that the drowned always return to the shore. After the sinking of a ship they come in a series of clusters, floating in the water with faces turned towards the shore. Sometimes, too, they are standing on their heads. The water supports the bodies so that they just bob up and down but don't fall over. So one wave after another pushes them towards the coast. They come in threes, fives or eights, apparently hanging together with the gases which the corpses emit. The drowned expect that the people on dry land will receive them. These pull them out of the water and bury them in the cemetery so their souls obtain rest.

Mummy once read to us a fairy tale by Wilhelm Hauff, which was terribly gruesome: 'The Cave of Steenfull'. Even now my hair stands on end when I think of the words which occur in it – 'Carmilhan! Carmilhan! comes the sigh out of the deep'. 'Carmilhan' was the name of a sunken ship, whose crew were drowned. I once saw a picture of a mother standing on a dismal shore where her dead sons began to stagger towards her through the sea. I have never forgotten the picture, nor will I ever forget Hauff's fairy-tale. Nor will I forget the picture of the Russians drowning in the Masurian lakes.

22nd January 1915

This evening there was a ring at the door. When I opened it, who was standing there? Covered in white dust, with white overalls and clogs, and a covered basket on his arm – the baker's boy. He held out to me our breakfast rolls, fresh from the oven and still quite warm. 'Well!' I said, 'why fresh rolls in the evening? We always get them in the morning.' The baker's boy laughed. 'Not any more now, Miss,' he said. 'We only bake in the daytime now. We can sleep at night. Do you know, there is too much flour baked in the German fatherland. Be sparing, Miss, be sparing, especially with the stomach!' And he was on his way, calling out as he went, 'Because of the war.'

Grandma thought it was a good thing for the use of flour to be restricted. I wanted to know whether more flour was being baked than in peace-time. Grandma didn't know. Willi said, 'Well, there are the soldiers! And any way, the German eats too much bread. So now he must eat less. This is true even in wartime.'

The newspapers keep giving the warning, 'Any one who uses cereals to feed animals is committing an offence against the Fatherland and is liable to punishment.' This warning is particularly important in our Eastern part of the country because we are nearly all farmers. Two thirds of the inhabitants earn their living on the land. Things are still very good for the farmers except for the small farmers and the daily wage-earners. But the big farmers and our many landowners, lords of the manor, and estate managers have plenty of everything and don't notice the war so far as their table is concerned. These have lovely white bread every morning for breakfast, sometimes containing almonds and raisins, with eggs, sausages, cheese, dark red ham with black crusts, smoked goose, various jams and I don't know what else. Anyone can drink fresh milk, anyone can have coffee or tea. In the tea they even put whole spoonfuls of fruit jelly.

With the big farmers the cattle are just as well off as the men. They still get fine corn and, although most farmers keep quiet about it, I know that they secretly fill up the mangers with it. By this means both cattle and horses have shining coats and full guts. The farmers ought to think of the poor horses at the Front, that have to go through so much and must not become weak.

But I must also say that the army authorities commandeer from the farmers all surplus horses that are not directly required for land work. These are the 'remounts'. Some farmers can hardly get over the sadness of seeing their horses led away. I too would grieve over a horse if it were taken away from me. I am terribly fond of horses and always feed them when I see them standing by the roadside, for example cab-horses or the old milk-cart horse. To that extent I am myself a sinner against the Fatherland. Sometimes I take bread or an apple out of my mouth and hold it out secretly in front of the old nag's muzzle. He is so lovely when he snuffles the morsel from my open palm with his lips as soft as butter. Once he snorted so violently that the bread was blown to the ground. As I bent down to pick it up he seized my pigtails between his teeth and nearly scalped me. I was indignant. The milk-cart horse is very old, said to be just 22 years. He has enormous yellow teeth.

27th January 1915

To-day is the Emperor's birthday. In every class-room at school there is a picture of Emperor Wilhelm II, with garlands of fir twigs hung round it. The great plaster bust of the Emperor that stands in the hall is decorated across the chest with a golden laurel-wreath. The teachers had arranged for us to wear black, white and red bows in honour of the day. Willi said to me, with a coarse grin, 'Don't forget – black, white and red bows on your shoes as well!' I answered that I would even stick a bow on my behind, whereat Hans Androwski, who was sitting with Willi at the writing-desk, burst out laughing. It was vulgar of me, though, and I shall not show Mummy this page of the diary.

We only had two lessons at school to-day and then we were let out. Before this the Headmaster gave us a long address in the hall, and we stood to sing 'Hail to you in your victory laurels'.

People used to fix long rows of candles between their double-glazing on the Emperor's birthday and light them in the evening. That looked very festive. And there was always a torchlight procession headed by the military band. And flags everywhere of course .... We had these to-day. The newspapers had written – 'Out with your flags! Any one who disregards the order of the day is a traitor!' My friend Dora Haensch and I walked through the streets and thought they looked lovely with all the flags. Also from our attic window the tenant, Frau Witkowski, had fixed a long black, white and red flag that fluttered in the wind with snapping sounds. The Emperor had asked through the Press that his birthday should not be celebrated very extravagantly. But see now! The papers published whole columns of charming stories about him: The Emperor once dropped his handkerchief during a troop inspection. A soldier immediately bent down, picked it up and handed it to the Emperor. The latter then gave some cigars to the soldier who accepted them with the words 'Thank you very much, Your Majesty'. 'You need not call me Your Majesty, my son,' replied the Emperor, 'just regard me as your comrade.' Another brave soldier heard this and immediately called out, 'give I 'un too, comrade Bill.' Laughing heartily, Emperor Wilhelm did as his 'comrade' asked.

If the Emperor is so friendly, couldn't one just write him a letter asking him to stop the war? I put this idea to our Marie who was just then sweeping, dusting and scrubbing in our dining-room. (It has a highly-polished wooden floor, coloured brick-red.) Marie was all for it, because her fiancé, who is a road worker and has received his call-up papers, would then no longer have to go into the army. She promised to bring me an elegant sheet of note-paper that has a golden edge and at the top two coloured hands clasping each other, one being the hand of Jesus and the other that of a young girl. She was given the note-paper at her confirmation. 'What a pity that you are leaving us on the first, Marie,' I sighed, for I thought the idea of the clasped hands so lovely that I wanted to say something nice to her. Marie at once began to cry and answered that she was not leaving us alto-gether. 'Altogether or only half,' I said, 'it is almost the same thing.' At this dear Marie smiled at me affectionately through her tears and asked whether I really meant this. I said yes. Then Marie said that she was so sad at the parting too and cried every night. This suddenly made me terribly sad, and I asked whether she loved Grandma so much then. Marie answered, 'Your

105

grandma, too. But I am so attached to you, Miss Piete!' I had never fully realised this before, and asked in embarrassment, 'But why?'. Then our Marie uttered these memorable words, 'Where in the world would I find such an angel!' 'Angel!' Marie said. Take note, diary – Angel! Our poor, funny, lisping Marie with her rats-tail plaits. Is this my 'familiarity with the lower classes', as Mummy said? Oh – what nonsense!

28th January 1915

Sometimes at school we are ordered, class by class, to visit a military hospital. Then, led by a lady teacher, we go to some hospital with gifts. In this way I recently came to know a hospital in a barracks a long way outside the town. It was an awful hospital! The wooden walls brown with age and all cracked, bedsteads of all shapes and sizes on loan, and very poor pillows. In the single dingy room the beds were so close to each other that we school children hardly had room to turn round. Suddenly some one said, 'Heavens! what's smelling? Is something burning?' Then I noticed that I was standing with my back to a hot furnace and the back of my coat was scorched brown. There was loud laughter, but I cried on the quiet afterwards. The coat was fairly new and it is out of the question for Grandma to be able to buy me another one just now. Grandma has grumbled, not so much at me as at the school, for the heavy costs which it entails. Now, for example, is the beginning of another National Wool Week, and we have to hand over to the army authorities old jackets, trousers, blankets, shirts, coats and woollens of all kinds. The good materials are made into warm clothing for the soldiers: the inferior materials go to the factories where they are pulverised and turned into paper and (I think) material for bandages. Again it is a matter of taking as much as possible to school. The teachers keep an eye on each lot given. There is a kind of competition between the classes to see whose collecting baskets are best filled. There is no way you can get out of it. I would dearly like to give my scorched coat to the National Wool Week.

1st February 1915

Dora Haensch ran up to me and called out, 'Do you know something?'

'No,' I said.

'The Zeppelin is here!'

That startled me. 'The Zeppelin? Where? Have you seen it?'

'I haven't seen it, but half the grammar school is on the way to the new hangar.'

It occurred to me just then that Willi wasn't back from school yet. We rushed to Grandma.

'Grandma, may we go to the aerodrome? The Zeppelin has arrived! I have to see the Zeppelin once in my life-time!'

'You will see one often enough,' said Grandma. 'It is much too cold to go so far. Do you want to get your ears frozen?'

'It is not really so cold, only 16 degrees,' I cried anxiously. 'What would Mummy say if I didn't see the Zeppelin! Because of the diary, you know?'

'It's always the diary,' muttered Grandma. 'If you want to get your nose well and truly frozen, then go.' I went to hug Grandma, but she said, 'Off you go!'

I put on two pairs of knickers, coat, muff, scarf, cap, gloves and even my old, disgusting gaiters. Then we were off at a run out of the house, over the temporary bridge, across a field, past the starch factory – and then we didn't know which way to go.

'Which is the way to the aerodrome?' asked Dora. 'The aerodrome? .... Wait a moment .... somewhere over there. Yes, near the Royal Forest.'

'Thank you so much!' said Dora and stood still. 'Look here, I'm going back. We have always got lost if we went too far.'

'Come on, be a sport!' I coaxed, for I was determined to see the Zeppelin. 'If we don't know the way, we can ask.'

We kept on asking the way. Every fifty metres we stopped to ask. In the end we did in fact land up in front of the airship hangar, which was tremendously tall and made of corrugated iron. An aircraftsman, a non-commissioned officer with the black cap-band of the Flying Corps, stood in our way. He grinned when he saw Dora. She blushed and said, 'It's no laughing matter to be so cold!'

The N.C.O. then began to laugh outright and said, with a crafty look at Dora's face, 'My dear child, there is a little drop hanging from your nose that is quite frozen.'

Dora became even redder. The N.C.O. accompanied us as we walked on.

'Look at that lorry!' I said. 'It is carrying such long iron bottles. It's supplies of water for the Zeppelin.'

'Really?' murmured Dora, staring as if hypnotised at the bottles. 'Water, do you think?'

'That's right!' said the N.C.O. 'For bleaching hair, Miss.' It was obvious that he was making fun of us.

Suddenly a sentry appeared and saluted the silly N.C.O. He had pulled a thick knitted round cap over his head and wore a black winter sheepskin. On his feet he had enormous fur shoes with buckles, that looked like slippers. He had leather gloves on his hands, in which he held a rifle with fixed bayonet.

'We only want to see the Zeppelin,' said Dora timidly, pointing to the great sliding doors of the airship hangar.

The sentry and the N.C.O. smiled.

'Yep,' said the N.C.O. pleasantly, 'so would we like to see it, but it isn't there. We certainly expected it, but it had to make a forced landing. Now it will not be coming.'

We turned round disappointed. It was already beginning to get dark. The ground crunched under our feet. Just then we noticed that the aircraftsman was walking behind us again, and suddenly he said to Dora, 'Let's drink a cup of hot tea together, Miss.'

Now Dora had said to me three days previously that she would like to have an admirer like the older girls in our class. To please her, I said to the N.C.O. 'A hot grog would be better, please,' Dora hissed. I couldn't understand that. She is already 15 years old and a very pretty girl.

So we went to an inn and drank some grog, and got really warm. The N.C.O. introduced himself as Herr Lehmann from Elberfeld; he was a teacher at an intermediate school. In the light he looked very nice, quite strong, and no longer very young. I noticed at once that he had made an impression on Dora; she was self-conscious all the time. He accompanied us as far as the station and promised to dine the next day at Haensch's Station Buffet, in order to see Dora again. He kissed her hand on leaving.

Blue with cold we ran on home and I finished up by our old tiled stove. Willi welcomed me with a big Hallo and asked gloatingly whether I liked the Zeppelin. I answered, 'Absolutely wonderful! So gigantic! Like a dinosaur!' and talked a lot of nonsense. But in reality I was far away, thinking of Dora and Herr Lehmann, and I crept almost inside the oven, where Grandma had kept some coffee and milk hot. My feet felt dead, almost frostbitten.

Now Dora too has a soldier like the bigger girls.

3rd February 1915

Our victory at Soissons has increased the fear in Paris of an aerial bombardment. According to a statement in the Cologne News the Chief of Police in Paris has ordered that the shutters in all lighted dwellings are to be closed from sundown to sunrise. The lighting-up of shops and public houses is prohibited. The street lighting is reduced.

My Christmas parcels which I sent out into the blue have found recipients. I received another Field Postcard.

'Dear Young Lady! Many thanks for your lovely Christmas parcel. The woollen muffler keeps me very warm and the eatables tasted very good. I was in transit from hospital to the Reserve battalion when I received your lovely parcel from the Red Cross. Greetings from a stranger. Reservist E. Kolmsee.'

I was delighted. Now I have two soldiers to whom I can send parcels.

Before this I was at Dora's to ask whether N.C.O. Lehmann had actually come to dine at Haensch's Station Buffet. There I found Dora crying bitterly behind the big round iron stove. Prince, the lovely Dobermann, was sitting at her feet with his muzzle on her knee. I was alarmed, and asked gently, 'What's the matter? Is it because of the N.C.O.?'

I only dared whisper, because railwaymen and soldiers were sitting around eating, and they are always jealous of Dora's acquaintances. But Dora, still half sobbing, began to laugh and said. 'Good God, because of him – no way. I'm crying because of Prince!'

I put my hand under Prince's nose, but it was cold and moist. 'But there's nothing wrong with him,' I said. 'He's quite well.'

Dora dried her tears and answered that it was true there was nothing wrong with him; on the contrary, it would have been better if there was.

This seemed so absurd that I laid my hand on Dora's forehead. 'I'm not feverish!' she cried angrily. 'But they are taking our Prince away to-morrow. Just think of it – to-morrow! He is to go into training – as a first-aid dog.'

I was speechless. Our dog! Our best companion and guard on lonely walks!

'But why, oh why?' I cried. 'He can't do anything. He can't even properly give his paw! Prince, come here, darling. Give me your paw – come on now, give it! You see, he gives the wrong one! You can't send a stupid dog like that into the Field!'

But then Herr Haensch, who was at one time a police superintendent, came up and said that Prince would pass through the school for first-aid dogs with distinction. 'He is so good a dog,' he said proudly, 'that no police dog can match him.'

At heart we shared his opinion; we were only looking for an excuse not to have to let the dog go. For a long time I stroked Prince's coat. Dora cried again because it was Prince's last evening and it made it all so sad. I couldn't stand it, and begged her not to cry any more. In the end I got really angry and said, 'Stop that crying! You at least have the teacher – N.C.O., even if you act as if he doesn't mean anything to you. But what have I got? I have only Prince.'

'And haven't you got me?' said Dora, also becoming angry. 'And your brother Willi? And your beloved Gretel?'

But the truth was that at that moment I was completely indifferent to all humans. I loved this beautiful slim, black Dobermann and no one else. When I left I laid my forehead against Prince's head and kissed him. He kissed me back, that is to say he licked my cheeks and nose. I was quite wet. It is funny that you can suffer as much over a dog as over a human being.

4th February 1915

Prince has actually been taken away this morning. Dora and I couldn't pay attention in school, because we couldn't help thinking of him all the time. In the break we squatted close together on a step in the school corridor and talked about Prince's good qualities. At the same time we considered how we could manage to join him in the field as Red Cross nurses. But the sad fact is, we are too young for the war. If the war lasts a few years more, we could certainly take the nurses' exam. 'Another few years!' I groaned. Dora said all the nurses in the Field would be dead in a few years' time and more would be desperately needed. The first-aid stations are often under fire. We have lost many doctors, orderlies and nurses. There is a large number of medical personnel, especially doctors, who have the Iron Cross, Class I or II.

We don't think any longer that the war will end soon. Perhaps it won't end until we are all dead.

5th February 1915

On 1st February all stocks of corn in Germany were confiscated in order to stop misuse and profiteering, and to safeguard provisions for army and people. Many farmers are unhappy about this. For us too, as Grandma says, 'The breadbasket goes up and up.' We consoled Grandma, saying we thought that in the East we had enough potatoes, cabbages and turnips to keep us satisfied.

'We hope so,' said Grandma.

When we spoke about it to Hans Androwski, he remembered that Napoleon's Great Army in the Russian Campaign of 1812/13 perished mainly because of insufficient supplies of forage. It was therefore right, he said, for the War Ministry for Food and Agriculture to take steps to safeguard corn supplies and to ensure a proper distribution. I posed the question whether you could mix chopped turnips and such like with flour and so make the dough go further if necessary. Willi cried, 'Heavens, the child is crazy! Just save your breath, little one!'

I was annoyed, because my idea was a practical one and ought to help provide bread for the Fatherland. Androwski laughed. I remarked calmly 'Anyway, you could at least say "supplies of foodstuff" instead of the foreign word "forage". That will cost you ten pfennigs in the "foreign word" box.'

When Androwski actually went to put the ten pfennigs in Willi went off to his room, saying, 'Don't take any notice of my scatter-brained sister!'

'But she is quite right,' he said. That pleased me no end, of course.

10th February 1915

Bodies of sailors and pieces of wreckage from the English auxiliary cruiser 'Vicknor' have been washed up on the North coast of Ireland. As the cause of the sinking of the 'Vicknor' has not been officially published the Press Bureau declares that the ship may well have struck one of the mines laid by us Germans. In recent days bodies and life-belts from other ships have been washed up in this danger area off Rathlin Island and off the coast by Portrush. It couldn't be determined from what ships they came.

111

11th February 1915

My gift parcel soldier Emil has written me a wonderful letter. It runs like this:

Dear Young Lady,

It is so lovely of you to send me the beautiful card and wonderful parcel which I received, both on the same day. You just can't imagine how pleased I was to receive it. I sent the card off right away to my sister Minna in Hamburg so that she can see what love you have for the soldiers. My sister Minna has taken refuge in Hamburg from Pagulbinnen near Wischwill. You asked where I am – I am near the town of Lotzen in East Prussia, defending it from the Russians. We are 28 kilometres from Lotzen. We are 600–700 metres away from the Russians. It is very difficult to get anything here, for there is nothing to be bought. We have money from our pay, but there is nothing to buy with it. Otherwise things are pretty good – you are alright if you are alive and well. I have no fresh news to give you – everything is as before. If God lets me escape death I shall not forget you as long as I live. For the Russians are right into my home country. I have had an answer from my father and sister. But they have fled and have abandoned house and home. My mother has left too, and no one knows where she is. Now I must close. Here's to meeting you when it is all over. But if I am to die, it will not matter much, for I have nothing to leave behind. For life here on earth is nothing. God will know what each man deserves. Keep well – you will get what you deserve for your love. Most sincere greetings to you, Miss Elfriede, from the young soldier Emil.

He writes just as if he were my brother. Even if he makes a lot of mistakes in writing, he means it alright. Willi and Hans Androwski laughed when I read out the sentence – 'I am defending the town of Lotzen from the Russians.'

'What a gallant soldier!' cried Willi.

I said: 'Just imagine – you are sitting only six or seven hundred metres away from the Russians! What must that be like? Hardly any distance at all! And hardly anything to eat!'

I was just going to pack up another parcel for Szagun when the newspaper came and I happened to read that for the time being no parcels can be dispatched to the East. What fighting there must be there!

12th February 1915

Now I will tell you why Gretel and I looked for the Russian prisoners' camp.

Mummy had sent us a newspaper report concerning a letter from a soldier held as a prisoner-of-war by the English. It said in the letter:

'Dear Mother & Father,

By the time you receive this letter I could be dead, for I am writing to you as a very sick man. We were nearly all as fit as a fiddle when we were captured. Most were unwounded, and it was only through our absolutely inhuman treatment by the English that we became so ill that many are bound to die.

The prisoner-of-war camp was near Richmond. A few corrugated iron huts in which about 200 men were quartered. The other 500 prisoners (there were about 700 in all) had to sleep in tents, including me. After a few days the first of us began to cough or complain of stomach pains and fever, for the sides of the tents were sopping wet with the heavy English mists and the conditions in the damp tents were frightful. In our first weeks here some of the earlier arrivals died. And now the death toll increases from day to day. Last week we had – as true as I am still alive – 46 deaths, all without exception being from inflammation of the lungs, influenza or dysentery. If only we got a little bit of good food, things might be alright. But what we are offered is real dog's food and hardly ever properly cooked, often in quite incredible condition. Those who still have some money (most had it all taken away) can get hold of some food at their own expense, but everything is terribly dear.

Most of us have only the clothes that we stand up in. It is quite impossible to change underclothes and so we wear the same things continually day and night, for you can't get anything here.

I am writing this to you, dear Mother & Father, so that it can be published in the German newspapers. This long letter has cost me a great deal of effort and has exhausted the rest of my strength. But now you know at least how we are treated here and what awaits those who have the misfortune to find themselves prisoners-of-war with the English. I would a thousand times rather die on the battlefield with my comrades!'

We were all shocked by this letter. We have always looked up to the English as a nation of gentlemen. Fräulein Gumprecht, who often comes to have coffee with Grandma, immediately exclaimed, 'I have always said – "Behind a stiff collar lies the shabbiest character!" God smite England!'

Gretel, who was close by me, drew me aside and whispered, 'Do you think we shouldn't look after the Russian graves any more?'

We thought it over for a long time. Then we decided we would not repay evil with evil, but would uphold German honour. With this object in mind we determined to seek out the Schneidemühl Russian prisoner-of-war camp and to see whether the prisoners there were treated anything like so badly as the German prisoners in England. If things were not alright with them we would inform the Red Cross. We said nothing about this of course: we simply asked if we could go for a walk.

'Don't be late back!' warned Grandma. We rushed off. 'Phew, how cold it is!' cried Gretel, bending her head down between her shoulders. I thumped her heartily on the back to warm her up. Sometimes I rubbed my own nose and cheeks, which ached with cold. 'If only I knew whether it's much further,' said Gretel, after we had walked a long time.

'For sure,' I replied. 'They have purposely placed the camp at a distance so that the Russians cannot so easily attack us.'

We came to a piece of waste land, where a detachment of our 149th were doing rifle-training. Then the command 'Stand easy!' was given, and all the soldiers slackened off. The poor lads were obviously miserably cold, for all at once they stamped their feet like mad, rubbed their eyes, cheeks, noses and fingers and beat their chests with their arms like freezing cab-drivers. Now they had noticed us. They began to smile at us. Many of them waved, others threw kisses to us. Two snowballs came flying towards us. 'Come away!' said Gretel anxiously.

We quickened our pace and came to the country lane, then a field-path, then another lane. The frozen sand almost crackled beneath our shoes. The wood here was very thin, pines with high, diminutive crowns that we call Polish pines. Suddenly we were frightened stiff. A sentry holding a rifle came out from behind a bush and called, 'Halt! Where are you going?'

'To the Russian camp,' I answered.

The sentry said, 'No one is allowed to go to the Russian camp.' I summoned up my courage and said that we only wanted to see the camp from a distance. The sentry said that we were not allowed even to see it from a distance. In the first place there was a high fence with barbed wire round the camp, so that we couldn't in any case get near the huts; secondly, dysentery and influenza were prevalent in the camp; thirdly, women and girls were definitely not allowed near the men. Now that was pretty flattering to us. But for better or worse we had to turn round and act as if we were going back. But we did not go back, for hearing that dysentery and influenza were prevalent in the camp just as in that English one at Richmond had made us really suspicious. So we crept forward under cover like the Indians until we suddenly discovered a huge encampment, hut upon hut, roof upon roof, a complete town of low buildings. It was however still quite a way off, and we saw at once that soldiers were guarding the hutted town. It was only possible for us to see the camp because we happened to be standing on a hillock and had an open view of it.

Suddenly a shot rang out, then another and yet more. We jumped down from the hillock and clung to each other. We were so scared that we were trembling. Not far away from us there was a rustling and crackling in the wood as from heavy running footsteps. I had once startled a stag in the Königsblick Wood; it sounded just like that as it ran off. Now we ran for our lives. We went more or less in the right direction, so that we eventually got back to the footpath and then to the lane.

'Oh boy, I'm hot!' gasped Gretel.

We looked at each other; we both had bright red faces. We had broken out in a sweat.

'What do you think that was?' said Gretel. 'Were they aiming at us or an escaping Russian?'

I said I thought it was meant for a Russian. 'Didn't you hear the crackling in the wood? Someone was running away!'

'Obviously!'

'There is dysentery and 'flu in the camp,' I said. 'That is why there are so many new graves in the Russian cemetery. But don't say anything to Grandma or your mother.' 'Not likely!' answered Gretel.

We pushed on vigorously to keep warm. It worried me to think that they could have shot at an escaping Russian. We discussed for some time whether he might have been lucky enough to get away or whether he had been shot. Gretel thought that if he got across the Küddow valley he would find himself in the swamp. 'Better then to be shot!' she thought.

'We could easily have hidden him in our cellar or in your attic,' I declared. 'Yes, especially in our cellar. No one would think of looking for a Russian in Frau Councillor Golz's cellar.'

'We'll look to-morrow to see whether there is a new grave in the Russian cemetery,' suggested Gretel.

We talked so long about the Russian that it seemed to us as if a friend of ours had been shot.

13th February 1915

We had no morning paper on Sunday. We found that no more newspapers were to be produced on Sundays. Paper shortage! Too many special news sheets! But Frau Schönfeld said reproachfully: 'They really must make the victories known!'

14th February 1915

I have read such a lovely poem by Goethe; it contains these lines:–

> .... But who is that disappearing into the bush?
> The trees close together behind him;
> The grass springs up again;
> The jungle swallows him up.[10]

I asked Willi to set the verse to music for me. Willi promised he would. But instead of that he set to music a poem by Nikolaus Lenau:– 'The soft light of the moon lingers over the pool, the restless pool'. Androwski, to whom he played it, laughed because Willi sang the words as he played, despite his breaking voice, and his voice kept going up and down. At the most beautiful point he croaked. I laughed too; then I played the treble part on a comb, blowing through tissue paper stretched over it. Then Androwski listened to it properly for the first time and declared that the new composition was so beautiful as to bring tears to your eyes. I exclaimed that Willi would make an even more beautiful setting for my Goethe lines. Androwski wanted to know what lines I meant. I began to recite them at once. 'And you like them so much?' asked Androwski and laughed again. I couldn't tell him that the passage reminded me of the Russian – or of myself – I don't know which.

Willi went on playing his latest songs; they become more and more lovely. With all this he is the worst pupil of our piano teacher, Frau Übe. I can play the piano better than he does, but neither of us enjoys practising any more, and the tedious Czerny will drive us to give up taking piano lessons altogether. Willi

116

skips practice anyway while he watches Lotte Voss passing by from the window. Androwski says that one day Willi will be sorry that he was too lazy to learn anything from Frau Übe. And yet Willi has his own technique, with runs and chords and silent pauses and changes of key. Strange, isn't it? Androwski thinks he has a natural talent.

I love my brother, although he is sometimes a pest. Early to-day for example. The wind was howling, the wooden window-shutters rattling, the trees in the garden sighing, whistling and creaking, with snow flying madly past in horizontal lines. I was glad that Grandma had not yet awakened me, and I pulled the bedclothes round me. Suddenly something big and heavy struck me on the head, then again and once again. Four or five pillows and cushions. In the doorway stood Willi, half-dressed and shaking with laughter. I hurled the cushions back. 'What time is it?' I asked.

'Late, anyway!' cried Willi cheerfully. 'We shall be late for school!'

'Jesus, Mary and Joseph!' I cried.

Grandma wasn't there. Her bed was empty, and the pillows lay smooth and undisturbed as on the previous evening. In the dining-room the lamp was still burning from last night. The coffee table was not laid. And Marie, who now lives with her sweetheart in the 'Herring Quarter', was also missing. Just as I was wondering whether I had time to make some coffee the door-bell rang. Who stood outside, completely covered in snow? Grandma! We asked in amazement where she had been. Grandma smiled guiltily and said that yesterday evening she had gone quickly to the station again and then had stayed there all night. 'Such an awful number of soldiers came, the ladies hadn't finished serving soup,' she said. 'So many wounded from the East ... My God, when you see how those poor men suffer! Get dressed quickly, children – I will write you a note to excuse you anyway. Willi, what are you standing around for – quick! quick! I'm not tired! I'll make the coffee!'

If I were Mayor of Schneidemühl I would recommend Grandma for the 'Order of Merit'.

15th February 1915

Grandma sent me a note from the station to-day: I was to go over there quickly, there was something to see!

I rushed over there.

There was a group of thirty infants, brought from the East by nurses, and next to them a pack of first-aid dogs. A forty minute stop! The infants were very nice; but the dogs! Like show-dogs! Thoroughbreds from head to tail! Such a wonderful breed of Scottish sheep-dog; long, pointed nose; intelligent eyes; upstanding ears; bushy tail and a strong, supple body on muscular legs. The coat – long and either black and white or white speckled with gold. I strained my eyes to see whether I could discover Prince. But there was no black Dobermann. Even without Prince I was delighted: wonderful animals! The dogs had on their backs a coat bearing the Red Cross. Little bunches of flowers were fastened on their coats and on their collars. The dogs were thirsty from their long journey and whimpering. I filled basin after basin with water for them to drink. I fondled the dogs as much as I could. Some of them licked me. One dog-handler said, 'You're not afraid of them, little girl?'

How happy I was! In their full field uniform the dogs look different. They have a collar from which two leather straps hang, left and right. The straps hold a folded cloth, which is rolled across the throat. Behind these hang two leather pouches with the Red Cross sign. Both pouches again are fastened with straps. In the pouches are bandages, medicines and refreshments. The dogs have to seek out the wounded after a battle, so that the medical services can get them into hospital; this also enables the wounded to receive first-aid and revival treatment. Many dogs which ran loose in town and country were caught and assigned to Red Cross duties.

Prince! You dear, lovely dog!

16th February 1915

Our 149th are to be transferred from the Western Front to Serbia. When I told this to Grandma, who was in the kitchen making potato fritters, with tremendous whirring and clattering, she said, 'Get away with you, girl, you're having me on.'

But Willi, who had been playing the piano in the best room, came also into the kitchen and said, 'It is true. It is good that our boys are going to Serbia; they can get their breath back there. The regiment is almost wiped out.'

'Grandma,' I said, 'they are saying to each other in the street, as they did in the early days of the war: "Every Briton must be smitten, wipe every Jap right off the map, bash every Frenchman in his trench, man, and Serbia, we'll curb yer".' 'Yes,' cried Willi with relish. 'They'll all gradually be killed off.'

'Stop your nonsense, children,' cried Grandma. 'They are all human beings, you shouldn't joke about it. Just bring me your plates, potato fritters should be eaten hot straight out of the pan, that's how they taste best.'

We found that was so. We ate the fritters with a lot of sugar and apple jelly. There was grated onion in them too. Hurra!

17th February 1915

I haven't yet given any description of our piano teacher, Frau Übe. Is it not funny that a piano teacher is called 'Frau Übe?' [Mrs. Practice]. So, she lives in a rather dark flat. The piano stands near the window where it gets the best light. The room in which Frau Übe gives lessons looks as if you wouldn't be allowed to laugh in it or jump on a chair. In fact neither Willi nor I have ever laughed there. Grandma says that Frau Übe is a brave woman for whom she has great respect. She has a daughter Doris who is already in the top class. Doris is reckoned to be the cleverest and most hard-working girl in the whole school. When Willi nearly got stuck in the fourth form she gave him private coaching. That got him through. Afterwards he even became a good scholar, especially when Professor Philipp became his friend. Because of his great admiration for Professor Philipp he has swotted like mad. Only with Frau Übe he did nothing at all; he learned absolutely nothing about playing from sheet music, found that practising bored him stiff, and skipped nearly every piano lesson, so that even I got furious with him.

But, heavens, these scales and studies! Frau Übe wants me to play Beethoven's Sonata in G Major, Op 49, No 2, at the next pupils' concert. I think the triplets are glorious, but I couldn't play in public; I would quite definitely fall off the piano stool with fear. I must ask Grandma not to send me to Frau Übe any more; I would rather go on learning by myself.

19th February 1915

Our forces have taken the town of Czernowitz. We looked for this town on the school map and found it between Dnjestr and Pruth. Dora Haensch was allowed to stick the little black, white and red flag in. The paper flags are attached to pins; we mark the progress of the fighting with them; just as they do at General Staff headquarters.

The German naval airship Parseval took off from a Baltic port on 25th January to bomb Libau and up to now has not returned. According to an announcement from the Russian General Staff it has been shot down and crashed into the sea.

Dora said, 'Perhaps that was the airship that we tried to get a sight of.'

Now it is broken in pieces, burnt, and drifting on the ice.

20th February 1915

Gretel and I couldn't rest. We wanted to find out whether we Germans treat our prisoners-of-war better than the English do. We decided to seek out secretly the Russian hospital that must be near the big camp. We had been given fairly precise directions to it. We trudged across a big field, covered in some places with thick scrub, and we were not wandering so blindly as the previous time.

'There it is already, I can see it!' cried Gretel and pointed to a long, straggling building that stretched across the field like a grey earthworm. The hospital was enclosed by a high, strong wire fence in which there were one large and two smaller gates. Ambulances could go in through the large gate. A flagpole carried the Red Cross flag.

The hospital consisted not just of one building but several. They were built like huts, some of wood, some of corrugated iron. The wooden buildings were painted dark green or dark brown. They had metal chimneys and pretty little windows.

'It looks alright,' I decided. We were very pleased. You could quite clearly see Russian patients through the windows. Everything inside was clean, simple and practically arranged. The wards were brightly lit with electric lights. The sick and wounded lay on camp beds and were carefully and neatly bandaged. Their bed-clothes were of white linen with blue stripes.

In the middle of the larger hut stood a white enamelled table. On it lay material for bandages, medicines and various appliances. A Russian doctor and two Russian orderlies stood around the table and seemed to be looking for something. They had Red Cross bands on their arms. Their heads and hair were covered with a clean white linen cap without a peak. They wore equally clean white overalls. Everything was extraordinarily clean. There were certainly no lice or fleas here.

'Tip-top, I should say,' said Gretel.

'Faultless,' I agreed. 'The Russians have nothing to complain about.'

'And we can't complain to the Red Cross!' said Gretel.

We laughed.

I took another good look at the hospital. In the surrounding area some Russians were digging a trench. Some of our soldiers were supervising them. As we passed by the Russians stopped in the middle of their work and smiled at us. 'Digging a grave?' I asked lightly. But we saw that the Russians were bringing old straw bedding here and burning it in the pit. 'For the purpose of disfection,' whispered Gretel. I couldn't help laughing, because she had said 'disfection', but I wasn't going to correct her; that sort of thing can be hurtful.

We went home quickly as it was beginning to get dark. I must add that at each corner of the encampment and not only at the main gate but also in the middle and on the sides of the wire fence there were sentry-boxes manned by German police. This time no one had turned us away or forbidden us to go any further as at the prisoner-of-war camp.

In the hall of our house there was a pleasant smell of baked potatoes. Gretel looked at me in amusement and (playing the part of Nurse Martha), said 'Are you satisfied, Lieutenant?'

'Ay, Ay, very good,' I said, in a rasping voice and giving a military salute. 'Will you come again to-morrow, Nurse Martha?'

'I'll see if I can. Perhaps I will. Good-bye for now.'

21st February 1915

At the station to-day I saw for the first time the strange boats that the sappers use to build pontoons. It was interesting. The boats are large and bulky, quite unlike our slender, elegant pleasure-boats. There is not much about them to describe. The keel is not pointed at the bottom, but flat and provided with regular little projections like buttons. Thwarts were non-existent – at least I didn't see any.

The trains again brought loads of machine-guns, which from a distance looked like children's toys. I soon went home, because it was too cold and the North wind blew such a mass of fine, icy snowflakes into my face that I was afraid it would get frozen. Willi was waiting for me with the news that a few days ago the Serbs Beliko Cubrilovic, Mickko Javanovic and Danilo Ikie, who had been sentenced to death for high treason in connection with the assassination of the Crown Prince and Princess, were executed in the courtyard of the fortress prison at Sarajevo. The execution took place without incident. Jaco von Milovic and Nedjo Kerovic, who were condemned to death, were pardoned, that is to say the death sentence was converted to life imprisonment and 20 years respectively.

When Willi had read this out, I asked, 'And what about the actual assassin, Princip?'

Willi read: 'Princip, the assassin of the Archduke and his wife, who, as is well known, could not be sentenced to death because of his youth, was given twenty years hard labour.'

I said, 'In twenty years' time he will still be under forty.'

'Yes indeed!' agreed my brother. He stared me in the face for some time and suddenly exploded.

'Why are you laughing?' I asked.

'Oh God!' cried Willi. 'I'm laughing because you are. I could see plainly that you were laughing inwardly.'

'I can't stand shooting people!' I said, and laughed because Princip too had not been shot.

25th February 1915

After lunch (which was jacket potatoes and herrings) I fell asleep on my chair. That has never happened to me before, except when I was an infant. Perhaps I have got consumption? Then I needn't go to school any more. That would be wonderful! I could play all the time.

When I woke up, my eyes happened to fall on a letter lying on the sideboard. It was addressed to me. I didn't know the handwriting. It was in large, firm letters. On the back it said – 'Sender, Minna Szagun, c/o Herr A. Schulz, Boat House, The Alster, Hamburg.' I tore the letter open and read:-

'Dear Miss Elfriede, a few days ago I heard from my brother on war service about the kindnesses which you have done him, for which I express my sincere thanks. When I read the lovely letter that you sent him I really shed tears of joy, for I thought of nothing else all that day but how God's strength guides us, and I commit our whole fate ever more to God the Three in One. Dear young lady, as you are my brother's benefactress I will tell you about ourselves and how good he is. For we live in East Prussia and were driven out by the Russians on 23rd November, having to leave behind our dear mother and all our goods and chattels, and could imagine what it was like for our mother when she was left without her main support. Up to now we know nothing about our dear mother, our uncle has made enquiries as to where the women from the neighbourhood are, we have no idea whether they are actually in Russia, so we are quite distraught, God alone knows whether we shall ever get together again. I and another sister have been asked by my relatives to go to Hamburg, I shall go into service from 1st March onwards, for in these days you have to work for your living, but I have always worked. I am 25 years old, my sister is 18, and I would very much like you to help my brother Emil to bear his burden in battle so long as he needs it. Somebody still in Königsberg received a letter from him today in which he said he thought it would not be long before he would have to be in the field. It is really sad what a burden we have to bear, but I think we deserve it, for you can imagine the suffering dear young lady, first my dear mother, second my very young brother whom it is doubtful whether I shall see again, and thirdly our possessions so that we have nothing with us to live on, 14 head of cattle, 5 horses, 8 pigs, and a lot of grain that our mother had thought to retain when so to speak she had to give up her living. The area from which we come lies North of the Memel and is called Pagulbinnen near Wischwill in Ragnit. Sincere greetings to you and thank you again, in God's name, from Minna Szagun.'

I turned the letter over thoughtfully in my fingers and wondered why war had to come upon the world. The Szaguns had so many cattle and so much corn – and now there's nothing left. In other regions it is the same; every one living in a frontier zone has lost cattle, corn, houses and people. I have seen a war photo in which a dead man hung backward on the barbed wire. He was fair and had lost his helmet in falling. His mouth was open and his lips collapsed. He had certainly not died instantly and had suffered and cried out for sometime; you could still see that from his mouth. The dead soldier could quite easily have been Emil Szagun. I should like to know the soldier's name.

Then Grandma disturbed me. She read out to me from the Schneidemühl News:-

'The landing party from the "Emden", which had landed in the Cocos Islands before the sinking of this best of all ships, had to look on helplessly as the noble ship went down. Now there happened to be an old schooner in the harbour. The landing party seized this foreign ship and, taking with them four machine-guns, steamed away. On the way, the party from the Emden forced a good, strongly built ship called the "Ayesha" to surrender to them and transferred from the schooner to the "Ayesha" (home port London). Lieutenant-Commander von Mücke took over the command of the ship. Then the "Ayesha" travelled through great dangers to Hodeida in the Red Sea (on the South West coast of Arabia). The crew will attempt to get through to Constantinople.'

The newspaper article ended with 'Three hearty cheers for the boys in blue of the Emden II.'

Grandma said, 'At least they were all saved.'

'At least that!' I agreed.

28th February 1915

I don't know at all just now what I have reported in the war diary. As Mummy is getting the pages typed, ready to be bound later on, they are in Berlin. I cannot look back through them. But I am pretty sure that I have written nothing much about the war in our colonies. They are in fact being gradually lost to us. First the Japanese seized Tsingtau in Kiaochow, China, but that was well before Christmas, about the beginning of November. I remember how upset all our friends were. Then came the German South Sea Islands and German New Guinea because we had few soldiers there, then the German African colony of Togoland. Now the Cameroons, German South-west Africa, and German East Africa are added to the list. German East Africa is defended by Colonel von Lettow-Vorbeck and his colonial troops, which consist of 3,000 whites and 11,000 Askaris (blacks). But what can the best colonial troops do against a hundred times as many English soldiers?

Perhaps all the German colonial possessions will soon be gone, but Fräulein Ella Gumprecht thinks we shall seize them back again at the end of the war. Fräulein Gumprecht's beautiful sister Sophie lived for many years in the colonies. She was married to an officer in the colonial troops. Sophie went to school with Mummy and they are still good friends to-day. A brother of

Fräulein Gumprecht also used to live in the colonies. He brought the strangest things back with him – poisoned spears, bows, quivers and darts, native jewellery, painted sounding-jars and plaited straw baskets, hairs from elephants' tails, ivory tusks, and a huge bare elephant's skull that was displayed in the office of the Gumprecht brewery. It lies on a lion's skin that is quite moth-eaten. Whenever I go to the Gumprechts, I gaze at it. I never feel comfortable with it; there is something gruesome about that skull. I always think, 'Poor elephant', and how happily he must have trumpeted through his trunk.

I cannot properly imagine colonial life, but I am frightfully fond of Sophie; she is beautiful and wears tight-fitting clothes, like a fairy. I saw a photograph of her in which she is sitting at the table in her bungalow, the only lady between handsome officers of the colonial troops. The bungalow is very elegant and has a long terrace leading into a garden. Sophie is wearing a white dress and has a giant white summer hat on. The officers have raised their glasses to her in admiration and she is laughing. Willi adores Sophie, but he hasn't dedicated anything to her as he has to Lotte Voss. So it is not quite as bad as that. Sophie is now in Berlin.

1st March 1915

The soldiers sing this marching song –

> Musketeers are a cheerful lot
> A happy brotherhood.
> They shout and sing their cheerful songs,
> To the girls they're really good.

The young lieutenants are even more cheerful than the musketeers. (Incidentally, nobody speaks of 'musketeers' nowadays; they are called 'infantrymen' or 'footsloggers'.) The officers often make whoopee in the Officers' Mess. Although this is quite a distance from our house the sound of the lively music reaches us. That is when a so-called 'Regimental dinner' is taking place. Sometimes ladies attend them, officers' wives and invited young girls from the town. There is dancing and a good deal of drinking. The merriment increases more and more. Recently it developed into a riot that was, however, hushed up. The tipsy lieutenants strolled through the streets during the night and threw bottles of ink at the Town Hall in the Neue Markt. It is understood that there were many arrests and that some were even transferred for disciplinary reasons. One of the lieutenants told Trude Jakobi's elder sister that he took part in all the foolery because he would sooner or later be dead, in a few weeks at the latest.

When I told this to Gretel Wegner she asked me whether I thought all this madness was right. I considered it for ages, then said: 'Well, they needn't actually chuck bottles of ink around, but it is obvious that they want to make merry in the face of death. It is just like having a glass of Schnapps before you die.' Gretel asked, 'Would you like to drink a glass of Schnapps before dying?' I laughed and said, 'If I could still swallow, I would rather drink soda-water with raspberry-juice.'

But I think it comes to the same thing, whether it's Schnapps or soda-water with raspberry-juice. Who wants to die! You would at least like to have a quick taste of life. Life is beautiful, in spite of war or anything else. The grass is lovely, the trees, the open air, the sky, the moon and the sun. And the animals, too – all these things are lovely.

10th March 1915

Instead of Spring coming, the winter has got even colder. We haven't enough coal in the cellar. Grandma has hung an old quilt over the veranda door to help keep the heat in the living-room. There is no stove in that room. We leave the bedroom door wide open because that is where the big tiled stove is. It reaches right up to the ceiling. It has a little china garland at the top. We put apples from the tree in my garden on the pipes. When they are soft and nicely browned, we put sugar on them. Very tasty.

What else shall I write? People don't now stand so often in front of the newspaper office. Perhaps it's too cold for them. It is just the casualty lists hung there that they still examine thoroughly. Here is an amusing item from our news-sheet:

The militiamen serving in enemy territory are so good-natured that their hearts often make fools of them. A Berlin militiaman who had a wife and children at home and therefore sympathised with what the people on whom he was quartered had to put up with, made the following complaint to a military doctor. 'I'm as good as married here! I live with a woman who has three children and is expecting a fourth in three weeks. I have to

126

dress the brats every morning, make coffee for them and their mother and then do the washing. When I get back to the house at mid-day I have to get dinner and sit down with the children and tell them stories. They and the young woman understand me alright, but I can't understand them properly. Then I have to clean up the whole show, because none of the relatives and neighbours give any help. All my pay goes on this and, what with getting the bread and the meat, the sergeant is always having to cough up a bit more, just so that I can keep the family satisfied. I know I'm being bloody stupid. But you can't go against your nature, can you?'

11th March 1915

Another collection has been announced at school. This time it is again for copper, but also for tin, lead, zinc, brass and old iron. Out of this are to be made gun-barrels, cannons, cartridge-cases and so forth. There is keen competition between the classes. Our class, the fourth, has so far collected the greatest quantity. I have turned the whole house upside down, from top to bottom. Our Marie doesn't half complain! 'Miss Piete is robbing us of everything!' I took old spoons, knives, forks, pots, kettles, a tray, a copper bowl, two brass lamps, old belt buckles and I don't know what else. Grandma clapped her hands and cried, 'The wench will bankrupt me! Better give your lead soldiers than take the last of my possessions!'

So my little army, with which Willi and I had so often played, had to meet their deaths. To avoid all the soldiers being sacrificed I drew lots for the candidates for death. Those on which the lot fell I took out from the four rows and laid on one side. When the drawing of lots was all over I placed the unlucky ones two by two in a large metal spoon and held it over the gas flame. The heroes in their lovely blue uniforms melted to death for the Fatherland, the lead became silvery, heavy and fluid.

'Into cold water, quick!' exclaimed Willi. I let the lump sizzle in a basin of cold water, while I sang 'The little woodland birds'. 'The others too,' cried Willi cruelly. 'There's no point in keeping them.'

It was awful! I melted the last of them too. I could easily have cried. But instead I laughed with my brother.

127

13th March 1915

Dear Mummy,

I must let you know that we must do something about Grandma's health. At ten o'clock yesterday evening Willi and I were alone in the house. Grandma was at the station with the Red Cross. I was darning my left stocking and Willi was just fetching a big book of head sketches by Leonardo da Vinci. Then there were several long rings of the doorbell.

Willi slammed the book down on the table and dashed into the hall to open the door. Then two Red Cross nurses brought Grannie in through the door. She could hardly walk any further and just dropped on to the sofa and closed her eyes. Grandma looked as if she was dying. But I'll tell you at once – she is alive. She had only fainted. It is all too much for her. The nurses think that too, and asked me to make a good strong cup of coffee quickly for Grandma.

When I came back from the kitchen with the coffee, Grandma was already sitting up on the sofa with her eyes open. The nurses undressed her and put her to bed and then she drank the coffee and I gave her a hot-water bottle. I had decided to watch by her bed through the night and after the nurses had gone I took my little stool and sat close to her. Willi at first didn't want to go to sleep, but when he saw that Granny was asleep he eventually went to bed. But Granny breathed so little and her mouth kept falling open. It was terrible. The moon was shining through the window and made a white streak across Grandma's face; then she looked again as if she was dead. Now and then I laid my hand gently on her heart; it was beating. That comforted me. Eventually I saw and heard nothing any more. I had gone to sleep on the stool – imagine that!

We called the doctor of course. He said, 'A weakness of the heart! Stay in bed, keep warm, and no work!' Now Grandma already says she wants to go back to the station. Just what can you do? Please, please, Mummy, write to her at once and tell her that she must stay at home for at least two weeks! In spite of school I can quite well do the shopping, cleaning and cooking; Frau Schönfeld will help me. I am doing alright at school, don't worry.

When are you coming to Schneidemühl again? Can't you come at once? Have you seen the Haber aunts Emma, Lieschen and Minna?

Your not so very happy daughter, Piete.
P.S. We do so long for you.

128

30th March 1915

Mummy has not come, because she cannot leave her music school. She has only a few pupils left and can't afford to lose them. I have done everything just as I told Mummy I would; after school – cleaning, shopping, cooking, and so forth. Sometimes I could only do potatoes with left-overs and chives, because there was not time to make a proper lunch. That was always the case when Frau Schönfeld hadn't time to prepare the meal. Marie doesn't come any more either, that is to say she only comes once a week, for three hours on Fridays. Grandma says she can't pay her for any more.

During this time I gave up thinking about the war diary altogether. I had to watch out that Grandma didn't attempt too much or even go off to the station. Dear God, I invented a hundred reasons to stop her doing that. I have even put the nurses on their guard so that they keep coming in turn to visit her. That at least stops her going out. Fräulein Ella Gumprecht came each day for coffee (I had to make it of course) and stayed right through till supper. Most evenings there was bread and sausage and Harz cheese, together with a cup of oatmeal soup followed by baked apple.

To my horror, during this time we had soldiers billeted on us. A captain and his batman. I gave the captain grandfather's former work-room with the roll-top desk and many books all bound in dark-green paper with brown leather backs. Willi had to sleep during this time in an attic room where he was frozen. The batman had the other attic room in which Gretel and I sometimes play secretly. It contains an enormous wooden box or chest full of old clothes and linen, a bed with a red quilt, a cupboard on three legs, a kitchen chair and a wash-stand with wash-basin and soap-dish. And an oil lamp. The batman found the room very comfortable. Every morning I placed a can of hot water for washing at his door, then I made breakfast for the captain and the batman. Sometimes I really groaned, because I had to do everything before school. I put the coffee under a thick cosy and covered the bread and jam with a plate. The captain had sausages as well. He brought his own ham and smoked-goose. The batman was a farmer's son and had more ham and fat in his knapsack than the captain. So they lived better than Willi and I.

Gretel and I had of course brought our dolls etc. down from the attic before the batman moved in. I often had long talks with the captain about the drill rules for captains and higher officers. This interested me greatly. Gretel and I now bring a captain into our soldier games, the captain's name is v. Vogelmann. He is a handsome officer and has a daughter called Lieselotte. Of course we don't say anything about the fictitious Captain v Vogelmann to the boys who play war games with us in the yard.

News from the Front: The Russians are advancing towards Memel in the East and are trying to enter Hungary in the South West. They have in fact taken the hotly contested Przemysl; but we shall soon recover that, don't you worry.

We were very sorry to hear to-day that our gallant submarine U29 under Lieutenant-Commander Weddigen had been sent to the bottom by an English tanker. Many people cried about this.

25th April 1915

I am thirteen years old to-day. Sometimes I would not like to be any older than I am, sometimes I would like to be twenty. My birthday guests were Hertha Müller, Maria Starke (Pastor Starke's daughter), Käthie Dreier and Dora Haensch. Gretel is still too little to join in the festivities with the big girls. We had a meringue pie with artificial cream, followed by rolls which Grandma had spread with egg, anchovy and even smoked-goose. We played games and sang songs by Hermann Löns. Hertha Müller has a book of songs by Löns; I can play them on the piano and sing most of them from memory. They are very beautiful, half happy and half sad. Our class is mad on these songs. When any one gets to know a new one, the others immediately learn it too. I want to ask for a guitar for my confirmation, then I can accompany any song on that. I already have a name for the guitar; it will be called 'El bobo', that is a Spanish word meaning 'the clown'. Then I shall have many coloured guitar-ribbons – there is a great craze for these at school. My heart throbs with joy when I think of the guitar.

I have forgotten to say that Grandma has for a long time been back on Red Cross duty. She has overcome the heart weakness. She recently took me with her to a young man who is dying. I had to carry the basket with red wine, malt extract, medicines, white bread, butter and a piece of ham. It was all very sad. The young man lay in a miserable room which was nearly empty. He was wearing a clean white shirt, that he had probably only just put on. His face was refined-looking and as white as porcelain, his hands looked like those of a dead man. He coughed terribly and kept pressing a kitchen towel to his mouth. The towel was spattered with blood. I forced myself not to look away, although I found it quite difficult. The poor young man's mother thanked Grandma exuberantly and said, 'Our Eric has only a few days to live'. She said that in front of her son! I was convulsed with horror and sympathy, but the young man listened calmly and simply said, 'What I am most sorry about is that I can't be with the army any more. Not even the Reserves. What can the Army Command begin to do with a consumptive! Just think of it!' Then he couldn't speak any more for coughing. I cast a glance at Grandma and lied, in front of the young man, that I knew of another soldier who had had consumption but became quite well and eventually joined up again and served with the 149th. He opened his eyes wide (lovely, bright blue eyes) and said, 'no, that surely can't be true! Do you know his name?' – 'Of course,' I cried, 'Paul Zohn!'. That was another lie, of course; I had once known a little boy called Paul Zohn; he never had consumption, but was fat, round and healthy. But guess what Grandma did! She didn't let me lie on my own – she said, 'He even won the Iron Cross!' The poor young man was silent, his mother began to cry a little and destroyed the whole lovely lie, saying, 'Eric would love to do that – to win the Iron Cross. But what can't be won't be. The Good God will take his soul into heaven.'

I was so furious with this religion that I would have had no objection if the woman had been struck dumb on the spot. Mummy has at times spoken so strongly in support of the white lie. You can't tell a dying man with such a strong will to live as this one that he hasn't the slightest crumb of hope.

28th April 1915

Our school grounds adjoin the Friedrichsgarten military hospital. Among the wounded is one who is the darling of Class IVb, to which I belong. If any one were to ask who is the one greatest character in Schneidemühl I would say 'this soldier'. His face is as flexible as those of the little monkeys that sometimes sit on barrel-organs. His mouth is a yard long; when he laughs it gets even longer. That is how we always see him – laughing. Always and unceasing we see him thus. War cannot defeat a soldier like this who can laugh in spite of his wounds. He is literally covered in bandages from head to foot, forehead and back of the head, chest, left arm and left leg. Yet he seems to take pride in the bandages, keeps looking down at them with pleasure and brushes off every particle of dust. Nearly every day I bring this man cigarettes that Grandma gives for him from the stock at the station. It is a real joy to see what pleasure this gives him. But he shares them out fairly with his fellow sufferers and puts the last in his mouth. When we come out of school at mid-day and walk past the hospital window on our way home with our school-bags under our arms, he watches us quite sadly.

I asked him one day whether he liked being a soldier. He nodded laughing and answered, 'I love it.'

I immediately beamed as he did and said, 'I would love to be a soldier too.' 'Ah, that's great,' he said with amusement. 'Next time we'll go to the Front together!'

29th April 1915

Mummy wrote a letter saying (I quote) –

'What do you say to our blockade of England? Perhaps the blockade is our best weapon. You know of course that England secretly smuggled weapons and munitions to her coasts from abroad under neutral flags? That is why the German Naval Command gave warning that from 18th February every enemy or suspicious merchant vessel encountered in English waters (except North of the Shetland Isles) would be destroyed by our submarines and cruisers without regard to crew or passengers. Have you given weight to this important step in the diary, Piete?'

No – shame on me! I had quite forgotten it. Strange to say, I had either not properly taken in the news of the blockade or had read it hurriedly, which means that I have become negligent in writing about the war reports. I got involved lately merely with music – songs by Hermann Löns, my brother Willi's songs, and soldiers' songs. Also some of the classes in our school have been practising for a pupils' concert under the guidance of our music teacher. We sing some wonderful songs. One especially I shall never forget, the words go like this –

> Life withers like the grass
> And the flowers in the field;
> The wind that passes over them
> No lasting trace doth yield.

And yet God's grace remains
As man's eternal stay;
He who keeps faith within his heart
Shall never pass away.

Now I ask you, God: will you really cause every dead soldier to rise again, so that he doesn't pass away: I mean dead Englishmen, French, Russians, Slavs, Turks and of course Germans? Why do you never give me an answer? Poor Eric is now dead, you know who I mean. Grandma brought the news home. Will you give him the Iron Cross? I do hope you will reward him. I am not going to his funeral because I don't want to see his mother. He has died so quickly – as if killed – for the Fatherland. For the beechwoods, the rivers and the meadows. For a town, for a village, for whatever men hold dear.

But Eric? Dear God, help me.

1st May 1915

Hey, we have led our teachers a pretty dance to-day, because it is the first of May. We have them on in fact not only on 1st April but also on 1st May, because it is such fun. We told Fräulein Becker that the seam of her dress had opened up at the back. She spun round like a top to look at her rear and we shouted 'First of May! First of May!' We declared to our drawing mistress Fräulein Plascuda that the stuffed squirrel that we were to draw was quite moth-eaten. She took it out of the drawing cupboard and examined it on all sides. At once – 'First of May! First of May!' So it went on all the morning. I even had Grandma on. And Gretel of course. I told Willi that unfortunately the piano was broken, three strings having snapped. How he rushed to the piano! I let him try all kinds of notes before I burst out 'First of May! First of May! The cat's laid an egg!'

'Silly goose!' he cried angrily. 'You stupid, daft, green, slimy frog!'

I soon collapsed with laughter. Then I sparred with my brother, but he had no wish to join in and said he had a headache and would rather go and lie down. That hurt me again.

3rd May 1915

This morning Grandma slept longer than usual and I awoke

because Willi sauntered out from his bedroom (in his night-shirt) through the parlour and the dining-room with his arms stretched up towards the sky and shouting in a strange tone of voice 'Huhuuuu'. I was about to be convulsed with laughter again when I noticed that his face was fiery red. He is normally always pale. I asked him if there was something wrong, for he was just like a ghost. But the rattle in his throat continued, as if he was going to choke, and he went on with his 'Huhu!'

I woke Grandma and she ran to him and caught him in her arms: he literally folded up. She laid him on the sofa and told me to fetch a blanket, with which she covered him. Then he lay there scarcely able to breathe.

And what do you say to that, Diary? The doctor has decided that my brother has scarlet fever.

I was immediately isolated. For the time being I am put in the same attic room in which Willi slept when we had billetees. So that I don't get frightened at night Gretel is allowed to sleep with me in this room. We have to share a bed. My friend is quite big and strong: we shall have to squeeze terribly close.

20th May 1915

A lot has happened. My brother has still got scarlet fever. During the night, while Gretel was sharing my bed I thought she had caught it too. She was as hot as at least ten stoves. She also began to cry out 'Huhuuuu!' just as my brother did. Like a great owl. I ended up on the bedside rug because she pushed me out of bed in her sleep. So I made myself as comfortable as I could on the floor, pulling down one corner of the bedclothes to cover myself with. But that didn't suit Gretel and she kept pulling the bedclothes up again while I was fast asleep. It was a really 'mind-boggling' night, as Willi once said; I was glad when it was over.

Next morning I said to Frau Wegner. 'Do put Gretel back in her own bed, I guarantee she has scarlet fever.' Frau Wegner was very shocked, but Gretel had no trace of fever, was full of beans and wanted coffee. Then Frau Wegner concluded her daughter didn't have scarlet fever, at worst just a bit of a cold, because she did in fact sneeze.

A new experience began for me, for Grandma boarded me out because of the danger of infection. I went to the girls' boarding house in Güterbahnhofstrasse. I was in a real boarding-house for the first time in my life. Many girls, big and small, sit together at one table here, including Willi's 'Empress' Lotte Voss. Now I can look at her every day, as much as I like. And really she is as beautiful as a fairy in a story-book, a fairy made of wax or china. She is very elegant and serious, and hardly speaks a word. I wonder how Willi could converse with her: it is better for him to go on worshipping her from a distance. Throughout the time I only spoke one sentence to her, 'Will you please pass the salt?' She answered not even with a sentence, just one word, 'Certainly'! I am really hopping mad with her. She could at least have asked me just once how my brother was and whether his scarlet fever was better. After all he has written such lovely music and poetry in her honour; in all her life she will have nothing else as beautiful.

> 'Tear not apart the golden threads
> That closely bind together our hearts!'

But I don't see any golden threads that bind her heart to my brother's heart, not even a piece of cotton. Such is love!

Meanwhile our ally Austro-Hungary has asked the Italian government not to make war on us – we have enemies enough. It has offered to Italy, in return for their permanent neutrality, the South Tirol region and the city of Trieste. Ella Gumprecht is very indignant and says it is not necessary for Austro-Hungary to 'creep on its belly' to Italy. Grandma thinks the same. She says, 'We are winning on all fronts and can do without such grovelling.'

We are not so very victorious at present. Our forces are engaged in terrible fighting in the West. Fortunately we have taken Hartmannsweilerkopf. A lot of blood flowed there. The fighting in the Champagne is now dying out. Willi's friend Hans Androwski says that the 'barrage' has been used for the first time. I imagine a 'barrage' must be horrendous. The shells probably rain down ceaselessly on the soldiers like drum-beats. Now when trains come from the West with soldiers who are being transferred to the Eastern Front, their uniforms are dirty and torn. Their spiked helmets are no longer enamelled black, but are painted field-grey. The Belgian and French soldiers wear flat steel helmets. I have even seen a few German steel helmets too. The soldiers don't say much, they are just hungry and thirsty. On the station there is ever more and more soup made, with meat or sausages. There are hardly enough supplies coming in. Many soldiers complain of lice. Some of our lady helpers at the Red Cross have got lice too now. They have to go for medical treatment at once.

24th May 1915

I am forgetting to write about the war news because I find the young ladies and high school girls in the Hoppenrath Boarding House so interesting and have made friends with some of them already. There is one young lady who can in fun run like a cab-horse as seen from behind. It is killing – people split their sides with laughter. I should like to see Lotte Voss running like a 'cab-horse as seen from behind;' I think I would be as much in love with her as my brother is. But she looks through me as if I didn't exist; nothing of a 'cab-horse' about her!

Mummy has reminded me about the diary. I certainly want to write in it, but nothing has happened to raise our spirits. On the contrary, yesterday our former ally Italy sent a declaration of war to Austro-Hungary. They are supporting the enemy Entente as from 23rd May. Poor Emperor Franz Joseph has had the following poster printed:–

'To my people!
The King of Italy has declared war against me. This is the beginning of a breach of faith, the like of which is unknown to history, by the kingdom of Italy towards its two allies. After an alliance lasting more than thirty years, during which it was able to increase its territorial possessions and enjoy undreamed-of prosperity, Italy has abandoned us in our hour of danger and gone over with flying colours to the camp of our enemies.
We have not threatened Italy, we have not damaged its image, nor have we impugned its honour or acted against its interests. On the other hand we have faithfully performed our duty as an ally, and have provided protection in the field. We have done more; when Italy cast its covetous eyes on our frontier we committed ourselves, for the sake of the alliance and preservation of peace, to great and painful sacrifices, sacrifices which were particularly close to our paternal heart.'

Finally the Emperor wrote:

'I rely on my people, for whose unequalled spirit of sacrifice my innermost paternal thanks are due. I pray the Almighty that he will bless our colours and take our righteous cause into his gracious protection.
Franz Joseph.'

People in the town are furious. They can hardly grasp the fact. Besides this there is a terrible new weapon: poison-gas! I cannot find out who first brought it into use, although any such thing is obviously a matter for court-martial. It was used in the bloody fighting along the Yser–Ypres Canal on the Western Front. The soldiers now carry so-called 'Gas Masks' in battle; these are ugly, snout-shaped grey-green masks with glass windows to see through and a supply of oxygen for breathing. When a poison-gas alarm is raised at the Front the soldiers immediately snatch their masks from their belts and cover their faces with them. But the warning often comes too late; the gas has already drifted through the trenches and kills the soldiers. Poison gas is already being used all over the place; there are said to be particular kinds, for example green gas and yellow gas, one being more terrible than the other. The soldiers are almost more afraid of gas warfare than shrapnel, mines, machine-guns and dum-dum bullets.

Instead of moving towards peace, the war gets worse and worse. There is no end in sight. Yet the soldiers still sing the old songs as they pass through our station. I can no longer listen to them.

I write love-letters to my brother. They usually begin with 'Dear Little Golden Willi', because of the 'golden threads' that refuse to act as binding. Unfortunately I don't receive any answers because letters from Willi would carry scarlet-fever germs. I don't get to see Grandma any more either; and she doesn't do station duty either, but is busy looking after Willi. Today I did a 'window walk' past my brother, because I could no longer bear the separation. I whistled our own special whistle. Then Grandma appeared at the window, pulled the curtains back and smiled and waved to me. God, was I happy!

Later I met my 'Sergeant' Jule Haensch, who joined with the other children in our soldier games in our yard. He called out to me: 'Unfaithful tomato!' I ran into the yard. They all immediately shouted, 'Play with us! Play with us!' Gretel was there too; she was looking after a 'wounded soldier' on a chicken-ladder. This chicken-ladder is our stretcher; we have put a sack over it as a tent-cloth.

I saluted and called, 'Hallo, Nurse Martha!' Gretel jumped up and called 'Hallo, Lieutenant von Yellenic! Where have you come from?'

I kissed her hand, clicked my heels and said, 'I am just on a through transport for Verdun. I have come with my company from Gorlice-Farnow. We have taken over a hundred thousand Russian prisoners.'

137

Jule thought this was an exaggeration and said, 'Now then, not really a hundred thousand!'

'You haven't read the war despatches then Sergeant!' I snapped out at him. 'It is quite true. We Germans have taken up to 150,000 prisoners at Gorlice in the East and captured countless machine-guns and cannons.' But Gretel's brother Fritz didn't want to know anything about the actual events of the war; he was only interested in getting me to join in. I explained again that I was just passing through.

'Let's just pretend that you have to take temporary command of our battery,' said Fritz. 'We are pretending to be horse artillery.'

The 'horses' on which they were tearing around were roller-skates. All the boys have roller-skates, Jule Haensch has just got his for his birthday; they shine like silver. To be sure, I took command and shouted, 'Squadron No. 1 mount! At the gallop, away!' and the squadron rushed off. Immediately upon my first command Jule's right skate got caught in the left one and he crashed at full length on to the concrete. There was a big bump on his temple, which immediately swelled up like half an egg and turned blue. His nose was bleeding, and we laid him on the stretcher, but he immediately turned round and brought up all his dinner. We were terribly shocked.

Fritz Wegner and I wanted to take him to Haensch's. He just swayed and moaned, he was so bad; so we took him under the arm and dragged him across the yard and down Uscher Strasse to his father's buffet. Frau Haensch put him to bed at once and sent Dora to the doctor. That was an awful fright! I was glad to sit down again with the big girls in the Hoppenrath boarding-house. I could hardly eat, although there were jacket-potatoes with sweet and sour sauce, which I like so much. I couldn't laugh any more. What have I done through my silly war games!

26th May 1915

At school Dora Haensch passed me a note saying, 'Jule has concussion. The doctor says he mustn't move.'

If Jule should die .... He is Haensch's only son! Dora is their only other child. And all just because I gave that stupid order! 'Squadron – mount! At the gallop!' Dear God, don't let Jule die! Dear God, let me die instead of him! It wouldn't matter so much with me, Mummy still has three sons. I am so sorry for the

Haensch family; the fat papa with the enormous moustache, the fat mamma who also has a tiny moustache, my sweet Dora and above all Jule.

In the past, when our class were still quite little, we had a fellow-pupil called Toni Renkawitz who was the niece of the Polish provost Renkawitz from Usch. This Toni one day leaned her arm on the desk with a pen holder in her hand. Then she accidentally pricked herself with the pen in the temple near the left eye. She must have actually pierced an artery, for three days later she was dead. First she went blind, and then died from blood poisoning.

Afterwards I had to go to a flower shop in Wilhelmsplatz to order a wreath on behalf of the class and I felt very proud. Maria Starke, the pastor's daughter, and I were to carry the wreath later on. On the day of the funeral we all travelled to Usch, twenty-five children and the teacher. There lay Toni Renkawitz in a white coffin in fine white lace: she was dressed like a bride with crown and veil. Her thick black plaits lay right and left of her chest. She was like a lovely wax doll. Her folded hands were also like wax; she held a silver cross. All the grown-ups, even the provost who had to give an address, sobbed and cried. Only we schoolchildren didn't cry; I don't think we realised that Toni was dead. Yet Grandma had pressed her best white lace handkerchief into my hand, murmuring, 'In case you can't help crying!' But I didn't cry, only thought that Toni Renkawitz had never looked so lovely, and that she was certainly not our Toni because she was always laughing and had red cheeks.

I can't help thinking of this funeral now. I am going mad with fear for Jule Haensch. Just let me die instead of Jule, dear God. I will never again play at war with the boys, never again! I'll just play 'Nurse Martha and Lieutenant von Yellenic' with Gretel.

14th June 1915

Hurrah, Przemysl has fallen. Didn't I say we are always victorious! (Nearly always.)

Of course we are let off school. French and mathematics have gone by the board.

And Jule Haensch is well. He is even roller-skating again already (in secret). And the best is, Willi is well too. Our house in Alte Bahnhofstrasse has been disinfected. I was allowed to go back home the day before yesterday. What a joy that was! But

139

the house seems quite strange to me; I act like a visitor. Even Willi seems different, so long and thin. He has very little hair; it fell out during his illness. I shall have to get accustomed to everything afresh, even Grandma and Gretel.

I haven't seen Gretel for ages. She flushed with joy when I said 'Good-morning' to her in the stairway.

'I still remember how I saw you for the very first time in my life,' she said. 'That too was here in the stairway. You were sliding backwards down the banisters, something I had never seen before in my life. And you had Willi's blue shorts on.'

I had always thought that I had first seen Gretel with her celluloid doll in her lap on the steps at the back of the house.

'Perhaps you were so little that I hardly recognised you in the stairway,' I said.

'No, it was dark,' explained Gretel. That could be; there is no light in the stairway. When evening visitors come, Grandma puts an oil lamp near our door in the corridor, so that the guests don't break their necks. I can find the steps in my sleep, and in any case slide down the long banisters. Nothing can happen to me there.

Willi wanted to know what Lotte Voss had said. That was very awkward for me for she hadn't said a word about my brother. So I followed Mummy's example of a 'white lie' and said Lotte Voss had spoken very well of him and often sent greetings to him.

'But what exactly did she say?' Willi wanted to know.

I lied that she said his compositions were very beautiful, and that he was the nicest boy that she knew in the school.

Willi said nothing and had such a lovely quiet smile on his face that I would have loved to put my arms round him. Then he took a sheet of fine paper out of grandfather's roll-top desk, on which he had written some new verses for Lotte Voss, which went like this:–

> Two Little Verses
> (*written during my illness*)
>
> Lotte, all my tears, my songs,
> Flow around thee constantly;
> Two words only they contain –
> Me and thee and thee and me.
>
> Moon, heaven and earth in the rapid course
> Of time will fade away,
> But these two words, just me and thee,
> All heaven and earth outweigh.

Willi asked me to give the sheet to Lotte Voss. That was really most awkward for me. But I promised I would. I have just now slipped the envelope containing the poem into the hands of Lotte's friend Mia with the request to give it to the marble queen.[11]

1st July 1915

Mummy has written to-day –

'Dear Piete, The latest pages of your diary have reached me. I have read them and given them to Fräulein von R. to type.

My criticism: It is really no longer a war document but a private diary. Is there any point in going on writing? That is what I quite seriously ask both you and me. What has happened to the historically important news from the Front, but also in Galicia where our heroes after Przemysl have now taken Lemberg too.

Moreover I haven't read a word about the sinking of the English passenger steamer 'Lusitania' by our submarine "U20". That was, as I now belatedly discover, on 7th May. I can understand that during Willi's illness and your stay in the Hoppenrath Boarding-House you had little inclination to write, but events of such far-reaching importance as the death of nearly two thousand passengers surely ought to get a mention in your diary. The event has finally brought us near to the entry of America into the ranks of our opponents.'

Mummy is right. But I really didn't know what I ought to write about the 'Lusitania'. This was a passenger steamer like the big liner 'Titanic' which struck an ice-berg a few years ago and went down with all hands, and with the ship's band playing 'Nearer my God to Thee'. But it says in the newspapers that the 'Lusitania' flew no flag.

'S.M.S. "U20" at 10 minutes past 3 fired a torpedo at the ship which was hit on the starboard side at the level of the bridge. A second even bigger explosion followed this detonation. The Lusitania quickly listed to starboard and began to sink. It is thought that the second explosion derived from the ignition of a large quantity of ammunition with which the ship was laden. The Lusitania was carrying an enormous quantity of munitions, much foodstuff and 4 million marks worth of gold to England. 120 of the passengers were American. They had chosen to embark for England in spite of the warning of the German Ambassador in Washington, Count Bernstorff. It is said that among them was the American millionaire, Vanderbilt.'

Two opinions, one saying this, the other saying that. I preferred to write nothing.

3rd July 1915

The Red Cross canteen at the station has been closed. Nobody knows why. Grandma thinks it is because big troop movements are taking place in secret. Many military trains come through, but unostentatiously. This is exceptional. Yesterday 50 enormous military motor vehicles came through, all grey enclosed vehicles. You couldn't see what was inside.

4th July 1915

We hear that the wounded from the East are being transported by waterway in order to relieve the railway. A hospital barge carries from 35 to 65 wounded. The air is better on the rivers than on the railway; and, besides, the wounded are not disturbed by the constant rumble of the train.

It is said that the Red Cross canteen may be closed for good – it consumes too much bread. In the town bread is no longer sold without so-called 'bread-cards', nor any rolls or biscuits. The bread cards are issued every fortnight in different colours and with different numbers and distributed to individual households by the 'Municipal Bread Commission'. So many heads, so many cards. For each bread-card you can buy two loaves and 60 Pfennigs worth of rolls. There are either five-pfennig or three-pfennig rolls. Two loaves and twenty three-pfennig rolls have to last each person a fortnight. When once the bread-card has been used, you get no more bread.

The loaves look different from those in peacetime. Whereas there used to be white bread made from wheat meal, now there's 'war bread' made from rye meal and potatoes. This bread is marked with a large K – Kriegsbrot [war bread] or Kartoffelbrot [potato-bread]. In addition every loaf shows the date on which it was baked. New bread is not allowed to be issued. The dark bread tastes better to us than the wheat bread. The 'Russian bread' that was on sale at the beginning of the war, and that Willi and I liked so much, has disappeared. In the bread that the prisoners now get in the camps there is potato-peel mixed with bran and animal-feed for the sake of economy. England, so the newspapers say, will not 'starve us out'; we'll see to that.

Military music can be heard coming from the Horsemarket. A bandmaster is practising there all kinds of songs and trumpet calls with his wind section. I am sitting at the window listening to it. It is said that the military bands had a part to play in the great Masurian battle which Hindenburg won. They were ordered to keep playing 'Fortissimo' so that our soldiers couldn't hear the screams of the Russians in the swamps. Even so there were quite enough German soldiers driven mad. Even to-day many field-greys talk about it. It makes us sad to think that the Red Cross canteen is to be closed. The soldiers need it. I think of one Sunday afternoon when two pale soldiers came to the door. Their uniforms looked awful, but both wore the Iron Cross. I had gone to the station with Grandma; I then picked out a few particularly thick sandwiches, filled two mugs with coffee and handed them to the soldiers. 'Thank you very much, oh thank you so much!' After a while one of the soldiers placed his hand on my arm. 'Could we possibly have another slice, little girl?' I gave them some more bread. A few moments later, as I was washing up coffee cups, I felt a touch on my shoulder, and the other soldier was looking imploringly at me. 'Oh miss, could we have some more bread!' I was surprised, but said nothing and handed them some more bread. Whoops! It was gone in a few bites. They looked again with ravenous eyes at the basket full of bread, but hadn't the nerve to ask for more. Then I went over to them and said quietly, 'Are you still hungry?' – 'Yes, yes!' They ate more, and the bread vanished inside them as if in a sack. The nurses began to show surprise too. Then one of the soldiers began to explain. 'Excuse us, but nothing has passed our lips since the day before yesterday. On Saturday we thought our end had come.' The other soldier said 'My mate and I have been in Serbia, fighting. It was bad enough in France and Russia – but still worse in Serbia.'

'Gosh, Willi,' I thought, 'what a false idea we have of the fighting in Serbia!'

'One fine day there we got separated from the Company and wandered for eleven days in the mountains without finding a house or a village. Luckily we had some army bread and sausages. There was enough water, but nothing like enough to eat. Then we came across some Austrian patrols, attached ourselves to them and stayed with them.' They buckled their packs on again, donned their helmets, and shook hands gratefully. We gave them some more cigarettes, pipe tobacco, and at their special request a pair of socks each; we also wrapped up some more bread for them.

They had hardly gone when a blond soldier as tall as a tree stuck his head through the door followed by other laughing soldiers. 'Just come in here, lads,' cried the blond one, 'it's just like mother's parlour – lovely and comfortable and snug!'

Yes, and now the 'comfortable and snug parlour' is going to be closed to our soldiers! And what when they again shout 'We're starving!' or want a plate of hot soup? Or a slice of bread and dripping or sausage? And all because of the bread shortage in the town! The rule is 'Every district to be responsible for its own food supplies'. Unfortunately Schneidemühl was recently designated as the main town of the district. Other main towns have a good many villages and rural areas around them. But we? Nothing but a few suburbs and open, sandy areas; potatoes, rye and turnips. And 40,000 prisoners in the camps. What bread they consume! If they did but know that they could easily do us all in if they wanted to! Most of our men are at the Front and there are none too many soldiers in the barracks now. But perhaps the prisoners don't want to escape? The war is over for them and they get fed too.

14th July 1915

It's dear Willi's birthday to-day. I have given him a music manuscript book and an indelible pencil. In return he produced a present that he had made for me during his illness; a perfectly lovely little garden on a cardboard base, with a stream made of silver-paper, little hills of moss and delicate little trees, a proper bridge and a tiny little arbour. Best of all were very small animals that he had put in the garden, coloured china deer, a stag with antlers and above all two miniature china dogs. I was enthralled, and could hardly stop looking at it. The whole thing looked like a Chinese pleasure garden.

20th July 1915

A Field Postcard from some-one unknown:–

'Dear child – you are a child, aren't you?

Yesterday after a long time I received with great pleasure a parcel. My pleasure was all the greater when I opened it and found the lovely warm stockings and the nice little poem. I cannot unfortunately return your kindness but I offer to you, and to your dear parents, who no doubt encouraged you in this, my sincere thanks, and I promise that we will not let the Russians rest until we can return to the homeland as victors over Russia (even if we have to march without stockings). I send you from Russia a real German soldier's greeting!

Paul Liebenau, N.C.O. in the Militia,
Major Lubitz's Detachment, Goslawitza.'

This Herr Liebenau is doubtless a teacher. I have searched my brains to think what stockings he can have received from me; I have only once put a poem in with a pair of stockings, and that was at the beginning of the war. So this gift parcel has been nearly a year on its way.

I was at the station a little while ago. It was sad without the Red Cross Centre. As I was coming away I saw a stretcher lying on the platform with two perplexed orderlies standing by it. On the stretcher lay a Russian officer. He had drawn his legs up and seemed to be in pain. His big dark eyes looked around questioningly and in fear. One of the orderlies said to me, 'Don't go too close to him, he may have typhus.' As the orderlies didn't know where to take the sick man, I drew for them on a piece of paper the way to the Russian military hospital.

In the evening I went to the Rohleder hospital with a bunch of flowers. Many of the wounded there know me. They raised their heads and greeted me as I went in. When they saw the flowers they all wanted to have them. It's funny isn't it? Men wanting flowers! But I laid them on the bed of a very badly wounded man. He smiled and quietly said, 'Thank you!' The other wounded men had been watching; one of them said, 'That was well done, Missy!' I was very happy. Later on I noticed that the badly wounded man was holding the flowers against his forehead; the leaves of the flowers helped to cool his fever.

A nurse put her arm round me for a moment and said 'You can stay until Vespers if you like. We shall set up the pulpit at six o'clock, and then Missionary Töpper from Kiautschou will preach.'

But I didn't want to stay, because I am still angry with religion. My goodness! Even the Emperor Franz Joseph has called upon God to give victory to his forces. On how many nations exactly is God to bestow victory? I would be only too glad if he would at least make these severely wounded men whole again. (And then the consumptive Eric!)

28th July 1915

For nearly three weeks we have been on 'Long holidays'. They are lasting longer than usual this time because many school children have to help with the early harvest work. It is hot, and the days in our little town are lovely. Each house has a face that I know. In one house the Rotkugels live, fat Herr Rotkugel and two fat sisters with even fatter bosoms and red-painted cheeks; their hair is artificially curled. Many officers and soldiers go to Rotkugels. They can drink Schnapps there. In another house the butcher Johr, who is a Jew, lives. He also sells horse-flesh. Opposite to him lives another Jewish butcher, Gabriel.

There are many Jews in our town. They have their church, called a synagogue, in Wilhelmsplatz. I have never been inside the synagogue; only men are allowed in and they have to keep their hats on. Some of them wear little round caps on the back of their heads. The women, it is said, sit at the back of separate balconies. On feast days many Jews stand solemnly talking together in the little green forecourt by the synagogue door; at the Feast of the Atonement they kiss one another. The leading Jews wear round hats. Some particularly pious Jews have long, twisted locks of hair on each temple, called 'Pajes'. There is a Rabbi (minister) and a synagogue servant. In Schneidemühl it is rumoured that the Jews plotted the war a long time ago. Nobody believes this nonsense any more. Willi and I greet our Jewish fellow citizens with particular politeness if we know them or if they greet us. Leo the grown-up son of Moses, the scrap-dealer, always greets us first, because we are the grandchildren of the late Councillor Golz (our grandfather). He once said that Grandpa helped his father in some way – something to do with building matters, I think. We always smile at each other when we meet. Willi would like us to invite Leo to join us at our table in the Fatherland Café, when we have cream puffs and coffee there; he thinks that would please Leo. I would find it good fun, anyhow, for it would give people something to talk about; they always look down on old Moses when he passes through the streets with his son and their barrow. Leo is a very good-natured person.

146

A few days ago Willi and I went up to the old Jewish cemetery, which neither of us had ever seen before. But I was astonished to see it! All the graves were plain, most having broken columns with Hebrew inscriptions. On most graves there was just grass growing. There was only one grave of some splendour that belonged actually to an old Jewish beggar-woman. When she was found dead in bed, there was a black woollen stocking full of gold coins under her pillow. Then the most beautiful gravestone was bought for her. Grandma says the Jews attach no importance to graves; this is in accordance with their religion. They have no pictures in their Synagogues, because God said at one time, 'Thou shalt not make any graven image'.

Fortunately our religion does not require this, otherwise the wonderful pictures by the great masters showing Jesus, the Virgin Mary, God the Father, and the Holy Ghost as a dove, would never have been painted. And there would not exist the beautiful figures illustrated in our History of Art, for example the Pieta of Michelangelo, etc.

29th July 1915

The ladies of the Patriotic Women's League, including our Mayoress and Grandma, are making an attempt to get the Red Cross Centre re-opened. The soldiers passing through are always calling for bread. Ever since the telegram came from Bromberg, 'Close immediately Red Cross Centre Schn. Station', it has not been opened at all. But Grandma says, 'Just wait, things will soon change. We're not giving in!'

Zeppelins fly over our town nearly every day; they look like gigantic silver cigars. I am now so accustomed to the sight that I hardly ever look up any more. 'Zepp 35' often comes over. The Zeppelins are frequently engaged in bombing raids over England and Paris; they cause great destruction.

I am sitting writing in the garden. The sun catches me on the neck beneath my broad-brimmed panama hat. The hat belonged to Grandpa. How good the summer is! I am looking at the old apple tree – 'my' apple tree! – I look around in my garden at all the pretty flowers, the stripped strawberry plants with their green leaves, the red-currant and gooseberry bushes, the robust potato plants. This year I am going to take all my garden produce, both fruit and flowers, to the soldiers in the hospital. Grandma doesn't mind.

At this moment Dora Haensch arrived with the news that her father is giving up the station buffet and is taking the lease of the Rinkau Woodland Restaurant near Bromberg. I nearly fell off the seat with the shock. What am I to do if Dora leaves? She is my favourite school friend, for Gretel doesn't go to the Empress Augusta Victoria School but to the local council school and is much younger than I. I am now thirteen years old.

It is evening. I said to Dora, 'Come for a walk! Let's do some thinking!' We took with us the Haensch's new dog Strolch, a lively little shaggy dog. But that was a mistake, for Strolch jumped up at every cyclist and every car, in short everything that moved, and barked enough to drive us mad. We didn't manage any sensible conversation because we had to keep whistling him and holding on to him.

Just as we were behind the old shooting-gallery, an army car came dashing down the road.

'Dora, the dog!' I shouted. 'Hold on to him!' But Strolch had already broken loose and made a dash for the car. There were four infantry officers in it.

'Strolch! Strolch,' we shouted.

Strolch didn't listen, but barked with joy and jumped straight at the car.

I just groaned, 'Oooh!' Then it was all over.

Strolch turned two or three somersaults and then lay still. There was a cluster of walkers around him and also the officers who had got out of their car. Dora stood as white as wax, staring at the little dog's blood-covered coat. I put my arm round her, my stomach felt as if it had turned over. The little old Professor Zerbst was there too; he said to us – 'Oh God, the poor little dog is dead!' The people looked inquisitively, first at us and then at the dog. One of the officers said sympathetically, 'Does the dog belong to you?' When we nodded, he unfastened Strolch's collar and handed it to Dora. Then we both began to cry terribly.

Strolch had a hole in his throat the size of a fist, and a gash in his side from which his innards burst out.

'This is worse than your moving to Rinkau!' I sobbed. We couldn't stop crying; we laid Strolch in the gutter, covered him with leaves and wild flowers and went home arm in arm, crying.

So ended the 'lovely summer's day!'

30th July 1915

Uncle Bruno writes from Beverloo (Belgium) that the horses of his artillery detachment have a chest infection.

Last night we had a wonderful moon. I woke up because the moon was shining so bright through the window. I raised myself up a bit so that I could see it. In the summer I sleep on the veranda on an old chaise-longue, then I can see the stars and the moon clearly through the tall window. Everything was deadly quiet, not a footstep in the street. The only sound was the gentle, friendly ticking of the long-case clock in our living-room.

All at once I heard this wonderful song coming from the station – first quietly, then gradually getting louder – 'It is laid down in God's own plan, That from his dearest must every man Be parted ....'

The song rang out through the night, ever louder, fuller and more magnificent, reaching the heavens. I curled up in my bed with sadness and began to cry just as I did at Strolch's death. More and more voices joined in – finally it was a great choir as at a concert or in church. Why were the soldiers singing in the night? And why this particular song? It is not really a soldier's song. Were they soldiers at all? Were they perhaps bringing dead soldiers in army coffins into our town? Were there parents, widows, orphans and fiancées on the train? Were they crying like me?

Suddenly I heard Grandma in her bedroom quietly blowing her nose. So she was crying too. I crept up to her bed on tiptoe. When she recognised me in the light of the moon, she said, 'What do you want, child?'

I answered 'Can I come into bed with you for a while?' (I had never been in Grandma's bed before.)

She was silent for a moment, then pushed the bedclothes back and said, 'Come on then!'

Then I snuggled up close to her breast and cried a lot, and Grandma pressed her forehead against my hair and cried too. So we cried and cried, although the soldiers at the station were by this time singing another song, a cheerful one:–

> When we march away,
> By the King's gate go we;
> Dark brown maiden
> You stay at home,
> And so, little maid, you must wave good-bye.

149

Beneath a fresh green lilac tree
There sits a finch that sings and sings,
'Wave, keep waving, maid, to me'.

Neither of us asked the other why she was crying so bitterly.

2nd August 1915

It is a year since the war began. How much longer will it last? I
ask, as does Mummy, 'Am I really to go on writing this war
diary?' The war may last for ever, and I go on scribbling like the
historian Pliny, whom we are just now studying in history
lessons.

I spoke about it to Hans Androwski. He said, 'If you want to
know what I think, you should go on writing.'

'Why on earth should I?' I asked in despair. 'You must bear
witness,' said Androwski. 'If another war comes, people will
quite forget this one.'

I was indignant and cried, 'There'll be no more war after this
one!'

'And why not?' asked Androwski.

'Because every one will have their bellyfull of war,' I cried,
'especially the soldiers.'

'Soldiers will always be soldiers and obey orders,' declared
Androwski. 'If the Fatherland is attacked they will fight. They
will also fight if the government wants them to.'

We argued for at least an hour. Willi took Androwski's side,
which made me so furious that I became quite red in the face. In
the end they both pressed me so hard that I promised to go on
with the war diary but only when something special happened.
Unfortunately something is happening right away – that is, the
whole town is full of soldiers again. Billeting and more billeting.
At one time I would certainly have liked this, but now I should
like some peace and quiet and not be always writing.

The council school is closed on account of occupation by the
military. (Gretel is lucky, she doesn't have to go to school now.)
The class-rooms are crammed with soldiers. Every family in the
town with a spare room has billetees. The field-greys go from
house to house with billeting notices in their hands. They came
to us too. Both our attic rooms and Grandpa's office are occupied again. The old 'mangle-room' in the yard, a wooden shed
in which we put the 'wringing items' through an ancient mangle

after a wash, is a proper barracks; seven men at present sleep there on sacks of straw. They cover themselves with horse-blankets, what we call 'saddle-covers'.

In the evening we all sit on the Wegner's seat in front of the house, drag more chairs out and sing songs with the soldiers or listen to their stories from the Front. Sometimes the soldiers flirt with Gretel's elder sisters, but in a nice way, and the sisters put up with it, because we all know sure enough that the contingent has to go to the Front in a few days' time and the soldiers will probably be killed.

5th August 1915

The soldiers have now all gone – to the East Front!

Gretel and I are playing a new game, as I no longer organize war games with the boys. I have moved the green garden table from the summer-house into the middle of Aunt Otter's garden and set up the two green benches on it, one on top of the other. This is my aeroplane, a 'Fokker-biplane'. It is called 'The Flea'. I have used one wheel from Gretel's old doll's pram for the propeller and another for my steering-wheel. An old rootstock is my machine-gun, with which I can fire through the revolving propeller. This is what the actual fighter pilots do. I sit between the two wobbly benches on the table in the role of 'Lieutenant von Yellenic', and then the action starts. Gretel acts the part of 'Nurse Martha' down below and waves. I wobble with the benches, turn my wheel and fly higher and higher, describe circles and am attacked by enemy flyers with machine-gun fire, to which I reply with a furious 'tack-tack-tack-tack-tack'. I am usually the victor, but it sometimes happens that I wobble so much that I collapse to the ground together with the towering benches. This means that I have been beaten and I either crash or save myself at the last moment in a forced landing or by parachute. The first time it all collapsed it made such a frightful row that everyone indoors rushed to the window, including Willi and Grandma. Grandma called out, 'What has happened, Piete?'

'Nothing,' I cried. 'I've just been shot down!'

'What did you say?' said Grandma.

'Shot down!' I shouted. 'We are playing fighter pilots!'

Willi, up at the window, laughed in his broken bass voice. I heard Grandma say to him 'That kid will break her neck one day! What goings on for a thirteen-year-old, and in the third form!'

The nice thing is that Gretel is always very upset when I crash. It is just as if it were real to her. Every time she goes quite pale and runs to me and says, 'Lieutenant von Yellenic, are you hurt? Have you broken anything? Your skull possibly?'

And I hobble on her arm to the hospital. That is the summer-house, and she tends my wounds there.

8th August 1915

Somebody else wanted to care for me in the summer-house – namely, Aunt Otter's new billetee. (All of Schneidemühl is again full of soldiers.) Aunt Otter's billetee is a proper medical orderly. He is blond and good-looking, really likeable. He came into the garden with Aunt's permission as I was swinging in the hammock on my own, reading. He at once wanted to know what I was reading, and I said 'Goethe! The Sorrows of Werther'. 'Good Heavens!', he said, 'Goethe!'

He looked at me in a most interested way, as if he could not imagine me reading Goethe. Then he twisted one of my plaits in his hand. I let him do it because I thought he was just playing. But it was quite another thing when he began to stroke my breast (I really haven't any yet) and even my hips and legs. I saw what he was up to of course. And what did I do? Oh, I had a marvellous dodge. As quick as a flash I swung round in the hammock and simply plunged out of it on to the ground. He was so dumbfounded that he hardly grasped what was happening as I shot past his legs on all fours out of the summer-house. I ran out of the garden and slammed the garden door behind me. I'm just furious with the orderly! It is the first time a man has looked on me as a girl.

9th August 1915

Quite forgot to write about it – the Red Cross Centre on the station is open again. Grandma does the rounds, 'like a true sergeant', as she says, and supervises the new set-up. We cannot serve any more bread, only coffee. It doesn't matter – it is a help! I spend a lot of time at the station again. It is crammed with soldiers clamouring for coffee. Sometimes we have got through 80 or 90 buckets of coffee for one single train. The sweat ran down our faces, we hadn't a dry bit of clothing left on us. But when a soldier smiled at us and gave us such heartfelt thanks, we felt repaid a hundredfold for our efforts.

There was 'Russian music' on the platform to-day. There were five German Territorials acting as comics. One soldier stood in the middle with a deadly serious face, beating time with a stick. Two other soldiers played one tune after another on a mouth organ out of a gift parcel. The fourth played plaintively on a clarinet. The fifth was playing the fool on a remarkable instrument which at first I took for a 'Russian' one. I looked at it more closely and decided that it consisted of a long piece of wood, two little bells, a tin can, two tin lids and four pieces of wire. This instrument was as big as a well-built man. The soldier who played on this wonder of craftsmanship, had another stick which he applied with great dexterity to the wires and tin lids. He also marked the beat by striking the whole instrument on the ground. This gave out a unique sound of clanging, clattering, humming and jingling, that you could quite easily have taken for a foreign instrument. I was allowed to give the musicians three cigarettes and a cigar each, they were very pleased at this. Many soldiers and reservists came to listen. They were all in good spirits.

10th August 1915

Our Emperor Wilhelm II issued the following message of greeting to the German people on the anniversary of the beginning of the war:-

'A year has passed since I had to call the German nation to arms. An unprecedented time of blood came to Europe and the world. Before God and history my conscience is clear; I did not wish for war!'

When our headmaster, reading out the Emperor's message in the hall, reached this point, many voices called out, 'No, certainly not! No, by God!' The Head went on reading and came to this passage –

'What lies before us if the fate of our nation and Europe comes to be determined by a foreign power is demonstrated by the afflictions of our beloved province of East Prussia.'

Then some of the girls, those who were refugees from East Prussia, began to cry.

'The enemy forces,' the headmaster continued, 'who were so cocksure of reaching Berlin in a few months, have been driven back in the West and the East. Countless fields of battle in

153

various parts of Europe, and naval battles in waters far and near, demonstrate what German wrath in self-defence and German military skill can achieve. No violation of international law by our enemies can undermine the sure foundations of our conduct of the war. Town and country, agriculture, industry and commerce, science and technology vied with each other to alleviate the privations of war. Understanding the need for interference in the free market of goods, and wholly concerned for the well-being of their brothers in the Field, the nation strained every nerve to ward off the common peril.'

At this point Dora, who sat next to me, nudged me and whispered: 'That is quite true! A wonderful addresss!' 'You can certainly say that!' I agreed. We were all inspired. The Emperor finished his appeal with these words –

'So shall we honourably sustain the fight for Germany, right and freedom, however long it may last, and before God, who will continue to bless our arms, we shall be worthy of victory.
General Headquarters 31st July, 1915.
Wilhelm I.R.'

The whole school, both pupils and teachers, jumped up and shouted at the top of their voices 'Hurrah! Hurrah! Hurrah!' I once again felt sad that I could not volunteer to be a soldier.

When I got home, Willi had a sheet of white paper spread out on the table and was writing on it in his best hand-writing –

Achievements of the first year of the War, 1914–15.

Enemy territory occupied:	180,000 square kilometres		
In Belgium:	29,000	"	"
In France:	21,000	"	"
In Russia:	130,000	"	"

Sum total of –	
Prisoners taken by the Germans	1,695,400
Canons captured by the Germans	7000–8000
Machine-guns captured by the Germans	2000–3000

I pointed to the machine-gun total and said, 'Just put another nought on that!'

But the figure was high enough for Willi. I pointed to a crumpled letter on which his elbows were resting, and said, 'What is that?'

'A letter from Minna Spatz-Huhn,' he answered with a grin. I opened the letter and was shocked to read that my soldier Emil Szagun has received a bayonet wound in the chest.

'He will live alright,' wrote his sister Minna, 'but I hardly dare think about his return. Dear Miss Elfriede, we will just put all our trust in Him who made heaven and earth. He can help us. But I do give you most sincere thanks for the kindnesses which you have shown to my poor brother for he has told me how pleased he was with them.'

I was quite overcome with fear. A bayonet wound in the chest! I will ask Grandma to send Szagun some wine. But then how is she to send wine to the Front? We don't know the address of the hospital for one thing. If I find it out, I will write him a long letter and send with it a photograph of me standing in the garden smiling all over my face, with my little cat Minka in my arms. Perhaps that picture will make him a little happier. But no, I can't say 'happy', but it will surely cheer him up a bit.

I haven't yet said that my school friend Bertha has given me a kitten: she is six weeks old, snow white with light grey streaks and blue eyes. Her little claws are still small and pink, but sharp as needles. She has occasionally scratched me by accident, and it has fetched blood immediately. I made a bed for Minka in an apple box, and she lies there sleeping for hours on my old dolls' cushions. She drinks out of a little milk bottle with a rubber teat. There were once sugar-sweets in the bottle, which Willi and I shared. But Minka can already sip luke-warm milk quite well from a saucer. She gobbles up little balls of liver sausage that I make for her, as if her life depends on it. Willi and I love Minka a lot. I sometimes kiss her, which makes her purr with pleasure.

2nd September 1915

Gretel's birthday! It always comes on Sedan-day! In theory we have to go to church again to celebrate the old victory of 1870/71, but we have so many new victories to celebrate in the meantime that Sedan-day has simply become a day of remembrance of the Reformation. Warsaw fell on 5th August, Ivangorod has been captured by the Austrians, Nowogeorgiewsk surrounded, the left bank of the Wieprz cleared of Russians by Field Marshal von Mackensen's divisions. I was just going to write condescendingly, 'What does Sedan matter now!', but people could just as well say, if there came to be another war, 'What does Warsaw matter, or Ivangorod?' Androwski was right when he stressed the importance of writing about all victories. 'You must bear witness,' he said. Now I am not really a witness of the fall of Warsaw, but it is certainly important that some one should write something about the background of the war as well. I went dutifully with pencil and paper to Grandma who was counting the last jars of pickled beetroot in the corridor cupboard.

'Grandma, what's the price of eggs?'

'Whatever next?' said Grandma, taken aback.

'I need to know for the purpose of the diary,' I explained.

'Are we having eggs this evening?' asked Willi, who came up to us, having just picked up the word egg from our conversation.

'Yes, just imagine, every one gets a bit of a shock because they have become so cheap,' said Grandma half in fun and half in annoyance.

'Eggs get dearer and dearer. They used to cost 60 to 80 pfennigs a set – that is fifteen. Now it is 1 mark 80.'

'And butter?' I enquired.

'Formerly 1 mark 30 a pound, now 2 marks 20.'

'A hundredweight of potatoes?'

'Six marks.'

'Outch!' cried Willi.

'Yes,' sighed Grandma, 'before the war a hundredweight of potatoes cost less than two marks.'

'And a pound of semolina?' I asked.

'Semolina?' answered Grandma slowly. 'If only we could get a sight of semolina ....

'A pound of pork, if you want to know everything, to-day costs 1 mark 50. Mutton 1 mark 10, Veal 1 mark 20, but that won't last much longer, then we shall pay three times as much. Meat gets scarcer and scarcer, all the housewives complain. But I don't see why we have to stand here in such a draught; our hair will be blown away. Come into the living-room!'

When we were in the dining-room, Willi said. 'And now you must write in your diary what my name is in Spanish.'

I answered that I wasn't interested in that because he was a German schoolboy and his name was Willi-Gunther Kuhr.

But he twirled his hips like a Spanish dancer, stamped his feet in the Spanish fashion and grandly announced his new name: 'My name is Don Guillermo Gutirrez Golaz!'

I collapsed with laughter. Willi remained deadly serious and demanded that from that day on I should use the short form of his Spanish name – Gil instead of Willi.

I laughed and said that all my laboriously saved pocket money would then find its way into the 'foreign word' box, for 'Gil' is not German but Spanish and therefore a foreign word. And he could 'get lost!'

10th September 1915

Our 'heroes' cemetery' has grown enormously. It is situated in the woods. A broad path between dark fir trees leads to the entrance gate, which is beautifully carved. Beyond – mound after mound.

I went to the cemetery with my school friend Trude Jakobi; I held a bunch of roses in my hand.

'There is an open grave,' said Trude.

You could still see the marks of the spade in the earth. Six short shovels were stuck in the heap of sand close by. I dropped my roses into the bottom of the hole. 'Now when a soldier is buried he will sleep on my flowers,' I said.

Just then a funeral cortège came through the gate. In front was a platoon of soldiers marching with shouldered arms. Then followed the army chaplain, and then the hearse with the simple black coffin. Next came the comrades carrying a large wreath. The soldiers with the rifles took up position by the open grave. The coffin was lifted from the hearse and carried to the grave. A command rang out, 'Company! Present arms!' The soldiers stood as if rooted to the ground. Slowly the coffin was lowered with ropes into the ground. The Chaplain said a prayer, the soldiers removed their helmets. A new command – 'Present! Ready! Fire!' Three shots were fired over the coffin. The six men walked up to the grave, took hold of the spades and shovelled earth on to the top of the coffin. There was the sound of dull thuds. 'Now his face is covered,' I thought. 'Now his chest, his trunk, and now the whole man!'

We turned away and walked homeward. At the gate we met my good friend the cemetery gardener. We asked quietly, 'Who was that?' 'A pilot N.C.O.,' he answered. 'He crashed over Plöttke.'

'An accident?'

'Certainly an accident. But you never know – they sometimes drink too much. And then, there is no longer any good material for aircraft – or so they say.' 'So they say!' sighed Trude.

I asked, 'Had he no relatives? There were only soldiers there.'

The gardener shrugged his shoulders. 'I've no idea. Maybe they couldn't wait any longer.'

11th September 1915

A field post-card from Szagun:–

'Dear friend, I am letting you know that the bayonet wound is getting a bit better and I can now eat. If only the food were better!
                    Yours sincerely, Emil.'

What does it say in the hymn? 'Glory, laud and honour' to God!

Italy and Turkey have been at war with each other since 20th August, but the Italians have so far suffered defeats all along the Isonso Front.

Truly Germany is faced with a whole world of enemies. In all, 21 declarations of war have been exchanged.

18th September 1915

'We have managed to conquer everything but the lice!' boasted a militiaman to-day at the Red Cross centre, after he had 'treated' his shot thumb with Grandma's brandy remedy. 'In Galicia there was hardly a night when we could sleep. Scarcely had we closed our eyes when one of our mates jumped up with an oath and shook out his tunic. And soon there we were all on the hunt for lice. I once had a marvellous idea, but it turned out badly. We were billeted in a Russian barn and were pleased to be there. No fox-hole for once! A quiet night! What a hope! We were all soon cursing the lice. "Let's clear all the old straw out, lads," I said, "and bring in fresh. The roof of the barn is covered with straw – off with it; it is, so to say, chemically cleaned by the fresh air." So we climbed on to the roof in our shirtsleeves and underpants, some barefoot, some wearing one boot, some two. One man slid off the smooth straw and nearly broke his leg. We had no ladders or ropes. But the straw came down all the same. Now the new camp was set up – everything good and ready! And then? Now we had still more lice! It was swarming with lice! What could you say? The Russians sometimes run away from our gunfire – but not so the lice! These creatures are loyal!'

158

20th September 1915

Our Marie is quite distraught. Her sweetheart has to go into action. He is in the reserve battalion of the 149th. Willi couldn't suppress a smile when he heard of Marie's grief; he went to the piano in the next room and sang with great feeling a song that our soldiers often sing at their departure:–

'To-morrow must my sweetheart leave me.
Perforce must go, perforce must go!'

I immediately joined in, regrettably, just as loud and with just as much feeling:–

'Out in the open the birds are singing,
In the dark green woods hear the song of the birds!'

Then we bawled out together:–

'Oh it is indeed so hard
To be thus torn apart.
Especially if there were no hope
Of returning in your heart!
Farewell, farewell,
Farewell, farewell,
Farewell till next we meet'.

Grandma said, 'Children, aren't you ashamed of yourselves? Our Marie has the finest lad in the whole district and is not yet married. If her Albert is killed, she will receive no widow's pension. We must explain to her that she should immediately make a wartime marriage'.

Willi and I were filled with enthusiasm for this. We immediately produced ideas for a wedding-dress for Marie.

'With a veil and a crown of myrtle', I said joyfully.

'Now then!' said Grandma, wagging her head from side to side.

'Oh yes!' cried Willi, 'She can have my lace bedspread, that will give her a bridal veil reaching the ground!'

'I will hold her train!' I shouted triumphantly. In reality of course I wouldn't hold the train; with us that is done only by small children; but it was so lovely to imagine myself walking behind our Marie holding the edge of her train.

'Stop your nonsense, children!' scolded Grandma. 'But what could we give her for a present? She might like bed-linen – but, good heavens, we have given nearly all of it to the hospital and only have left what we really need.'

'A wall-clock!' suggested Willi.

'A striking one!'

But Grandma thought a striking clock would cost too much money; she was nearly bankrupt after the third war loan.

We racked our brains, until I cried out, 'A Bible!'

We still have a lovely Bible, almost new, that was Grandfather's. (We also have Great Grandfather Haber's very old and yellowed Lutheran Bible of 1854 with its worn leather binding.) So we all decided on Grandfather's bible and a bottle of Cholera-brandy that Grandma always made herself from Great Grandfather Haber's well-known recipe. But then it occurred to Grandma that you couldn't very well give a Lutheran bible to a catholic, so that was no good.

Grandma has already on this very same morning urged Marie (as if she was a 'lame horse') to arrange a war-wedding at once. But Marie said her young man is an evangelical and she is catholic, and – at this she sobbed her heart out – they could not therefore get married.

'There you are!' I said triumphantly. 'It's religion all over again!' What on earth does it matter! I just don't want to know anything more about religion; now it means that Marie cannot marry her fine young man and will probably continue life as a young widow without a penny of pension for the hero's death of her Albert. That's an injustice – no doubt about that! Willi was taken with a fit of laughter at my indignation, from which he couldn't recover for a long time. He is the silliest person I know.

22nd September, 1915

Wednesday – my unlucky day!

At school the terrible news spread through all the class-rooms that the recently established military hospital in our old Freemasons' Lodge 'Borussia' was on fire.

Oh, what a huge fire it was!

The pillows and bedding were thrown out of the windows into the Alte Markt by the hospital staff and volunteer helpers. The wounded were pulled out of bed and carried on stretchers or in people's arms into the Lodge garden and into the Alte Markt. There was much screaming and groaning.

The fire brigade arrived in response to a telephone call, and pumped on to the fire such water as the machine contained. The water pressure was so great that it threw the glowing red tiles high into the air.

The fire lasted over an hour and a half before it was finally extinguished. The Lodge, that beautiful building, now looked horrible. The woodwork of the roof was gone. The windows were nearly all cracked with the heat, the walls blackened with smoke. The inside – bare, brown, charred and full of ash; burnt-out bedsteads, twisted appliances, and everything black and wet. And it was still glowing beneath it all.

Our Lodge! How many festivals and coffee-times had we shared here; Grandpa was a mason. On his watch-chain, which he wore on his stomach, there hung a gold pendant engraved with the ruler and compasses symbols. If ever I have time I will describe a 'Rose Festival' in the Lodge in which my brother played a special role.

And now the fire! The wounded were transferred to another hospital. Such excitement! It was a sad time. Grannie cried about the Lodge. Grandfather's funeral took place from the big Masonic Hall in February 1912. A choir of masons sang:– 'In the dark house below is peace and rest for the weary'. A mason struck the coffin loudly with a silver hammer and asked the dead grandfather some question, but I don't remember what the question was. It was all very solemn.

24th September 1915

Is it possible – the proceeds of the Third War Loan amount to twelve billion and 20 million marks! I must write that again in figures: 12,020,000,000 marks. Oh, dear diary, that includes Grandma's sacrifice. Emperor Wilhelm has sent to Dr Helfferich, the Secretary of State to the Treasury, a telegram beginning with these words:–

'I thank you for the news of the brilliant outcome of the plan for the Third War Loan and I congratulate you on this latest result of our entrusting to your guidance the financial conduct of the war'.

1st October, 1915

The autumn holiday has begun. The big schoolchildren have again been installed on the farms and estates to help bring in the harvest. Willi's teacher wanted my brother to take part in the harvest work too, but our doctor says that since having scarlet fever he has a weak heart and water on the knee and there can be no question of harvest work for him.

Many prisoners of war, English and French, were waiting at the station to-day. I don't know why they were brought here; perhaps they were to help in the big fields. The French struck me as the best-looking, with their refined, intelligent faces. Most of them wore boots that were bound up with string. Some had no shoes at all, but only soles cut out of any sort of material and bound to their feet with string. Their toes and heels poked out from their coarse stockings and footwrappings. I decided to speak to one of the Frenchmen in my poor school French, and said – 'Oh, Francais, tu as été fait prisonnier par les Allemands! Ce n'est pas bon! Un Francais ne doit pas se faire prisonnier par les braves Allemands!'

The result of that was that all the Frenchmen around began to laugh loudly, to point to me and begin to pour out French on me like water-mills. I fled as fast as I could into the Red Cross centre, the prisoners calling after me, 'Petite mademoiselle! He, petite mademoiselle, venez encore une fois! Venez!'

6th October, 1915

The French have had to abandon the unsuccessful offensive in the Champagne. It was quite the most frightful and bloody of the whole war. They had once more gathered all their strength and like one man hurled themselves with heroic gallantry against the grey wall of our German troops. All the soldiers arriving at our station from the west say this. They are full of admiration for the French.

Is this reversal indeed the beginning of the end of the war?

To-day there was a gipsy in German infantry uniform at the Red Cross centre. He was yellow-brown, had blue-black straight hair, gleaming teeth and black, lively eyes. The soldiers were talking about the town of Vilna; the gipsy meanwhile was rolling a cigarette and listening. 'The finest things in Vilna were the churches', said a Saxon, 'with their many turrets and little windows and inside, the altars with lights and sacred pictures. I have never seen such beautiful pictures! We kept gazing in astonishment and thought; "How is it possible, here such magnificence and outside such poverty!"'

'Oh, it was great in Vilna!' murmured a thin beanpole of a territorial, 'only a pity that the pavements are so narrow; at most only two people could pass each other.'

'The pavements in Vilna are wooden,' interjected the Saxon, 'and rotten and slippery!' Suddenly he stared at the gipsy who was slowly scratching himself under his tunic. 'You've got a louse on your skin, lad, haven't you?' he said. 'Mind you're not chucked out by the nurses! We don't need lousy louts here'.

The gipsy's dark face grew darker still with anger. 'I haven't got lice and I'm not a lout'.

I was immediately on the side of the gipsy and cried, 'No squabbling among comrades!' 'That's right, lass!' cried the Saxon, once more in good mood. 'It is time for us to be on our way. Jump to it, quick march!' And he blew through compressed lips, just like a trumpet, the signal for the attack, 'Potato soup, potato soup!' whereon they all stormed out of the place laughing. The gipsy was the last to go. I gave him my hand, and he bent down and whispered in my ear, 'Have you ever seen a louse, little nurse? I could present you with some!'

I had to laugh. I wasn't cross with him.

1st December, 1915

I haven't written for a long time.

Bulgaria declared war on the Serbs on 14th October, and now stands on our side in the violent struggle with them. So there is no end to the war, but fresh troop movements! Would you have thought when the war began, that the little Serbian nation would hold out so long against the superior power of Germany and Austro-Hungary. Our soldiers say that the Serbs continually withdraw into trackless mountains and open fire from there.

The King of Bulgaria, our new friend, is called Ferdinand; his War Minister is General Naidenow. The Central Powers (that means us) together with the Bulgarian forces, immediately opened the second great field movement against the Serbs. On 9th October the fortress of Belgrade was seized, then the Serbs were defeated in the battle on the Amselfeld (west of Pristina) and driven back into the mountains of Albania and Montenegro. This gave rise, of course, to a true delirium of victory on the streets of Schneidemühl.

Now winter has come. The autumn holiday has long since ended, and the harvest is everywhere gathered in. We are already

163

in the month of Christmas. A great oak cross which was given on Hindenburg's birthday in October to drive nails into, stands in the Neue Markt. Silver and iron nails can be driven into it. When it's full of nails it makes a copy of the 'Iron Cross' which our soldiers wear on their chest for bravery in face of the enemy. Such crosses of nails and 'Iron Hindenburg-statues' stand now in nearly all German towns; the hammering of the nails brings a lot of money into the country's war chest. When our cross was erected, regimental music was played – 'Germany above all'. Our Mayor made a speech which ended with the words, 'And now every blow of the hammer is in honour of our warriors, for the assistance to our war weapons and in everlasting remembrance!'

Also in the Neue Markt two French siege-guns have been placed as trophies of victory – giant, fat objects. I looked at them and thought to how many poor soldiers they have brought death.

I will not write any more, my nose has just started to bleed violently.

24th December, 1915

Christmas eve! I have tied a sky-blue ribbon round my cat Minka's neck. Mummy has come from Berlin for the festival as she does every year. Willi and I are very happy and hardly let her out of our sight. She wears a dark blue woollen dress that fits closely at the hips and is fastened with a million tiny buttons. When I showed Minka to her she was delighted. Minka behaved really splendidly. She performed all the clever tricks that I had taught her. First – 'Minka, how do cats go?' whereon a long 'Miau!' follows. Then – 'Minka, make yourself look beautiful', whereon Minka goes up on her hind legs with both front paws high in the air and reaches for my outstretched hand. And then still more, until Mummy said, laughing, that was enough and Minka was ready for the circus.

Grandma has stopped me wearing Willi's blue sailor trousers; she wants me to behave more like a young girl. So my pig-tails, which used to dangle and were always untwisting, are now worn pinned up over my ears in thick coils and I have exchanged the beloved trousers for a fairly long and modest pleated skirt. I can't really say that I feel any better in it. In other respects I carry on as before, washing up the dirty cups for the soldiers at the station, polishing the tables at the Red Cross centre, carting

steaming coffee (always in two buckets) from the kitchen to the
troop trains, cutting and laying out bread (we now have permission to provide bread again), distributing cigars and cigarettes,
knitting and sewing for the field-greys and taking the much
sought-after gift parcels to the poor wounded.

Emil! I have heard nothing more for weeks from my Szagun,
in spite of sending many parcels, cards and letters.

Night-time. I am writing in bed with the light from a pocket-
torch; Minka is rolled up in a ball by me and purring. All the
household is already asleep. Oh, our Holy Night!

Only Willi and I went to church; Mummy wanted to finish
decorating the Christmas tree in the Christmas room and
Grandma was preparing the seasonal food. There was no
Christmas goose this year, and no carp in gingerbread sauce with
almonds and raisins. There was no smoked hare either, but only
an imitation! I mean – so-called 'imitation hare' consisting of
ordinary minced meat. There was nothing else to be had this year
in the market or in the shops. But with brown sauce and mashed
potatoes it tasted lovely or, shall we say, middling lovely.

Then before we had actually started eating, but just as we were
standing in front of the lighted Christmas tree and about to sing
with due ceremony 'Silent night, holy night', there was a ring at
the door and Grandma went to open it. She was a long time
coming back and we were very curious to know what kept her.
Suddenly the door opened again, and guess who came into the
room in the middle of the light from the Christmas tree? Uncle
Bruno, Grandma's son, sergeant-major in the Horse Artillery and
acting lieutenant. He had leave for Christmas. Oh, what a
surprise!

Mummy rushed straight to her brother, put her arms round his
neck and hugged and kissed him, Grandma was quite white in the
face and wept tears of joy so that she had to keep using her handkerchief. Willi hopped, skipped and jumped in his crazy way to
show his joy, I kissed Uncle carefully under his moustache
(which smelled of tobacco and was prickly), and Minka, the
sweet little animal, had to be put into his arms of course. We
nearly missed singing our Christmas carols; the singing was
tremulous. The whole room smelled of the army, oiled boots and
weapons. Uncle had brought a present for each of us; I got a
book of stories by Wilhelm Raabe, Willi a collection of short
stories by Adalbert Stifter, Mummy the novel 'Der Stechlin' by
Theodor Fontane, and Grandma a piece of lace fabric. We were

so pleased- with the presents that we again nearly forgot the Christmas dinner.

Grandma called out agitatedly, 'Will there be enough meat, children?' but as there was a big dish of potatoes and even red cabbage with apple on the table, we all had plenty to eat. And to drink, too, for Uncle had brought with him from France some real Burgundy (bought, not taken as booty). We looked with amazement at the French bottles as if we had never seen Grandfather's wine cellar, in which there were many bottles of Burgundy, for he loved to have good wine to drink with a good meal.

Now every one has gone to sleep. The scent of Christmas tree and extinguished candles comes from the drawing-room. I think of the hundred thousand snow-covered trenches and dug-outs and the Holy Night of all the soldiers. I am sad and happy at the same time, and could cry. Oh, not now that song from the station, '... in the homeland, in the homeland, there we'll meet again!' Oh no, not that!

25th December 1915

Uncle Bruno's army equipment interests me greatly. He has long brown leggings and strong shoes, a polished sword-belt with field-grey buckles, a helmet, a forage-cap and artificial-sheepskin boots that are quite worn out. I got into the boots and hobbled round the room in them. 'But they are very heavy!' I said.

'Because of that I'll leave them here,' replied Uncle Bruno. 'I don't need them any more.'

That gave me an idea but it was such a cheek that at first I dared not put it to him. At last I asked Uncle if he would give me the old army boots. 'Certainly, but what in the world can you begin to do with them?' said Uncle with a smile. 'You definitely can't wear them!' 'Yes I can!' I declared. 'When I have left school I want to be a dancer. Then I will do a dance called "The dead soldier". Perhaps it will have some other name, I don't know. Then I shall wear these boots on the stage.'

Uncle was so astounded that he shook his head 'What ideas you have, child!' he said. 'You certainly couldn't dance in those heavy boots. Just think: Terpsichore! That's just the beginning. And secondly, that's a terrible subject that you have thought up. What is it supposed to mean? You can't dance a dead soldier.'

I sat down in front of Uncle crossing my legs with the boots still on, and placed Minka in my lap. 'It is to be a soldier who has risen from his hero's grave,' I said, 'because he hears the call to a new war. Do you know, Willi's friend Androwski says that soldiers will always fight if the order for a new war is given.'

'To be sure,' Uncle agreed. 'Otherwise they wouldn't be soldiers.'

'Exactly,' I cried. 'Even the dead soldier rises again, just because he has to fight.'

Uncle said, 'There will always be wars. That is a law of nature; otherwise the world would finally be destroyed by over-population.'

'Then wars exist to cause death?' I said, horrified.

Upon this we had a long philosophical discussion (Uncle is a doctor of philosophy). He talked a lot about the philosophy of Nietzsche. I couldn't answer to this because I don't yet know much about Friedrich Nietzsche, except that he was mad, but I decided to go to the library immediately after the holidays and borrow the book 'On the Genealogy of Morals', of which Uncle spoke. By this time though he was rummaging again in the pile of books that he had brought with him in his rucksack. He reads and reads; I do believe he even reads on horseback instead of commanding his battery. He tells us absolutely nothing about the conduct of the war on the Western Front, but speaks simply about the cathedrals that he has seen, and the artistic monuments in enemy countries, of which he has brought many picture postcards and photographs. He likes best to sit in the arm-chair next to the Christmas tree, reading and smoking his pipe; then he even hums a little tune to himself as if to be a soldier were the nicest occupation in the world, really comfortable.[12]

29th December 1915

Uncle went back to the Front again to-day; his leave is over. Grandma and Mummy took him sadly to the station, but showed wonderful cheerfulness.

I have freshly polished the boots and hidden them in the clothes cupboard in the loft. In doing so I discovered that Grandma had tucked away there a heavy sword belonging to Uncle Bruno; I immediately drew it out of its sheath and examined it closely. There is still some yellow oil in the groove ground into it, so Uncle had recently greased it.

I put the sword back in the cupboard. Nowadays a sword's only purpose is for parades. It is a hindrance in the Field. The weapon of this war is the M.G., the machine-gun.

1916

1st January 1916

Now we are in the New Year. I am writing 1916 in large figures in the diary.

Mummy says, 'What will it bring?' The same question as last year. It says in the newspaper:–

> We are maintaining what we have gained by our victories. In the East, following unprecedented fighting, German and Austro-Hungarian armies have advanced as far as the Duna. Kurland, Poland, and large areas of Lithuania and Wolhynia have been seized by us. In France and Belgium our forces form an unshakeable wall against which the enemy beats his head in fierce but vain offensives. In the Orient the Dardanelles have been surrendered by the enemy. In Egypt and Persia the pillars of British resistance are beginning to crumble. Serbia has been annihilated and its old King Peter, deprived of land and people, has fled to traitorous Italy. Success upon success, wherever the German eye looks over the mighty field of battle. General of Infantry v. Besler, who is at present Imperial German Govenor-general of Poland, writes from there truthfully, 'At the close of a year full of heavy fighting and outstanding successes of the federal Austro-Hungarian army, we can look forward to the future in fullest confidence. Our military and political situations justify us in the hope that in the coming year we can reap the fruits of the mighty efforts with which our combined armies and nations have astounded the world.'

5th January 1916

A Field postcard from Szagun. He is back with his unit in the East.

'Dear Friend Elfriede,
This is to let you know that I have received your parcel and

169

yesterday the letter and I offer you my best thanks for them. For they give me very great pleasure. I wish you a merry Christmas, so far as it can be in wartime. I could do with some warm underpants if you have any to spare. I am now out of hospital and often feel the cold. Dear friend, don't be cross with me for not writing for so long, for I was on sick leave.

Most sincere greetings, from Emil.'

I was so pleased at the sign of life! I got some lovely, long, warm underpants from the Red Cross, packed them in a parcel with some foodstuff, and wrote –

'My dear soldier, how glad I am that you are still alive. Here are the underpants that you wanted. I hope you will spend many pleasant hours in them.'

I was at first amazed that Mummy and Grandma laughed out loud at my letter; Mummy even wiped away tears of laughter. Then I had to laugh too, but I sent the letter off all the same.

1st February 1916

Mummy has left, life is back to normal. Marie's sweetheart has been sent to the Front without them having a war-wedding. Marie has given notice to leave Grandma's service because she has gone to her Albert's parents to help the old people with their farm work. They have a small-holding and cannot easily get labour. Marie said she could quite well take the place of two farm-hands. She cried a lot when she took leave of us. Grandma gave her a lovely present. She kissed Grandma's hand and mine too. Since then Willi bows to me and kisses my hand too when we meet or when we part. We always kiss Mummy's hand as well; that is quite usual with us. The Poles do it in any case, and of course the officers. When Willi kisses my hand he does it in fun of course and I say graciously 'Good morning, Gil!' or 'Good-bye, Gil!', because he wants that and I like to show him a kindness.

Another thing: We are no longer piano pupils of Frau Übe! Without us saying a word, Grandma declared two days ago that she could no longer afford to pay for piano lessons. We acted very sorrowfully, hung our heads and expressed our deep regrets. But hardly was Grandma's back turned when we jumped for joy. Now I shall practise the piano for my own sake, that will be much more fun, and Willi in any case plays his own compositions

170

in any spare moments and they are more difficult than old Czerny's finger exercises. I don't really know about that. If you really practised Czerny's confounded exercises properly, you would soon have a marvellous technique. Androwski deplores that Willi will never acquire this technique. Willi says he will study counterpoint later on instead.

The job of cleaning our house in Alte Bahnhofstrasse now falls to me, as we have no Marie. I have to wash-up and dry, do the dusting, the shopping and so on. Our washer-woman helps with the window-cleaning. Gretel Wegner helps me clean the kitchen – that is really good fun. We clean the kitchen very thoroughly, placing the two old kitchen chairs upside down on the table, as Marie always did, scrub the floor, then dry it with floor-cloths which we wring out, polish the stove and scour the saucepans. In all this we play our favourite games of course; it all goes better as a game. Grandma often has a good look round the house and is well satisfied. She said once to Fräulein Ella Gumprecht, 'Piete is a very good replacement for Marie.'

Fräulein Gumprecht answered: 'Have you had a look under the beds and the cupboards too? It is usually a case of "On top, fine!" But underneath – oh dear!'

Gretel and I just looked at each other. We were not a little angry! After all I am still just a schoolgirl, have to go up to the second class at Easter and I do duty at the station into the bargain. I also want a little time to play, apart from writing the war diary, visiting, practising the piano and going for walks.

9th March, 1916

Germany has declared war on Portugal. Why??

15th March, 1916

What a to-do in the town to-day! There is a whole crowd of chattering women standing in front of the baker's shop excitedly brandishing their bread-cards. Words of abuse are being hurled on all sides blaming the baker and all bakeries for the bad times and so on. A fat woman in a black woollen shawl was particularly prominent. 'I've bin standin' 'ere on me two feet nigh on two hours,' she shrieked, 'and there ain't no bread! A mean trick is that – enough to drive you up the wall. A baker! Hugh! Open up your shop this minute!' She began to hammer on the shop window with her fists. When the other women saw this, they followed suit and shouted, 'Open up! Come on, open up! We can't stand here taking root!'

Then along came a policeman who tried to calm the crowd. The fat woman first of all cast an astonished look at him and then scornfully turned her back. The policeman – I know him to be a terribly uncouth and uncivil type! – seized the woman who was also carrying a milk can in her arms, by the collar. Then she fell down. And then all hell was let loose! I was just on my way to the dairy when I witnessed the commotion. The fat woman got back on her feet, raised the milk can and smashed it angrily into the policeman's face. As if this had been the signal for the attack, all the women fell upon the policeman. He blew his whistle and a second policeman came running to his assistance. But this one too became caught up in the general rough-and-tumble and was so beaten up by the enraged women that he turned tail and fled. The baker saved the situation by opening the shop, utterly flabbergasted as he was. The whole mob stormed inside. I shudder to think what terrible language the embittered women used on the baker! I heard them shouting for a long time: 'Bread! Give us bread! Our children want something to eat!'

26th March, 1916

I spent nearly all this afternoon painting my cat. I very much wanted to have a picture of her. When I had finished her portrait I romped around with her all over the house. I got her so excited by scraping a willow twig along the floor that she jumped at a tassel on a chair and clawed at it and bit it until it shed bits of wool and silk. I lay at full length on the carpet and laughed. Minka spread her legs, raised her tail like a flag, put her head on one side, rolled her eyes wildly, and gazed at me sidelong. 'Minka, you sweet animal, you ought to have your photograph taken like that!' I cried. Minka jumped at my hand, growled and bit my finger really hard – I enjoyed it. At this moment she is lying on a yellow cushion on the sofa. Just now I had to yank her off Grandma's best hat with mourning-veil, which she had sought out to sleep on.

Grandma has gone to a meeting of the Patriotic Women's League. She has not been able to prevent the soldiers now having to give something out of their pay for their bread, drinks and soup. Willi and I have the responsible job of fetching the box with the day's takings from the station each evening and bringing it home for safety. It is fun to go to the station late in the evening. Just then the train returns from our pleasure resort Königsblick, bringing back all the Schneidemühl excursionists, especially the lieutenants and their girl-friends. I know various girls who keep company with all the officers. I hear that they sometimes take money for it. There are some very pretty ladies; one of them is the sister of a school friend and twenty-two years old.

28th March, 1916

At the station tables with roofs over them have been set up on every platform close to the tracks. Coffee is given out to the soldiers from these. The old Red Cross canteen has been enlarged by means of another disused railway carriage placed so that both carriages form one long, continuous room. The inside of the canteen has been painted white with marine enamel paint, the benches and tables are bright yellow. Also new cooking facilities have been installed, lovely and clean with shining stove and shining saucepans. Even electric lighting and running water have been put in. Really useful. I rather regret the old canteen – it was so cosy.

But the field-greys sit together in the same brotherly way in the big canteen, eating, drinking, smoking, writing field-postcards and relating their experiences. I listen to them; you keep learning more about the war. There were recently two soldiers there whom I particularly took to, one tall and dark, the other short and fair. I filled their empty glasses and spread plum jam as thick as my finger on their slices of bread, so that the jam was dripping down from the sides. The short one told this story:

'In France – I forget the name of the place – the sentry suddenly announced that the enemy was aproaching with several regiments. Panic stations! We immediately prepared for action. Our lieutenant was a typical raw-blooded young aristocrat; he said to the oldest sergeant, "Sergeant Stiebel, if I am killed, you take over the command. I carry a leaden case under my tunic; take it off after my death and send it to my parents. Here is the address." He handed him the note with the address, but that was the end of him. A piece of shrapnel landed right there and killed him outright. It had missed Sergeant Stiebel; he must have been protected by a guardian angel. Then all hell was let loose.

173

Orders could no longer be heard for the loud gunfire. Comrades were falling to my right and left. My father is a baker; whenever a swarm of flies came into the bakehouse, he would take the leather fly-swatter and swipe at them, six or seven at a time. Death came in France too just like a fly-swatter. I was wounded, in the head and the right shoulder. I didn't notice it at first. Later, as the medicos were carrying me away, I received a shot in the right thigh'.

The tall soldier said: 'I just want to tell you about the blowing up of a bridge'. 'No, don't talk about that', said the short one. 'You know what ...' 'Let me tell it', said the tall one defensively. 'We were a group of thirty men detailed off to blow up this bridge, because the Russians had to cross there with reinforcements. Our N.C.O. was laying the explosive charges himself. All at once his spade hit something hard in the trench. He dug carefully around it. Suddenly an ear-splitting explosion! I was flung a distance of several yards. When I came to, the bridge had gone and of my twenty-nine comrades only dismembered pieces remained – arms, legs, trunks – all in the water, and blood, blood, everywhere. Our N.C.O's head had been cut off as if with an axe and was bobbing up and down in the current – just as if he was out for a walk – his cap sitting askew over his ear with a strand of hair hanging out. His face wore an expression as if he was about to say "Well, I never!" And all around the head was covered with blood. That was the beginning of my nerve trouble'.

Suddenly the tall, vigorous-looking man began shaking violently. His eyes became glazed, his nose twitched, his face went yellow. This lasted about two minutes. Then he recovered. We refreshed him with wine, which we always had at hand for emergencies and took him to the sick bay. The short soldier watched him go and said sadly, 'There is nothing more to be done for him. The hospital doctor in Königsberg stuck a pin in him right up to its head and he felt nothing'.

I felt so sorry for the sick soldier. The short one had now left too; other soldiers were sitting in the canteen and telling other stories, but I didn't want to hear any more. I kept thinking of the head bobbing up and down in the river. Suddenly the short soldier came back in, pressed a card into my hand and whispered: 'There, little miss. My poor comrade sends it. He is bad, he is suffering another of his attacks. He says, you mustn't be cross with him, but he cannot give you anything better. He liked you so much and he says Good-bye!'

I looked in confusion at the card in my hand. It was a simple coloured field-postcard with a variation on the song, 'I am standing in midnight darkness'.

I have thought for a long time about the sick soldier sending the message that he liked me. Perhaps it comes from the fact that I shall soon be fourteen years old.

25th April, 1916

Easter is over. To-day is my birthday; fourteen years! I have gone up into the second class. Only another two years now and school will be behind me. We have received some new girls into the school. There is one that I like particularly; her name is Gerda Conitz and she is the daughter of a village school-teacher from Studsin near Kolmar. She always comes by train, quite a long journey. She has long, thick plaits just like mine, only as fair as ears of corn. She has her plaits fixed round her head like a crown. She said to me, 'Do yours up in the same way!' Now I wear my plaits fastened up like 'Connie's'. Perhaps God has sent me this classmate as a replacement for Dora Haensch, who is now actually moving early in the summer with her family to Rinkau near Bromberg, where they are taking over the Woodland Inn. I am to go and stay with Dora in Rinkau in the long holidays.

It happened to-day, right on my birthday, that for the first time in my life I was present when a soldier was arrested. I was in the Haensch's buffet, calling for Dora. Two soldiers came in. One of them, a giant-sized infantryman, was stone-drunk and shouted to Herr Haensch, who was standing behind the bar, to bring him some beer. Herr Haensch said, 'I can't give you any more alcohol.'

The infantryman cried, 'Beer isn't alcohol, man.'

'You'd better leave that to me,' answered Herr Haensch.

The soldier was then about to help himself to beer. Herr Haensch seized him by the shoulder and pushed him back. The soldier quick as lightning unsheathed his bayonet and closed in on Herr Haensch. Dora and Frau Haensch called out loudly for help; other guests jumped up and took hold of their chairs as weapons. Herr Haensch ran through the back door to the station guard-room; I wouldn't have thought that the fat little man could run like that. The second soldier had meanwhile sat down at an empty table and stretched his legs right out in front of him. Then he said half aloud to his drunken companion, 'Get away, quick'. Then the soldier took to his heels and was gone. A few minutes later Herr Haensch returned with a sergeant and two guardsmen. They were astonished to find the bird had flown. But the second soldier was still there, a young man with handsome well-formed features who had in complete calm picked up a newspaper. The sergeant went up to him and asked him in a friendly way to give the name of his companion.

The soldier remained seated and said in a tone of indifference, 'You can't give me orders, sergeant; I'm not going to give my friend away.'

I saw the sergeant frown. He went up close to the soldier and said something to him quietly. Then the soldier jumped up, his eyes blazing and, quite hoarse with excitement, cried, 'You're a rotter, sergeant! I didn't want this filthy war, I was forced into playing soldiers. So there! If you have anything to say to me, please say it in a proper military manner. Anyway, however long you bully me, I shan't give you the name of my companion!'

The veins in the sergeant's face swelled up. He said quite calmly, however, 'Do you know what offence you have committed?'

'Certainly!' cried the soldier.

'What exactly are you in civvy street?'

'A student of politics if you know what that is.'

'You have resisted authority and have been guilty of disobedience,' stated the sergeant calmly. 'Do you know the consequences?'

'I am no fool,' said the soldier, who stood bending forward over the table and gripping its edge firmly with both hands. His knuckles were quite white.

The sergeant kept trying to make the best of the matter. He put his hand on the other's shoulder and said in a soothing tone of voice, 'Come, my friend be reasonable. I don't want to have to arrest a subordinate. So what is your companion's name? To what regiment does he belong? Answer me now!'

The soldier shook the hand from his shoulder and said angrily, 'You're a shitbag!' 'That's it!' replied the sergeant, who had gone pale. 'That changes everything. You are under arrest. Your sword-belt!' The soldier made not the slightest move to comply with the order. There was a deathly hush in the refreshment-room. The sergeant suddenly shouted, 'Don't you hear me, you shameless fellow?'

'I hear you alright,' said the soldier coldly. 'And I understand just what you say. But please understand me too – I don't betray comrades!'

The sergeant turned to the two men accompanying him, and said, 'If he won't comply we shall have to use force. Fix bayonets!.' And to the soldier – 'For the last time: your sword-belt!'

In face of the glistening raised bayonets the soldier undid the strap holding his bayonet. He was so pale that even his lips were white. The sergeant seized the belt, the guards took the soldier between them and all four left the room.

Excited speech broke out in the buffet. Everyone was indignant with the arrested man. Dora drew a deep breath, took my hand and put it against her chest, saying, 'Just feel how my heart is beating!' Her heart was beating like mad. 'Oh, Piete, thank God that they've gone, eh?'

'Yes,' I said.

Dora looked at me hard. 'You said that in such a strange way ... did you enjoy the end of it?'

'No,' I said. 'I didn't enjoy it at all. I just don't know which was right, the sergeant or the soldier.'

'Now, just a moment,' cried father Haensch, really angry. 'There's no question about it. The sergeant of course. If discipline fails in the army – then that is mutiny.' And he angrily gave me a hefty slap on the backside.

I went home quite perturbed. I was sorry for both of them; the sergeant and the soldier. Because the soldier wouldn't betray his foolish, drunken companion, I was even more sorry for him than for the sergeant. The latter had after all only the fear arising from a refusal to obey an order. I was most of all sad on my own account. I can never quite decide what is right and what is wrong in this war. I cheer for our victories and am beside myself because there are dead and wounded. I heard yesterday that, hidden away in the forest, there is said to be a military hospital where soldiers live who have had their faces shot away. They must look so frightful that ordinary people cannot look at them. Things like that drive me to despair.

2nd June, 1916

A frightful naval battle has taken place in the Skagerrak. It lasted two days, from 31st May until yesterday. A part of the English fleet under the British Admiral Jellicoe and an even greater part of our German fleet encountered each other by chance in the Skagerrak. Our fleet was commanded by Vice-Admiral Scheer and Vice-Admiral Hipper. We faced the English with 16 big battleships carrying heavy guns, and 6 cruisers, ships of the line, torpedo-boats and destroyers. I don't know how many ships the enemy deployed.

Dear diary, we were victorious in the biggest naval battle ever yet fought. The English fleet lost 1 ship of the line, 5 pocket battleships and 10 destroyers. We lost 1 ship of the line, 1 pocket battleship, 4 light cruisers and 5 torpedo-boats. Although we lost many ships, our loss of tonnage is far less than that suffered by the English. The special news sheet reports a frightful total of dead and wounded on both sides. That is the worst of it.

The English established conscription for youths and men between the ages of 16 and 41 some time ago. They bring in from the colonies and dominions all those liable to military service. Thus many Canadians, for example, are fighting in the British army. We hear also at home of the introduction of a new liability to service affecting those from 16 to 50 years of age. Willi and Hans Androwski would then become involved. Women are working in all the German munition factories. The male workers are nearly all at the Front. When the women come home in the evening they are too tired to bother about the children. This is bad when the children are small. When they are bigger they all try to help with the housework. It goes without saying that this is a duty in wartime.

Grandma says, we women are an 'emergency force'. Many women and girls sell their lovely long hair to provide money for the Fatherland. 100 grammes of hair fetch 2 marks. The hair is used for military purposes.

3rd June, 1916

And now what do you think has happened? A soldier has shot another for the sake of a girl.

A much nicer thing is that my school friend (who shall be nameless) asked me to play the piano while her big lovely sister and two of her friends were drinking coffee in the next room with three young lieutenants. 'You ought to make a little background music,' she said. 'My sister thinks it is so lovely when you sing and play the piano.' So I just played and sang in the other room

178

some beautiful songs such as 'Death and the Maiden', 'The oak wood roars', 'I like to carve the bark of every tree', and so on.

5th June, 1916

Minka is missing! For God's sake, where is Minka? I have looked everywhere without finding her. I went finally to all the people we know throughout Alte Bahnhofstrasse, asking 'Have you seen a white cat with little patches of light grey and a blue ribbon?' They all said no, looking at me sympathetically. Minka has never before been missing for a whole day and night and another half day. Once in the winter when she got out she came back covered in dirt and without her little collar; she was trembling and sneezing and we placed her on a woollen blanket in the luke-warm oven. She immediately went to sleep there. Afterwards she licked herself perfectly clean and was warm and happy. But now?

10th June, 1916

Our kitten is dead. Shot by a wicked neighbour. His own daughter told me about it on the way to school. Willi and I are inconsolable. Minka was evidently playing with the neighbour's pigeons on the roof of the shed, that is to say she sprang in the air after them as they took off. Then the man got a gun and shot her dead. I cry and cry. Willi sits at the piano and plays out his grief for Minka in hymns of praise and sorrow. When he played Minka's little lullaby that I often used to hum to her in fun, I slammed the piano lid down. After a while we searched all Minka's favourite places, sofa, rugs, bed-covers, cushions, for white hairs that she had shed. We soon had quite a bundle of them. Then we dug a token grave under my old apple tree. Gretel helped with the grave and shed floods of tears. With grandma's sharp kitchen knife we suitably carved a wooden tablet which we placed on the grave. On the tablet in thick ineffaceable letters was the following –

Here lies our sweet little Minka
Born 14.7.1915
Shot 10.6.1916
Sleep, dear Minka, sleep!

That evening I was feverish – 38.4 degrees. That night we swore revenge on the man who had killed Minka.

17th June, 1916

A letter from Mummy in Berlin:–

'Dear Willi, Dear Piete,
How terrible what has happened to Minka, you have my heart-felt sympathy. My poor darlings! What you have planned to do in "revenge" has my full approval – a postcard every weekend with the appropriate verse that will be a repeated accusation. Maintain a humorous manner! And you, Piete, are cutting out silhouettes as well. That's wonderful! Let me see the verses, so that I may enjoy your ingenuity.

Now for something important: please tell Grandma that I have given notice to leave the Conservatory Rooms at 18 Genthiner Strasse on 1st October. I have found a 3-room flat at a good price in the adjacent Steglitzer Strasse; it has a bath-room (with gas water-heater), kitchen and little drying-loft, and I immediately settled for it. A camp bed can be put up in the drying-loft if needed. By the time of the move I hope to have sold the last of the instruments. It is pointless to try to keep the Conservatory going. My loyal partner, the conductor Franz Rumpel, has found a new position in Vienna, while his daughter continues as my singing pupil and secretary. So I will carry on teaching in the new rooms and I am sure that my name as a singing teacher is well enough known to ensure me a constant flow of new pupils.'

We were dismayed when we read this letter. Mummy's beloved 'Leading School of Music and Drama'. She had the best teachers and owned some valuable instruments, for instance a Blüthner piano and two Steinway grands. But some of the teachers have been killed, some are fighting at the Front and there are hardly any young people left with enough time and money in wartime to study music. I looked at Willi and he looked at me. Feeling very sympathetic to Willi – for he looked so downcast – I called him 'Gil'.

This is one of the bad effects of the war. Many people are becoming enormously rich through it, because they derive massive incomes from war business; they are called 'Profiteers'. Others – like us – are impoverished.

20th June, 1916

The great battles of arms in the West, despite untold numbers of dead on both sides, bring victory for our German troops. Thus Hill 304 was captured with the loss of a thousand men. The Forest of Caillette and Fortress of Vaux are in our possession too.

While we gain victory after victory, the German social democrats want the war to be brought to an end at once. The leader of this so-called 'left wing', Karl Liebknecht (whose name I at one time understood to be Lieb Knechthund), called out during the May Day festivities in the Potsdamer Platz in Berlin, 'Down with the War!' He was sentenced to two and a half years in prison. This has led to demonstrations in many German towns for Liebknecht, peace and bread. The social democrat Rosa Luxemburg also belongs to the Left Wing, the 'Spartacus' League. Just like Karl Liebknecht she calls for an end to the war. There are many artists who want it too. For instance the painter and illustrator Käthe Kollwitz. She paints mothers embracing their starving children and young men enthusiastically joining up to die a hero's death.

I can no longer imagine how the war will be brought to an end. The enemy countries want to go on fighting and they force Germany to train fresh reserves and keep the army corps at full strength. The Emperor and his generals naturally want first to gain the final victory. Moreover, the war has become so enormous, a colossus that really can no longer be halted. Where are you to make a start? For example, the English and the Russians in the Persian Gulf. Androwski says they are interested in the oil-fields. The fact that the English General Townshend was driven back by the Turks and us at Kut-el-Amara has not achieved much; the Russians immediately advanced in the North East.

Then in the West. When I think about it: Verdun! The fighting couldn't be stopped there. We have brought the big 38 cm. guns into position there. The French are protecting Verdun with every kind of weapon. The soldiers say that the countryside around Verdun is like a moon-scape with a thousand craters. No trees, no bushes, no houses, no birds – nothing but shell-holes, dead bodies, wounded men, barbed-wire entanglements, trenches, dug-outs and firing: barrage-fire, heavy bombardment, cannon-fire. Living soldiers rest their rifles on the shoulders of their dead comrades and shoot until they too fall victim to the firing. Do you know, dear diary, that there are 'flame throwers'? These are sprayers of fire that lay a blazing carpet of flame over attacking soldiers or cover the trenches with flames. Then men are burnt alive in them.

181

And then – the Russians in the East. They are still after a long time undefeated, but throw more and more men into the Front. Just now a mighty offensive is beginning at Narotschsee, near the Rumanian border, under General Brussilow, the commander-in-chief of the Russian South Western army. In addition to the Linsingen army units our Austro-Hungarian allies stand in opposition to the Russians, but the Russians are so superior in strength that the situation is quite dangerous. Even the two heads of the German field forces, General Ludendorff and Field Marshal v. Hindenburg have said so. General Brussilow wants to make amends for East Prussia with this new offensive. Men's lives count for nothing there. Now tell me, dear diary, how is the war to be brought to an end?

The machine rolls on and on over almost the whole of Europe, even over our African colonies; no one can stop it. Watch out, America is beginning too; it has already sent us two notes threatening to break off relations with us. No, the war cannot be ended at the Emperor's behest. How on earth can it be settled?

The poet Matthius Claudius has written a poem that ends with the words –

'Sadly it is war and I want not
To carry any shred of blame therefore.'

The soldiers are singing a song with a new ending –
'For this campaign
Is not an express train'.

The chorus originally went like this –
'For this campaign
Will soon be over
And once again
I'll be back home with you'.

Every soldier wants to be back home. But *how*? In August 1914 we really thought the war would be over by Christmas. People were like children, just like me.

10th July, 1916

It is very hot. Gretel and I often go bathing. We have a 'Municipal River Bathing Station' on the Küddow; very beautiful. There are wooden bathing huts, spring-boards, a swing and gymnastic apparatus. Behind it, where the river is dammed to form a basin, is a weir, about a metre high. Over this flows clear, ice-cold, water like a carpet. Below the weir there is stretched a steel cable that you can hold on to. It is fun to force your way right up to the weir and let the mass of water rush over your head and back. You don't hear anything. Sometimes you hardly get any air. One of my aunts was nearly drowned there at one time; she called out for help and the bathing superintendent saved her.

Gretel and I think bathing in the Sandsee is even better. Indeed the long path through the fields and the woods is beautiful. Willi and I once built ourselves an Indian wigwam in the woods; we set up a circle with thick brushwood, a double wall of branches all the way round with sand, moss and the heaviest possible boulders in between. But Willi lost the urge to finish building the wigwam, because it so often rained at that time, so our building became ruined.

The Sandsee woods consist almost entirely of a type of pine-tree that has a blue-blackish green colour. There is juniper too. And there are many 'deers'-paws' in the moss – little yellow fungi that are called 'chanterelles' in Berlin. You can also find edible mushrooms there, but these grow mainly in the mixed woods around our favourite pleasure resort, Königsblick. Not so long ago Königsblick was called 'Modlewobrück' and the next village was called Modlewo or Modilewo. But since we 'Germanise' everything, Modlewobrück has become Königsblick; King Frederick II (Old Fritz) and later Emperor Frederick III, the father of our Emperor, are said to have been there and viewed the beautiful green landscape of the Küddow. Otherwise we have a lot of sand, as I think I have already mentioned, but meadows also and vast fields of rye, barley, potatoes and (a little) wheat. The soil that is almost the best is used to grow sugar-beet. We have sugar-beet (molasses) factories and starch factories. A lot of potato brandy is distilled around here. Men often get drunk on it. It is terribly fiery stuff. I once nearly burnt my throat.

In the Königsblick woods I have watched roe-deer and stags and wild boar, in the Sandsee woods there are thousands of rabbits, hares and deer. There are loads of fish in the Sandsee; because the banks are crumbling and weedy a lot of carp live there. And in the lonely lake around the Hammer estate and inn our wonderful birds – herons, osprey, snipe, ducks, all kinds of bitterns and even cormorants – nest; but I have never yet seen

183

any cormorants. Once I was swimming on my back in the Hammersee and let myself simply float on the water, and a heron flew over me quite close and quite unconcerned.

We also have a lot of storks, even black storks which are very rare. When Grandpa was still alive, I saw a 'Stork parade' one autumn when I went for a drive in the country with him and coachman Schulz; I must describe that at some later time.

I live in beautiful surroundings. Sometimes I think I would die if I were deprived of them, but when I leave school I am to study singing with Mummy in Berlin so that I can eventually help her in the singing school. But home-sickness will always draw me back to Schneidemühl because I love Grandma so much. Grandma is like a mother to me, while Mummy in Berlin is a kind of fairy, a queen whom we adore.

18th July, 1916

Our airmen have bombarded Harwich, Dover and Calais. Yesterday there was a big air attack on the Russian naval base at Reval. In our stationer's shop there are post-cards on sale with photographs of our best known air force heroes. Whenever I have saved up 20 pfennigs I buy myself an airman post-card. I am going to allot a whole album to them; that should be interesting later on. I have already had to put a cross, indicating death, against many of the photographs.

Leaflets shaped like planes have been distributed among us, with the following message –

'If this leaflet were an air bomb, how would you react? Act in the way indicated in the accompanying explanatory pictures.'

On the back are pictures with the following captions:

'Go indoors – Get into a corner, preferably behind a wall-post – Go into the cellar – Lie down in a trench – Go calmly into surrounding houses.

When Willi read the leaflet and looked at the drawings, he said – 'I think I'd rather creep straight into our family vault!'

28th July, 1916

In the middle of the summer holidays things became serious. Dora Haensch, Julius (Jule) and their father and mother have left our town. They have moved to Rinkau near Bromberg to take over the Woodland Restaurant (foreign word! should say 'Inn'!) and have taken all their possessions with them. When I asked Herr Haensch why he did this, he said he could no longer manage to keep the big food business of the station buffet going. 'People want to get something substantial in their stomachs,' he said, 'and I can only offer them piffling stuff. Supplies are nowhere near sufficient. In Rinkau I have only drinks and pastries to worry about. I can manage that alright.'

In the autumn holidays I am to go and stay with Dora. On the last day Dora and I held hands the whole time; we couldn't let go of each other's fingers. When we looked at each other we gulped down our tears, which we didn't want to show. I stood on the platform as the Haensches got into the train for Bromberg. Just before the train left they all leaned out of the window once more to shake my hand for the last time. I thought now it was essential to make light of it and laughing I began to sing '... in the homeland, in the homeland, there we'll meet again', whereon Jule was seized by a fit of crying and dropped his head on to his arm.

'Come on, Sergeant Haensch!' I cried. But there was no more fun in it and therefore no more self-control; Jule simply cried all the louder. Then Mother Haensch began to cry too, tears as big as peas. Even Papa Haensch had tears in his eyes. Only Dora and I didn't cry. Dora stuck her lovely black mop of hair out of the window as far as she could and laughing sang –

'Though parting from each other
We can our tears restrain
Because we have the certain hope
That we shall meet again.'

Then the train moved slowly off. I waved as long as I could see anything of it; then it was just the size of a worm, then just a point. And then nothing.

For me, now, it was as if a part of my childhood had ended.

Compose yourself, Lieutenant von Yellenic!

5th August, 1916

We have carried out our revenge and sent the nasty neighbour open post-cards with pictures of him and Minka in silhouette form stuck on. Under each picture there is a verse, for example–

'For powder and shot for use in the war
There is, no doubt, a very great call,
So, Sunday hunter, do not waste it
On a target that is so small.'

or

'If you kill the domestic cats
You'll hear in the roof the squeak of the rats.'

or

'First comes his stomach, then close behind
Himself with his shotgun you will find.'

The last verse was the one that annoyed him the most. We have been told that he showed the card around in the house.

Frau Schönfeld's brother Fritz, who has been serving in the Pioneers since the beginning of the war, came home on leave today. He has volunteered with a group of friends for bridge-building in Egypt.

'Cross your fingers for me, that I may get away from the Argonne,' he said to me, while we were playing a game for two in the summerhouse with his well-thumbed playing-cards. I can understand him being fed to the teeth with the terrible static warfare in the Argonne, in which he has been taking part for months. At one time he was buried for eight hours. There was frozen silence all around him, a silent numbness up to the neck. When he was rescued he was put into hospital suffering from shock. He is now on convalescent leave. How wearily he spoke! I listened to him and later I gave him a nice tobacco pipe and a pouch of tobacco which I had begged for him from the last collection of Red Cross gifts.

7th August, 1916

The Schneidemühl schools are again partly full of the military. Billeting everywhere, in our house too. A captain and two privates. The soldiers speak to me differently now because I wear full-length skirts and have my hair done up.

Sometimes I am again called on to provide 'tea-time music' when my classmate's big sister invites a few lieutenants and their girl friends for coffee. Yesterday I met a young air force officer on the stairs. He stood and greeted me and asked whether I too was 'one of the party.'

I said no, I was just the pianist. He laughed and said – 'Oh. But that's a pity.'

'Why a pity?' I asked.

But he just laughed and disappeared into the room.

1st September, 1916

I've finished with the war diary! I really cannot bear it any longer. The war is never-ending. I can't go on writing when my hair is grey. Now on 27th August Rumania declared war on Austro-Hungary. Just a day later we on our side declared war on Rumania. Then on 30th August our ally Turkey followed suit, declaring war on Rumania, and to-day comes Bulgaria's declaration of war on Russia.

In former times, when we were something like 'a great family', there was a silver bowl in our drawing-room in which visitors put their visiting-cards. That's how it seems to me with these everlasting declarations of war – every one declaring war on every one else. The only thing missing is the bowing and kissing of hands. 'Allow me – please – my declaration of war!' – 'Respectful thanks! Allow me – here is mine!'

I was so beside myself that I rushed to Willi who was busy swotting Latin homework with Hans Androwski and his school friend Andreas Zorn. All three listened speechless to my angry outburst, until Willi grinned and said to Andreas Zorn, 'Look, this positively meek person is my sister Pliny'.

'What?' I cried, thinking I had misheard him.

'Pliny!' repeated my brother emphatically.

'My name is Piete!' I said in astonishment.

'She is our female Pliny,' explained Willi.

'That is to say, she carries out historical research and sets down her – ah – findings in writing for posterity. Then her opinions will earn the respect of all nations. It will be interesting to read what she has to say about all this.'

Androwski collapsed into laughter. I gazed at Willi, then said, 'I have finished with writing the war diary. I swear it!'

'Don't swear!' cried Androwski, still laughing. 'You have already sworn one false oath. You will promise me at least at intervals to carry on ...'

'... spitting,' interrupted my brother. 'Pliny will write. Whatever happens. Posterity wants to know how this spectre of war continues.'

When he said 'spectre' I suddenly felt sympathy for the war. I could even find it impossible to go on living without it. I said, 'How can the war help it if mankind has created it?'

'Pliny is right,' solemnly declared Androwski. 'Let us praise the war that makes men tough! There's no finer death in the world then to be slain by the enemy! Say nothing against the poor spectre and its henchmen! We, we alone, are to blame! And I tell you, one day I shall have had enough of this ruddy life!'[13]

'No', I cried. 'You mustn't say that. Life is beautiful; I mean all of nature; the animals, the wind, the grass ...'

'My sister has a thing about grass,' said Willi, chuckling. 'She is obsessed with it. She has said she wants to be buried in an open field, with grass over her stomach.'

'It seems you share my attitude to life,' said Androwski, laughing again. 'You have nothing against death.'

'That was just to do with school and also the war,' I said. I was cross with Willi for giving away my secrets.

'Exactly, exactly!' cried Androwski. 'We think the same.'

I left the schoolboys to their Latin swotting, whistled for Gretel and went for a walk with her – over the Karlsbergs.

'Pliny!' That's the limit!

2nd September, 1916

I must add that Grandma has received the Red Cross medal for her work at the Schneidemühl station, together with the good wishes of our Emperor.[14] I am horrified that I forgot to write about this (I beg your pardon, Grandma. I am very sorry! Such an important event! Whatever has come over me?) The medal is made of a metal like silver. On one side are the words. 'For services with the Red Cross'. Our Mayoress, the ladies of the Patriotic Women's League, and all the members of the ladies' club and the masonic sisterhood have given their congratulations. A few ladies have sent flowers. Grandma looked at the medal and said, 'When we have won the war I will wear it at the victory celebrations.' Then she put it back in its velvet box and locked it in the writing-table drawer. She put Mummy's telegram in with it. Mummy had telegraphed 'You have earned it, Mamma! Very pleased! Good luck. Yours. Grete.'

Willi said: 'At last!'

Otherwise everything was just as usual. I soaked some salted herring in water and baked it till it was crisp in the nearly dried-up pan, and we had jacket potatoes, followed by shrivelled baked apple with sugar. The sugar was actually saccharin which I had ground to a white powder. We have to go sparingly with sugar.

3rd September, 1916

Now comes blow upon blow, as they say. Mummy has read the latest pages of the diary which I sent her and has written a letter to me. I will copy a part of it, because I cannot otherwise explain why the war diary is really to finish.

'I don't understand,' wrote Mummy. 'How you could do it; background music for what are obviously love-sessions of little Schneidemühl tarts! Has the war so confused your ideas of morality? I am furious with you! Does Willi know about it? I hope not, otherwise I am bound to have doubts about my son's morals. Not a word to Grandma about this, do you hear? You will of course have nothing more to do with your classmate. As for the war diary, which was begun with such great hopes, I am not interested in it being carried on in this way. I would be ashamed to show it to my circle of friends. You are fourteen years old and big enough to know why.'

When I had read this letter, I felt awful. Was this really what I had been doing? Willi sometimes calls me 'Stupid!'; perhaps he is right. When I was nearly nine years old I once asked our 'Religious Knowledge' teacher what were King Solomon's concubines. The teacher thereon gave me such a dressing-down that the whole class was shocked. He said he knew just how 'perverse' was the motive of my question and that there were some children who are absolute 'snakepits'. I had no idea what I had done, indeed I thought the teacher would praise my interest in the lesson on religion.

It had never entered my wildest dreams that my classmate's sister and her friends were entertaining the Air Force officers in 'love-sessions'. I had thought that they were really having coffee and cakes – and, yes, perhaps would do a bit of kissing. The big girls nearly always do a bit of kissing with the soldiers. It is only too clear – they are off to the Front, and in any case will be killed or wounded. Many women kiss the soldiers out of sympathy. I know of course what else goes on between men and women. But in this instance I hadn't thought about it. I pretended to be Lieutenant von Yellenic playing background music for his friends in the Casino for fun, just as in the novels of Tolstoi and

Dostoiewski the gipsies played music at the tables of the guests. I imagined myself to be Lieutenant von Yellenic in the role of a gipsy; I convinced myself that he was one.

Who can know what has happened in the past of one's own family! It is said of my earliest ancestor that he was a leading piper in the army of King Frederick; he perished one winter in the Polish forests. Perhaps he too was a gipsy. Why else are we all so gifted in music and dream the wildest things that no other people dream? The headmaster once said that I disturb the whole class and the other girls would no longer be allowed to associate with me. The simplest thing would be for me to turn on the gas some time when I am alone in the house. Then my dear soul would be at rest.

Of course I am not going to break off friendship with my classmate. What has she to do with the goings-on of her older sister? On the contrary she is a good girl and so loyal! In any case I will not write any more of the diary for Mummy. A pity. (Because I love Mummy so much!) But I have promised Willi and Androwski to go on with it till the end of the war and that it will be just for our eventual children. Besides, I can improve my style with it. I have for example become quite a good friend of the subjunctive. I write the best essays in the class. To prove this I got a 'first' in oral and written German.

Now I feel completely empty; I am neither sad nor happy. Seemingly another 'war victim'. I shall have to bury myself. I could after all play that sometime with Gretel – being buried! Lieutenant von Yellenic, killed on the Eastern Front!

4th September, 1916

I have written to Mummy:–

'Darling Mummy! You can be sure that I shall no longer play music for T's sister. About what you say I had no idea – definitely not. If I had known, I would not have gone to T. in the first place. I can understand that you don't want to have any more of my diary; actually you have not for a long time wanted me to go on with it. I simply don't strike the right note any more, at least not for general reading. It is because I no longer have any enthusiasm for the war as most other people do, Ella Gumprecht for example. At every moment I think about soldiers dying everywhere, not just Germans, but also French, English, Russian, Italian, Serbian and I don't know what other

190

kinds of soldiers. Or they come back as cripples. I am afraid that Willi also will one day be called up. Many grammar-school boys who volunteered have already been killed. Please forgive me over and over again for causing you so much worry. I do love you so terribly much, dear, dear Mummy. Have you enough bread to eat? We are alright, but food is getting scarcer all the time. Women go into the villages to stock up, although it is forbidden. But what are they to do? We sometimes get eggs from Studsin; Frau Conitz the teacher's wife always packs me up a few fresh ones when I visit Connie. Unfortunately you don't yet know Connie at all. She is, after Dora Haensch, my best friend in the whole school. I recently received a whole 'fifteen' of eggs from a strange farmer's wife in Studsin. Frau Conitz had asked for them. Just then a military policeman came along and in my anxiety I pressed the bag containing the eggs against my chest. Frau Conitz said quite pleasantly, 'Piete, carry the bag just as carefully as if it contained new-laid eggs; the washing has only just been ironed!' She did indeed save me; the policeman didn't notice anything, and we had a good laugh afterwards. Good-bye, darling Mummy, keep a bit of love for me – in spite of my idiocy. Your daughter Piete.'

6th September, 1916

I can go to Dora's in Rinkau near Bromberg in the 'potato holidays', Grandma has given her consent! The Haensch's have invited me. They now have a horse and cart. I have already told Dora when my train arrives. I have brought the trunk down from the attic and polished it with boot-wax until it shone. I am packing a sailor-suit, a light summer dress, underclothes, shorts and a blouse. I shall wear strong shoes, and pack sandals and also a pair of heeled shoes that Mummy has left off because they don't look so nice any more. They fit me and I can dance well in them. I learnt to dance at my friend Käthe Dreier's birthday party. I often dance with Gretel. I can already dance Waltzes and the Polka quite well, especially the Krakowiak. That is a Polish dance in which the floor resounds with the crashing of heels.

Potato holidays, 1916

While the school boys and girls are helping the farmers dig potatoes, I have come to Bromberg. I came past many barbed-wire entanglements and empty trenches. The trenches have never been occupied; they are partially silted up again. I thought a great number of rabbits must live under the barbed-wire entanglements; they are as safe there as in Paradise.

Herr Haensch was waiting for me at Bromberg railway station with a yellow-painted cart; the horse was pretty old, fat and good-natured. He is a gelding and is called Gustav. I was so happy that my heart started beating madly. We went first along a main road and then through country lanes. Then we turned into a lovely wood of mixed broad-leaf trees and conifers. When we had gone a long way, the horse going at a nice jog-trot, the Rinkau Woodland Restaurant came in sight, quite a big building with a long extension for a ball-room and out-houses for horses and carts and tools. In the open doorway on the terrace stood dear Dora; she ran towards me and we clung round each other's necks. Frau Haensch came out from the kitchen too; she has become even a little fatter than she was. Jule had not yet come back from school. What a joyful all-round greeting there was! Dora is well-tanned and with her black curly hair is even prettier than before. I had to have a good look at everything and ended up in an attic room with a flowered wall-paper and a well scrubbed pinewood floor, an iron bedstead, an old wardrobe, a table and chair and a chest of drawers for my underclothes and my writing things; a mirror in a brown frame reaches from floor to ceiling but it is actually partly blank. If you look out of the window, you are looking in to the dark forest. There is also a wash-stand with a huge china wash-bowl, a tooth-cleaning glass and a water-jug. Dora and I danced around the room and could hardly contain ourselves for joy.

Then we had lunch with the staff in a corner of the terrace; afterwards we ran into the wood. Dora also showed me a meadow that belonged to the forestry people; the horse was allowed to graze there and roll around and rest. There was already quite a crowd of excursionists there who had come on foot or by coach from Bromberg to Rinkau to take coffee. Dora showed me the tables with white cloths on which cakes were laid out for sale – plum, apple and gooseberry tarts with artificial cream made with semolina, sugar and egg-white, which tastes nearly as good as the real thing. Herr Haensch said to me, 'If you like, Piete, you can help with the selling of cakes. Most people come at about three o'clock, and we always need nimble hands then.'

I didn't need asking twice. So many people came that I could hardly serve portions of cake quickly enough. The cakes had always to be paid for at once, so that no mistakes were made in the amount. At first Dora helped me with the cake-selling, but then there were suddenly so many customers that the two waitresses could no longer cope on their own and Dora had to run to and fro fetching jugs of coffee, milk and tea from the kitchen. 'It will soon be like Schneidemühl railway station,' I said laughing. Dora nodded to me with glistening eyes.

Suddenly Jule, my old 'sergeant', appeared. He was carrying under his arm a bundle of books strapped together, and he looked much taller than he used to. We greeted each other at once, but a bit awkwardly. 'I've got something for you,' said Jule, and produced a large cigar-box. It contained a fully-grown slow-worm, but it looked almost dead; only the forked tongue flickered a little. It had a little red cut on its back. I asked what was wrong with it. Jule said that the farm-hand had gone over its back with the scythe while cutting grass. He had then hung it over the handle of the scythe and was going to throw it away, but Jule had called out that he wanted to have it for the 'visitor'. So he presented me with the slow-worm. We christened her Rebecca. I placed her in Jule's old empty aquarium in which I had put moss, roots, stones, earth and an empty jam jar with water. Rebecca came to when she felt sand and moss under her and slowly coiled up under the lumps of root. I covered the aquarium with an old tray. Dora, Jule and I kept watch on the snake. It was interesting to watch her. She wouldn't eat, although we put all kinds of beetles, insects and even little butterflies in front of her in the aquarium. She probably felt like a severely wounded casualty or even a prisoner.

15th September, 1916

Now Rebecca is eating. I put a long, hairy caterpillar in her glass house and she swallowed it down. Strange, because it was such a big caterpillar and prickly too. Then I took Rebecca out and put her on the table in my room in the roof. She crept slowly around, but didn't glide underneath. I talked to her and stroked her back carefully. She wriggled a bit, but allowed the stroking to go on. Sometimes she raised her head with her black shiny eyes. I found my snake strangely beautiful and let her glide over my wrist and creep into my half-closed fist. The warm hiding-place probably suited her well; she slipped into my fist as far as she could and held herself quite still. Then I put her round my neck; her head and tail reached right into the hollow of my neck; and she lay still, not sliding down. That made me very happy. I walked about with my new necklace and showed it to all the Haensch family; they could hardly believe it and admired it greatly.

In the afternoon, when the coffee customers arrived and were buying cakes from me, there was absolute horror when some ladies discovered that I was wearing a live snake as a necklace. One young girl even dropped her plate, shrieking, with good plum tart, cream and all. Then Herr Haensch forbade me to display Rebecca in front of the customers. He said, 'Nearly every one is afraid of snakes. It is a fear as old as the story of Adam and Eve.'

What nonsense! I should very much have liked now to show people how harmless a snake can be unless it is an adder and is trodden on.

16th September, 1916

Something interesting! Rebecca was missing. I searched everywhere for her in the attic. Then I saw her tail on the floor between the looking-glass stand and the wall. When I pulled her out she was wrapped in a spider's web, her whole head and body. A wonder she wasn't suffocated. I cleaned her up with a moist piece of cotton-wool, and she lay on the table. Suddenly she raised the top half of her body, opened her little jaws, and a bright red bead rolled out from her throat over her tongue and fell on to the table – a drop of blood. At the same moment Rebecca recovered from the scythe-wound on her back. She twisted herself like lightning, I could hardly hold her. Then I just let her play in the aquarium, gave her a lot of caterpillars and insects and weighed the lid of the box down with a stone. She is as lively as a fish in the water.

17th September, 1916

Yesterday evening I got at least 50 young Poles and their girls to drink beer. It happened like this.

The Poles from the neighbouring village of Nimtsch (it is nearly all Polish) had announced a Saturday evening dance at the Haensch's. The long dance-hall had been decorated by the Poles with garlands of fir, bunting and fiery red paper-roses. About seven o'clock in the evening half of Nimtsch arrived in flower-covered rack-waggons; the first waggon contained all girls and young women, the second one the young men in brightly polished top boots, dark trousers and snow-white shirts. Some wore handsome waistcoats with buttons and braid. And then they all took their seats in the ball-room, the girls in an endless row of chairs on the right and the young men on the left. They acted as if they had never seen one another before in all their lives, so stiff and distant they were. Many were quite red with embarrassment, especially the girls. They chatted with one another without casting a glance at the young men.

Herr Haensch stood waiting behind the bar. It occurred to no one to get up, go to the bar and ask for a glass of beer. At last the music began to play, concertina, clarinet and fiddle. Now the dance would get going. As if at a command all the young men rushed across the room with a noise like thunder and clapped down on their left knees in front of their chosen ones. This delighted me enormously; I was quite overcome. Then the girls began to come dancing on to the floor with the young men on their arms and it was all under way. But very formal, as in dancing lessons. At first they danced a kind of cotillon, always prettily done with changes of step around the room. Then there was the Polonaise. Finally they all held each other around the waist and sidled around with the Polka step. Then the young men brought their ladies back to their seats, clicked their heels, bowed and turned to go back to their chairs. It went on like this for a whole hour, sometimes a waltz, sometimes a Polka, sometimes a round dance (with figures!) and then the orchestra put their instruments down, indicated an interval and disappeared.

Then Herr Haensch came to me and whispered angrily in my ear. 'Would you believe it, Piete; I haven't sold a drop of beer! A wasted evening!'

Then I had an idea. I sat down at the old piano (heavens, what a clapped-out box of tricks! Willi would be horrified!) and beat out the first Krakowiak. Oh diary, you should have seen it! Back over to the girls rushed the young men, down on one knee again, then – 'Up, jump, one, two, three – up, jump, one, two, three! – always in 3–4 time and round and round the room with 'Yuhe!' and 'Ole!' the stamping of feet and clatter of heels, such swinging and twirling of the girls and romping around that the lamps quivered and the beer glasses behind Herr Haensch rattled. You might have thought, 'Now the floor will give way!'

And I, wicked girl, played on and on! I well knew that I ought to stop; the couples had long been getting tired. But the Polish men were too polite to interrupt the dance without being asked, and the girls were too shy to give up on their own. They had to keep going as long as the music went on. I didn't stop until they were all boiling hot, the sweat pouring from the young men's brows and the girls nearly fainting. Then the dancers, men and girls, rushed to Herr Haensch and the bar. He just could not fill their glasses quickly enough, while Frau Haensch sold the girls one bottle of lemonade after another. Herr Haensch soon had to broach a second barrel of beer. Jule fetched from the cellar one case of soda-water and lemonade after another. I didn't dare play any more, but restrained myself. I had a bad conscience.

When the orchestra came back, no one wanted to dance any more at first. Some couples went into the woods to enjoy the night. It wasn't until an hour later that the dancing began again. Before we went to bed Herr Haensch said to me he had never sold so many drinks before.

Dora and I talked for a long time about how nice it was to see the Poles kneeling in front of the girls. I wanted so much that it should stay like that in our part of the country, Poles, Jews and Prussians together. I didn't know it otherwise, it had always been like that and ought to stay the same way.

Chopin was a Pole too of course, and Willi and I like nothing so much as his music. But many soldiers and officers say that we would attack the Poles. Just why though? It is a very good thing that at least the abuse of the Jews is over; nowadays there are Jewish officers in the army.

19th September, 1916

Mummy's birthday! With the help of Frau Haensch I have sent off a parcel of cakes, bread, sausages and bacon; Frau Haensch has given it all to me.

In the afternoon Herr Haensch sent me to a house in the forest near Nimtsch; I was to hand over a police-dog that Herr Haensch had been training for police service. The dog is to guard the forester's house in these uncertain times. He is still young and is called Wulli. I went off with Wulli on the lead and handed the dog over. The forester's family were very friendly to me; I had to drink coffee (from roasted barley) at the table and eat mountains of cakes sprinkled with almonds. They still get enough to eat in the country, although not as much as they used to. Then it became dusk and the forester said, 'You had better go back now, miss, or it will be dark. You know the way alright?'

'Of course,' I said. 'I came that way.'

But as I was walking back along the forest path towards Rinkau, suddenly I was at a loss. One path looked just like another. I thought, 'This is the right way!' It was certainly well used, and so I walked on and on until it was pitch dark and I could no longer recognise anything at all. I could no longer even see whether I was on a path or wandering in all directions between the tree trunks.

Suddenly I heard a crackling; it sounded like stealthy footsteps and I immediately thought, 'A Russian patrol!' My heart nearly stopped beating. All around was the stealthy movement, this almost inaudible crackling; I nearly died of fear. To keep up my courage and to confuse the enemy sentries I began to whistle, as loud as I could, one soldiers' song after another, mostly 'The little woodland birds', so that the Russian patrol would think I was an armed soldier. At the same time I kept groping my way forwards, praying to God that he would just let me find my way home. I thought, perhaps it's all because I made the Poles collapse with tiredness and got them to drink so much; such are the thoughts that come to you when you are half dead with fear. Finally I thought some one was walking right close by me; I felt him near me. I couldn't whistle any more, my lips were tightly closed.

Suddenly a light came towards me, a pocket-torch which kept blinking on and off. The voices of Dora and Jule called out, 'Piete! Piete!'.

Then my knees gave way and I simply dropped. As before in school, when I fainted, there was a buzzing in my ears. It wouldn't have taken much for me to faint again. I could only chirp 'Here I am! Here!,' but Dora said later I had growled like a bear, with quite a deep, hoarse voice. Would you believe it! We laughed till we cried afterwards about the 'bear'.

But when I was in bed I felt ashamed of myself. Fie! The devil of it! That any one could be such a coward! Lieutenant von Yellenic in the face of the enemy! For shame! I didn't tell any one in Rinkau about my fear.

Strange, but I don't want to stay in Rinkau any more. I should like best of all to go back to Schneidemühl, to Grandma and my brother Willi. I'll take Rebecca with me. Yes, I want to be back at home. I am going back to-morrow.

30th September 1916

High time that I was back in Schneidemühl! Dear old 17 Alte Bahnhofstrasse, lovely yard, lovely garden. I took the aquarium with me, but Grandma was so horrified with Rebecca that she threw her out of the window into the garden. When I came back from my first day at school she was missing. I have looked for my little snake until my eyes are dropping out, but can't find her anywhere. I have turned over every leaf in the garden and looked under every bush. Nothing! Willi tried to console me by declaring that Rebecca was happier now. 'No longer a prisoner of war, as you yourself have said,' he declared.

I have cleaned out Jule's aquarium and put fresh plants in, in case I find Rebecca again. But I know well that she will like her freedom better than me. I could keep crying over it.

Cowardice and crying ... I must let Lieutenant von Yellenic die. I have prepared Gretel for it. She was dumbfounded.

1st October, 1916

There are new entrants in my class again. They are not refugees. Connie and I have become still closer friends. We are united in that after the war we want to stay in close touch. After the war ...! Will that ever happen? Our town is full of the military. Every big girl has at least one soldier friend. They are principally airmen with us now. It is said that the Schneidemühl 'Albatross Factory' turns out a hundred fighters and bombers every month. There are constant forced landings over the town. Many coffins of airmen are brought to the goods station, where they are loaded into open goods wagons and sent to the relatives. Then the military band plays sad tunes, like 'Jesus in whom I put my trust' and 'I had a comrade'. Every time I fight back the tears.

There is scarcely one of our larger buildings that has not been converted into a military hospital. Ambulances and, recently, military hospital-cars are constantly going past with wounded and delivering them to the hospitals. I don't go so often to the station to help in the Red Cross canteen. Grandma has organised so many helpers that it is better for me to get on with my school-work or, in any spare time, do household jobs such as mending mountains of underclothes or darning stockings. I hate mending and darning. Doing the washing and ironing and cleaning the rooms are much better.

This winter, and perhaps a year later as well, Connie and I and several of the girls from the high school will learn ball-room dancing with dancing-teacher Kleinschmidt. I am pleased about that. I would like most of all to be a dancer rather than a singer. If only I knew what to wear for the dancing-lessons; I have hardly any more good dresses. My school outfit is a discarded sailor's blouse of Willi's and a pleated skirt from an old dress of Mummy's; but the skirt is already pretty worn. Grandma says I must not 'cause any grey hairs' over the clothes for my dancing-lessons. The clothes for my confirmation the year after next will cause her far more anxiety. She says that for the 'examination dress' she would if necessary sacrifice the curtain material which at present hangs in our drawing-room window. I asked whether I could have new shoes, perhaps with buckles and heels for the confirmation. Grandma thought there wouldn't be enough money for special shoes. Because of the leather shortage we girls wear cloth sandals, the soles of which are formed by three cut-out pieces of wood. The pieces of wood are bound together with remnants of strips of leather which are nailed on and keep the soles flexible. But they make a mighty clatter when you walk in them; I can no longer walk silently through the woods to observe the animals, as I am mad on doing. The ground is already too cold to go barefoot. Winter is coming on early.

10th October, 1916

No one shouts 'Special News sheet! Special News sheet!' in the street any more. We read the war news in the newspapers or on the placards at the newspaper offices. At present there is a great battle going on on the Somme; our forces are trying to break through the English and French positions. Every inch of ground is heroically contested. The earth is strewn with thousands of soldiers' bodies. Rivers of blood are flowing at St. Quentin and Cambrai. There is not so much fighting now at Verdun, 'the Hell of Verdun'. I think the offensive which cost so many lives has been abandoned as hopeless. The French commanders at Verdun were General Pétain, who was later relieved by General Nivelle, and General Joffre. That is what is so terrible about the war; that so many battles are fought in vain. And the victims ...?

Among the soldiers you see more and more old, bearded, fathers of families and young-blooded warriors. I sometimes think they put schoolboys into uniforms much too big for them.

They have poor, starved-looking faces and are so thin! I picture my brother Willi in uniform. O Lord in Heaven, don't let my brother become a soldier! This time the scarlet fever effects won't count for anything – they need every one!

If only we had a bit more to eat! But bread and flour are so scarce, and it is no better with any other foodstuff. At present our week's ration per person is half a pound of coffee-substitute and half a pound of margarine; 125 grams of butter for a grown-up. Sometimes there are coupons for half a pound of rolled oats, half a pound of pearl barley and half a pound of semolina. But when the stocks are sold out people may have been standing in queues for hours at the shops all for nothing. The supplementary ration for heavy workers allows for 50 grams of bread and 125 grams of beans a week. How strong men must get on that!

Recently there was a wonderful smell in the house when we came home from school. Willi sniffed and said, 'Oh, I say! Oh, I say!'

Grandma, with a mysterious air, placed a stewed bird with jacket potatoes on the table.

I cried, 'Grandma, a pigeon!' We hadn't had roast pigeon to eat for years. 'Now just eat it!' said Grandma and went on behaving mysteriously. She carved the bird and put a little piece on each of our plates. We could hardly peel the potatoes fast enough, so keen were we for the meat. It tasted wonderful; we thought we had never had anything better. Grandma smiled when we had eaten it all up and said, 'Guess what you have been eating!'

'A partridge!' cried Willi.

'A young pigeon!' I said.

'A crow.' said Grandma. 'A farmer from Kolmar sold it to me.'

So for the first time in my life I have eaten a crow.

11th October, 1916

We are having good fortune in the East at least. The Russian Brussilow-Offensive has been wrecked near Korytnicza. We have won! We have also beaten the Rumanians; we have driven them back over the Danube. But whatever is happening at sea? We read to-day in the newspaper office window an announcement in red lettering –

German U-boats begin economic warfare off the coast of U.S.A.

Hans Androwski, who was standing near me with Willi, said 'That means war with America!'

Willi cried irritably 'The devil! The Devil,' and spat angrily behind him. But he had actually spat accidentally onto the coat-sleeve of an elderly gentleman – a good mouthful! We quickly sank to the ground! The gentleman simply held out his coat-sleeve in silence. Willi stammered 'Oh! ... I beg your pardon ... Oh!' took out his handkerchief and wiped the spit off. The old gentleman answered not a syllable. Just gazed at his sleeve and twisted his mouth a little into a smile. We slunk off. On the way we began to laugh.

Something funny is always happening to Willi. One night recently there was a great 'plump' as if a sack of potatoes had fallen down. When I rushed into Willi's bedroom, he had fallen out of bed. He was crawling around the floor in his striped night-shirt, asking in confusion 'What's happening? What's happening? How did I get here?' But I couldn't answer for laughing.

In the summer holidays Mummy, Willi and I were walking one time through the Sandsee Woods. It was raining and we had umbrellas up. Then the sun came out and we closed the umbrellas. But Willi still held the closed umbrella up as if it were open. When I asked, wondering, what he thought he was doing, he looked, as if shocked, into the air and cried, 'Hey there, where has my brolly gone?' Mummy and I fell into each other's arms laughing. On the same walk Willi kept a few paces ahead of us while discussing with Mummy the manuscript of his novel 'In the land of the Klingstein (Mexico!).' Suddenly there was a dull thud. The poor chap had rammed his forehead against a tree. So he had to put up with our laughter as well as the pain.

15th October, 1916

Uncle Bruno is here. He has got three days' leave. Grandma nearly fainted with joy when she saw her son suddenly standing at the door. She was as white as a sheet and her arms hung down limply. Uncle took hold of her, put his arms round her, kissed her and led her to the sofa. Then she kept saying 'Bruno! Bruno! Bruno!' and I ran into the kitchen and quickly made some strong coffee. But the coffee is not really strong because it is only roasted barley. Still it was hot and did us all good. We were quite overcome with surprise and joy.

Uncle has brought in his pack a flat, blue-grey steel helmet which he found on the battle-field. It is a Belgian steel helmet; it has two smooth holes in the front as if made by a bayonet, but the steel is too hard for that to be possible. It also has a deep indentation near the holes. The leather lining is encrusted with blood, and the leather strap is just the same; it is stiff and hard.

I took the steel helmet carefully into my hands and looked at uncle. Uncle said, 'It lay upside down on the ground like a basin full of blood'. 'And the soldier?' I asked. Uncle answered, 'He was no longer there. The medicos would have taken him away.' When I looked more closely inside the helmet, I saw that on the edge of the neck there was a name scratched with a sharp object. The name read, 'van Glabeke, César.' So he was a Fleming.

Van Glabeke, César – César van Glabeke. This man is no longer alive; I am holding his helmet in my hand – a German girl, one of those who killed him. I pictured his mother. I immediately resolved firmly to write to her. Perhaps a letter will reach her if it is addressed to a Madame van Glabeke, Flanders, Belgium. Uncle will tell me the name of the area where he found the helmet. Unfortunately there is no regimental number in it.

20th October, 1916

Uncle has gone away again. Grandma pretends not to cry, but I know she does. I have written a letter to Madame van Glabeke in French and told her that I have possession of her son's helmet and that I am so sorry about the whole thing. I wrote –

'La guerre est un désastre;
Dieu ne la veut, ma famille
désire la paix.'

I addressed the letter to the French Red Cross in Paris.

I would have loved to write to Madame van Glabeke that I cry over her César every night. I think of the wreath of glass pearls that hung on the wooden cross of a dead Frenchman in Schneidemühl prisoner-of-war cemetery and on which were the words –

'A toi mes pensées
et mes larmes
tous les jours.'

202

It is really something for a German school-girl to cry over a dead French soldier. You ought not to cry out of sympathy – that is certain.

Lieutenant von Yellenic, you are crazy! Simply war-crazed! You must really be allowed to die.

24th October, 1916

News Extra: On 21st October the Austrian president, Count Stürgkh, was assassinated by a man named Friedrich Adler. There was a crush of horror-struck people in front of the newspaper office. An officer of the Jäger battalion shouted: 'Away with all socialist swine!' I didn't like to ask whether he meant Count Stürgkh or the assassin Friedrich Adler. It says in the News Extra that the assassination took place in a Viennese hotel. By shooting.

I read it as quickly as I could to Willi and asked why the President would have been shot. Willi answered that Count Stürgkh favoured the continuation of the war. I said, 'So do most of the people!' Willi said, 'But not the reds.'

In the window of the newspaper office hung a photograph of Count Stürgkh: a proud man with a pointed beard sprinkled with grey hairs. He wears spectacles and looks a bit like my late grandfather Eduard Golz, so serious and severe.

A photograph of the assassin was also displayed. I can't imagine at all that an assassin could look like that. He looks like a professor, has a thick moustache and likewise wears spectacles. His face is not proud, but gentle and sad. You can't imagine that he has any idea how to handle a revolver. Will he be shot now too? When I asked my brother that, he cried, 'Murder is murder!'

I fetched Gretel up. We played until evening, 'Big party at Yellenic Castle' (Lieutenant Yellenic is at present staying with his parents in Hungary), to which we had invited 66 guests. I had scribbled the names of the guests on 66 pieces of paper and placed them around the table. The pile of paper represented the guests. We drank tea and coffee (in reality there was nothing in the cups, although we had secretly taken Grandma's best cups from the sideboard), ate pyramid cakes with whipped cream (but only pretending!) and carried on furious conversation.

Afterwards we danced a polonaise all round the house, Lieutenant von Yellenic dancing with Nurse Martha, and then we danced a very noisy Krakowiak, for we were alone in the house. Willi and Grandma had gone out.

26th October, 1916

Yesterday a lieutenant in Air Force uniform greeted me in Posener Strasse. I turned bright red. It was the young lieutenant who had previously spoken to me on the stairs when I was engaged in playing music for my school friend's sister's coffee party. I mean, for the parties with officers. And he had asked whether I was one of the party too.

I contrived to go into Teuffel's bookshop as quickly as I could. Then suddenly he was in the bookshop too and was thumbing through a pile of newspapers near me. He said, 'It's lovely to see you again! You are the young lady who plays the piano so nicely, aren't you? "Pieteken" is your name, isn't it?' Then he introduced himself, 'My name is Werner Waldecker and I come from Bielefeld.'

I was struck dumb and couldn't answer a word, but just looked at him. I must have seemed utterly stupid. I never know what to say at times like this and am so cross afterwards that I could almost kill myself. It didn't seem to matter at all to him, however; he smiled and said he would like to have an éclair with me in Fliegner's the confectioners. Then I got my speech back; I stammered (imagine it!) that I would like of all things to have an éclair but unfortunately hadn't enough money on me. He laughed pleasantly and said that would be a real pleasure, and when I had bought my arithmetic book and he a pencil we went to eat éclairs. They have enormous éclairs at Fliegner's and the whipped cream, although it is artificial, tastes nearly as good as real cream.

We talked about flying and Lieutenant Waldecker told me that he flies a Fokker machine. Over our éclairs we very quietly sang the 'Airman's March' and laughed when we came to the part –

'In the air, in the air
That is where you get the spice
Up to the heavens, up to the heavens,
Hip-hip-hip-hurrah!'

Lieutenant Waldecker asked whether I would fly to heaven with him. I misunderstood him and thought he was offering me a trial flight in his Fokker machine. In my stupidity I answered that I really preferred horses to aircraft. He asked what in the world horses had to do with it. I realised then that I had said the wrong thing and now asserted that I just liked horses very much. 'Horses are better than people', I said and went as red as a lobster again.

'Dear God,' cried Lieutenant Waldecker, 'You are the strangest girl who ever crossed my path!' I became furious and said that I hadn't crossed his path at all but he had crossed mine and besides I had had enough and wanted to go.

'Pity,' he murmured.

When we parted outside Fliegner's the confectioners, he kissed my hand and asked whether he might hope to see me again. 'Not likely!' I said; I was sufficiently occupied with my dear brother Gil (I absent-mindedly said 'Gil'), we played music together, and then I had school-work to contend with.

'Pity!' he said again with a little smile.

He has blue eyes and soft fair hair. He also talked about his mother.

2nd November, 1916

Diary, my dear diary, the soldiers at the station say that our wonderful Emperor wants to make peace. They are excited and keep talking about it. A reservist put his arms round Grandma, kissed her with a large smack on both cheeks and cried, 'Mother, mother, good lady! Now we're for home! Quite definitely! The Emperor is making peace!' Frau Schönfeld, who was just then stirring the potato soup in the cauldron, looked up in astonishment and said we definitely hadn't yet gained enough ground. The soldier, laughing, cried 'What, dear lady, have we never gained enough ground?'

It is true, we are winning ourselves half to death. Rumania too is nearly overcome. The Allies are not advancing any further on the Somme, although Australians are fighting together with the English and the French. In Russia there is talk of revolution. But is there anything in it? For years people have talked of peace but it has never come. We are everlastingly eating turnips, queuing for bread and spreading meal-pap with mustard or marjoram on the slices. We sometimes go to sleep in school through weakness; the teachers have even allowed us to sleep for an hour with our arms on the desks and our heads on our arms.

And winter is now coming with a vengeance too. It is snowing with thick flakes. The little children go sliding in the frozen gutters in the streets. I would love to go sliding too, but I am now too big, unfortunately. All the bigger girls walk up and down Posener Strasse between 4 and 5 o'clock in the afternoon; they go 'courting' with the grammar-school boys and lieutenants.

I must confess, dear diary, that Willi and I have started this 'courting' too, and frankly we find it great fun. Willi wants to see his 'Empress Charlotte', who goes walking with her friend Minna and other girls from the Hoppenrath boarding-house. Yesterday I met Lieutenant Werner Waldecker too; he was walking between two 'ladies'. When he saw me he bowed politely and gave me a military salute. I nodded coolly; unfortunately I again went as red as fire.

We sometimes meet Andreas Zorn and Hans Androwski too. I think Androwski has grown more manly of late; he resembles a picture of Franz Schubert (with glasses), rather ugly but intelligent. Andreas on the other hand is good-looking; most of the girls in my class fall for him. Willi is the best-looking; he is now nearly as tall as Uncle Bruno and has wonderful dark hair and a handsome face. A true artist. Only in his nightshirt you see how spindly he is.

4th November, 1916

Now the newspapers too are speaking of the Emperor's desire for peace. He has written to Reich Chancellor v. Bethmann Hollweg – 'Peace – a moral act!'

These words were written in blue on a sheet of paper behind the window of the newspaper office. I would have gone really mad with joy. But it was simply too cold. Suddenly I couldn't feel my thighs any more; my legs absolutely folded up under me. For any reason or for no reason at all I could easily have burst out crying. I staggered home with stiff legs. Grandma said, 'Is something wrong with you, child?'

I said, 'Grandma, it is really peace. But I just don't know ...'

Grandma said, 'You are absolutely frozen. Take your shoes off and put your feet in a bowl of cold water.'

Now I wanted to have warm water of course. My feet were as white as chalk. When I held them in warm water I writhed with pain. I drew them out again at once and hopped on each leg alternately around the room. Grandma cried 'You see, you see, that's what I just told you. But the youngsters always have to know best.' She made me some warm milk and honey. I drank that up in one gulp. Then I felt better. But only a little.

20th November, 1916

Mummy and Granny are writing to each other a lot, because they are afraid that Willi will be called up next year. A few boys from his class have already been enrolled. Mum will try to get Willi an interview at the army cadet college in Berlin. A young acquaintance of hers, Teddy von Roszinsky, is actually in the Junker cadets; that's what gave her the idea. Willi would have to stay there as a scholar for quite a long time, so that he might no longer have to go to the Front. It could be that the war was over by then. Frau Schönfeld's brother Fritz, who is on leave again just now, shrugged his shoulders when I mentioned the cadet college. We were both sitting in Frau Schönfeld's parlour eating potato fritters. He said, 'Miss Piete, don't you believe it! Only the Junkers get in there, those who have a "von" in their name. The "top drawer", you know, the aristocracy. Your dear brother hasn't a chance. He is just middle-class.'

That annoyed me immensely, that my brother should be 'just middle-class.' An artist! Besides, I don't want my brother to become a soldier. Such a dreamer would get into the midst of the field of fire right away and be knocked out with the first salvo. That's for sure.

25th November, 1916

What is now happening again? It is said that we have made Poland into a 'state'. The Central Powers, and thus we, however, retain the supreme command in Warsaw and Lublin, where we have general government. I haven't read anything about it in the newspapers. But I have hardly read the papers at all lately, only casualty lists.

26th November, 1916

Jesus God, I have forgotten to say that on 21st November the old Austrian Emperor Franz Joseph I died, the one who once said, 'There's nowt that doesn't happen to me.'

He had been Emperor of Austria since 1848. When he was younger he had a wonderfully beautiful wife, Empress Elisabeth, called Sissi, who had her own imperial circus and rode a white stallion, a Lipizzaner, putting it through its paces. Some madman stabbed her in the back when she was walking all unsuspecting with her lady attendant by the Lake of Geneva. Fräulein Ella Gumprecht says the assassin was an Italian anarchist; she also says that Grandma in her young days resembled the beautiful

207

Empress. There is supposed to have been nearly a riot once in Bromberg because some people thought Grandma was the Empress Sissi walking through the streets incognito with an attendant; but the attendant was only Grandma's sister, our Aunt Clara Schwarz, who lives with her family in Bromberg. I think it is wonderful that people believed Grandma was the Empress Elisabeth.

In the window of the newspaper office there is a picture of the new Emperor of Austria; he is called Karl I.

At school we had a service of mourning for the dead Emperor Franz Joseph. We can't yet properly come to terms with the new Emperor; he looks as if he will collapse under the weight of the enormous crown and the coronation cloak. He certainly couldn't stop a runaway horse. Our coachman Schulz could. I was sitting next to Schulz on the box of our carriage when the horse ran away, because just then a traction-engine came along the street with a terrific clatter. The horse lifted both his front legs high in the air almost on top of the traction-engine, then lashed out with his back legs and shattered the footboard of the box so that the planks just flew around our ears. Grandpa, who was sitting behind in the carriage, shouted, 'Schulz, hold the reins tight.' Schulz did, too. The traction-engine driver stopped the rattling engine, but nothing else stopped. God, how that steed rampaged! But our Schulz! You should have seen how that little man got the horse under control! I held on tight to Schulz with both arms, otherwise I should have been thrown up in the air to come crashing down again.

It must be a heavy responsibility to be crowned Emperor, and in the midst of war too. Willi grinned when I talked to him on these lines, and said, 'Don't worry! You will never be crowned Empress.'

1st December, 1916

The fortresses of Douamont and Vaux, which we had captured, have been taken back from us by the French. They penetrated our lines on a broad front. There is talk of three quarters of a million dead on both sides, said to have been the cost in lives of the offensive on the Somme. If 750,000 dead were laid next to one another on the ground, what a field of corpses that would make!

Grannie said, 'The coffin-makers are getting rich on the coffins they have to send to the Front.'

That is not so. Most soldiers are laid without coffins in quickly dug graves and are covered with shovelfuls of earth. But I don't talk about that with Grandma because her son is stationed on the Western Front.

Dear God, I address these words to you. You cannot surely find any pleasure in seeing me running uselessly about here, getting one black mark after another at school, arousing Mummy's anger and being really superfluous while so many wonderful men are being killed at the Front. For instance as early as 26th September, 1914, soon after the outbreak of war, the notable modern painter August Macke was killed, and on 4th March this year Franz Marc, one of the best of all painters, who painted the Red Deer and Blue Horses, fell at Verdun. On 26th September, 1914, our beloved poet Hermann Löns fell in the battle of Rheims, after writing in his diary the previous evening, 'The sun is setting angrily. It is yellow.'[15] I know all his songs by heart. If I could stop the war, I would willingly die, dear God. It says indeed in the Bible that you accept particular people as sacrificial offerings to save a town or a whole nation. May I become such a sacrifice? You see, dear God, I am just now reading a book by the writer v. Oppeln-Bronikowski, called the Rebel, about an unhappy lieutenant. Now look, if the hero, that is the lieutenant, has to die at the end of the book, then I shall believe that is a sign. Then my sacrifice is accepted by you. You can indeed not speak; therefore I will hear your voice through the book, The Rebel. I am then the rebel, and you will bring the war to an end, whether we are the victors or not doesn't matter at all. Listen, dear God! I will hear you clearly.

3rd December, 1916

God has let the hero in the book die. This means he has accepted my offer. I have cried so much over the poor people in the book! Now I am going to die, so that the dying at the Front ceases. If a child (that is what I really still am, dear God, isn't it?) offers herself as a sacrifice, then you *can* make the war cease, then you *must* keep alive all the soldiers who are now still in good health and have a future! I am serious about this, dear God. Are you too?

I will now wash myself, lie on my bed and turn on the gas ring-light. It has four jets, so it will happen quickly. Willi has gone to Androwski's and Andreas Zorn's. Grannie has been invited to a coffee party at Frau Leonhard's and won't be back for three hours. It is all perfectly quiet here.

Keep faith with me, dear God! I will keep faith with you. That is a vow, God!

At night, 3rd December, 1916

It has all gone wrong.

Do you know, dear diary, what happened? Just listen. So – I did everything just as I described and turned on the four taps of the gas light. I had closed both the bedroom windows and the door and bolted the hall door from inside so that when Grandma came home she would first have to fetch the locksmith and that would leave me more time to die. I heard the gas gently hissing as it issued from the open taps. I lay still for some time just thinking of Grandma. It occurred to me that she had once said that if I had to die she would die too. It was a lovely thought that Grannie and I would lie together in one coffin, she quite old and I quite young. I imagined that her arm would be placed around me. Suddenly I became a little dizzy, but it was quite a pleasant feeling; then I was nearly going off to sleep when – imagine it – I suddenly heard Grandma talking and laughing happily in the yard with Frau Wegner and Frau Annchen Schönfeld. They were all three talking quite merrily together. Then I was instantly overcome with fright because for some reason Grandma hadn't gone to Frau Leonhard's at all but had come straight home. Can you understand such a thing? Grannie goes every Thursday to each of the members of her sisterhood in turn and is never back home before seven o'clock in the evening. Whatever went wrong?

There was nothing else I could do but immediately throw the windows open as quickly as possible and unbolt the hall door. I had first of all turned off the gas taps. It had made me terribly dizzy; I knocked up against everything and even overturned a chair that I had stumbled against. A fine how-d'ye-do! When I tried to pick up the chair, I fell against the table, but I finally managed to stand the chair up. Luckily the ladies kept laughing and talking in the yard quite a long time so that the smell of gas wasn't as strong as it had been. I even had time to close the windows again.

But in spite of this Grandma immediately noticed the smell and said, 'Why is there such a strong smell of gas?'

I acted stupid and said 'What smell of gas?'

'Oh, it absolutely reeks of gas. And why?' said Grandma irritably. 'Have you been cooking and not turned the gas tap off properly?'

I ran into the kitchen and pretended to be at the controls of the gas stove. I could now act as if Grandma was right and called out, 'Yes, the tap was not turned off. I had made myself a little coffee.'

'Dear child,' said Grandma, 'just think what might have happened! You could have been dead!'

That's just how it should have been. Why didn't God want me?

Grandma went on to say, 'We can't thank God enough! He has sent you a guardian angel!'

A guardian angel! It was an angel of war, an angel of death! Albert Dürer painted it. There is a picture of it in our art history book.

11th December, 1916

At school the heating is bad. From yesterday we have been given 'cold' holidays. Our bedroom stove is heated by a single briquette which we have wrapped in three newspapers. The tiles of the stove do in spite of this give off a little heat, so that Grandma can keep the blue jug of barley coffee warm in the recess. When it is dark, Gretel and I press thin tissue paper on to the tiles and stretch it out over them until it clings to them. Then when we take it off and carefully crumple it in our hands, glorious sparks fly up, blue, yellow, green and gold. Then I sing the Löns song to Gretel:–

And as the fire burns
The sparks are flying.
I had a guiding star
But I can't help crying
Because my star has set in the dark, dark night
And no more smiles on me with its friendly light.

Sometimes Gretel then leans her head on my shoulder, closes her eyes and says, 'Go on singing.' Or we open the door of the stove and see the briquette glowing at the back of the cavity. I tell the story of Mogli, the Jungle Boy, to Gretel. The story is by Kipling and I know it nearly by heart.

I am actually becoming a first-rate ballad-singer and story-teller, whether I want to or not. But on the whole I want to.

During the main breaks at our Empress Augusta Victoria School I always have to tell stories. Hardly does the bell go for break when the girls shout 'Come on, Piete, tell us some more stories!' Then we race to a particular corner of the school yard, they all collect around me and I tell a story. An endless story. When Willi and I were smaller, we used to play it with our paper dolls; it was never-ending just like the game of Nurse Martha and Lieutenant von Yellenic. I keep thinking out fresh possibilities for the school stories. The girls are fired with excitement every time. The more's the pity that we are now on 'cold' holiday.

23rd December, 1916

We have bought a tiny fir-tree and dressed it with our old Christmas decorations. On top is placed our only candle. The third wartime Christmas.

The German Admiralty wants to extend the so-called 'total U-boat war round the whole world', as a giant fence against the attacks of the Allies. No one speaks of peace any more. On Christmas Eve we shall have turnip and potato purée with horse-meat balls in mustard sauce. Grandma has baked wartime gingerbread and oatmeal cakes. They are iced with real sugar. Willi and I fetch our mother from the station to-day. I hope the train will not get stuck in the snow. We have heated the place as far as we could, so that Mummy doesn't get frozen. We have warmed her bed with hot-water bottles since the morning. Willi is sleeping in the dining-room on the sofa, Mummy in Willi's bed in the office, as from long habit we call it, because Grandpa's former cylinder bureau stands there, a gigantic piece of furniture with a green-covered folding-table and half a million compartments. Grandpa always used it for drawing his building plans, writing out bills and paying the builder's wages.

25th December, 1916

I have had for Christmas some mittens and a white rabbit-fur collar, but best of all the thick book on which the whole girls' school has gone mad; it is by Agnes Gunther and is called 'The Saint and her Jester'. I have even begun to read it on Christmas Night although I had previously borrowed it from Hertha Müller. It is wonderful.

It seems that Mummy doesn't love me as much as she used to.

Willi declares that I am mistaken. But I don't know! She asked me whether I still kept up the war diary. I stammered, 'Yes, a bit. But not properly now.' I was afraid she wanted to read it; then she would read all the nonsense about the gas-light and Werner Waldecker. Luckily she only said, 'Hm!'

I know Mummy has always loved my brother Willi (she now calls him 'Gil') better than me. Willi loves Mummy more than anything in the world. When he was nine years old, he once wrote a letter to her, over which she laughed till she cried. She kept the letter. I had to copy it for Grandma. Here it is (with all its mistakes of grammar and spelling):–

Whitsun is a great festival,
My Mummy is the best of all!
Three cheers for her, my Mummy who
Sings so beautiful and true!
There's no one better the whole world over
In wood and meadow or field of clover.
She is so frightfully, frightfully good.
God shields her in his father hood.
When she comes, put out the flags!
Even the sky dons its glad rags!
Darling Mummy, when you come
Do please bring me for the sum
Of 1 Mark 25 a box of cunjuring tricks
Your loving son and budding poet, Willi.

Mummy laughed especially over the last sentence.

But I am Grandma's child. We never talk about our love for each other, but we know it in our hearts. Every evening Grandma massages my head because I so often have a head-ache since the affair with the gas-ring. But I think she does it just as a kind of fondling. She sits on a chair, while I sit on a footstool at her feet, with my back between her knees. Then she kneads, presses and massages my head, forehead, temples and neck. That feels good. It is wonderful to be massaged by Grandma. Her hands are so warm and soft; they smell slightly of onions, that is so homely. We often sit for some time in the dark, hardly speaking, while she massages.

Mummy thinks I have become as thin as a lath. But who has not gone thin in this war? Gil has legs like a stork. We queue for one loaf of bread.

Map showing the position of Schneidemühl after the First World War, with the establishment of the Polish Corridor.

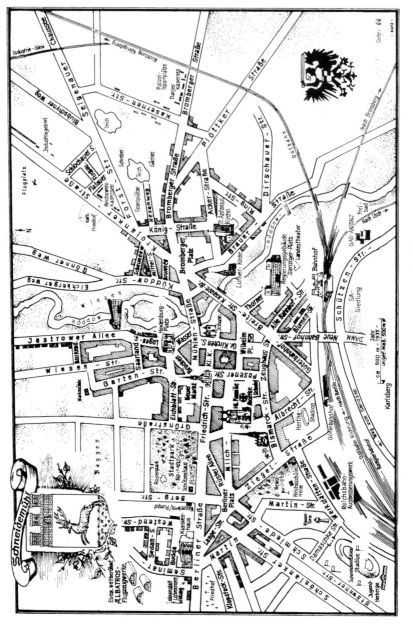

Street plan of Schneidemühl

Family photograph from 1915: Piete (seated) with (left to right) her mother, brother and grandmother.

The House at 17, Alte Bahnhofstrasse

The main square in Schneidemühl – referred to by Piete as the 'Neue Markt'

The river Küddow, photographed in 1996, now having the Polish name 'Gwda'

Notice concerning Piete's mother's music school in Berlin. The note in
the top left hand corner is in the hand-writing of Piete as an adult
(Jo Mihaly)

1996 photograph of the one-time Helene Lange Schule, originally called
the Kaiserin Auguste Viktoria Schule (Piete's school)

The Infantry Barracks in Schneidemühl, built by Piete's grandfather as
indicated by her inscription in later life on this postcard.

Schneidemühl railway station as at the beginning of the First World War.

The station photographed in 1995 – with the Polish name Piła.
The translator's two sons appear in this photograph.

Gloria Victoria!

„In der Heimat gibt's ein Wiederseh'n."
(Soldatenlied.)

Das Lied wird auch mit folgendem Anhängsel gesungen: (von*) nach*))

The soldier's song which haunted Piete as she heard its sound coming
from the station. Words from the chorus formed the title of her diary
when it was published and thus the title of this book. The same words are
quoted in Christabel Bielenberg's best-selling book about the Second
World War, *The Past is Myself*, and feature prominently in her sequel,
The Road Ahead.

At the Red Cross canteen on the station. Piete is holding the coffee-pot
and her grandmother is standing second from right.

Notification of award of Red Cross medal to Piete's grandmother
(see page 188).

The German cruiser 'Karlsruhe' with the captured English ship 'Bowes Castle' (see page 44 and Note 4)

Wounded soldiers being taken from a hospital train – illustrating a description on page 61.

Dogs in training for medical service – see pages 109–110 and page 118.

Dreier's wine shop – see pages 75, 90, 268 and Note 6.

Song composed by Piete's brother Willi and dedicated to Charlotte Voss –
see pages 69, 135, 140, 239 and Note 11.

Loge Borussia, Schneidemünl

Masonic Lodge built by Piete's grandfather and damaged by fire while in
use as a military hospital – see page 160.

1995 photograph, showing the above building as a survivor of the
Second World War destruction.

Above

Entrance to the prisoners-of-war cemetery mentioned frequently by Piete – e.g. pages 42, 46, and 317–319.
The Polish inscription, photographed in 1996, reads thus –

War Cemetery, 1914–1918 Soldiers of the Allied Armies died in the German prisoner-of-war camp of Piła. In this cemetery are approximately 3,000 graves in which are buried Russian, Polish, Latvian, Lithuanian, Belgian, British and Jewish soldiers. These people of various religions, Orthodox, Greek Catholic, Roman Catholic, Muslim, Jews, united by the same fate.

Respect This Place.

Left

Advertisement for Kleinschmidt's Dancing School. See page 253, 261-2, 266 and 281.

Part of War Memorial in Church of St. Nicholas, Bielefeld, showing
the name of Werner Waldecker – see, inter alia, pages 204, 222–3
and 249–50

Advertisment for Fliegner's café, visited by Piete with
Werner Waldecker.

At the home for sick children where Piete was employed towards the end of the War. Piete is on the right, holding the child Annemieken, one of her favourites – see page 305

Photograph taken soon after the end of the War:
left to right, Piete's grandmother, brother Willi, Piete and Ella Gumprecht.

1917

1st January, 1917

Take note – New Year! I solemnly write '1917'. Yesterday we celebrated New Year's Eve. Uncle Bruno has not been granted any leave. He has written a long 'Active Service' letter. We were not at the New Year festivities at the station, but celebrated with red currant wine that we had obtained from Frau Annchen Schönfeld. Then we stood at the open window and made a little good luck wish at the passing of the year, raising our glasses and shouting at the top of our voice, 'Here's to the New Year! A good New Year!' I thought of Lieutenant Waldecker too, and whispered 'Best of luck! Best of luck!' You are allowed to wish good luck to a stranger.

3rd January, 1917

How lovely my mother is! I admire and love her because she is so brave. As the times have become so bad and she can no longer earn enough as a singing teacher, she has taken a secretarial job in a Berlin branch of the Dresden Bank. She goes 'to the office', as she says, every day, gets up quite early and has to start work at 8 o'clock on the dot. Then she works until 5 o'clock in the afternoon, travels on the tram to her new little flat in Steglitzer Strasse, eats the supper which she has prepared beforehand, and awaits the few singing pupils. Later on she sinks into bed dog-tired, to be up early again next morning for the office. She does this without complaining. Magnificent! Some of the higher bank officials, who are very polite to her, are almost afraid of her and even help her on with her coat as if she were a Countess.

Mummy is now really afraid that Willi will have to join the Army. Uncle Bruno has become a lieutenant and serves with the 54th Field Artillery Regiment. Willi is to go to Berlin as soon as possible, before he gets his calling-up papers. Mummy hopes, through the von Roszinsky family, to get him accepted into the Cadet Corps. The Roszinskys have a lot of respect for my mother. Then by the time Willi gets his officer's certificate perhaps the war will have ended. Up to now Willi has not yet passed his 'Abitur'. Mummy thinks he could get through that alright in the Cadet Corps.

I am amazed that Mummy wants to keep her youngest son out of war service; she was always such a German patriot and enthusiastic about our Imperial family and the many victories. I cannot imagine Schneidemühl without Willi. Besides, how will it be when he has to part from his 'Empress Charlotte'? Willi is to go to Berlin at Easter at the latest. Hans Androwski, with whom we discuss everything, shook his head and said, 'Oh boy, poor Kuhr! It's crazy!'

Androwski always wants to hear Willi's compositions and my poems. He leans back comfortably in the arm-chair, gazes into space and wears a happy look. I have of course written a number of new poems, sometimes with a melody as well, but I just give them to Gretel. Usually they are lively dance songs and we sing them when we are alone and invent dances for them. The song that we sing and dance most to is called 'Marlene'.

In the meadow did Marlene stand,
A little red rose.
The Junker took her by the hand,
The little red rose.
He said, 'So lovely are your charms,
I long to hold you in my arms.'

'Oh sir, you may not,' Marlene said,
The little red rose,
'At home to a young wife you are wed,
A little red rose.'
But still he said, 'Such are your charms'
... and so on.

It has four verses. but Androwski, regardless of these, declares that I will one day be a writer. But I want to be a dancer. Mummy would really like me to learn to sing, she wants to train my voice for alto parts and later I am to help her with the re-establishment of the singing school. But I have no wish to be a singer or a singing teacher.

On Christmas Eve when we were sitting at the table under the lamp, Mummy read to us a book by Hermann Hesse, 'The Latin

Scholar'. Gretel listened with us too; at the same time she was knitting stockings for Frau Schönfeld's youngest brother Arthur Zühlke, who was wounded on the East front and is in hospital. Arthur sends me regularly from the hospital service post-cards which are very amusing and which I always answer right away; you never know how soon any one who is severely wounded will die.

I write regularly to four front-line soldiers. One of them is still, thank God, the warrior Emil Szagun. I send parcels to all of them. But what really can you send? Perhaps a little of our already scarce sugar, wartime chocolate (awful stuff), cigars (from the Red Cross), articles which we have knitted with war-time wool, post-cards to write, and also pencils, a tooth-brush, whitening for cleaning teeth, horribly scratchy brown green clay soap – and so on. But I think the 'Mushketeers' (as they call themselves half in fun), are pleased simply with the thought from the homeland. They are so brave, so ready to give their lives for the Fatherland without complaining. The Russians would very much like to start a revolution in their country. They would like to see no more men sacrificed, and when I think our heroic airmen Oswald Boelcke and Max Immelmann were also shot down, I can only think as they do – peace. Instead of that the High Command have ordered the formation of German Air Hunter Squadrons. The gas mask has been prescribed for the troops. During attacks the steel helmet must be worn instead of the simple forage-cap and old-style helmet, as it gives better protection against shot. So it's more and more war!

In my wardrobe I secretly preserve the flat Belgian steel helmet of the dead César Glabeke, that Uncle Bruno brought back from the Front. Sometimes I get it out and look at it.

10th January, 1917

Mummy goes back to Berlin to-morrow. Her leave from the office is over.

Yesterday was an interesting day. We had been invited to coffee by the factory owner Herr Gruse. The invitation was especially intended for my mama, the sister of his old friend Dr. Bruno Golz. Uncle Bruno and Herr Gruse have often had philosophical discussions with each other, smoked cigars and talked about books. Besides us several ladies and gentlemen were invited. The servant girl was wearing a black dress, a white lace

217

apron and a white lace cap. Tea was served in really thin cups, and there was chocolate cake and wafer-thin slices spread with smoked salmon. What joy it was! Herr Gruse is just as tall as Uncle Bruno and very elegant. He treated me like a lady and kept putting fresh bits on my plate as if he knew how hungry I was for the lovely things to eat. At the end, when all the people were crowded together in the cloak-room, getting ready to go home, he asked me whether I liked listening to music. I said that my mother, my brother Willi and I positively revelled in music. Then he led me quickly to a wonderful grand piano in the music-room and said that he would one day play something for me, if I liked. He asked what I would most like to hear. I answered, 'Chopin and Schubert.' He said, 'I am glad of that. I will get out Chopin's last Scherzo and some of Schubert's Impromptus.' He added softly, 'I cannot play myself, I haven't the necessary technique. This instrument is a mechanical one. But I can regulate the volume and the tempo according to the composer's directions. The piano is my great joy.' I stammered, 'I can imagine that,' but actually I couldn't imagine it at all. I just cannot picture what a mechanical instrument is; I only know musical-boxes with revolving cylinders, fair organs and gramophones. And of course barrel-organs, which I like terribly. I think it is so amusing when every now and then the air-supply in a barrel-organ gives out and some notes hang as it were in the air. But a mechanical grand piano, that looks just like a real one? I hope Herr Gruse is not just joking, and will really let me hear Chopin and Schubert on it. When I told Mummy about the grand piano, she took a deep breath and said she didn't approve of such an inartistic absurdity. She sat down at once at our piano, placed her lovely, slender hands on the keys and began, 'Do you know the country where the lemons grow?' I joined in immediately; but because I can't sing as high as Mummy, I sang the high notes just an octave lower. Mummy stopped playing after a while and began to laugh. She said, 'Now then, my treasure, we will fix it alright!' I asked in astonishment what she meant. She answered that one day she would train my voice properly in Berlin. Again I thought that I would rather study dancing than singing. I often dance in front of the mirror. My polite brother says indeed that they are contortions, but I shan't give it up. Why has fortune sent me the soldier Glabeke's helmet and Uncle Bruno's army boots? There must be some meaning in it. I have actually told Uncle Bruno that one day I would invent a dance that portrays a soldier rising from the mass grave, or something like that. I don't know yet exactly how I shall do it. In any case I would rather study ballet than singing; but I am not telling Mummy that yet.

Willi drew his chair up close to Mummy and listened in rapture as she went on singing so beautifully. I leaned my head against the back of my chair and listened just as attentively. My mother has a wonderful voice; because of her voice-training she can sing Soprano, Mezzosoprano or Alto equally well. The method of teaching is her own invention.

What lucky people we are!

15th January, 1917

A Russian prince recently murdered the monk Grigorij Jefimowitsch Rasputin. He shot him at a social gathering. Rasputin is said to have been a terrible man, a real Satan, who for years held the whole of the Tsar's court and thousands of people, especially women, under his spell. He was the Tsarina's confessor. Special news sheets came out immediately. People say that revolution will break out soon in Russia. I asked Grandma whether the Russians would then depose Tsar Nicholas. Grandma didn't know and sent me to Richter's shop to get coffee-substitute, oatflakes and semolina on the last coupon of the ration card. I was furious because I wanted to read more of my Christmas book and it was so cold outside. You have to wait ages outside the shops before you get inside. I recently waited an hour and a half outside Rüger's, the butchers, because it was said that they were giving out a bit of sausage. Willi never has to queue; he is so cunning that he always pleads schoolwork as an excuse. I am very bad at deception and would rather get my toes frozen. I have really bad chilblains because my shoes are no good. And I cough too. 'My dainty little sister coughs like an old cab-horse,' piped up Willi.

I became furious and shouted at him, 'Cabbage head! Tell me rather what benefits a revolution will bring, other than bringing the war to and end.'

'Well, the workers and peasants will then have enough to eat.'

'Haven't they enough to eat then?'

'Too little! Too little!' cried Willi.

I think our farmers are poor too, that is the small farmers and the farm-workers. If you go into their houses, you see at once how poor they are. Most of them just have salted potatoes with barley coffee early in the morning. At mid-day they have butter-milk potato soup with baked onions and, if times are good, some baked pork cracklings. In the afternoon a piece of home-made bread with turnip-treacle, which is black like tar, or with a little dripping. In the evening bread and dripping and cracklings again and a plate of potatoes or swedes. Sometimes they fry mush-rooms which they have gathered and beat a few eggs with them because they do always have hens in the garden. The mushrooms taste gorgeous, especially the little 'deer's feet' or morels that grow in the woods around the village of Erpel. I have gathered them myself with our former maid Emma. Our workers likewise earn very little; despite this, they nearly all have a colour-print picture of Emperor Wilhelm and the Imperial family hanging in their rooms. Sometimes the picture is surrounded with a garland. With us the people are nearly all German nationalists, including the poor. Androwski thinks that is because of the nearness of the frontier; national feeling is usually strong in frontier districts, out of fear of the neighbouring country, sometimes from pride as well. I cannot imagine Revolution ever breaking out here in East Germany; we have no Karl Liebnecht and no Rosa Luxemburg here or any one else who would tell the people to revolt.

27th January, 1917

The Emperor's birthday! During a walk to-day over the Baggen, which is uncultivated marsh, I met our former coachman Schulz. He was sitting on a farm-cart drawn by the old brown nag and carrying a load of peat. I was delighted and called out, 'Schulz! Schulz!' He shouted 'Whoa!' and pulled in the reins. He was very pleased too. 'Come up here, young Miss Piete, my child,' he said, and slid along the wooden seat to one side. I climbed up over the front wheel on the cart and pushed up close to our Schulz. He still has the same heavy moustache, though it is now nearly white, and the whole man is smaller and more bent than ever. I noticed too that he was still wearing the ancient brown woollen waistcoat that he used to wear over his blue and white striped shirt in grandfather's time. Mother Schulz has darned it at least a hundred times and knitted new cuffs for the sleeves. It's funny, but I was so pleased that he was wearing this old woollen waistcoat. It was as though it made everything just the same as it used to be when we lived in the white 'Villa Golz' in Zeughausstrasse, with the Schulz's in the coach-house in the yard. At the back of the coach-house was the stable in which our two shiny brown horses usually stood; later it was just one horse. We always had brown horses, the last was a gelding. They were called Hans or Liese.

Next to the stable was the place for the black coach itself, which had blue upholstery and a black leather covering which could be buttoned up. The horses' reins hung there too, black leather for everyday use and white, fine-woven ones for festive occasions.

When I was little I was so fond of Schulz that I was always climbing up the steep steps to his flat, where he lived with Mother Schulz. I really think I was more fond of him than of my own grandfather. Yes, definitely, I liked him better! I used to beg cigars from Grandpa for Schulz and carted cakes, sweets and great pieces of sausage into Schulz's kitchen; I got our maid to cut off the bits of sausage. At Easter I would give him an Easter egg and he would give me a thin white sugar egg with a red or bright blue edge; on the egg there were two sugar doves, these also were pink or sky-blue. I never dared nibble the doves; I always used to hang the egg on the wall above my bed until such time as it broke up or Willi pinched it and ate it up.

Mother Schulz's face is all wrinkled and her cheeks are as red as Christmas apples. She has a married daughter named Gustel Neumann. Gustel was my wet nurse because my mother didn't have time to breast-feed me; she had to manage the music school in Berlin. I loved Gustel too and Gustel loved me. They were happy times.

Now Schulz calls me Miss and addresses me as a grown-up. I am still the 'boss-child' as it is customary to say in the East. But I am anything but a 'personnage'.

When we stopped in front of the archway which leads to Schulz's present flat I jumped down from the box-seat and just quickly greeted Mother Schulz together with Gustel and a troop of children. The eldest of Gustel's children is called Friedchen after me.

In Schulz's parlour there is a life-size oil-painting of my grandfather. I go rigid every time I see Grandpa looking down at me so solemnly. Schulz had asked Grandmother for the picture as a memorial; it has a place of honour over the oil-cloth sofa. Mother Schulz poured me a cup of coffee and was pleased for me to eat a large roll with dripping. It tasted wonderful, just like ham. Then I walked home through the dimly lit town.

221

I long for Mummy. She goes every morning in darkness now to the 'office' instead of her old 'Leading school of drama and music'. I just hope nothing will happen to her!

19th February, 1917

Greta Dalüge and Trude Jakobi called for me to-day to go skating. We arrived at the skating meadow half frozen. It is flooded by the Zgordalina, a little tributary of the Küddow, and frozen over. Sometimes a silvery tuft of grass pokes through the ice; this makes the surface a bit uneven. There are long rows of benches without backs, on which you can sit to fasten your skates. Towards four o'clock in the afternoon the sun was already fiery red and setting. The ice glistened like Grandma's pearls. Many people, muffled up in thick coats, caps and woollen scarves, were skating up and down; the men held their arms folded across their backs; the women and girls sometimes had their hands in muffs, sometimes they skated arm in arm. A lot of girls screamed and went down with a plop. I was about to set off in dashing style, but – whoosh – down I went right at the start. When I tried to stand up my skates failed to grip and I kept on sitting down hard on my 'prime joint'. I was very embarrassed. Greta and Trude laughed out loud, so that I laughed too. They helped me to my feet and supported me, and for a while we got on famously. Greta gave the orders – 'Left – right – left – right!' and we skimmed over the ice. An ancient gramophone scraped out the skaters' waltz. The sun became redder and redder, and our cheeks stung with cold. The girls let me go and I described a breath-taking curve of my own, and then – as the devil would have it – in making just such another breath-taking curve I crashed down on to my rump and slid at least three yards while my left skate shot off my foot. My skate flew out and my left leg went up in the air like the mast of a ship. Someone shouted 'Hullo, young lady!' and there came shooting up to me – Lieutenant Werner Waldecker!

Greta and Trude curled up with laughter; Lieutenant Waldecker laughed too. But I was nearer to crying. I could hardly stand up for pain either; it felt as if my back was broken. Lieutenant Waldecker helped me up and I staggered over the ice to the seat, while he looked for the skate that had flown off me. He said, 'Shall I screw it on again?' I didn't want to make a fool of myself and nodded with clenched teeth. Then I had to give him

222

the skate-key, which I wore on an old black bootlace round my neck; but my fingers were so stiff with cold that I couldn't get it off. He took his fine leather officer's glove off and unfastened it, winking at me and smiling in the process. This made me angry and I cried, 'No! I've had enough! Don't bother about the key. I want to go home.'

'Not without me!' said Lieutenant Waldecker. 'If you really do want to go, we will first go and have some éclairs at Fliegner's!' Greta and Trude immediately wanted to come too, but Lieutenant Waldecker said in a commanding manner, 'Company – right turn! Quick march!', which was as much as to say – 'Come with us? Not on your life!' Then they left us, and skated off laughing with folded arms.

It was nearly dark when we got to Fliegner's, the confectioners; the street lights were already lit. I was suddenly terribly happy. Lieutenant Waldecker found a corner table and hung my skates on a hook next to his. There were no éclairs left. We drank mulled claret and ate sweet cracknels. I told Lieutenant Waldecker about Mummy; he was very interested in her and admired her courage. I asked whether he liked being in the Flying Corps. He answered, 'Very much so,' and I looked at his shoulder-pads and thought that without his finely tailored uniform he might not look so handsome. Suddenly I imagined him crashing in his aeroplane and being killed. Every week indeed some airman crashes near us; they are then taken, accompanied by a military band, either to the war cemetery or to the goods station, where their coffins are sent off to their relatives. I can't bear to hear the funeral marches any more.

Lieutenant Waldecker looked at me and said, 'What is going on in your little head?' I said I had just been thinking about something. Then he wanted to know what it was, but with the best will in the world I couldn't tell him. He took one of my plaits in his hand and untwisted it a bit so that the hair fell over his fingers. 'Dear girl!' he said. 'Such wonderful hair! I should like to see it all undone. May I one day?' I said I really must go home now. He brought me to the door of our house. In the lobby he was suddenly going to kiss me, but it struck me at once that all the lieutenants kiss the girls they take home. So I quickly said, 'Good-bye,' and ran up the steps.

When I got upstairs I pushed away my brother who immediately wanted to lead me to the piano so that he could play to me a new composition, the third 'Reed Song' by Lenau. It was still unfinished and I wasn't at all interested in it at that moment. I would have liked best of all to be alone, turn out the light and think.

Of course I would have liked to let Lieutenant Waldecker kiss me. Very much even! I really was a goose – God, what a goose!

25th February, 1917

Since Rumania entered the war against us we have black, white and red victory flags nearly all over Rumania on our school map. The main Rumanian cavalry force is as good as wiped out. Bucharest fell as early as 6th December. Then at last we had another victory holiday and went for a stroll.

To-day Grandma fainted outside Johr's the horse-meat shop in Alte Bahnhofstrasse. Herr Johr, who is a Jew, and the shop people carried her inside and sat her on a chair. But because she was too weak to stay on it they carried her into Johr's living-room and laid her on a sofa. Then she came round again there. Herr Johr, good man that he is, got his horse harnessed, and drove her home himself. Willi and I were shocked to see Grandma so pale and cold. Frau Schönfeld, who was with us just then, made a cup of coffee and put real sugar in it instead of saccharin. Although there is no more real bean coffee, the heat did Grandma good. She drank the coffee in bed and said, 'Now I am warm again, children.' That made us happy.

I drew the old stool up to Grandma's bed and swotted physics; thus I was able to do my homework and look after her at the same time. I find physics interesting, and chemistry equally; we do crazy experiments at school. However, I like the history of religion and art better than anything except German. And nature study of course. I got 'very good' in these subjects in the Christmas exams.

It will soon be Easter. Then I go up into the first class; that is the last class in the high school. After that there is just the college of higher education, that I have no wish to attend; I don't want to go on studying. What's the point? Especially if I am going to take up an artistic career. The higher education college is for girls who want to become teachers or doctors or something else in the academic line.

26th February, 1917

The papers are full of news about citizens' revolts in Russia. Willi shouted, 'This is the Revolution!' and ran off at once to

Androwski. I whistled out of the window for Gretel. She looked out through her door and I was astonished to see that she was holding in her arms her old celluloid doll with fair curly hair. I particularly wanted to talk to her about the revolution in Russia, but then I thought 'God, she is still little', and she asked whether we were going to play upstairs in my place; we do still play at Nurse Martha and Lieutenant von Yellenic. She came upstairs at once, but neither of us looked at the doll any more. It sat stiffly on the window-sill.

We played at revolution. Lieutenant von Yellenic had to return at once to the Russian Front, because the military situation in the East had become uncertain. That was in our game anyway. The train came in (that was Grandma's bed), I swung on to the foot-board of the carriage (actually the bed-rail) and held my hand for some time to the peak of my cap (my temple) in a military salute. Nurse Martha ran along the train waving and shouting a fond farewell – 'Good luck to you again, Lieutenant von Yellenic. God preserve you! Come back again safe and sound!' She was actually nearly crying.

27th February, 1917

The Russian workers and peasants have seized the fortress of St. Peter & St. Paul in St. Petersburg and set fire to the Palace of Justice. Special news-sheets were on sale in Zeughausstrasse. I hadn't a single farthing in my pocket, but Grandma had heard all about it from the soldiers at the station. She said that many soldiers gave a cheer and had danced Cossack dances on the platform. Fräulein Ella Gumprecht, who has become accustomed to come regularly and punctually for coffee, said that it was a disgrace and a scandal and that these soldiers ought to be arrested on the spot. 'Weren't any officers there?' she cried indignantly. Grandma said that there were some officers there and that they had given sharp orders. Beyond that she knew nothing.

This year I join the confirmation class under Superintendent Schammer. Dear God, we are getting more and more grown up. One thing is certain; Willi will be called up this year if he can't soon get into the cadet school. Mummy has already sent a request to the grammar school asking for Willi to be allowed to leave at Easter. She said that Willi was moving to Berlin. Mummy and the 'von Roszinsky' family have managed to arrange for my brother to secure a place in the Corps. What will it be like when my brother goes away and I no longer hear him playing the piano? The house will be empty. Thank God I still have Gretel and my school friends, especially Connie. At Easter there are to be many new girls; it's very exciting. Our class is doing better and better. According to the teachers we are a particularly cheeky class, but Fräulein Becker says we are just at the stage of 'developing our personalities'; I think that is frightfully good. Jolly decent!

16th March, 1917

Russia no longer has a royal family. On 2nd March Tsar Nicholas 'surrendered the throne', as it says in the paper. A so-called 'Provisional Government' has been formed.

Androwski came in, crimson with joy, threw himself into the chair at Willi's writing-table, and cried, 'Boy, oh boy, it's said that the Russian soldiers have formed a brotherhood with the peasants and those who don't want any more war! They have distributed their weapons among the civilians. If only they can carry it through!'

I was open-mouthed. I just asked, 'Will Willi now not have to go to Berlin to join the cadets?'

Willi, quite pale, was standing next to Androwski. 'I shall still be going to Berlin!'

'Whatever are you going to do there if the Russians pull out of the war?' I said angrily.

Willi thought the Entente would go on fighting even if the Revolution in Russia led to peace in the East.

I squatted on the carpet near to Androwski and asked him what would happen to the Royal Family. Androwski looked at me through his round spectacles and said quite calmly, 'They will be shot.'

My heart began to beat like mad; I really thought I would drop down dead. Instead of that I suddenly saw a bright red light in front of me; I stood up and felt as if I had no more life in me. Androwski asked a question. I burst out: 'They mustn't shoot those who are responsible for the war. That is just like an act of war – to shoot!'

'Oh?' said Androwski, and he too stood up. 'And what should the people do with the guilty ones in your opinion?'

I felt still more like a spirit between heaven and earth and said, 'They should set them to work in the fields like the peasants.'

'You are crazy!', cried Willi. 'What on earth are you thinking about? Them with their millions! Don't you know that the Tzarina said that the Russian people will only work under the whip? What do you think of that? Can a nation put up with such treatment?'

I couldn't think what to say. I am not yet quite fifteen years old. How can I know whether the Royal family should be shot? According to Jesus you definitely shouldn't shoot them. 'Thou shalt not kill!' Definitely!

18th March, 1917

Tsar Nicholas and the Tsarina Alexandra have been arrested.

19th March, 1917

We have only a few potatoes in the cellar now. When we come to the end of those, what then?

Grandpa's former builder Tiedtke has chopped some wood for us in the shed; he earns a little this way. Grandma always adds a few potatoes for his sick wife, who has for years been confined to bed. To-day she could only say, 'Here is the money for your wood-chopping, Tiedtke, but I have no more potatoes to give you, or I shan't have enough for the children.'

Tiedtke answered, 'That's a'reet, Missus. Us can manage wi'out tatties.'

The families in Germany live mainly on turnips. We in the East call the turnips swedes. Grandma always puts carraway seed on the swedes. I can't help it – I like eating swedes, but I hardly dare admit it. Everybody complains about the turnips. Anything that has any nutritional value at all finds its way into the soup kitchen for the soldiers. Just what do the 45,000 prisoners in the Russian camps eat, that's what I'd like to know? Gretel and I still go past the camp sometimes and quietly put a few eatables through the fence, when the guards are looking the other way. I think they look the other way on purpose. In any case we have never been stopped again.

I always look into the prams when mothers with their infants have to stand in queues at the shops. Oh, such pitiful-looking babies! How will the mothers produce milk in their breasts when they themselves go hungry? The poor little mites sometimes look as if they are at death's door. I have indeed thought that next

227

year, when I leave school, I will take a course in the care of infants and children in the new municipal babies' home, just for the sake of helping these children a bit. I can't go straight to Mummy in Berlin because I am too young; I shall be staying another year in Schneidemühl – that is, if we are still alive. The war goes on in spite of the Revolution in Russia. The American President Wilson and Pope Benedict XV wanted to mediate between the warring powers. But what have they achieved? The Entente demands of Germany that our Alsace-Lorraine should belong to France because the Alsatians speak French more than German. In addition, the German army would have to surrender in spite of its victories. The German High Command would never agree to that. Diplomatic relations between America and Germany have been broken off. Emperor Wilhelm has had no luck with his peace offer either. Our enemies believed the German government just wanted to mislead them. The situation has deteriorated all round.

20th March, 1917

This letter came to-day from Mummy for Grandma:

'Dearest Mamma! I am writing in great haste! I enclose a specimen application for Willi's entry into the Cadet Corps, of which he should immediately write a fair copy on best quality paper. He need not now send the fair copy. He can bring it with him. He should get on with writing it at once, so that he can work on it quietly and not in the tumult of his departure. You don't need to send bed-linen with him, Mamma. But if at all possible, get him to bring some bread. Otherwise there will be a panic in the first week. It is Saturday to-day. I came to the end of my bread yesterday. There are only three thin slices for me to take to the office for breakfast on Monday morning. Could he also possibly bring a pound of sugar? And a little fat. Those are the three most pressing needs. I will expect Willi in the course of next Sunday, mid-day or in the afternoon. I must close now – the office break is over. So no more for to-day. Heaps of love!'

Then there was a postscript –

'The office irks me terribly. But I *must* cope with it. I *will* cope with it.'

I had to read the letter out loud to Grandma because her eyes have got worse and she couldn't make out Mummy's thin pencilled writing. The letter was scrawled on the back of a sheet of official paper with the printed heading –

'Enquiry into the safeguarding of children's milk supplies. Provision for households with children up to 14 years of age (born after 3rd November 1901)'

Below this it read –

'Do you obtain milk direct from a cow-shed within the Greater Berlin area? If so, from which one?'

It struck me as quite funny that there should be a cow-shed even in Greater Berlin.

My brother must now leave Schneidemühl or he will be called up for military service immediately. He has already got his leaving permit from Schneidemühl Grammar School. In the words of one of his compositions, 'It is just as if it didn't exist . . . '

Easter 1917

The place is empty. I took Willi to the station. He carried a big card-board suit-case. This is new and looks like leather. Grandma tied a washing-line round it as a precaution against it bursting open. Willi's suits, underwear, shoes, books and writing materials are packed in the suit-case. Grandma also added a whole loaf of bread, some sugar, fat, a horse-meat sausage, a pound of semolina, a pound of flour, and a packet of home-roasted barley-coffee, as well as six hard-boiled eggs that Connie's mother gave us for Willi. The train left for Berlin. It was all black. There were lots of soldiers on the train, and as it drew out they sang 'In the homeland, in the homeland, there we'll meet again!'

I didn't cry. I ran quite a way alongside the train, as it departed with my dear brother. The 'Field-greys' laughed when they saw me running like that, and shouted 'Hey, little miss, mind you don't fall! Hey, Missy, little sister!'

When I couldn't run any further, Willi and I waved to each other until he was out of sight. I shouted. 'Wave to Androwski, he is standing on the station bridge!'

Willi looked up at the bridge where our friend Androwski was standing and waved frantically. The train thundered under the bridge and I saw Androwski run to the other side. Then the train went on round the curve and was gone. Dear old Gil!!!

229

25th April, 1917

On the 6th April America declared war on Germany. That too now! Our soldiers had earlier chalked up on some railway coaches, 'Declarations of War accepted here!' We could easily have dropped down dead with excitement. The trade unions are now calling for strikes. There is even said to be some student unrest.

I am fifteen years old to-day. My brother wrote me a lovely letter.

9th May, 1917

I haven't yet said that I am now in the top class of the Empress Augusta Victoria School. We have received many new pupils; most of them are from the country. We 'old girls' were at first curious, but now we have made good friends with the new ones. I particularly like Irmgard Kenzler from the Adlig Liebenthal domain, a manorial estate near Erpel. Irma has a cherry-heart mouth and laughing dark eyes; everyone falls in love with her. The most interesting of the new arrivals is Miriam Borchardt from Deutsch-Krone; her father is an African explorer. Miriam has long flowing brown hair, a high forehead and looks like a classical painting. Her eyes are large and serious. She comes from a very rich house and possesses a real organ on which she plays Bach, Corelli and Pergolesi. But mostly Bach. I was struck dumb with amazement when I heard that she plays on her own organ. There is another of the new girls that I like – Martha Zwieg from Flatow. She keeps looking at me. We will certainly become friends. But my best friend is still Connie with the flaxen hair. The other day during the English lesson, when it got deadly boring, Connie and I plaited our long pig-tails together, and then the teacher suddenly asked me a question. As I had to stand up Connie was of course forced to stand up as well, so there we were, standing at the desk with our heads fastened together at an angle. The class soon died with laughter but we got a black mark in the class book for 'gross misbehaviour'.

Irma Kenzler wants me to go to the Liebenthal Estate with her to get to know her family. But I would rather get to know about the running of the estate, the cow-sheds, the teams of horses and the fields. Herr Kenzler employs young trainees and an overseer. For Irma's young brothers and sisters there is a young governess living in. She is said to be exceedingly nice. When I asked Irma whether they still had enough to eat at Liebenthal, she laughed and said, 'On a big estate like that?' So it is a definite 'yes'!

12th May, 1917

Our form mistress is also a new arrival in Schneidemühl. She used to teach in Allenstein, East Prussia, and she is called Assistant Teacher Fräulein Olga Kutschelis. She has brown eyes and pinned-up dark hair. It will be exciting to see how an unknown form mistress turns out. We are in any case glad to be rid of our strict form mistress of the second form.

But what about this? When Fräulein Kutschelis was entering our names for the first time in the form register and I gave my name, she stopped short and asked casually, 'what did you say your name is?' I stood to attention and announced meekly, 'Elfriede Kuhr, known as Piete.' Fräulein Kutschelis looked me straight in the face before writing down my name. She smiled a little. It is obvious to me that the Head had warned her about me. Fräulein Kutschelis looked at me again and said, 'Why are you still standing up, Elfriede? Please sit down.'

It was only then that I realised that I was still standing at my desk and that she was staring at me. It seemed to me absolutely wonderful. I knew at once that I would love this form mistress. You sense such things immediately.

Lessons with her are interesting. She gets us to take different parts in reading classical authors. For instance we are at present reading Goethe's Hermann and Dorothea. At first you feel a bit awkward, but you soon get used to it as if you are standing on a stage. It even becomes good fun. For the first time I don't find a classical author boring.

But when Fräulein Kutschelis asked us the other day what were our favourite books and Mirian Borchardt said in a saintly voice 'Goethe's Iphigenie', I was annoyed at such grand speaking. I thought that Goethe's Iphigenie couldn't possibly be a favourite book at our age. I considered frantically what I should say, and when Fräulein Kutschelis asked me for my favourite book, I blurted out, 'Tom Sawyer and Huckleberry Finn by Mark Twain'. The class burst out laughing; Fräulein Kutschelis shook her head a little and smiled. I would have liked best to say, 'I read Friedrich Nietzsche and Hermann Hesse and poems by Nikolaus Lenau and Storm and Eichendorff'. But what would be the point?

231

15th May, 1917

A letter to Willi.

'Dear Senor Guillermo Gutierrez Golaz of Schneidemühl,

It is really lonely just now. Yesterday and to-day I have been mending curtains. Because I miss you I have annexed some of your belongings – among other things, your arm-chair. It stands now in front of my writing-table, which is not a writing-table at all. And then I write on your writing-case, which I treat like biscuit-ware. I have polished it with shoe-wax, and now it shines like new. I haven't touched the piano since you left. Sometimes I hum your songs a little. Write to me often, won't you?

I have been praised at school and in Art History I got a two-plus for the Pyramids and the Fields of Death at Memphis. I wonder if I shall ever go there?

I have been for the first time to-day to the confirmation class with Superintendent Schammer. It was a frightful bore; I nearly went to sleep and kept looking out of the window where the weather was at its best. If it continues like this it will be alright. My faith has been on wobbly legs ever since they started praying 'God send victory to our forces!'

Lotte Voss is now wearing a red dress with her red hat. She walks to and fro arm in arm with her friend Minneritati. She recently wanted to know from me what Androwski said about her. I lied that I had no idea; I am definitely not going to betray our friend. Otherwise she is the same as ever. I think she could at least ask how you are getting on. Have you now been admitted into the cadet officers? You don't write anything about the cadet establishment. Why not? Do tell us about it.

Something else that is new; it is Spring! The chestnut trees in Alte Bahnhofstrasse have got tiny little green leaves. There ought not to be any war in Springtime!

I can't help thinking all the time that it is wonderful beyond measure for you to be in Berlin with Mummy. Androwski and Andreas Zorn send you greetings as to their old friend. I cautiously send you a kiss, Senor Guillermo Gutierrez Golaz, known as Gil! Your loving sister, Piete.'

13th June, 1917

Grandma's birthday. Gretel and I extended the dining-table on both sides and covered it with an enormous damask cloth. Then we laid out the best service with the little swallow pattern and folded serviettes for sixteen people. Frau Schönfeld made lots of coffee. We had previously baked little cakes sprinkled with artificial nuts and chocolate cakes. We had eked out the artificial nuts with grated boiled potato; it tasted like real. A war-time recipe. Many guests came. The ladies appeared by arrangement with bunches of roses. Old Professor Zerbst, who always used to give Willi and me sticky sweets out of a tin which he pulled out of his coat pocket, was there too. The sweets were quite hot from his body and Willi and I were frightfully nauseated, but were too polite to say 'No thank you', and stuck the sweets in our mouths, to be spat out later on. Thank God the Professor spares us his gifts now that we are grown up.

The talk at the table was about the Revolution in Russia. Fräulein Emma Gumprecht said in a loud voice: 'Have you heard that that red swine Lenin has turned up in Petersburg? He was in Switzerland, in Zürich, if I am not mistaken. Now I just wonder how the rogue got through the Front to Petersburg!'

One lady suggested that General Ludendorff had sent him into Russia in a sealed carriage so that he could more quickly make peace. That aroused Fräulein Gumprecht's anger. She adores General Ludendorff nearly as much as Chief of Staff General Paul von Hindenburg and she nearly upset her coffee-cup as she cried, 'Never! Never on your life! That is a lie! Our Ludendorff would never do a thing like that!'

There was a great uproar at the table; everyone was shouting and talking at the same time. Fat old Frau Leonhard, whom I like very much, folded her hands across her stomach, and asked genially, 'Now, children, do tell me, whoever is reigning in Russia?'

Only Professor Zerbst knew the answer. He placed his pince-nez on his nose and said, 'A man called Kerenski. He is the Minister for War and is mobilising fresh forces against us.'

That gave rise to further indignation. Fräulein Gumprecht completely forgot what she had said against the 'red swine', and cried: 'Yes, what's the use of this fellow Lenin, whom Ludendorff is supposed to have sent to Petersburg, if he allows Kerenski or whatever his name is to build up new Russian armies? He should at least be making peace!'

All the ladies accepted this and nodded their heads emphatically. I thought Fräulein Gumprecht so comical that I fled to the kitchen to join Frau Schönfeld and Gretel and cried with laughter.

233

20th June, 1917

This war is a spectre in grey rags, a death's head out of which maggots crawl. Fresh heavy fighting has been raging for months in the West. There are the battles of the Chemin-des-Dames, the Aisne and in Champagne. The whole area is in ruins, blood and slime everywhere. The English have launched a horrible new weapon – armoured vehicles on rollers, that surmount every obstacle. These war-machines are called 'tanks'. Nothing is safe before them; they roll over and flatten every gun-battery, every trench, every position, to say nothing of soldiers. Anyone wanting to take refuge in a shell-hole has no chance any more. Then the accursed poison-gas. The English and the French don't yet have any really gas-proof masks with oxygen supplies like the German soldiers. But there is also a poison gas that eats into uniforms. What a way to die! We have retreated to our 'Siegfried Line', but have first, for strategic reasons, laid waste all the area surrendered. I am so sorry for the earth, I mean simply the natural surroundings. What have they done? Why do we destroy them?

When I asked Superintendent Schammer about this in the Confirmation Class, he said, 'We must entrust ourselves in all humility to God, my child. He will make everything alright in the end.'

I said. 'Where is God then? He can't help seeing what mankind is doing. Surely he can't remain silent.'

Superintendent Schammer gave me an answer that I can't begin to accept. What he said was, 'Don't keep questioning, dear child, but *believe!* Believe! That is everything!'

14th July, 1917

Gil's Birthday. I crochetted for him a white tie out of linen thread which I took from a torn bed-sheet. And I bought a whole lot of music paper. He has never written one word about it, although he still sometimes composes a song. But, dear diary, the matter of the top-notch Cadet Officer School is a great wash-out, just as Fritz Zühlke once foretold. Because my brother is not an aristocrat, it was politely suggested to Mummy that she should take her son back. And the recommendations of the Roszinsky family counted for nothing. I think this was a great blow to Mummy. She is so distinguished, much more aristocratic than ten dozen noblewomen put together. And now this!

But the stay in Berlin has actually been of some use. Through Mummy's intervention Willi has been provisionally registered unfit for war service because he retains a weak heart resulting from his former scarlet fever. It says also on the certificate that he has 'water on the knees'. Now to my joy Willi is coming back to swot for his school-leaving exam. He will go back to the Grammar School to his well-liked Professor Philipp. They are both friends. I think the relationship is similar to mine with Assistant Mistress Fräulein Kutschelis. We idolize her, I most of all. Because of our strong affection for her we have become a model class and swot like mad. For my last paper I again had a 'very good'.

To my horror Mummy has asked in a letter about my war diary. I can't possibly show her what I am writing. But I realise my shortcomings. Thus I haven't yet mentioned that nearly all the world has now declared war on us, for example Greece. We had always thought that Greece was our friend. Throughout Germany we respect Greece; the humanistic grammar schools bear witness to that. The Greek King Constantine has left his country; he probably didn't want war with Germany.

Now detachments of troops are off again; the station is full of soldiers; once more I drag buckets of coffee around and help serve soup. There is billeting in the town. We have a major and his batman. The batman sleeps in the attic, the Major in Willi's room, which is now empty. He is an elderly man and looks a bit like Uncle Bruno. He looked around in Willi's room, spotted Grandpa's classical library, pulled out a volume of Kleist and asked whether he could read it. Then he hit upon the story 'The Earthquake in Chile' and settled down with it in the corner of the sofa. 'You don't know,' he said to me, 'what it means to an old soldier to sit in the corner of a sofa and read Kleist.'

'Oh yes!' I said, 'I know exactly.'

'How do you know that?' he asked with a laugh.

I told him that I knew how the soldiers suffer, that we constantly have transports passing through here, including wounded. Moreover the Front was at one time quite near; even now we still have old barbed wire entanglements behind the town. There are also many military hospitals in Schneidemühl which I visit. I have indeed seen many wounded and dead. I also said that besides our 149th Infantry Regiment we had a Territorial Reserve battalion and airmen and airship crews. The airship 'Schütte-Lanz' had at one time come down over

Schneidemühl and a soldier of the ground staff who was clinging to the mooring-rope crashed on to the fence of the grammar school and the points of the iron railings pierced the middle of his body. I said too that a large number of aircraft crashed here because they had been imperfectly constructed. And that the soldiers now all looked wretched and dirty and had tatty uniforms and only one wish, to be able to go home. I carried on just like a book without any punctuation marks – full stops, commas or dashes – and also said the soldiers often told me about their experiences at the Front.

'It is one's patriotic duty not to talk about experiences at the Front,' said the major after listening seriously to me. 'If soldiers want to talk to you about the Front, please tell them that they are giving away military secrets and that is a punishable offence.'

I exclaimed that the soldiers must certainly not tell what it looked like at the Front; I knew that alright. And that it was important for me to know everything because I had been writing a diary of the war since 1914 at the instance of my mother. I told him also that my brother calls me Pliny in fun, after Pliny the historian. The Major laughed out loud at this and asked if he could see the war diary some time. But I didn't want to give it to him. He suddenly gave a deep sigh, and said, 'Yes, yes, the war!' and put the volume of Kleist back with the other books. 'What could you recommend for me?' he said, pointing to the rows of books.

I was dismayed because I had probably spoiled his enjoyment of 'Earthquake in Chile' and stammered, 'You wouldn't just as soon read fairy tales?'

'Fairy tales?' he said, looking at me in astonishment.

I pulled out a volume of Hans Andersen's fairy tales and said it was a very valuable first edition. The major smiled again at last, cried 'Marvellous!' and sat down with the book in the old sofa-corner. Then he said, 'Now tell me, which fairy-tale should I read; I'm not very conversant with them these days.' I quickly suggested half a dozen tales. The Major suddenly looked completely happy. To-morrow he must be off to the Front with his regiment. He couldn't say which Front of course, but it is quite obvious that he is bound for the new Balkan Front.

15th July, 1917

It is summer holidays. Saying good-bye to the class affected me badly, to Fräulein Kutschelis especially. Six long weeks! Fortunately I have invitations from several friends, from Connie to Studsin near Kolmar, from Irma Kenzler to the Adlig domain at Liebenthal and even from the organist Miriam Borchardt to Deutsch-Krone.

I like being with the Conitz family. I am always so happy there. The jolly Mother Conitz, who is so like Connie. But Connie's father too is a dear man. At home he usually wears a straw-coloured peaked cap and a light cloth jacket; he always has a tobacco-pipe in his mouth. He has dark, almost black, hair and dark eyes like his eldest daughter Gertrude. I don't think I have ever seen such a beautiful girl as Gertrude; tall and slim, with a skin like porcelain. And she is so placid! Connie has confided in me that her sister has a great sorrow: her fiancé has been killed in the war. But Trudy doesn't speak of him and his name isn't mentioned at home, because it would be painful for her.

The teacher Conitz is a silent man. In the morning he gets on his old bicycle and cycles to school with the pipe in his mouth. Frau Conitz and Trudy meanwhile look after the fruit and vegetable garden. They have a cow called Ceres who gives good milk. Trudy and Connie churn the milk into butter in a tall, narrow wooden vessel; the butter-milk remaining is lovely and rich. But best of all are the little bowls of thick milk, with a yellow skin like cream, on which we spread black bread-crumbs and sugar.

Connie's father has many beehives made of woven straw in the corner of the garden near the black-currant and gooseberry bushes. When he is working with his bees he wears a gauze mask with a leather neck-shield and extra gloves. He is surprised that the bees don't sting me. They even crawl over my bare arms and sometimes buzz around my head, but they do me no harm. I move carefully if they settle on me and I enjoy it.

I have already milked Ceres, but I cannot do it well. At one time I accidentally got the stream of milk right in my face. How they laughed at me – especially Frau Conitz.

On one evening walk we passed an enormous field of potatoes; they were in full flower. One section had bright violet flowers, another white ones. The evening sun stood behind the field and cast long rays across the sky. Then Frau Conitz spread her arms, took a deep breath, and cried, 'Look at those potato flowers, girls – how beautiful!' I have seen thousands of flowering potato fields in my life, but never before realised that they could be beautiful. Now I suddenly found that they are beautiful, just as Frau Conitz

237

said. I was quite astonished at the beauty of the potato-flowers. Frau Conitz bent down and picked some white and lilac flowers and fastened them on my chest. I shall never forget that.

The last time I was at Connie's, the teacher's house was full of billetees; Connie's cousin Kürdchen and two young officers. One is a lieutenant who has red hair, light eye-lashes and freckles, and is in love with Connie; his name is Lieutenant Pruss. The other officer is tall, dark and thin. He is always looking at the beautiful Gertrude. Cousin Kürdchen is an infantry man; he is going to be a teacher. I think he is a little in love with me.

In the evening we play round games. This is the fashion everywhere in the war; hardly have a few young people got together when – round games! The loser has to give a forfeit to the forfeit-holder, we say; a ring or a bracelet or a pencil. Later on the 'judge' is appointed. Then the forfeit-holder takes one of the forfeits out of the basket and says to the judge, 'Your worship.' The judge answers, 'Who is speaking?' Then the forfeit-holder says, 'What is the owner of this forfeit in my hand to do?' The judge can then impose any duty that he likes, without knowing who the victim is. For example, 'He is to hop round the table three times on one leg.' Or (what is still more difficult), 'He is to go out into the street and make a bow to the first person he meets.' But he might also say, 'He is to go down on one knee before so and so and kiss him.' The latter is the favourite. Every one must do as the judge says. One time when the dark lieutenant had to kneel in front of Trudy and give her a kiss, Trudy laughed and turned her head, saying, 'I'm not kissing any one.' Then she had to go into the corner and stand 'in shame' for a minute, and then eventually allow herself to be kissed. It is war-time after all and young folk want to enjoy themselves while they have the chance to do so. (Foreign word – chance! But who thinks of that nowadays?)

17th July, 1917

Mummy and Willi have returned from Berlin to-day. Grandma has in all haste got the Major's room ready for Mummy. The major and his batman have left. I have put clean sheets on the bed for Mummy. Willi will sleep on the veranda; we have put a chaise-longue there. 'Hans Andersen's Fairy Tales' were still lying on Willi's roll-top bureau. The major had placed a lime-leaf between the pages as a book-mark; he had actually read 'The Story of the Christmas Tree'.

Mummy and Willi look pitifully pale and thin; they must have had less to eat in Berlin than we have. But Grandma said cheerfully, 'I will soon feed you up again.' There was presently a thick pea soup for supper with potatoes and a few lumps of fat. Willi told us about the Cadet Officer School. Later he said to me on the quiet, 'Am I glad to be away from there! So far as they were concerned, I was just a shoeblack!'

I am furious. My brother! (The bastards! Excuse me!)

22nd July, 1917

Willi has just paraded in front of his 'Empress Charlotte's window, but she didn't put in an appearance. He sent her his composition, 'I am the monk Baltramus', which he wrote out really beautifully and embellished with a dedication. When he met her at length in Güterbahnhofstrasse, she shook hands in an embarrassed manner and said, 'I thank you for the song!' Willi suggested a walk in the municipal park, but she made the excuse of having school-work to do. Typical Imperial behaviour! It is holiday-time. What school-work can she have!

Mummy is sitting in the summer-house writing articles about the art of singing.

I am pining for Fräulein Kutschelis, who has gone off God knows where. It is some comfort for me to go for a walk with Willi and Androwski. I am writing a letter to my old friend Dora Haensch. Dora writes to say that her father may perhaps take over the canteen at Schneidemühl railway workshops, which lie at the other end of the town near Meveshoh. Oh yes, more good news! Prince is back. Prince, the doberman, who was enrolled for medical duty. 'He keeps creeping into the stable,' says Dora. 'You wouldn't recognise him, he is very shy, and if any one cracks a whip, his whole body trembles. He really thinks it is a shot.'

30th July, 1917

I must add that our Reich Chancellor Von Bethmann Hollweg is no longer Reich Chancellor. He asked Emperor Wilhelm for his release because General Fieldmarschal Von Ludendorff was going to resign his post in the Army Supreme Command if Bethmann Hollweg continued as Chancellor. Emperor Wilhelm naturally gave priority to the Army and dropped the Reich

Chancellor. Ludendorff wants to carry on the war unconditionally and not surrender an inch of German territory. One Dr. Michaelis is now the new Reich Chancellor, he was formerly responsible for food supplies in Prussia.

A terribly confused situation! Our forces have, in support of the Austrians, repelled the Russians who had resumed an offensive. Our dear brothers-in-arms are truly in a fix, but we are in the same fix in the West, for the Tommies in Flanders are fighting dreadful battles with superior equipment. The newspapers speak of mass attacks at Langemarck and Verdun. It is Verdun again and again! Whenever I hear the name, I think immediately of a waste of shell-holes in which one dead man's skeleton leans against others. No trees left, no bushes, no grass, no flowers, no birds, no habitation.

We simply see the soldiers coming to and fro between Schneidemühl and the Front! They are so dirty and quite unshaven and haggard. None of them complain. They just crowd around the Red Cross coffee-urn, or preferably swallow spoonfuls of our thick soup and great chunks of bread and dripping, or sometimes just dry bread if we haven't any dripping.

1st August, 1917

Mummy asked, 'How is the diary going?' I said, I still put down the most important things but didn't get much pleasure out of writing. 'Stick at it,' said Mummy severely. Then we all laughed, because Willi got back on to his 'Pliny' theme. It was a sultry evening; we were half asleep. Mummy had just taken her shoes off and was enjoying the feel of the cool ground against her bare soles.

Suddenly she stood still as if fixed to the wall, pulled a face, went white as chalk and began to limp. She quickly crumpled up with pain and took her foot in her hand. 'Children,' she said calmly, 'I have just trodden on a nail! It's gone right in!' And then she repeated: 'A nail! Gone right in!'

Willi and I were scared stiff. I rushed up to Mummy, knelt down on the ground and carefully took hold of her foot. It was such a lovely, dainty foot with quite red nails. I had never seen Mummy's foot bare before. What did I see between two toes that had curled themselves right up with pain? A pea! I picked the pea out, held it up high, swung it to and fro in front of Mummy's eyes and whispered in the same tone of voice as Mummy's, 'A nail, children! Right in!'

240

We laughed till we cried. Long after we had gone to bed I heard Mummy laughing in her room.

3rd August, 1917

Our new bomber squadrons have bombed London and some other English towns. The High Command has ordered that we should keep building faster war-planes. The Zeppelins are no longer viable; because of their size and their inflammability they are too easy a target for the enemy. The American forces are now fighting in all the Western theatres of war, but they don't seem to be good soldiers. It is said that when young Americans are taken prisoner they are like big children. Very naive.

The Russians are making things difficult for Germany. Kerenski, who is now the first Minister for War of 'Red Russia' has re-organised the completely shattered Russian army and sent it into action against us. It is said that many of our soldiers, and even more of the Austrians are going over to the Reds. German sailors have mutinied, but the mutiny has been quelled. Who would ever have thought that German sailors would mutiny – the Fleet, our Emperor's pride.

Fräulein Ella Gumprecht refused to believe it all. She says it is lies put out by 'the Left' to undermine the good spirit of the German fighting forces. 'Our soldiers and sailors fight to the last drop of blood,' she said.

But Irma's mother, Frau Kenzler, wife of the Lord of the Manor of Liebenthal, once said to me when we were together in her room reading news of victories, 'The reds are our only salvation! They will put an end to this mad slaughter. I tell all our people that they should vote "left".'

I looked at her in amazement and stammered 'Does Herr Kenzler think – I mean – does your husband – oh, I beg your pardon! I mean –' Then Frau Kenzler interrupted me and said sadly, 'Ah, my child, no one here thinks like that. What can be done! You had better keep quiet about what I have said to you'.

'Yes,' I said.

Frau Kenzler kissed me and I tried to get back quickly to the stables and the foal's paddock. Hans Androwski had never dared to say anything like that. When Willi, he and I discuss the Revolution in Russia, Androwski says he doesn't think it is a proper revolution. A proper revolution would have immediately put an end to the war. But Kerenski is even mobilising fresh

241

forces. That is 'Betrayal of the working-classes'.

I don't understand much about the revolution and the working-classes. I just always feel sorry for the soldiers, the wounded and those who have to die. How many millions have there been already? I don't know, no one knows. And the horses get shot in great numbers, and poor dogs like Prince tremble when a farmer cracks his whip.

10th August, 1917

Mummy's holiday from the office is over. She has gone away again. Her work in the bank has begun again for her. No more of the former 'Leading School of Music and Drama'. Farewell, Mummy, farewell!

Willi and I stroll past the knacker's yard and ask the knacker whether he has any horse-meat to sell. There is no fresh meat there. Moreover there is a terrible stink in the knacker's yard and great fat blue flies swarm around. I like the knacker. He is a quiet, tall man with brown eyes. I think he is a Pole.

20th August, 1917

Dear Diary, I must tell you something that really shook me. I came back from a walk to-day as it was getting dark. I went up the stairs, opened the door into the hall and crept on tip-toe into the kitchen to see on the quiet what food I could lay my hands on. There I saw an old woman sitting on the coal-box crying; she was sitting all bunched up, her head on her knees and her hands covering her face. Her thin white hair was gathered into a meagre bun and she looked so hopeless, so terribly sad, like the refugee women from East Prussia, who used to pass along Zeughausstrasse, and she seemed lost. I didn't recognise the woman on the coal-box at first. Suddenly I realised it was Grandma. I was paralysed with shock; then I crept quietly out and back to the front door. Outside I acted as if I was running up the stairs whistling loudly. I deliberately made quite a lot of noise, called out 'Grannie, I'm hungry!' and rang the door bell to give her time. Grandma acted as if nothing had happened. She just said, 'The door wasn't locked, child!' I pretended to be surprised, and said, 'I hadn't noticed. I am so hungry. Can I bake some potatoes?'

'Oh,' said Grandma, 'the potatoes are all gone. I've only a

242

crust of bread and a few apples.' I said that that would be wonderful, I was just dying for bread with apple.

I shall never forget how Grandma sat on the coal-box crying. And I have often behaved so badly to her, and when Willi and I were alone we have referred to her as 'the old girl', or 'Oldie', because at school everything is so up-to-date. Oh Grandma! I do so love you!

Now I can't help crying myself.

2nd September, 1917

In Russia everyone is fighting every one else. Germans and Austrians against Russians, and Russians against Russians. All the Russians who still support the Tsar and the Tsarist régime throw themselves in unison like tigers upon the 'Reds', who are for socialism. The Cossacks, loyal to the Tsar, fight most fiercely of all. The Russians are mutually destroying themselves after we have forced the Kerenski army back behind the Sereth.

Everything is going to pieces on the Italian Front. The Italians lost thousands of dead and hundreds of prisoners at the Isonzo.

I don't know whether I have already written that now in France a General Pétain has taken over the Supreme Command of the French troops. I am no longer particularly interested in that, but Mummy insists that our descendants must be informed about everything. Then they must also be informed that Willi and I pinched some potatoes on the marshes to-day. Willi stuffed his trouser pockets full and I stuck them under my sailor's blouse; I looked as if I was with child.

I must confess something else. Gretel and I recently from sheer greed stole from Frau Zahl in the baker's shop. Some kind of delicious-looking sugar-snails were laid out there; they made both our mouths water. When Frau Zahl went into the back room for a moment, I seized a snail as quick as lightning and hid it in my old shopping-bag. Then Gretel did the same, quick as the wind; so we had two. Frau Zahl didn't notice anything and we ate the snails later in the summer-house. With delight! We kept gazing at each other and laughing as we ate. We felt no remorse at all. As I was licking my fingers, each tasting better than the other, I said to Gretel, pointing to myself, 'Look – a snail-eater!' Gretel clapped loudly and said, 'we children have got to look after our nourishment.' I am of course no longer a child, and stealing is still stealing. Perhaps I shall regret it later.

To-day is Sedan Day, and Gretel's birthday. She has grown quite a lot and wears her hair fastened in 'snail-coils' over her ears. (Snails again!) It seems all snails to me at present. Willi said yesterday, when he had eaten some egg-flip (that is, baked potato with egg), 'That tasted really fatty, folks!' How we laughed! There was absolutely no fat in it, simply pure frying-pan and salt.

8th September, 1917

I have been with Lieutenant Waldecker, Lieutenant Leverenz and my friend Trude in the forest. First we had coffee at the 'Little Castle in the Forest', and then we walked over the Sandweg to the village of Küddowtal and on to Königsblick. It was still warm; the sand on the woodland path was golden yellow as at the sea-side. I told Lieutenant Waldecker how Willi and I had whooping-cough as little children and were taken with Mummy and Grandma to the bathing resort at Kolberg. Whooping-cough was supposed to be cured by good sea air. But Mummy and Grandma wanted to bathe in the sea. Willi and I watched from the terrace of the hotel by the shore as Mummy and Grandma waded into the sea; they wore knee-length bathing-costumes and bathing-caps with frilly tops and also bathing-shoes which were laced right up to below the knee. As they went deeper and deeper into the water I began to think that they would drown and broke out into a loud roar. No one could console me. The spectators by the balustrade laughed themselves silly, but there was one nice couple who sympathised with me. But when they went to stroke me and calm me, I cried all the louder. My loyal brother imme-diately burst out crying too, and we bawled and yelled the whole time until Mummy took pity on her youngsters' misery and came dripping out of the sea.

Werner Waldecker laughed and said, 'How pretty you must have been – a tiny red-head with freckles!' He put his arm round my shoulders and gave me a quick kiss on the nose. I said nothing. Lieutenant Leverenz, who had seen it, raised a warning finger and said in fun, 'Now then – she's a minor!' But Lieutenant Waldecker drew me to one side, smiling, so for a time we were walking by ourselves. He kept bending forward and looking at me so lovingly; under his officer's cap, which he had set at an angle, his hair gleamed yellow and gold like the sand. We held each other's hand. I had to tell him more about Kolberg;

how my brother and I had left our little papier-maché donkey on the shore in the rain and found it again next morning all sodden and secretly buried it under a beech-tree in the big churchyard of Kolberg. When I was going to stop telling the story, Waldecker called out like a little boy, 'More! More!' and, quick as lightning, kissed me at various points, my plaits, my temple, my shoulder, every single finger of my left hand. We were eventually in the deep forest of Königsblick. Then I suddenly held him back and whispered, 'Quiet! A deer!'

A deer came quite calmly across our path, an enormous animal.

'The things I experience with you!' whispered Lieutenant Waldecker. He gazed after the lovely deer and went quite pale. Lieutenant Leverenz and Trude appeared on our right; I couldn't believe that they hadn't seen the deer. We walked together to 'The Stone'; that is a memorial to the Emperor Friedrich who once stood here looking over the Küddow meadows. We sat down on the hillside and looked across the Küddow which flows in many shimmering bends through the meadows. The sun was beginning to go down and the river shone beautifully. A few ducks were swimming downstream. They left little ripples behind them; sometimes they buried their heads in the mud by the river-bank. Lieutenant Leverenz kissed Trude longer and longer on the mouth, but Lieutenant Waldecker just looked at me smiling and murmured, 'only a minor!' and pressed my head against his shoulder.

We returned home on the red 'Rail-car', as the little railway between Königsblick and Schneidemühl is called, and arrived in Schneidemühl with many other excursionists at 7 o'clock in the evening. When we parted at the stairs to our house, Werner Waldecker whispered in my ear, 'I love you!' I looked at him, but just said 'Thank you!' Then I jumped for joy. On my honour, I leapt into the air with true happiness. So crazy can I actually be!

9th September, 1917

I should like to be alone. I should like to go far off and be alone. I don't know what I want. Life is tedious; I just wander about. I hope school begins soon, then I shall see Fräulein Kutschelis again. And my class-mates. Part of the time I have been at Connie's in Studsin, and part of the time at the Liebenthal estate

245

with Irma Kenzler. Frau Kenzler, who is always sad, likes me to sit with her much of the time in her room and read to her while she does embroidery or needlework. It often has to be my own poems or stories. I have already read the 'Story of the Queen without a name' to her three times. It's a bit of a bind. I would rather be with Irma and her little sister Waldtraut in the fields or the stables or in the foal's paddock. The other day Waldtraut crept into my bed early in the morning; she pressed against me in her thin nightie and clung her arms round me. It was a funny sort of feeling. I had to tell her stories about gipsies.

At Liebenthal I am allowed to sleep in a guest-room with bright blue walls and a white varnished bed with a bright blue quilt. The dressing-table is also varnished white with a touch of gold. When I think, as I lie there, about my old bed whose foot-rail serves me (in the role of Lieutenant von Yellenic) as my charger –. But that is all out-dated! Nowadays Grannie and I are always hunting bugs.

When evening comes, the whole Kenzler family, together with governess, manager, supervisor, trainees, and billetees or other guests from the neighbourhood usually gather at the giant hearth of the old Hall. A brown bearskin lies in front of the hearth. Around it are leather armchairs in which you sink right down. The light is turned out and there are only the flames playing around the logs of wood. Then they all like me to sing. Mostly folk-songs ('And when the fire burns, sparks fly –'). I wished I had a guitar; I would soon learn to play it. Then I could accompany my songs. I have already drawn on arithmetic paper a diagram of all the scales of the guitar, I have copied this out of the 'Guitar Handbook'. In the spirit I play on the six strings of the guitar – EADGBE. You can indicate the strings of the guitar with the sentence – 'Every aged dame goes bloater eating'. The guitar would always be called 'El Bobo' with me, 'The jester' as I liked to call it years ago. God, how old I have become since then!

10th September, 1917

I wonder whether the war has perhaps some meaning? Otherwise God wouldn't allow it to last so long. It has now become a sort of permanent institution; you can no longer remember properly what it was like in peace time. We hardly think about the war now; I do still write about the war news, simply because I promised this to Mummy a hundred years ago. Nothing more is said about the war at school either, except perhaps when another friend or relative has been killed. 'Victory holidays' have long been a thing of the past. Some one occasionally shifts the black, white and red drawing-pin flags on the map in the class-room, although it is really no longer of any interest to us girls. At present the flags are stuck a little behind the Siegfried line, and so withdrawn. This means we must have surrendered some territory.

What really interests us girls are the boys from the grammar school and of course the officers on the 'Posener'. I am not lying; it is true. Only I sometimes still hang around at the station fence and watch the troop trains and hospital trains coming and going; when I have time I also help the Red Cross ladies carry the urns of coffee and soup. Or I spread bread for the soldiers with dripping.

But I still like best to play at Nurse Martha and Lieutenant von Yellenic with Gretel Wegner. That means, we play with at least a hundred people who of course don't really exist; we have invented them, and that is what is so good about it. We know these people well, their qualities and peculiarities, and their names. Lieutenant von Yellenic is often madly in love with some imaginary lady, but mostly with Nurse Martha; only she is unfortunately married to a major and so he can only worship her from a distance.

Coming back to reality, everyone is trying to get hold of food. We have new potatoes in the cellar; I got Herr Kenzler to send us a whole cartload. We have some turnips too. Of bread and fat, of course, very little – hardly any in fact. I now have a good wheeze for making egg-flip. I scour the large saucepan with a well hardened piece of bacon-rind, sprinkle salt on it, then put in the slices of boiled potato. If I am careful, they don't burn. We usually have an egg somewhere in the cupboard; I beat that up with water, flour, salt and pepper. If possible I add an onion or chives. Willi and I think egg-flip tastes grand; we even think it really tastes of egg. I put so much water in that the lump of egg remains a bit moist like scrambled egg.

8th November, 1917

Revolution! Revolution! Lenin has brought about a revolution in Russia! Kerenski's army is now finished. Willi and Androwski applauded thunderously by banging on the table with the flat of their hands like students, Willi even stamped his feet. He shouted, 'Perhaps I shall not be called up now!' I hopped about too, although the whole thing was not a hundred per cent clear to me. But when two are rejoicing, the third joins in.

I asked Androwski whether the war now had acquired an 'ethical value' as most people declared. Androwski said, 'The best we can expect is that this damned human race learns to think – at least in Russia.'

'Not in Germany?' I asked.

'I don't see any hope of it so far.'

I wanted to know why the Russians were cleverer than ourselves. Androwski answered that the German men had for generations eaten out of the hand of the Emperor and the Empress and the German women were stupefied by the cooking-pot.

'Do you mean me?' I said laughing, and Androwski went red. Later my brother said to me, didn't I know that Androwski was in love with me. I was thunderstruck. I had never thought that Androwski saw in me anything other than his friend's sister. Willi said patronisingly, 'Of course, you are still only a kid!' It struck me immediately how Lieutenant Werner Waldecker had whispered 'a minor!' We haven't spoken to each other again since that day. I just know that he goes out walking with a certain lady who has a bad reputation in Schneidemühl. But she is very beautiful and they make a fine couple. I also know that he goes to her coffee-parties. Perhaps I could get in as a pianist again. Then I might 'accidentally' meet him on the stairs.

I am by the way practising the piano again. At present Variations by Carl Maria von Weber, 'Vien'quà, Dorina bella'. Willi is rehearsing a new composition. I must see that he doesn't forget the old songs, for he cannot write them down. At least not so beautiful and lively as they come on the piano. All his songs have a distinctive, wonderful ending. When I made mention of this once to Androwski, he looked at me thoughtfully and said that Willi would never bring his great talent to fruition; he was too easy-going to persevere with a real study of music. 'He would at least have to study counterpoint and composition. But I know my Kuhr! How he dreams his way through life! He will waste his talent.' I counted up all the composers who were ill and weak and yet have left a great work behind them. Sometimes Androwski's pessimism makes me sick.

248

2nd December, 1917

When I entered the class-room, Greta Dalüge and Trude Jakobi were parting from each other. They had shocked faces and were quite embarrassed.

I asked, 'What's the matter?'

Trude Jakobi stammered, 'Don't you know? Werner Waldecker has crashed.'

'Dead?'

'Yes. Dead. He was to have gone over to Bielefeld tomorrow. To his mother.'

'When did it happen?'

Trude didn't know.

I put my school-bag under the desk and took my coat off slowly as if nothing had happened. After a while I was able to speak again and asked whether she knew any more.

'About the accident,' I said.

But all she knew was that Waldecker had taken off from the airfield that morning and soon afterwards had crashed.[16]

'Alone?'

'Yes. Those aeroplanes are no good, as you yourself have said. Waldecker said so too – those machines.'

I didn't get much out of the lessons, but made more response than usual, so that no one would notice that the news affected me. I just kept thinking, 'Dead!' A gaping black hole.

I picture his face, the flashing eyes, the merry scornful laugh, the wisps of fair hair under the cap worn at an acute angle.

Is all that shattered, broken to bits, broken in two, smeared with blood, the skull in pieces? The same as with the old farmer who once in the sight of Grandma and myself was crushed against the station building by a run-away horse and lay there with a broken skull? Does his head now look like that? Werner Waldecker's head? What did he whisper in my ear, at the same time touching my ear with his lips? 'I love you!'

What am I to do now? Dear God, what am I to do? How am I to hide my feelings in front of people, in front of Grandma, Willi, Androwski, my friends – and all? How am I to go on living?

3rd December, 1917

I have bought a rose. Roses are dear now; it was the last of my money. It was very cold out-of-doors. I waited in the Güter-bahnhofstrasse from half-past one until half-past three. Sometimes I thought I would die of cold. There were not many people about. Who goes along Güter-bahnhofstrasse around mid-day anyway!

About half-past three there was a distant sound of drums. In exact time with the steps of the marching soldiers. My heart gave such a leap that I pressed my fist holding the rose against it. Then the sound of wind instruments; Chopin's Funeral March. Then silence. Then the drums got nearer. Then, 'I had a comrade'. I think I groaned. Then they arrived.

First a detachment of soldiers in Field uniform, then the Padre. The hearse. A few curious people were walking alongside the funeral procession. A flat brown coffin; the wreath from the Flying Corps rested on it. Under the wooden cover there lay Lieutenant Werner Waldecker.

I ran forward and threw the rose on to the coffin, but it slipped down and fell on to the street. Lieutenant Leverenz was walking between three officers who were Waldecker's comrades. He looked at me solemnly. I quickly looked again at the coffin. It had gone past. Behind it and the officers marched a second detachment of soldiers; two rows with rifles, the others without any weapons.

The procession turned through the open iron gates of the goods yard. There stood a detached goods van, reddish brown with open sliding doors. At the sides, in the background of the van, a few cases in a pile.

Lieutenant Waldecker's coffin was lifted off the hearse and placed on the ground in front of the goods van. The first two rows of soldiers stood beside it. The padre opened a little black book and read something. Then the command, loud and clear, 'Helmets – off for prayer!' Click! It was done in precise military fashion. The padre said the Lord's Prayer. Then, 'Present – arms! Attention! Level arms! At the ready! Fire!'

A threefold salute.

A minute's silence. The air smelled of gunpowder. And: 'Helmets – on!' Click! Again as by the book. Then four soldiers lifted Lieutenant Waldecker's coffin into the goods van, pushed it back into the middle, carefully placed the wreath and jumped out. Two railwaymen in shabby uniform coated with black soot closed the doors of the van to right and left. ('Let's go and have éclairs again at Fliegner's! Would you like to?' ...)

I had picked up the rose from the street; it had not once been trodden on. I stuck my nose into the rose and ran bent down

along Schwarz Weg to the fields. No one must see me! Especially
the girls from the Pension Hoppenrath or those from Posener
Strasse! Just what am I to do?

I heard the music of the soldiers fading into the distance. What
were they playing?

The little woodland birds
Sang such a wonderful refrain;
In the homeland, in the homeland,
There we'll meet again!

Why have you allowed this to happen, dear God? Oh why?

20th December, 1917

We have had the Christmas school reports. My report is bad.
Mathematics and French unsatisfactory. Fräulein Kutschelis got
me to carry a pile of exercise books to her flat. It was the first
time I had been there.

'Sit down, Elfriede,' she said. I sat down in one corner of the
sofa and she in the other. She asked quietly, 'What is wrong with
you, Elfriede? Or would you rather I said Piete? I find you have
changed and it worries me. You are falling behind in your performance and you no longer pay attention in class.'

I looked at her really bewildered, for what she was reproach-
ing me with was something I had not myself realised. Both of the
'unsatisfactory' markings in the report were indeed pretty awful.
I had not expected them. But it didn't upset me at all. The main
thing was that in both Fräulein Kutschelis' subjects I had 'good',
in German very good and in English good. Nothing else
mattered.

Fräulein Kutschelis said, 'You won't get your school-leaving
certificate. Do you know that?'

'No.'

'Unless you make a special effort in this last quarter. Have you
any worries?'

I again said, 'No.'

Fräulein Kutschelis looked at me a long time. Then she turned
my face round gently to hers. I thought, 'You just mustn't cry!'
and sat as stiff as wood.

'So!' said Fräulein Kutschelis. 'I do so much like my pupils to
succeed – especially –' She hesitated for a moment and then to
my astonishment said – 'especially you.'

251

'Why?' I said.

I wanted her to say, 'Because I love you.' But of course she didn't say that. But she pushed the exercise books up together on the table (such an ugly table with a dull red velvet cloth) stood up suddenly and said, 'Be sure of this, and depend on it. There is no point in having to take the exam a second time. Fundamentally you are in advance of most of the others. Only these two subjects – Why does Mathematics strike you as so difficult?'

I told her that I had been ill through all the early groundwork of mathematics. I had never caught up with the subject.

'But you had special tuition with Fräulein Doris Übe.'

'Yes indeed. In spite of that I never grasped it – or immediately forgot it again.'

'But in your Michaelmas report you had "Satisfactory" for mathematics and also for French, both written and oral. And so 3 plus. What has made your marks so much worse? Are you unwell?'

'Definitely not.'

'But you like German?'

'Yes. Very much. I should like better than anything to read and write all day. Especially to write!'

'Yes, yes,' said Fräulein Kutschelis with a sigh. 'Your essays are good! Do you know, I know your essay on autumn almost by heart? And what do you write at home?'

'Poems. And short stories. I once began a novel. And – a war diary.' Fräulein Kutschelis asked if she might look at the war diary some day, but I stammered that it was simply a family story. And war news taken from the papers. And then I gradually came over faint and it all went dark in front of my eyes. Fräulein Kutschelis washed my forehead with Eau de Cologne and dabbed my throat and my wrists, and after all this I had to swallow some cold tea. She was terribly kind and considerate. Like a mother. She thinks I am not having enough to eat.

23rd December, 1917

In Brest-Litowsk the first peace negoations with Russia are taking place. There are no longer any distinctions of rank in the Russian Army. Anyone who is a lieutenant or a captain is addressed as 'comrade lieutenant' or 'comrade captain'. Imagine that in the German army!

Uncle Bruno has got leave for Christmas; he suddenly appeared at the door in full battle-dress. Grandma nearly fainted for joy. As Mummy arrived to-day too, the family is suddenly complete again. Uncle thinks the war is getting near the end; in Rumania there is talk of a cease-fire. In the West the fighting goes on. The English, who had broken through the Siegfried Line, have been pushed back again by the German troops. They have lost many tanks in the Cambrai area. We in the hinterland are no longer greedy for news of victories; all we are interested in is how to get hold of the food we need. I spend most of my free time queuing up at the shops. Grandma has sewn a piece of horse cloth into my coat as a lining. But she can't sew a lining into my shoes; I have chilblains on most of my toes.

Well, it doesn't matter. At least we have a little Christmas-tree and war-time gingerbread, and flaked oats macaroons have also been baked. On Christmas Eve there will be a carp; Herr Kenzler has sent us one by his coachman. We shall cook the carp in Polish fashion, that is with peppermint sauce, sultanas and beer.

25th December, 1917

I was anxious about Christmas. About the church-going and the singing. I was not sure that I would not be thinking of every-thing, of everything again, and be unable to stop crying out loud. Then fortunately Grandma said that she had thought of something special as a Christmas present for me. I could join the winter course that had just begun with Herr Kleinschmidt the dancing teacher and take dancing lessons; she had already arranged it. 'Because you seem so gloomy,' said Mummy laughing.

I was over-joyed.

'I would really rather be a dancer than a singer,' I exclaimed.

'I think you will like to carry on my singing-school one day,' said Mummy. 'Just think – have I ever seen you swing a leg gracefully in a dance?'

'No,' I answered perplexed, and everybody laughed. Willi performed his comic hop, skip and jump again until the Christmas tree was nearly overturned by the vibration. Grandma cried, 'The silly chump will be setting the room on fire,' and everybody laughed all the more.

29th December, 1917

Uncle Bruno was happy all through Christmas. He visited his old friend Gruse (the gentleman with the 'mechanical grand piano'). We were all invited to tea. When I just surreptitiously ran my finger over the lovely smooth surface of the piano, Herr Gruse came up to me and said gently, 'Who wanted one day to come and listen to some music? I would have liked to play some Chopin for you.'

My God, I should just think so. I am still only a teen-ager. But I am so pleased that Herr Gruse actually wanted to play Chopin for me. I promised to come one day.

Dear Diary, I have written a letter to Lieutenant Werner Waldecker's mother. I addressed the envelope to the Postal Directory Office at the town of Bielefeld with the request to forward it to Frau Waldecker. I said in the letter that she was not alone in her sorrow. I had so loved her son because he was such an innocent person. I said that I had written many poems and a story about him. But I didn't say that I possess a faded red rose in a little black box.

1918

We are in the fifth year of war.

Uncle Bruno has been posted to Hanover, so is no longer at the Front. Mummy went away much earlier; the 'Office' did not grant any longer leave. Willi, Gretel and I have stripped the Christmas tree. I wrapped the coloured glass birds with silken tails in tissue paper and cotton-wool that we have not been able to replace for three years; it is now quite grey with age.

It is cold. The wind is coming from Siberia. Gretel's brother Fritz asked me to-day to go to Witkowski's mangling-room.

'Why?' I asked.

'You will soon see,' said Fritz.

In the corner of the room stood a giant mangle with which all sections of the house, front and back, smooth out their washing. Fritz swung on the long cylinder which is full of heavy stones and asked whether I would take part in 'a certain event'; I always used to be their leader in war games, he said.

'Leader of whom?' I asked, although I knew very well what he meant, but I was so tired and hadn't the slightest desire to join in anything.

'Of us boys, of course!' said Fritz. 'It's a wonderful plan!'

So I then had to ask what sort of a plan. Fritz answered, 'We are going to catch rabbits, behind the earthworks where the barbed wire entanglements are.'

I said, 'How will you catch rabbits?'

'With Paul's dog. Paul has trained him for rabbiting – he is crazy on them.'

'What rabbits are to be had?'

Fritz said that whole colonies of rabbits live there. Little pines and clumps of heather were now growing between the wire entanglements and they have made their burrows underneath them.

'Paul's dog is first-rate at it. We hunt the rabbits out of the

255

burrow and as they emerge he quickly gets one by the back of the neck.'

'And then?'

'Then –' Fritz demonstrated with the edge of his hand how you kill a rabbit with a sharp blow behind its ears.

But I had known that for a long time. I thought it rather nasty. I said, 'I'm not killing any rabbits.'

'You don't need to. We'll do that. You only have to come with us.'

'But why? You do it on your own!'

Fritz didn't answer for a while. Then he said that I would just be there; it was no fun without me; I was the leader.

I suddenly understood the boys fully. We had all played war games together; now they wanted everything to be the same as before. For some reason it just made me terribly sad. 'And Gretel?' I asked. Fritz laughed and said, 'But we're not saying anything about it to her!'

I wanted to know then what they would be doing with the dead rabbits, and Fritz said, 'Eat them! What else? Oh boy, it makes a wonderful bit of meat, and no mistake! Each of us takes just one rabbit home; he can then say he got it from the farmer.'

'A whole rabbit? A present from the farmer? Are you out of your mind?'

'Oh well, you can say you have done some job in return for it. Chopping wood, digging potatoes out of the clamp, or some such!'

I couldn't think. Fritz asked whether I would now join them.

I said, 'If I can take a rabbit back for Grandma, then I will.'

'That's settled!' cried Fritz.

He wanted to kiss me, but I said, 'None of that!' I was astonished that he wanted to kiss me; I now realised for the first time that he was really quite grown up. We arranged to meet the following evening at the barbed wire entanglements, in the sand pit between the knacker's yard and the wire.

11th January, 1918

I think I am ill.

We met in the big sand-pit, the three boys, Paul's dog Karo and I. Karo is a black mongrel, a cross between a hunting-dog and a milk-cart dog, quite big, with floppy ears. He has a good-natured face but an ugly mouth. You can also see his red gums and he slobbers. For instance, when I took a sandwich out of my coat pocket and began to eat it he slobbered over my coat. We sat silent for a long time in the pit. It was already nearly evening. We began to get cold and all the boys looked at me. They were waiting for an order from me, but I hadn't the slightest desire for a hunt. I thought of the deer that I had pointed out to Werner Waldecker; there is no animal that I don't love. I am sorry for the rabbits. What a damnable situation! I looked again at the sticks that we had cut on the way, pretty thick cudgels that were used for hunting.

'Now, shall we?' asked Fritz at last.

'Away!' I cried and jumped up with one bound. We dashed across the field towards the barbed wire. Paul held Karo on the lead, and he tugged like mad so that he snorted loudly and nearly choked. When we reached the military area which had never actually become involved in warfare we all began at the same time to scream 'Brr ... Brr ...' and to beat the barbed wire and the weather-worn stakes with our sticks. It made a terrible racket. I had arranged the outcry with the boys beforehand.

'Let Karo loose,' I called. And the dog rushed like the devil through the gaps in the barbed wire. We heard his yelping as he drove the rabbits out of the reeds and chased after them. We could tell from his yelping and howling that he had caught a rabbit. Then Paul blew quickly on the dog-whistle and Karo actually came creeping under the barbed wire with a rabbit in his mouth. Paul said 'Bring!' and Karo laid the rabbit down at his feet. It was still twitching a bit. Paul struck it behind the ears with the edge of his hand – it was immediately dead and hung from his fist like a sack.

I took no further part in the hunt, but just stood thinking that the rabbit was now finally dead. Again it seemed awful to me.

Karo brought a second rabbit that was even bigger than the first one. Then a third. Something red glistened on Karo's black coat and I saw that it was not rabbit's blood, but that he was bleeding from a number of wounds.

I shouted, 'Stop! Paul, stop the dog! Hold on to him, he is bleeding. He has blood all over him!' Paul was so shocked that he stood still and didn't move a hand. When the captured rabbit suddenly tried to jump away, Fritz killed it with a blow behind the ears.

'Ow!!' he cried and raised his hand to his lips. 'It was like a bull! A neck as hard as iron!' 'Stop!' I cried. 'Stop at once! And hold on to the dog, Paul! Come on, Karo, come here! To me!'

I enticed Karo, who was just about to slip off under the barbed wire again, held him tight with both arms and pressed his head to my breast. Then the three boys came running up, Paul hooked the lead into Karo's collar and looked in dismay at his bleeding coat. I knelt on the ground and tried to stem the blood with my handkerchief. 'That was the barbed wire,' whined Paul. 'Oh dear, Piete, what shall I do! Father will go mad if he sees the dog in this state!'

We picked up the rabbits and went back to the sand-pit. We sat down there in a circle, with the dog pressed between us. I kept stroking his head and pressed the handkerchief against the wounds, but the blood kept flowing. Paul was crying. He said, 'I can't take Karo home like that – can't possibly!'

We considered what we could do and decided to shut him up overnight in the shed behind the slaughter-house. He could sleep in the hay there and lick himself better and Paul could tell his father the dog had run away. In the morning we would go and fetch Karo and Paul would tell his father he didn't know where the dog had been and got injured – probably hunting.

'But I am not going to the shed alone,' sniffed Paul. 'You must come with me.'

I said immediately, 'You can rely on me, Paul.' We arranged to meet just after school on the railway station bridge; we also decided that we would take for Karo any food we could get hold of and also a bottle of water, for he would be hungry and thirsty.

So we stood up and walked to the shed at the left of the slaughter-house, Karo tugging at the lead all the time. I made up a warm bed for Karo in the hay, which was three feet deep, and told him to lie down. But he stood up again as soon as he saw us going to the door of the shed. We had to use all our powers of persuasion to get him to 'stay'. I stroked his head again and kissed him between the eyes. I felt just as much like crying as Paul.

Then we bolted the door, but could still hear Karo howling and whining and scratching at the door for a long time behind us. We agreed that each of the boys could take a rabbit. I didn't want one. When Paul offered me a half of his rabbit I had to turn away to avoid breaking down.

At home I couldn't swallow the least bit of supper in spite of Grandma pressing me. I said I felt bad and went to bed. When I drew the featherbed around me, I couldn't stop crying. I nearly choked with crying. But nobody heard me.

12th January, 1918

We went to the shed at three o'clock. Each of us had secretly taken some food for Karo; I had also a beer-bottle full of milk and water. It was cloudy and cold. The valley had a covering of dirty snow. When we arrived at the slaughter-house, the knacker was standing there. He was leaning with folded arms in the open doorway and looking towards us. He didn't move. The longer he stood, the slower we walked, at length we hardly moved as if we were attached to an elastic cord which kept pulling us back.

'Hello!' cried the knacker. 'A bit slow, aren't you? Is the dog yours?'

I began to run forward, then the boys followed suit. I stared at the knacker. He pulled my school hat half over my eyes and said, 'He has gone! Do you understand? Rats have seen him off!'

'But how – how?' stammered Paul; he was white as chalk and trembling.

The knacker looked at him sympathetically and answered that the rats had been driven crazy by the smell of blood on Karo's coat; they had half eaten him.

Fritz shouted in fury: 'Parasites! Body-snatchers! Dirty, filthy beasts!' For some time we did nothing but shout abuse.

The knacker bit his underlip and said 'Hold on. You are in the wrong. You are real poachers. Do you think I didn't know about it?'

I was frightened. If the knacker said anything to the game-keeper or the police, we would be in real trouble.

Fritz asked, 'Where is the dog?'

The knacker said, 'In the lime-pit.'

Paul began to cry again. I stretched out a finger and touched the knacker's jacket until he looked at me sideways. 'You won't give us away, eh?'

'No, I promise,' he murmured. 'Now just get off home!'

We slunk away to the sand-pit. We sat down again. I dropped down at full length in the snow and remained lying there. I would gladly have died. Then I should have known nothing more. I closed my eyes and asked Fritz whether he saw any stars. Fritz said he didn't see any.

15th January, 1918

The American president Wilson has submitted to the American

259

Senate a peace programme with fourteen points. Germany would be forced to make peace and would surrender all power. Just think of Ludendorff's position in this!

1st February, 1918

Willi has received his call-up papers! The plea of 'Water on the knee' and 'Muscular weakness of the heart resulting from scarlet fever' is no further help to him. The Staff-doctor has passed him as fit for military service. Willi was furious. He said that he and the other recruits were examined stark naked in the ice-cold barracks. The doctor just pressed his abdomen and sounded his lungs, that was all. 'Sound as a bell,' he declared.

Willi spat and said, 'The great fop! He just wants fresh cannon fodder for Emperor Wilhelm!'

Androwski chuckled angrily. He is excused military service on account of his short-sightedness. 'Kuhr,' he said, 'you must have made a sublime spectacle – naked! A model of Olympic divine youth!'

I laughed '– and weighed just half an ounce,' I quipped, quoting from the 'Suppenkaspar'.

'Don't get shoved into the footsloggers!' said Androwski. 'Not the infantry. The Air Force would be best. Ground staff of course. Office work best of all. Really! Office work. Just tell them you have fabulous hand writing.'

'Just tell them!' mocked Willi. 'You've no idea! Everything there goes by opposites. there's no sense in it at all. Prussian Army. And now I'm stuck in it.'

'Just let Uncle Bruno hear that – or Mummy,' I said. 'To them "German national" is still the tops. And if you fall with a cheer for the Fatherland you will die as a hero in their eyes.'

'What kind of new tone is this?' mocked Androwski. 'Miss Piete – the new Pliny. Are you suddenly writing the history of the war from a different point of view?'

I went red again and exclaimed that to-day every one of any intelligence knew what had happened to the enthusiasm for war. I don't want any more soldiers to die. What purpose is served, for what and for whom? What use has it been to the Russians to perish in the Masurian Lakes? They can no longer die for the Tsar. He too is now worth nothing. Millions of dead for nothing – I repeat nothing.

Androwski thought that the millions had by their death brought about the Revolution.

'Through their death?' I cried. 'If that is what it costs I don't want any more Revolution!'

'What then?' asked Androwski, and Willi bit his fingernails irritably.

I couldn't give any answer. Nor could Willi. He stopped biting his nails and grinned foolishly.

'Just tell me,' I cried indignantly, 'why millions have to die before you have a revolution? Can it not be brought about by reasoning?'

'That would be the simple solution!' declared Androwski. I had no idea whether he meant that sarcastically or seriously. I think he meant it seriously. But now it is too late. We must just make sure that there is never another war in the future. We must never again fall for the humbug with which the older generation has bewitched us. We were still only children, still at school. And everyone at school, led on by the headmaster and the other teachers, shouted hurra. Our parents and relatives have become poor because they have given up all their money, jewellery and valuables for the war-loan. Grandma maintains us by means of the few marks brought in by the rent paid by the poor people who live in our house on the Berliner Platz. They are even poorer than we are and some can hardly afford the rent any more. Anyhow, Grandma lets old Tiedtke live there rent-free, and our former cook, too. About ten people are cooped up there in two miserable rooms. I think I would rather die. But that is no solution. It is better to live. Definitely.

1st March, 1918

It is certain, I shall not be going up to the top class. Fräulein Kutschelis has told Grandma this. Grandma hasn't scolded me; I can go to dancing-lessons just the same. The dancing-lessons take place in a hall in the Bromberg suburb. It is an ugly, plain, lengthy hall that smells of beer. But what does that matter? It is wonderful. I know all the dances that we began with – Viennese Waltz, Polka, Mazurka, Polonaise, Gallop and our Polish Krakowiak. I can just about manage those. The Minuet, Pas D'Espagne, Quadrille and the long, solemn Square Dance are more difficult. If only we had at least proper partners! But the good dancers have been called up and the younger ones are bashful young boys who are terribly clumsy and have to be helped to get going. Not every girl has a partner, so at Herr Kleinschmidt's request I stand in for a male dancer. The girls prefer to dance with me rather than with the boys and I pretend that I am Lieutenant Joan von Yellenic dancing with beautiful, elegant ladies at a big regimental ball.

I have bought myself a hard-covered exercise book in which I write down every dance-step and every command. So that I don't forget anything, I have worked out a dance code by which all the difficult steps can be portrayed. Herr Kleinschmidt already entrusts me with the tutoring of particularly inept dancing couples. He says I am a good helper. Once I asked him whether he would give me private ballet lessons. But he said he only had a licence to teach ball-room dancing, not ballet. I was very disappointed, especially because he thought I was too old for real ballet lessons; I should have started at the age of five or six. I said sadly that I could never become a dancer then.

'Do you really want to?' he said, smiling. I said that I had already worked out dances for the stage and had decided to take ballet lessons secretly in Berlin along with singing lessons. I would earn the money for it myself. 'Just so!' said Herr Kleinschmidt thoughtfully. We spoke for some time about the possibilities of a dancing course. In the end he said there are five basic positions in ballet; he would show me the first one now. And he began to demonstrate in his fine, soft, patent-leather heel-less shoes the first position together with its associated arm movement. 'Toes pointing out, knees straightened and turned outwards, thighs also turned outwards – thus!' I am blissfully happy. Herr Kleinschmidt now always finds a few minutes during the dance lesson to take me through the five ballet positions. The dance pupils don't pay any attention to it. But I! I! I practise at home in every free moment and I nearly sprain my legs, which makes Willi laugh himself sick. Every joint hurts.

15th March, 1918

Strikes against the war everywhere. General strikes in Vienna, in Berlin, Hamburg, Kiel and in the Rhine industrial area. Workers' councils have been set up in the munitions factories. But, dear Diary, you don't know yet the best and greatest news of all; on 3rd March the Treaty of Brest-Litowsk brought peace between Russia and us. The Bolshevist leader Leo Trotzki, a friend of

Lenin and enemy of Kerenski, had already declared, before peace
was concluded, that the war was over. Now it is really over.
What will become of the thousands of Russian prisoners in our
Schneidemühl prison camps? Will they now be allowed to go
home? Willi says only socialists and bolshevists can return to
Russia because Lenin is now engaged in establishing the
workers', peasants' and soldiers' state. Any one who will not co-
operate is shot or deported to Siberia. Then there will be new
refugees, this time from Russia. Endless chaos! A lot of troop-
trains from the East are coming through the station. This time
they are again singing '– in the homeland, in the homeland, there
we'll meet again!' But a sergeant whom I asked answered, 'It's
not so simple, Miss. We've all got to go to the Western Front
first. Any who survive that can then sing "there we'll meet
again!"'

17th March, 1918

Grandma, Fräulein Ella Gumprecht, Frau Schönfeld and Aunt
Otter are racking their brains over what I am to wear for my
confirmation. I need two dresses: one for the day of the public
examination in church and one for the actual confirmation. I am
pessimistic – my brother Gil even more so.

Yesterday Grandma and Frau Schönfeld went into the town
and after a long search bought a remarkable piece of material; it
looks just like these silky-shining, glistening sticky sweets with
stripes right through. The colours were just like those too: bon-
bon red with white and green.

'O God!' sighed Willi.

'At least that will provide a blouse with sleeves,' I declared.
'What sort of a skirt am I to wear with it?'

Grandma said resignedly that Aunt Louise Otter's old black
silk skirt could be borrowed and taken in a bit. I howled with
rage and afterwards ran into the yard to call for Gretel and go
for a walk with her. I had to relieve my anger. On the same
evening by lamplight began a great cutting-out operation, but this
time it was for the confirmation dress. Grandma had sacrificed a
brown and green curtain from the trunk which stands in the attic;
this, decorated with a narrow black braid was to become the
confirmation dress. Frau Annchen had bought the pattern; a half-
length dress with a waist, long sleeves and a little round cut-out
at the neck. The sleeves are gathered in at the lower end and the

skirt is wide-sweeping. 'I will also lend you my gold necklace with the cross and diamonds', said Grandma anxiously. I looked at her and thought that I loved her above all and that it was disgraceful of me to cry with disappointment over the bon-bon silk.

18th March, 1918

Willi has to join up. He is called up for the Flying Corps and will belong to the 75th Fighter Squadron. When he went off with his composition trunk, my heart was like a lump of clay. Willi turned around once more in the street and said, 'Adieu, dearest!'

To make him laugh, I shouted as of old, 'Foreign word – Adieu!'

He actually laughed a little. I quickly called out after him: 'Come on leave soon!'

Before he went away he had written in my poetry album: – 'I hear a gentle sound of golden harp-strings – the harmony of our hearts! Little sister, from your Willi-Gil.'

I always want to call my brother Gil now, because he likes the name so much. He doesn't want to be called Wilhelm like the Emperor any more, but like a Mexican. There is a revolution now in Mexico. Gil is enthusiastic about the uprising in Mexico and has pinned the photographs of all the Mexican freedom heroes to the wall-paper over his bed. We have yelled like mad –

Yo soy puro Mexicano
Viva Mexico!

And someone like that is now a German recruit!

Palm Sunday, 1918

Evening. We confirmation candidates have been confirmed to-day in the town church. It was a sunny day. I wore the rep-curtain dress with the black braid. We girls had a small garland of myrtle in our hair. Gretel's mother had cut the myrtle from the pieces in her window; Frau Schönfeld and Gretel had bound them into a bunch. On my feet I wore lovely featherweight little fabric shoes with tiny heels, which Grandma to my delight had magically conjured up from some corner; they are a perfect fit, and I immediately resolved to wear them for all my dancing lessons. Grandma and Frau Schönfeld looked at each other and smiled, but Fräulein Ella Gumprecht burst out laughing, the silly goose.

I carried Grandma's black 1862 hymn book with gilt edging; a delicate lace handkerchief had come from Aunt Emma Haber in Berlin, and Grandma had made a little cross out of real violets and placed it on the handkerchief. Her heavy gold necklace with a cross in which a diamond sparkled hung on my chest. From every street came the darkly clad confirmation candidates, the boys wearing long trousers and a twig of myrtle in their coat-collars. It looked as if all the town were on their way. I saw Fräulein Kutschelis too and all my friends and acquaintances. Mummy had not been given leave from the 'Office'; she had written a very loving letter. I also had a Field Post Office letter from Uncle Bruno, in which he promised me Adalbert Stifter's book, 'Aus der Mappe meines Urgrossvaters'. Gill of course had no leave.

For the first time we were allowed to take part in the Lord's Supper. But, dear diary, I had expected to be deeply moved by it. Instead of this I kept thinking anxiously of our toilet; I was bursting for a pee. It was dreadful. I was terribly afraid it might happen in the church and I just hoped that not too many people would be standing at the door of the church to congratulate me. I hardly know, really, how I got home. In the end I was tripping alongside Grandma with very short steps.

This made the confirmation coffee all the more welcome. Grannie had invited my best friends and laid the extending-table which was drawn out into two rooms. It was nearly collapsing under the quantity of flowers, coffee-pots and war-time cakes. There was artificial cream made from semolina and sugar. Every girl brought me a present, but what nearly bowled me over was that Irma Kenzler brought me from her parents a brand new big guitar. 'El bobo' – my instrument! I could hardly speak, but sat with 'El bobo' in my arms smelling the scent of varnish and wood. Connie, who had known about this wonderful present, has embroidered for me the first ribbon for it, with the words 'You lie in my heart'.

And then, there was my confirmation motto, 'Be faithful unto death and I will give you the crown of life'.

2nd April, 1918

I do miss Gil. Sometimes I try to play his songs on the piano to remind me of him. I can't do it well without music. I often sing

265

them quietly to myself. And if I go for a walk with Gretel we sing them as we walk. Gil has only once had leave, and just then I was at Connie's in the school-house at Studsin near Kolmar. Connie is now allowed to take dancing lessons too with Herr Kleinschmidt; we are such good dancing-partners that Herr Kleinschmidt calls us 'the classical couple'.

We have a marvellous pianist. When he plays it is absolute magic. There is simply nothing nicer than dancing; at those times I think of nothing else.

I must tell you about the experience I had recently with my confirmation shoes. We had a dancing-school ball and I wore the rose-coloured blouse from the examination day and Aunt Louise Otter's altered black skirt, with Grandma's little black shoes, which had made Fräulein Emma Gumprecht laugh so much. Hardly had Connie and I started walking arm in arm down Zeughausstrasse when a group of urchins stood pointing at my shoes and grinning.

'Whatever's the matter with them?' I whispered to Connie. 'Is there anything on my shoes?' Connie looked down at me and said, 'No, nothing. Everything's O.K.'

But to my dismay more and more boys joined the group, making remarks about the shoes and shaking with laughter. 'Just look at those! Coffin shoes! Coffin shoes!'

'What are they saying?' I asked; I was standing struck with fright.

'They say "coffin shoes",' whispered Connie. At first I couldn't understand it at all; but when the urchins neighed more and more with laughter and began to hop around me on the pavement, Connie suddenly grabbed me and whispered, 'Come back home! Quickly! You must put some different shoes on!'

'But why?' I said. I had lost my cool. 'It seems they are really coffin shoes!' Connie whispered and forcibly turned me round. 'You know, the sort that people wear in their coffin.'

I nearly collapsed. That was why the horrid Fräulein Gumprecht had laughed so much! Grandma and Frau Annchen had also looked strange. But where had Grandma got the shoes from? Oh God of all Righteousness – and I went like that to my confirmation! At least no one had laughed then; it was such a solemn occasion. Connie and I ran back to our house as quickly as we could; I took the shoes off at once on the stairs. Grandma was working in the kitchen when I burst in like a bomb and hurled the shoes towards her. I overwhelmed her with questions and reproaches. At first she was quite calm.

'Calm down,' she said at last. 'You wanted to have nice shoes for confirmation day. Where was I to get hold of any? Then it occurred to me that I could enquire at the undertakers. All they had were black shoes like those. Who would recognise them as coffin shoes if you wore them with your confirmation attire? And they only cost three marks. So I bought them. I thought they would do nicely for a special day.'

I hurled the coffin shoes into the coal-scuttle. Then I put on my old buckled shoes with linoleum soles and dashed out of the house with Connie; I couldn't get soon enough to the dancing-school ball. At least there was no such wretched poverty there.

Connie said on the way that she was sorry for Grandma. I cried, 'Oh! Rubbish!' I was terribly ashamed of the coffin shoes and was afraid that the big boys in the street would now always call things out behind my back.

That is the story of my 1918 confirmation shoes.

22nd April, 1918

I am the only one not to have received the school-leaving certificate. Fräulein Kutschelis didn't look at me as she handed me my report; she just said, 'A pity, Elfriede, that you couldn't manage it.'

I took the report and said, 'What would you advise me to do?'

'Stay on another year,' said Fräulein Kutschelis. This time she looked me in the eyes. 'One of my most gifted pupils must really have a school-leaving certificate!'

Good, I will do what she wants, but I do it without any inclination. It's horrible to have another year of school with younger classmates. And what purpose will this year of repetition serve? I shan't learn any more mathematics and I can catch up on French if at any time I need to speak it. But before my class breaks up for ever we want to celebrate our old comradeship. We were a fine group even though some of the teachers say we were not outstanding.

We have written a 'Beer News', for which I have contributed most of the text. Our drawing mistress, Fräulein Plascuda, has painted the title page; wonderful to say, we were all excellent at drawing, and because of this Fräulein Plascuda had a special liking for us. Many of the girls, including me, also contributed some vignettes and comic scribbles to the 'Beer News'. It is being distributed to all class associates and to our teachers. We shall have a public reading of it on Wednesday. Kathy Dreier's father, who has the big wine business in the Neue Markt, has invited us to a 'forester's cup'. It will be a wonderful festival.

Then it occurred to us that we could collect together the marvellous bunches of flowers that many of us had received at the end of the school exams and bring them to Fräulein Kutschelis. We will take them quietly to her room. I suggested giving her a farewell serenade. The proposal was taken up with enthusiasm. We began immediately to practise for it. These are the songs that we are going to sing: 'You remain in my heart, you, you are always in my mind', and 'Oh, how can I ever leave you', and finally we will sing the soldiers' favourite song, 'I had a comrade', with the refrain 'In the homeland, in the homeland, there we'll meet again', for Fräulein Kutschelis has been our most loyal comrade, and we all hope that we shall have a chance to see her again; she is leaving our town to take up an appointment as assistant mistress in a modern grammar school.

1st May, 1918

It is all over. Farewell party, Beer News, and the flower serenade for Fräulein Kutschelis. The farewell song with its 'Meet again' made me choke. I felt I was losing Fräulein Kutschelis in the same way as I had lost Werner Waldecker, and in the middle of the chorus I turned my face to the wall and couldn't help crying out loud. Fräulein Kutschelis put her arms round me and said, 'Child! Child!' But it was no good; it made me cry still more, although it was terribly embarrasing. So I left the dear girls and Fräulein Kutschelis and rushed home through the many streets crying. Luckily Grandma was at the station; I was alone.

15th May, 1918

We have now made peace with Romania in Bucharest. But what does 'peace' mean! Germany and Austria have also made peace with Russia, and yet the fighting in the East still goes on. General von der Golz has defeated the so-called 'Red Guards' of the revolutionary Russian army. The fighting has moved into the Ukraine. There is no cessation of hostilities. And Gil is carrying on with his training with the Flying Corps staff and it seems I never see Androwski since my brother went away.

I feel strange in the new class. How am I supposed to act among these youngsters? They are really only a year younger, but they seem like children to me. There is no laughing fair-haired Connie, no sweet Martha Zwieg, no interesting organ-playing Miriam Borchardt nor any of the other good companions. I know the class-work by heart; it doesn't interest me. There is a new teacher, a Polish clergyman, a curate; he takes Fräulein Kutschelis's subjects. He is tall and fat and wears the black alpaca coat of the clergyman, quite long and fastened with little buttons. He is certainly very clever, but I don't like him. He watches me and puts catch questions to me. Sometimes he makes out he is reading, with one hand over his eyes; but I can see clearly that he is looking at me through his fingers. Twice already he has taken me to task for something that took place in class but with which I had nothing whatever to do. I answered him back, and of course he didn't forgive me for that. But one other time when the class had done something, he called: 'Kuhr, stand up! How could you dare to perpetrate such nonsense? Don't deny it, for it was you!'

I looked at him coolly and said loud and clear,

'I don't deny it, Herr Vikar.'

'So you acknowledge that you are to blame?'

'Of course, Herr Vikar.'

The new class was struck rigid. The girls well knew that I had done nothing, nothing at all, but they were all too shocked and indeed too cowardly to come to my defence.

'I order you to go to the headmaster and confess to him your disgraceful conduct.'

'Certainly, Herr Vikar.'

At this I left the classroom, but I had no intention of going to the headmaster, but sat down on a corner of the wall in the play-ground and waited for the German lesson. The wounded soldiers who were looking out again from the hospital windows, laughed and waved across to me. I resolved to leave the school for good next time I am falsely accused. I don't need the school-leaving certificate any more.

Whitsun, 1918

On this Whit Sunday evening some soldiers at the station were singing so beautifully that Grandma and I opened wide the window on the veranda to listen. Grandma said, 'That is a

269

Catholic Whitsun hymn about the Holy Spirit. It is in Latin and I don't know what it means.'

'But how do the soldiers come to know Latin?'

'They learn it in their church.'

Grandma had been massaging my head again as she so often did. The stars were shining so bright that we hadn't turned on the light on the veranda. The great leaves of the tobacco plant that stretched half-way across the veranda rose against the bright night sky. Grandma stopped stroking my forehead and said, 'I shall not live for ever. When I go, you are to inherit my gold necklace with the cross and diamond which you wore at your confirmation.'

I was struck dumb with fear; then I said quietly,

'And Mummy?'

'I have other jewellery,' said Grandma. 'The cross is for you. And the old clock, that stops whenever a close relative dies.'

I thought of the clock with its white dial, its heavy weight and polished brass pendulum that swung to and fro. I have wound it up hundreds of times, always on a Sunday morning – it goes for just a week. I thought with dread that one day it will stop when Grandma dies.

Grandma continued, 'You might go and fetch great grand-father's bible; it is on the bedroom window-sill.' I fetched the bible and Grandma put it on her lap. 'Your confirmation text is a good one for you, but the bible has something more to say to you. I will now consult it on your behalf and whatever it says will in God's name be binding on you.' I became anxious and wanted to ask Grandma not to do this, but she was already making the sign of the cross over it and murmuring, 'In the name of the Father, Son and Holy Ghost. Amen. Now I will open the bible. Where my finger rests, that sentence is binding on you.' I held my breath and she opened the book at random and pressed her finger on a certain line. 'Turn the light on,' she said, 'and read it out loud!'

Pressed closely against each other, we looked at the bible. There it read, 'But thou child, shalt be called the prophet of the Highest: for thou shalt go before the face of the Lord, to give light to them that sit in darkness.'

My heart nearly stood still. Grandma told me to read the sentence again. Then she closed the bible and said, 'Take note of this. You will always find this text again, every time you open the bible. It is God's will that you walk in that path. Don't forget that'.

I leaned my face against Grandma's hand and rehearsed the text with her until I knew it by heart. I asked Grandma whether it would also be a part of my task to tell people that they should never go to war again.

'That too,' said Grandma.

'But why has God permitted the war, Grandma?' I asked.

She answered, 'You must never hold God responsible for the war. It is mankind that has made the war. We alone commit all the evil in the world.' 'But surely not natural disasters!' I said. 'Earthquakes, storms, floods, hail and so on.'

Grandma said these were God's punishments for us, but we simply took no notice of that and just complained about everything. But Moses and the prophets had always recognised God's punishments and warned mankind.

'And was it of any use?'

'None at all.'

Terrible. We never learn.

Whit Tuesday, 1918

Visited Gil in the Flying Corps barracks. An N.C.O. (very friendly, probably because I am a girl) asked me whom I wanted. But even before I could answer he said, 'It's Airman Kuhr, as I can see'. 'How can you see that?' I asked in astonishment. 'By the resemblance,' he said smiling all over his face.

So I was allowed to pass. I had to wait in the rather cold guardroom, in which a sergeant sat at a long writing-table rummaging among papers; there was also another older N.C.O. there.

I waited quite a long time; then my brother came. But what did he look like! Was this Gil? This long, pale being in loose-fitting uniform with concertina-trousers, thick boots and a crazy-looking helmet? And his lovely soft, dark hair cut short? Oh Gil, my brother Willi! I gazed at him flabbergasted. I was aroused by the fact that he didn't cast a single glance towards little me, but clicked his heels together in front of the table, his hands pressed against his wretched trousers, his backbone straight as a ruler, his head held stiff and high, staring vacantly into space. Oh boy, oh Diary! Like a corpse! I have myself played the part of Lieutenant von Yellenic like this and so drilled my boys in the yard, until they mastered the rules just like Willi now.

But that was in play. This is reality. My brother, the soldier!

271

Enough to make you spew! (Beg pardon.)

I couldn't feel any more pleasure. When Willi had obtained leave to go for a walk with me and we were at last walking outside on the high road (he still with this vacant look!), I couldn't discover the old way of speaking to each other. The first thing I said was pretty daft; I asked in fact, 'Do you really have to stand to attention in front of those idiots?'

'Why do you say "idiots"?' he answered placidly. 'That is the nicest sergeant we have'. 'It looks so silly when you stand to attention,' I said.

He answered, with some embarrassment, that it was like that in military service and that he would suffer arrest or loss of leave if he went against the rules. I could see that of course, but I felt somehow offended throughout the walk. In the end I couldn't check myself any more and asked outright whether he was not a little pleased that I had visited him in the barracks. Gil said he was very pleased, especially because I had brought him a packet of bread and butter from Grandma. I said, 'There is roast horse-meat on it: Grandma got it from Johr the butcher.'

'On the quiet?'

'No. It was advertised.'

Gil opened the packet in the lane and started to eat. After a while he said, 'Would you like some too?'

I said I had already eaten a slice in the kitchen with Grandma's spread. 'Grandma now puts marjoram in the spread,' I explained, 'It tastes better than mustard – is more piquant, you know, among other things.'

'Does the old lady still always make meat-balls when she gets horse-meat?' he asked, chewing. We can really no longer face the everlasting meat-balls, but then Grandma can also put strips of gristle and fat through the mincer; that produces extra meat and in addition she can make it 'go further' by adding soaked bread. Only, if you are always getting meat-balls instead of a joint, they stick in your throat.

I said, 'Yes, she still keeps making meat-balls. But for you she has just roasted a few slices of meat.'

'Fine', said Willi and ate up the last but one of the sandwiches. My mouth watered, but I said nothing. 'I'll take the other sandwich with me to the barrack-room,' he said, putting it away.

We didn't achieve any real conversation. He didn't ask anything about Androwski and not once did he mention the piano. I said, 'Sometimes I play your songs. I can't play them

272

properly without music of course – I simply strike a few chords and sing, you know. I have also composed a song for Gretel, a dance song that I have written. I play it on the guitar'. 'Have you?' said Gil. He had assumed that vacant look again, for we were already approaching the barracks again. Our time was up. And he kept looking at his wrist-watch. Previously he would have asked immediately how the words of my dance-song went and what the melody was like. Now – nothing!

'Good-bye, Gilly,' I said, when we reached the entrance to the barracks, and gave him my hand.

'Good-bye, dearest!' said Gil, pressing my hand. I should have liked to give him a kiss, but because a soldier was standing in the sentry-box outside the guard-room I refrained, so as not to embarrass Gil. Then I went home without once looking back. I dawdled all the way; I had no desire to go home.

16th May, 1918

The Kenzler children Irma, Waldtraut and little Otto came to-day to take me in their carriage to the Liebenthal estate. Then we went on to the Provost's house. The Kenzler family is actually Protestant, but Frau Kenzler thinks highly of the Provost. He is Polish. Frau Kenzler thinks he has the cleverest brain in the whole neighbourhood, and in addition he is a real artist on the organ and the piano. I was naturally very curious about this.

We travelled in their best coupé, which was drawn by gleaming brown horses whose tails and manes the coachman had plaited and waved. In honour of the day he drove with white reins and a white enamelled whip. Frau Kenzler sat on the blue cushion with me on her left side. Irma and Waldtraut sat on the back seat. Little Otto was allowed to sit next to the coachman. It was lovely looking over the fields in which the crops stood quite high. I would rather have sat up on the box too, but Frau Kenzler thought it was not the right thing for a young lady when we were going as guests to the Provost's.

The Provost's house is a handsome farmstead of red brick with black tarred panels as is common with us. The Provost was already waiting on the entrance steps. I liked him very much, a true Polish gentleman, radiant with kindness. The living-room into which he led us was large, low and light; it had four windows with gathered-up white muslin curtains. The table was covered with a damask cloth, the coffee service was of silver and porcelain. A life-sized cross of black wood took up nearly all one end of the room; Christ was nailed to it. This Christ was certainly a great work of art; his eyes were picked out with glistening bluish mother-of-pearl and his face was sorrowful, a wonderful masterpiece of Spanish carving. I was so scared by this cross that I could hardly look at it, or rather that I would have loved to gaze at it all the while.

Frau Kenzler asked whether I had noticed that Jesus was weeping. 'The Provost will certainly let you take a close look at the tear,' she said. 'Step right under the cross and you will perceive the tear.'

'It is a real pearl of great worth,' remarked the Provost. He smiled but at the same time looked sad. 'The Lord is crying over our world.'

Now I could see the tear plainly; it was attached to the black wood under Jesus's left eye. This tear nearly caused me to break down. Fortunately a little old lady, the Provost's mother, began to pour out coffee at the table and invited me to join the others. 'Help yourself, my dear young lady,' she said, and went on to offer cake with almonds on and cup cakes. The provost possesses land and poultry; that enables you to make good cakes. Frau Kenzler and the Provost discussed politics at the table and Frau Kenzler declared that she regarded our Emperor Wilhelm II as having lit the flame of war.

'Oh, there are a great many who have lit the fire,' observed the Provost. He turned the conversation again to the tear on the cross and said he was sure that the Lord in Heaven was weeping not pearls but real tears because we had so grieved him. Frau Kenzler spoke of the untold millions of dead in the war, among whom was also her beloved son Werner; therefore she could never cease to hold the German government responsible for the outbreak of the war. I could hardly swallow my mouthful of almond cake. To comfort Frau Kenzler the Provost said that the dead would immediately be welcomed as blessed spirits by the angels in heaven. 'Oh, it is true,' he cried fervently. 'The supernatural beings have laurels and roses prepared for the fallen in war – for all victims of the war, dear lady and my dear young lady. And *no* distinction between Germans, Poles, Russians, Serbs, French and so on – no distinction in God's righteousness between all the dead in East, West or South!'

Now, I would gladly have fallen on the Provost's neck! But then Frau Kenzler said wearily, 'Enough of that, Provost, I don't

274

believe it. I don't believe anything! I left the Church after my son's death. For have not *all* the churches blessed these terrible weapons? All I believe in now is the good sense of humankind. This will end the war and change everything.'

'We will pray to the Holy Spirit for that. Amen,' answered the Provost and extended both hands over the table to Frau Kenzler.

I was glad that, after a slight hesitation, she squeezed his hands. All this time I had been waiting for music; I now summoned up courage and cried, 'Please, please, play something on the piano, Provost; Frau Kenzler says you are a virtuoso. I would like it so much!'

The Provost agreed immediately, indeed he literally jumped up and hurried to the piano in his black priest's robes, put some music in place and began to play. I recognised it at once; it was one of Mendelssohn's 'Songs Without Words'. Peace was immediately established in the room. Everything seemed different. When I looked at Frau Kenzler I saw that she was crying but at the same time smiling. It seemed terribly sad.

20th May, 1918

An announcement: Because of the scarcity of material for outer garments in the German nation, a million suits of clothing for workers on the land, in war industries, on the railways and in other essential war work are being sought. The community association of Schneidemühl has to contribute 728 suits. Only 110 have so far been offered as gifts, so that over 600 more are required (so says a prominent newspaper advertisement).

'You could easily give Willi's old confirmation suit,' I said to Grandma. 'The trousers only reach as far as his calves now.'

But Grandma thought she could perhaps cut out from them some kind of sailor's outfit for me. She said, 'Leave it – you never know.'

I thought of the coffin shoes and shrugged my shoulders dismissively. But I didn't mention the shoes. I thought it beneath my dignity to say what I thought about the sailor suit. I am much too old for that.

21st May, 1918

The new class-teacher, the curate, was again watching me to-day through his fingers held in front of his face. If he thinks I didn't notice it he must take me for a fool. Thank God I have a photograph of Fräulein Kutschelis. Next time I will put it openly on the desk, so that he can't help seeing it. Another thing: Mummy arrived yesterday.

27th May, 1918

A terrible thing has happened in our family: our old Uncle George Otter, the Postal Secretary with the little velvet cap and the white pointed beard, has been burnt to death. Can you imagine such a thing? He had gone to Königsblick in the afternoon with his daughter, our Aunt Agatha, to smoke his beloved cigar for a while in peace. Aunt Luise never lets him do this; she always maintains that the cigar smoke settles in the curtains and then the whole flat reeks of it. So off he went with his daughter into the forest.

But who came back alone on the seven o'clock train but Aunt Agatha. She was utterly distraught and bathed in tears. As soon as she reached the stairs she called out in her high thin voice 'Papa! Papa!' so that we all rushed together in the vestibule. Aunt Luise shrieked, 'But Agatha dear, whatever is the matter? Where is Papa?' Aunt Agatha cried, 'He burned like a torch! Like a torch!' and threw her arms up in the air.

Weren't we horrified! Especially because we just couldn't understand it. So we crowded in confusion into the Otter's kitchen where Aunt Luise and Aunt Agatha were shouting at each other and crying.

Grandma said, 'Now control yourself, Agatha, and tell us from the beginning what has happened. Where is George?'

'Papa was sitting at the top of the hill smoking his cigar!' whimpered Aunt Agatha, staring in front of her as if she had seen a ghost. 'Good!' said Grandma. 'So he was sitting there. And where were you while he was smoking up there?'

'Picking flowers!' said Aunt Agatha crying. 'I was down the slope looking for flowers. When I happened to look up at Papa, he kept beating the ground with his hands – like this.' And she indicated with her fat hands how Uncle Otter had beaten the ground. Suddenly she cried out again in her high-pitched voice, 'And I called, "Papa, whatever are you doing? What is wrong? Have you lost something?" Then he stood up, and flames rose high around him. Flames!' She writhed again with horror and cried out again 'Like a torch! He stood still and burned like a

276

torch, and it was burning all around him too. Then –' She cried aloud. 'Then he collapsed without a word in the middle of the fire. All that bit of the wood flared up in an instant. And I –'

Grandma, deathly pale, said – 'And you?' 'I couldn't do a thing,' wailed Agatha wringing her hands. 'What could I do? I couldn't get through the fire. I just kept shouting, "Help! Help! Papa!"'

'And then?' said Grandma. She put her arms around her sister Luise and collapsed with her on to the kitchen chair. 'Then some people who were out there walking came rushing up and tried to put the fire out and pull him up out of it; they were much nearer to him than I was. But he was already dead. Dead! Dead!'

Grandma and Aunt Luise remained clinging to each other and crying bitterly. And Frau Witkowski came running up from the flat below, and with her head in her hands kept crying 'Is it possible! Is it possible!' Then Frau Schönfeld came too from the top flat, sobbing, 'My God! What a calamity!'

Willi and I didn't know what to do. I saw that Willi was even grinning with embarrassment. That of course was the most stupid thing he could have done. I threw him an angry look although he had just come on leave and I wanted to make the days as nice as possible for him. Luckily Mummy had gone for an evening walk and didn't have to experience the scene. When she arrived home she was naturally terribly shocked. She asked where Uncle's body was now. Then the hearse immediately went to bring him and four men carried a brown oak coffin up the stairs. The coffin was closed. Willi and I were sent out while Mummy and Frau Schönfeld opened wide the door of the Otter's flat and Uncle Otter's coffin was carried into the living-room. We heard Aunt Agatha crying out loud again, 'Papa! Dear Papa! Like a torch!' Willi whispered to me: 'Heavens, great snakes! Has she gone mad?' It was really unbearable.

31st May, 1918

Uncle Otter was buried to-day. Before the mourners appeared, Aunt Otter came in an old-fashioned black lace dress (even at this time still carrying her 'Patents' tied round her body under the skirt) and said to Grandma, 'Bertha dear, just call the children. You can just have another look at him before the coffin is closed.' We were just standing at the veranda window talking about the funeral, which was due to take place at 4 o'clock. Willi at once said anxiously to Mummy, 'Do we really have to? I would rather not see Uncle Otter.' But Mummy threw her head back with a severe look and said, 'Of course we must! First, it is Aunt Luise's wish and secondly it is the last respect that we can show to Uncle Otter in this world. Bear that in mind for all time!'

We were all in dark clothes. Willi, instead of his badly-fitting uniform, was wearing his old blue confirmation suit which had become much too short for him at the ankles and wrists; but we really couldn't buy a new suit. Then we went across the hall to the Otter's flat, where all the occupants of the house were already assembled. They were carrying flowers and wreaths. I was feeling a bit sick. The entrance door was decorated with a garland of fir. The brown coffin rested on two stools covered with a black cloth with silver fringes. The coffin was open, the lid leaning upright against the wall. The coffin was lined with white tulle and cuttings of myrtle. Uncle Otter lay in a black suit and his best white shirt with black loops in all the tulle. His hands were folded across his chest. They had a few red and brown burn marks, and the left half of his face had some red patches but not very bad. His white hair and the white pointed beard were a bit singed on the left side. But all in all he didn't look as if he had burned 'like a torch'. His face, which had always been round like Aunt Agatha's, now seemed to be narrower. His expression was if we no longer meant the slightest thing to him. A stranger.

We went close up to the coffin and looked down at the dead uncle. I just couldn't imagine how he had once laughed so heartily at the window when I called out to him from the yard that I no longer knew what there would be to eat for lunch; I thought perhaps pea soup with pig's ears.

To my astonishment and Willi's a crowd of people came to the funeral, even public service associations with their banners and a brass band that played 'Jesus in whom I trust'. The procession moved off from our house. I saw Gretel with her mother and waved to her. My family went in a closed cab that belonged to the coachman Fletschok. Aunts Otter and Agatha and Aunt Clara Schwarz from Bromberg, Grandma's youngest sister, went in another cab in front of ours. There were five cabs in all; in the last three were the oldest friends of our families. Then followed the mourners who went on foot. The bells of the church in the Neue Markt had been tolling for some time. On Posener Strasse I suddenly couldn't help thinking of Lieutenant Waldecker. I was all at once terribly sad. It is unfortunately true that the memory of the dead Lieutenant Waldecker made me much sadder than all this funeral. I couldn't help thinking how he had once played with my plait and said, 'I should like to see your hair undone one day!' I had a job not to cry. But it would have looked as if I was crying for Uncle Otter, and that would have been untrue.

Uncle Otter didn't want to have any more to do with us – you could see that plainly in his face. He had always been alone in his room; we never knew exactly how he passed the time. He was probably glad that he could leave the old flat in which he wasn't allowed to smoke. I hope he will be allowed to smoke as much as he wants to in Heaven; he really needs a little happiness.

Grandma said to Mummy, 'But Grete what do you think of the little Haber girls in Berlin not coming to George's funeral?' Then I remembered the three Aunts Emma, Minna and Lieschen Haber who used to have a little hat shop in Friedrichstrasse and had left Schneidemühl with the other refugees. The funeral procession went right past their little shop, that has now been closed for so long. Aunt Emma, with her red nose, always used to look out of her millinery-room, smiling and waving, when we girls came out of school.

After the funeral we had coffee in the Central Hotel, and ate war-time cakes with artificial cream. Willi scoffed four cakes; he grinned at me and I suppressed a laugh. Some of the men drank wine. Aunt Otter kept wiping her nose, which was quite swollen with crying, with a crochetted lace handkerchief. I felt terribly sorry for her; she was so tiny in her black dress. Strange to say I didn't feel very sorry for Aunt Agatha. I was even rather angry with her. I think I would have gone through the fire for my Papa.

1st June, 1918

I have just read the last sentence again. My Papa – I still remember how astonished young Gil and I were that time when our brothers Hans and Ernst turned up and spoke of 'Papa'. Our Papa lives in Danzig and has never, as far as I know, asked after his two youngest. Gil and I have no feeling for our father. So long as Grandfather was alive, Grandpa was the head of the family. Later it was Grandma and Mummy. We are a living example of the fact that a father is not always necessary in a family, if there is enough love there. Besides Grandma and Mummy I love dear Gil, and he loves me.

Aren't we lucky people?

10th June, 1918

What have I done to that Curate man? I like the Poles – no different from any one else; a fine nation and good neighbours. Why does this man hate me now?

I have left school.

For two days I was ill; Grandma put me to bed. I don't know what was wrong with me; perhaps it was Uncle Otter's death that caused my headache, perhaps the expiry of Gil's leave.

When I went back to school, the Curate asked, 'Where have you been for the last two days?'

I looked at him in astonishment and said, 'It says in the sick note – I was in bed.'

He compressed his lips and said, looking scornfully at me, 'But could you at the same time be going around smoking cigarettes in the evenings?'

'Pardon?' I said, thinking I hadn't understood him.

'Smoking cigarettes – with the soldiers'.

The girls in the class were now getting worried and looking at me anxiously. Suddenly a cold fury took hold of me. When I realised what a poor opinion of me the Curate had, I bent down for my school bag, seized the pen case, stuffed it into the bag with the exercise books, fastened the straps tight and lifted the whole bag up in the air. Then I flung it over the heads of my class-mates in the direction of the teacher's desk; there was a fair old crash. Luckily the straps held and nothing fell out. A deathly silence prevailed; even the Curate said nothing; he had fallen back into his chair and was red as fire. I walked up to his desk, picked the bag up from the floor, and left the classroom without a word.

For a moment I thought the Curate would run after me and shake me or perhaps box my ears, although beating is forbidden in our school. But nothing happened. So I sauntered along the old corridor, down which I had walked so many hundreds of times, past a few class-room doors behind which I could hear the voices of teachers and the high-pitched answers of the pupils, and down the broad staircase to the ground floor. I thought how Dora Haensch and I had once sat on one of the steps bewailing Prince who had been enrolled with the Medical Corps dogs. Then I took one last mistrustful look at the corridor on the right where the headmaster's room was – Headmaster Enderlein. I thought about his everlasting grudge against me – 'the naughty little girl with the horrible look' – and went out through the school door.

Now I was free. Never again will I go into the Empress Augusta Victoria school of Schneidemühl.

Perhaps I am grown up from now on.

Grandma didn't scold me when I told her all about it. She just asked what I proposed to do now. I said I should like best of all to take an exam to be an infants' nurse in the Municipal Home for Children and Infants; there were so many sick babies and so few to care for them. Grandma agreed with this. We decided to go the very next day to Mayoress Krause and ask her to speak for me with the matron of the home, as I am definitely still too young for an exam.

'Grandma,' I said, 'how ever could the Curate think such a thing of me?'

Grandma said, 'Who can see people's thoughts? You are no longer a child. We don't want to talk about it any more; it is over. But it is a pity.'

I asked what she would do if the school authorities took any steps against me. Grandma said she already knew what she would say. After a while I said, 'Are you angry with me, Grandma?' Grandma shook her head. Then I was happy.

12 June, 1918

The dancing lessons are finished. Herr Kleinschmidt wished me luck for my later dance studies. He seemed to have forgotten that he at one time said it was too late for me to take a proper ballet course. You have 'Lift', he said (that means in ballet terms, lightness in jumping), 'and great power of expression.' He thanked me for practising with the most awkward pupils and so helping him. I was very proud and wrote a long letter to Mummy.

In the afternoon I met Androwski on the way to the Sandsee. At first I was nervous about accompanying a young man, whom I didn't recognise at once, on a lonely path through the woods; then I was glad, for Androwski has stopped visiting us since my brother is in the forces. He blushed with pleasure and said he had just been thinking of me. I suddenly wanted to tell him about great-grandfather's bible and the text that Grandma had turned up for me. Androwski asked scornfully how I thought I could combine a dancing profession with my 'prophesying', 'Oh, that is simple!,' I cried. 'I can express everything in dance form – a dying child for example, or a mother who has to give up her son, or a soldier who has met with a bullet, or –'

Androwski laughed and kicked up some sand with the toe of his shoe. He declared he had never heard of such dances and doubted whether they would find favour with the public. He said he would like me to write books. In his opinion that was where my gift lay. I answered that I could do both – dance and write. Androwski went on casting up so much sand that it was like walking in a cloud and I began to cough. 'Besides,' he said, 'I think your calling to prophesy is absurd.'

Now I went red and said, 'Why?'

'I have nothing against you making propaganda for a good cause,' he retorted; 'that is close to my stand-point, that you should write. But don't bring into it God and the prophets. God is the illusory product of our human fears. We have invented God because we were afraid of the emptiness of our life, above all of death. No one wants to go into the grave to be eaten by worms, therefore we dream of the Beyond. You should understand that we escape, with our fantasies into an everlasting life of bliss – to the little angels!' He laughed bitterly. 'The little halleluja-singing and harp-playing angels!'

I said that the Archangels were definitely not such dainty little angels.But Androwski became more and more bitter. I asked him to stop, but he just talked all the more vehemently. He said that mankind's only duty was to work for his fellow men, to think and to try to save them from catastrophes. 'For we must work madly to save this race of ants from extinction,' he said. 'That is the only true prophesying and that is what the Russians are aiming at with their revolution.' 'Who has said that we must save this race of ants from extinction?' I asked.

'Now you want me to say, "The Bible!"' cried Androwski. 'But my answer to you is – Natural Science. Natural Science is the result of logical thinking. That is why it leaves God out of consideration.'

I spat out some chewed pine-needles which tasted abominable, and asked, 'Don't you believe in God at all?'

'Heavens, no!' said Androwski. 'There is after all something more rational, namely humanity. Revolutionary humanity.'

He expounded to me the length and breadth of what humanity is; it appealed to me very much, but I thought carefully about God and felt bad that I didn't know with what words to defend him. It is my fate that I never know what to say when the subject becomes tricky. At those times I think a thousand thoughts, following one another more and more quickly; in the end they get all mixed up and I lose the threads. While Androwski was speaking more and more interestingly about revolutionary humanity, I began silently to argue with God; I berated him because he had promised solemnly to Moses and the prophets that he would put words in their mouth at the right time. According to Grandma I am also his prophet, but he doesn't think of putting words in my mouth; on the contrary I become more and more stupid. At length Androwski and I walked on in silence till we saw the Sandsee in front of us. We sat on a seat there and watched the fish leaping out of the water. 'Are they just playing or are they snapping at gnats?' I said, but didn't expect any answer; and Androwski didn't say anything. After a while I said that on 1st July I would begin to work in the Municipal Home for Children and Infants.

'Oh yes?' murmured Androwski. He didn't seem to have any further interest in me and my plans. 'Do you think that's good?' I said. I so much wanted him to say something nice to me; I would gladly have run away.

Androwski answered, 'Yes, yes. Better than playing soldiers.'

'We don't play soldiers any more,' I cried indignantly. That was a lie, because Gretel and I still play Nurse Martha and Lieutenant von Yellenic in our spare time; but I decided in that instant to have done with the game. I suddenly had a strong desire for Androwski to fall madly in love with me; I moved close to him, squeezed his arm and smiled at him. He pulled away from me as if he had burnt himself and declared he must now go home and do some swotting for the physics lesson.

'Good, let's go!' I cried also jumping up. 'That was a lovely walk!'

But it wasn't a lovely walk, it was even a loathsome walk; above all there was the matter with God.

14th July, 1918

When I took Gil's birthday cake to him in the Flying Corps barracks, he said, 'Things are cracking up.'

'Listen,' I said, 'I am now a nurse in the children's home.'

Gil didn't think this any more interesting; he was preoccupied with the cake. 'Perhaps the war will soon end now,' I said.

'Very likely!' said Gil chewing. 'Things are cracking up.'

'Aren't you glad that it may soon end?' I asked.

Gil answered that he was anxious about the peace. 'Let's wait and see what effect the peace terms will have on us,' he said. 'They will make us quite small, quite small.'

'The main thing is – peace!' I cried. I told Gil that I had to work as the youngest infant nurse in the home. Gil began to listen more closely when I talked about my efforts with the guitar. I am practising all the scales and working out accompaniments. Wherever I am invited I take 'El Bobo' with me; they say at once 'Play something, Piete!' Then they sit round me in a circle and listen. As there are lovers nearly everywhere, I sing and play songs of love and yearning; sometimes I fancy I am a gipsy in a coffee-house and am now full of joy and now sad. Now and then I fall head over heels in love with some one; then at home I make up heartfelt poems. I then sing these to the guitar; no one realises that they are my own poems; most people think they are unknown Löns songs or such-like. In any case they listen to them quite attentively; the lovers kiss each other and sit holding hands.

But what are my songs compared with Gil's compositions! Mummy recently wrote that she got her pupil Fräulein Lap to sing 'What is the name of Queen Ringang's little daughter' and 'Sleep, sleep, nothing but sleep', in a house concert; it met with great applause. Gil looked at me wide-eyed as I told him this.

He eventually deigned to ask me how I got on on my first day in the Infants' Home.

'I put on a white apron and had to wash my hands with a brush,' I said, whereon Willi had to laugh.

'Do you still do ballet training?' he said. I answered that I didn't have much time left for training because of the work in the Infants' Home. I get up at six o'clock and work from seven in the morning until six in the evening. A thousand times a day I have to wash my hands in a solution of disinfectant; my skin is already quite sore from it. Grandma has bought me a box of grease to rub into my hands at night.

Suddenly it struck me that I hadn't congratulated Gil on his birthday, and I wished him much happiness in the year to come. 'Perhaps you can soon go to Berlin when the war is over.'

'I'll have to go into the Dresdner bank then,' said Gil. It sounded as if he was saying 'I'll have to go to the scaffold then.'

'But you could carry on with your studies,' I said. 'The best would be for you to go to the College of Music'.

'And who would pay for that?' said Gil, 'I shall have to earn.

284

Mummy has to earn too, because the Music School has gone to pieces, and Grandma has more or less lost everything through the war.'

That is right. But Mummy combines singing lessons with her work in the Dresdner bank without complaint, and we young ones can work even more. We talked about what you can achieve with effort. It was eventually time for Gil to return to the barracks, and my free afternoon was over as well. We kissed each other good-bye as no one was around. 'You and your freckles!' said Gil. I was immediately reminded of Lieutenant Waldecker and I rushed off. 'Till next time!' shouted my brother after me. He added, 'Thank Grandma very much for the cake!'

20th July, 1918

On the 16th or 17th July the whole family of the Tsar was murdered in St. Catherinesburg. Tsar Nicholas, Tsarina Alexandra, the beautiful Princesses and the young heir, who was a haemophiliac and often had to be carried because of bodily weakness. They were all collected together and shot. What a blood-bath! I imagine how the Tsar's family, who certainly loved one another just as much as our family, stared with horror as they saw themselves surrounded by soldiers pointing their rifles at them. And how the children screamed as the first of them or perhaps their parents collapsed streaming with blood, and what they thought during the seconds between salvoes. Then I think again how the Russians at first idolised the Tsar's family and were prepared to die for them and for Russia! Will it be the same with us, so that Emperor Wilhelm, the Empress Augusta Victoria, and all the Princes and Princesses, including the Crown Prince and Crown Princess Cecilia, are shot? Dear God, please, please, not that! If the Emperor is to blame for the war, he can surely be punished in some other way, dear God! You surely are for gentleness, are you not? Your son Jesus spoke of pity. He cannot possibly think differently from you! Just what is to become of Germany? There is talk of a big offensive of the Allies under the French General Foch and terrible losses on all sides at Soissons. As if the losses could go on getting greater and greater! So it looks like the end! And do you know, dear God? At first when war was declared people sang in front of the Emperor's Palace, 'Now thank we all our God!'

28th July, 1918

I no longer feel a stranger in the Infants' Home. I feel as if I have already for a long time been responsible for everything. Oh, these babies! Skin and bone. Little starving bodies. And such big eyes! When they cry it sounds like a feeble squeak. One little boy will certainly soon die. He has a face like a dried mummy; the doctor injects him with a saline solution. When I bend over his bed, the little one looks at me with great big eyes like a wise old man; yet he is only six months old. Quite clearly there is a question in his eyes – indeed a reproach. I am continually pinching gauze nappies for him; the cellulose ones cling fast to the children's bleeding behinds; they yell when you try carefully to remove the wet paper with oil.

The home has only a few nappies of real material. All the rest are lined with cellulose. But the bottle-feeding of the sucklings is ideal. Nurse Vera works in the milk kitchen; it has to be brought to exactly the right temperature with the help of big thermometers. Each child is given its due compound, but sometimes only rice or oatmeal gruel, or tea.

There is also a section for bigger children. The eldest is three years old. At first Sister Gertrude entrusted only this section to me. I had to put the children on potties, wash, comb and dress them and feed them at little tables. The head of one boy was covered with moist yellow scurf from which drops of puss were continually exuding. The first time I saw it I felt really ill; the boy disgusted me. Sister Gertrude told me to remove the moist scurf with a fine-toothed comb. I thought I could never do it; at the first attempt I was nearly sick; the boy also began at once to scream pitifully. Then it occurred to me to keep pressing cotton-wool soaked in oil on to the part of the head where the scurf was to be removed. Suddenly it ceased to make me feel sick; I was glad that the combing no longer seemed to hurt the little one. He stuck three fingers of his right hand in his mouth and sucked them hard while I removed the scurf bit by bit and kept putting fresh oily cotton-wool on the festering places. Eventually the skull was quite clear but with an angry redness; it glistened with oil and moisture from the sores. I called the sister; she disinfected the head and wrapped sterile gauze round it. Then I took the little boy in my arms and rocked him before putting him in his bed. He went to sleep at once, still sucking the three fingers.

2nd August, 1918

Families, especially young soldiers' wives keep bringing more sick children to our home.

I am again in the section for very ill nurslings, which I much prefer; one of the previous older pupils of the Empress Augusta Victoria School, Fräulein Hertha Quast, is now in the bigger children's ward. I admire Fräulein Quast greatly and I must confess I am actually a bit in love with her. She is proud, and when she is not in nurse's uniform she wears stylish clothes while I go around everlastingly in skirt and blouse. She asked me the other day whether I had known Gretel Wegner for long. I answered that Gretel was almost like a younger sister to me; I had got to know her when she was five years old. I was surprised that Fräulein Quast asked about Gretel; so far as I know she had never seen us together. But she did.

Hertha Quast said: 'It's remarkable that you find so young a thing good company. You can't possibly ever have a serious conversation with her.'

'Why not?' I asked, taken aback. 'Gretel understands everything I say.'

'And I have noticed you a lot in the home,' said Fräulein Quast. 'It seems as if you love these sick children.'

I laughed and said that it didn't just seem like it, I really did love them.

'Do you like the work here?'

'Very much. Don't you?'

'No,' retorted Fräulein Quast. 'Absolutely not. How could I like this terrible work?'

I couldn't understand this and asked why in that case she was here.

'I am filling my time in,' answered Fräulein Quast, 'You've got to do something useful, but I definitely don't enjoy doing this work.'

'Then I would rather read, play music or carry on studying, 'I said.

This led her to ask whether I sometimes went for walks, and without Gretel.

'Of course,' I said. 'I wander all over the place with my guitar, mostly by the Sandsee or in the Königsblick woods. Or I go across the fields. I imagine then that the fields belong to me and I have got to look after everything, the rotation of crops for

287

example and the pastures.'

This was so unimaginable to Fräulein Quast that she laughed out loud. 'You could go for a walk with me some time,' she suggested.

I was again perplexed at this; I couldn't imagine that she could have any desire to go walking with me. I naturally agreed and we arranged to go to the 'Little Castle in the Woods', on the next free afternoon. I am pleased about this.

5th August, 1918

Nothing will come of our walk for some time, for I have a month of night duty in the infants' home, starting from yesterday. The duty begins at 6 o'clock every evening and finishes at 6 in the morning, but after that I have to put in another hour in the milk kitchen, preparing the milk mixtures, filling bottles and attaching the right numbers to the necks of the bottles. During the night I have to organise the supply of nappies and put out the packets of cellulose. Also navel-bandages and gauze bandages have to be unrolled – in short, what with drying-out, supplementary feeds, sitting them on potties, taking temperatures and other services to the sick, there is plenty to do. The bigger children slept last night, but the sick nurslings were bad. Most of them suffer from bed-sores on their poor bleeding bottoms; I frequently put ointment on and I beg from the day nurses some of the scarce muslin nappies. When the babies are wrapped up comfortably and dry, I hold them in my arms a little while, rocking them until they are nearly asleep. Yesterday I was going to read a bit between times but I didn't manage to.

I am rather anxious about the milk kitchen. Nurse Vera has certainly given me full instructions about each mixture, and everything is also very carefully written down. But how easy it is when you are over-tired to make mistakes and get something wrong.

But I am also nervous about being on my own at night. There is no one in the big building other than me and the children, not even a dog. Only a telephone, so that if the worst comes to the worst I can call the municipal hospital. But the hospital is pretty far away. We have in the cellars, besides the milk kitchen, other rooms in which there are ice-boxes containing milk and milk products; next to these are stocks of vegetables, tinned meat and potatoes for the bigger children. The nursing staff are not provided with food; we take sandwiches and thermos flasks of malt coffee, tea or soup. These provisions might well attract burglars. And what would I do then?

I said the prayer that Grandma taught me when I was little, and came to this passage:

Oh, preserve me from all fear
In every danger be thou near,
May illness not disturb my sleep,
Let sounds of war their distance keep.

I just exchanged the words 'me' and 'my' for 'us' and 'our'.

10th August, 1918

It happened to-day at 9 o'clock in the morning (when I had stayed on longer at the home to bath the children because Nurse Vera wasn't feeling well) that little seven-month old Gerhard, who was in the bath-tub, suddenly contorted his whole body, his arms quivering, his neck dislocated, and all at once lay as stiff as a board in my arms. I immediately yelled for the sister, who quickly placed the baby on the nursing-table and rubbed him with a woollen towel, then put him back in the bath, while I had to pour hot and cold water alternately over his chest from a bowl. But he was motionless and stayed thus. The sister gave him another injection. We observed the child anxiously; then Sister Gertrude said, 'Telephone the doctor. Little Gerhard has collapsed; he is dead.'

I asked whether no more help was possible, for the little one had only a little earlier been kicking vigorously in warm water. But nothing more could be done. After the doctor had been I had to dress the little child in a little white shirt and jacket and put him back in his freshly-made bed; I was able to get a few green twigs from the front garden and decorate the pillow and bed-clothes. We spread a large net over the bed. Beneath it lay little Gerhard like a wax doll; his hands were like glass, quite transparent.

Mummy has just written me a really lovely letter to-day. She says –

'I wish you much happiness in your new calling, which will of course just be an interlude before more artistic work later on. But the experience you are now getting will be a help to you in many situations in your life, my precious Piete.'

11th August, 1918

The parents of little Gerhard have ranted and raved that the Infants Home is to blame for the death of their child. But that is not true; we looked after Gerhard according to instructions and with loving care. The bath-water had just the right degree of heat according to the thermometer and at first he was even enjoying his bath. Nothing wrong had happened, but he was just a war-time child and apparently not strong enough to live.

As soon as the parents learned that the child had died in my arms they began to get really desperate. They reproached Sister Gertrude bitterly for not ensuring that the nursing staff was sufficient. 'She is not much more than a child herself!' they cried, meaning me. It was terrible and I immediately wondered what I could have done wrong. But Sister Gertrude said, 'Nurse Elfriede is a great help to me, and I have every confidence in her.'

I was speechless because of her praise; it naturally pleased me, but I was still sad at heart. The parents' blame was worse than the insults that the Curate had thrown at me at school. Then at noon the parents took the child away in a white coffin.

Now I shall always mistrust myself when I have to bath infants. Two of our nurses are ill with influenza. So I have to help out although I am on night duty. Among the bigger children two girls are feverish. We have isolated them in a third room which was formerly Sister Gertrude's office. We have installed her chair, writing table and records cupboard in a corner of the broad corridor.

15th August, 1918

Germany is nearly finished, Dear Diary. We have suffered a terrible defeat at Amiens. Most of our soldiers surrendered to the English. At the station a sergeant said to Grandma, 'Well, Mother, you will soon be able to close our soup-kitchen. We are done for, fini, beaten!' When Grandma came home from duty at the station, she was very pale. 'Make me a strong coffee, child,' she said. I heated up so many roasted barley-beans that the coffee looked black. It did her good. 'You also look as if you are ready to drop,' she said. We looked at each other closely. 'There's nothing wrong with me,' I said.

290

16th August, 1918

Now the poor little worm that was all skin and bone, and whom the doctor injected with a saline solution, has died too. He had become my darling. I devoted every spare moment to him and he would look at me continually with his over-serious eyes like a wise old man. He never smiled. This dear little boy died in my arms too; he simply laid his head, which looked much too big for the skeleton of a body, on my arm and died without a twitch or a rattle.

I bedded him down in the nicest possible way under the net covering after arranging round him as many flowers as I could find in the meadow behind the Catholic Church of the Holy Family. Surrounded by these he looked horribly like a very old dwarf, who had been dead for a hundred years.

17th August, 1918

My dead little one caused me such a shock during last night's watch that my heart is still pounding even now. I had moved his bed out into the passage where it would be cooler, but went to him several times and looked at him sadly. Between three and four o'clock in the morning I suddenly heard a strange buzzing, such as I had never heard before. It seemed to come from his bed and I bent over the netting. True enough, the noise was coming from under the net; but there was nothing to be seen. The buzzing definitely came from the little dead one. This was so terrible that I went cold with horror. The buzzing was not constant in volume; for some time it would be loud, then stop for a while, then it would come again. Horrible! Was the child not really dead? Was he breathing with his lungs which had begun to live again? I tore the covering away and bent down lower. Yes, the buzzing came from his mouth, which was a little bit open. I summoned all my courage and strength and tried to open the tiny mouth a little wider so that the poor lungs could take in air more easily. Then, oh God!, a great fat blue-bottle crawled out, the sort of blow-fly that feeds on carrion. For the sake of the dear little dead child I was full of loathing and hatred for the fly. I couldn't help thinking immediately of the rats on the battlefields, these scavengers of corpses. I drove the fly out of the window and drew the net tight around the bed. Now no more buzzing came from my poor little boy. He was dead. Nothing other than dead.

The doctor who examined Grandma also listened to me and he diagnosed an over-strained heart and something to do with the ribs. I must stop work in the Infant's Home 'with immediate effect' and cannot return to work until he gives me a certificate of fitness. Now I could go walking with Fräulein Quast. I showed her some paths that she didn't know before; on the way I took my shoes off and went barefoot over the sand. Fräulein Quast couldn't understand that this didn't hurt me; I laughed and said that Gretel and I often went barefoot through the fields because the ground felt so pleasant. But I was glad when I got home again; it was too hot for walking, and my heart was also still beating hard.

What a pleasure! Dear Gil was on leave and was there with a nice young sergeant. Grandma was baking apple-rings and made coffee for the three of us. Sergeant Friedrich said that we were approaching collapse on all fronts. Gil rubbed his hands and uttered a loud 'Fine! Fine!'

'What will you do, Kuhr, when you are discharged?' asked Sergeant Friedrich.

To my surprise Gil said that he wanted to go to Berlin to the University. That was the first that I had heard of this.

Friedrich asked what he wanted to study. Gil answered, 'Philosophy and sociology. I should particularly like to go to Mexico one day.' 'That is not at all a bad idea,' said Sergeant Friedrich. 'Things are going to get ugly in Germany.' He looked at me. 'Revolution, you know!'

I said nothing and thought of the Tsar's family and what Revolution might be like in Germany. Suddenly I thought I must finish with the 'Nurse Martha and Lieutenant von Yellenic' game. I don't want the role of a soldier any more, still less that of an officer; that time is past. There will be Revolution; soldiers and officers have no future in that. There is no point in Gretel and me going on with the same old game – war, wounds, hospital, convalescence, casino dances – and again war, the Front and aircraft crashes and so on. And funerals too. But we couldn't really play anything but war games while there was no peace. Perhaps it is bad that Gretel and I are so happy in spite of everything, when we play Nurse Martha and Lieutenant von Yellenic; we forget how terrible life around us really is. We must stop this play-acting. There has certainly never been such a wonderful game in all the world; but now it must finish. We are no longer children. It's all over.

29th August, 1918

I broke the news to Gretel that Lieutenant von Yellenic has to die.

What a scene that was! I played the part of a postman and handed her one of our tiny little hand-written imaginary news sheets. I always write these myself. This one contained the following death-notice with black edging:–

The Officer Corps of Schneidemühl Air Station regrets the death in the air of its comrade Lieutenant Joan Graf Yellenic, Knight of the Order of Merit and Holder of the Iron Cross, First Class and Second Class, who met with a fatal accident yesterday during a training flight over our garrison. The transfer of his mortal remains from the Air Force Station to the Railway Station en route for Castle Yellenic in Hungary will take place at 3 o'clock to-morrow afternoon. The Officer Corps express to the sorely tried parents, relatives and friends its deep sympathy.

(Sgd.) v. Hocker, Commander
Commandant of Air Personnel, Schneidemühl

Oh, how shocked was Nurse Martha, and therefore Gretel! She was pretending to give a little ladies' party, sitting on our old sofa serving (pretend) coffee and (pretend) cakes. 'Do help yourself,' she said. When she had made out the death notice, she gave out a loud shriek, 'What? What? But that's nonsense!' and she read it again and again. Then she jumped up and went at least as white as her apron. I laughed inwardly, but was also a bit shocked, because I had not expected that her pain would be so real. She also began really to cry. I was dumbfounded. It was as if Lieutenant von Yellenic had been, not just a fictitious character, but a real living man. But nothing now could alter his death as an airman. To-morrow we shall enact my military funeral procession to the railway goods station. I feel quite worked up myself and am pleased with this climax of our game.

30th August, 1918

Night-time. You can't imagine, dear diary, how I have laid

myself out! No one was in the house. Grandma was at a meeting of the Patriotic Women's Guild – Gil at the barracks. In Gil's room, Grandpa's old office, there has been for a little while the camp-bed which used to occupy half of the attic room. I covered it with a cloth and with old sheets and pillows. I made up a life-size long figure – head, chest, legs, everything, and covered it with a black coach-rug just as if this was plainly supported by the body underneath it. Then I placed uncle Bruno's old army boots, next to each other in military fashion and sticking out from under the cloth. I had previously whitened the boots. Then, where Lieutenant Yellenic's head showed itself, I placed on it the dented, flat, steel helmet of César van Glabeke. Where the hands should have been, I placed uncle's old cavalry sword, point downwards, and also a little bunch of dried lilac that Mummy had brought from Norderney. I had made out of cardboard two Iron Crosses with black ink and white edge – these were the Iron Crosses, first and second class – and similarly a paper 'Order of Merit' which Lieutenant von Yellenic had won after his 80th 'kill' with his fighter-plane 'Flea'. I laid these three medals on Grandma's blue velvet pin-cushion immediately above the sword-handle. It looked marvellous!

Now I drew the curtains and lit two tallow-candles at the head of the corpse. They were in fact only two little stumps, but as they were stuck in Grandma's tall brass candle sticks, they looked like big funeral candles. After all this I closed the door of the room.

Meanwhile Gretel had dressed up as the mourning Nurse Martha, wearing Grandma's black dress, which we shortened with safety-pins, and her black widow's hat with a long black crêpe veil. She had put on the thin black face-veil below this and a white handkerchief in her hand. My God, I had always pictured her like this as Lieutenant von Yellenic's widow; but we could never marry because she was the adored wife of my command-ing officer, Colonel v. Hocker. In this way she was unfortunately never my widow. Now we pretended that the officers and staff of the Schneidemühl Flying Corps were marching to the funeral of their imprudent but greatly admired hero of the air. I sat down at the piano and played a part of Chopin's Funeral March, which is so terribly sad. Then I beat dully in slow-march time on a saucepan muffled with a cloth. It sounded exactly like the drum-roll at a military funeral. Then the procession made its way from the bedroom through the dining-room and drawing-room to the door of the office. Nurse Martha stood, now red as fire, now white as a sheet, at the closed door. I rushed back to the piano and played 'Jesus, my protector and saviour, lives,' and Gretel instantly began to cry bitterly – genuine crying. Dear Diary! She was continually blowing her nose on Grandma's white lace hand-kerchief.

Now came the climax: I opened both wings of the door. Gretel whispered 'Oh God!' when she saw Lieutenant von Yellenic's corpse in full war regalia in the light of the candles, and I really must say that it looked just as if an officer was laid out there. I sprang to the piano again and played all three verses of 'I had a comrade'; then Nurse Martha sobbed as if her heart would break, for she had of course always secretly loved Lieutenant von Yellenic.

I fought with myself because I didn't know whether I ought to roar with laughter or cry. I was near to both laughing and crying, for it suddenly struck me that the whole affair resembled the carriage of Lieutenant Waldecker to the goods station. To regain my composure I adopted the role of Commander v. Hocker and whispered angrily to my weeping spouse, 'Stop your blubbering for this fellow!' Then I made a characteristic speech about Flight-lieutenant von Yellenic, in which I honoured his 80 'kills' of enemy aircraft. Then I quickly became another character from our game, namely Captain v. Vogelmann, a particularly kindly and well-liked officer, who gave the order, 'Three times – fire!'

To represent the volley of rifle-shots, I burst three paper bags which I had previously blown up, tied and placed ready. Thereon Captain v. Vogelmann took the swooning Nurse Martha in his arms and kissed her hand long, for he had understood everything.

And so we ended the game of Nurse Martha and Joan von Yellenic, but I was afraid it was not yet altogether finished with, for when Gretel had calmed down and we had put Grandma's things, especially her best widow's hat, back in the cupboard, she asked whether it was now all over, the whole lovely game. I said I didn't know for sure, for the war looked like being over soon, and Lieutenant von Yellenic could then no longer be an officer, especially in a revolution like the Russian one. Gretel thought we could pretend that they had mistakenly buried someone who was not really dead – that had often occurred in this war – and that Joan von Yellenic could perhaps take over the estate in Hungary after the war. That seems to me quite a good idea, especially when I imagine that he would then renounce his title and simply

295

become a farmer. But I really want to stop the game because we are now fully grown-up and our game has been essentially a childhood dream.

2nd September, 1918

Reformation Day, Sedan Day, and Gretel's birthday. I gave her three handkerchiefs which I had embroidered with her monogram. Frau Wegner invited me for coffee and potato fritters. But it was not a proper birthday party. We talked about Arthur Zühlke, Frau Schönfeld's youngest brother, who had most of his leg amputated in hospital. Gretel and I avoided each other's eyes most of the time. Something is missing. I would love to be back serving in the Home for Children and Infants. I wonder if any more children have died.

Grandma has a slight attack of 'flu; she is lying on the sofa and has to keep on drinking. Cases of small-pox have been reported from Berlin. There have been no more potatoes there for weeks. The street-lighting has ended. There is only a single light here and there.

10th September, 1918

Letter from Mummy.

> Children, this autumn is really getting me down. It rains, it pours, and it's cold. And just imagine, I have lost my coal-card. I must get in touch with the coal-merchant first thing tomorrow; luckily the man is devoted to me and will not leave me in the lurch. The soul-destroying work in the office is beginning to sap my strength. I long for freedom and music. But who thinks about a music course now? If the faithful Fräulein Lap didn't come for evening lessons, the piano would go to sleep altogether. I shudder at the emptiness of the music salons. In Berlin everyone is crying out for peace. But what sort of peace will it be? Can we honestly look forward to it? We shall lose everything if we are defeated. Our brave soldiers! Dear Gil & Piete, keep your fingers crossed for poor Germany. It must not be that so much blood has been shed in vain!

I feel sorry for Mummy. If Gil were with her, he could cheer her up a bit; instead of this he is still a soldier. Thank God he is now doing office work; they have discovered his wonderful hand-writing. Perhaps also Sergeant Friedrich is behind it.

I cannot go to Berlin before 1920. Mummy would like to build up the music school again first, so that there is 'the basis of a living' for us, as she puts it. She also wants me to take the exam for a children's and infants' nurse, so that in case of need I have an occupation. It is definite that I am to study singing under her. It is just as definite that I have to earn my living at the same time. What is most definite for me is that in spite of all my work I must find time to study ballet. That will need extra money. I have agreed with Grandma that after the exam I will take lessons in shorthand and typing. I will put my name down for a course at the trade school. I can't earn enough as a nurse. So it is better to get a job in an office as 'typing girl', as Mummy calls it. I will find a good job. Then I can help you a bit too, Mummy. You will see!

4th October, 1918

Gil came on leave to-day. How pleased I was! Since Gretel and I no longer play our game, I loaf around feeling useless, get heartbeat and coughing and long for something to do. Sometimes I even miss school, the girls and Fräulein Kutschelis. Unfortunately the doctor still bars me from service in the Children's Home. He says my heart is weak.

I asked Gil to go for a walk with me. We linked arms and walked over the Karlsberg. Sometimes Gil pressed my arm, sometimes I pressed his, as if we were a couple of lovers. I loved my brother particularly this day; I had been homesick for him for so long. It rained a little and our coats got wet. Gil's military coat threw the water off, but I was wearing my old woollen one, which had worn so thin that I felt every drop of rain through it.

Gil said, 'We had better go back. I'll take you to Fliegner's for an éclair.'

'Oh no, not that,' I said and sank my head on Gil's shoulder. 'I've got a sort of stomach-ache.' But that was a lie. I just don't want to eat éclairs at Fliegner's ever again.

So we trotted homewards in the rain. I asked Gil what the Entente would take away from us Germans when the peace terms were settled.

'Well, Alsace for a start!' answered Gil.

I can't understand that. I have seen thousands of soldiers from Alsace in the troop trains, who went to the Front to fight for

Germany just as much as a matter of course as the others. I asked Gil whether Germany was not the 'Fatherland' for the Alsatians. 'After all, the Alsatians are German,' I said.

'Even more so are they French,' declared Gil. 'I had never realised that before either; but I know it now.'

I asked what else the Entente would take from us.

'Schneidemühl, for example!' said my brother.

'Schneidemühl?' I stood still in horror. 'Why Schneidemühl?' I was really at the end of my tether. Gil said, 'Because they want to propitiate the Poles.'

'You are crazy!' I cried, pushing Gil's arm away. 'You are absolutely balmy. We have been living with the Poles for years. There has never been any trouble between us.'

'But now there is,' said Gil grinning. 'They are actually fed up to the back teeth with our war and they want to establish their own republic – when peace comes.' 'We also want to establish a republic when peace comes', I cried. 'Androwski has said that too. A humanitarian republic!'

'What sort of thing is that?' Gil began to roar with laughter. As we had already turned into Bahnhofstrasse, people looked at us in astonishment, because Gil was laughing out loud and I was furious. I reminded Gil of my conversation with Androwski and his views on humanism and revolution, but Gil was seized with laughter and couldn't stop; he was jumping up and down as he always does when laughing and in his soldier's uniform attracted unwelcome attention. In the end, after a long dispute about Schneidemühl and the Poles, he said I was shockingly un-informed, but he loved me in spite of this. And now he had to add that of course we would have to give up the colonies. The matter of the colonies was immediately obvious to me; I have never been able to understand why people have taken all the land from the negroes into their own possession. And Gil and I were always against the terrible injury that the Spanish raiders inflicted on the Indians, who were much nobler than the Spaniards and had an ancient culture. To-day they are put into so-called 'Reservations' where they can neither live nor die. My brother and I hate all inhumanity.

To return to the colonies, I think it is only right if Germany has to give up the colonies under a peace treaty. The only snag is that the colonies will then get new masters; so they just change their owners. Is there no escape then from this ghastly merry-go-round?

But Schneidemühl! Such a little town! Gil laughed and said, 'With the little town goes a whole German East, lovely big cities like Bromberg and Posen, railway lines and farmland, the cornstore of Germany.' 'But perhaps we shan't lose the war at all!' I cried in desperation. 'None of our soldiers are throwing down their weapons. They all obey the Generals' orders. They simply fight to the death for victory. And what then?'

Gil said wisely, 'You are mistaken, my child. We have already been defeated by the English – at Amiens, please remember. And decisively to be sure. Ludendorff says so too; so he doesn't want to carry on anyway. The Army High Command has requested the Emperor to offer the entente an armistice. Haven't you read that? And Count Herzling of course didn't want to continue as Chancellor. Prince Max von Baden is now Chancellor.

I had no idea that we have yet another Chancellor; I have not been so interested in the war news recently. I much prefer to read books or continue writing my novel.

We had reached our house, but remained standing outside although it was still raining. We simply could not part. Suddenly we heard Fräulein Ella Gumprecht and Aunt Agatha Otter talking loudly with Grandma; they had been visiting her and were now saying good-bye on the stairs. 'Just come away,' whispered Gil, and pulled me along. 'Let's not get mixed up with the old aunts; they've got Hindenburg and Emperor Wilhelm on the brain.'

'Narrow-minded old codgers!' I whispered maliciously and dashed along the street with Gil. 'We're against them, aren't we? Absolutely against narrow-minded folk!'

I accompanied Gil as far as the barracks. He told me on the way that in the battle of Amiens we had lost great quantities of war material and thousands of prisoners – fifteen thousand, he thought.

'That's fine,' I said. 'Those fifteen thousand at least haven't been killed.'

We kissed each other good-bye at the entrance to the barracks. The sentry at the gate grinned. 'Come on leave again soon!' I whispered.

17th October, 1918

It seems certain that my old friend Dora Haensch is coming back to Schneidemühl: the Haensch's are going to lease the canteen at Meveshöh. Then I shall see Jule again too and the dear dog

Prince. I often see Connie. As she still attends the school, she spends many afternoons with me. Out of our old drawing-boards and some wooden laths we have made two easels and we do some painting. That is our favourite occupation. I have been a few times to Miriam Borchardt's in Deutsch-Krone, to hear her play her house-organ. She plays Bach mostly. I then sit in a high, carved chair and sketch her beautiful profile with her long locks. Of course it is not a good likeness. But what does that matter? Once she took me into the old Deutsch-Krone church. She had permission to play the church organ. There was no one in the church. There was a little door in the organ; I slipped in to have a look at the instrument from inside. Miriam had no inkling of this; she thought I was sitting in a pew down in the nave of the church. Suddenly she started to play Bach's Passacaglia. I felt as if my head would split in many pieces. I opened my mouth wide and fell on my knees. With an effort I struggled out of the organ-chamber and for a long time I was deaf. I just kept opening and shutting my mouth and poked my fingers into my ears until I could hear properly again. Miriam was quite horrified and didn't laugh a bit. She is generally very serious.

Frau Kenzler has twice invited me through their coachman to the Adlig Liebenthal estate, but I have sent a message to say that I can't come because of Grandma's cold. That is the truth. Grandma is ill. She lies in bed so pale and tired; her forehead and hands are hot. I make coffee for her and give her rusks which I have got from the Red Cross at the station; it is the only thing that she likes. Sometimes she even pushes the tray of rusks away. She has told Frau Schönfeld, her only confidante, that she can hardly bear the thought of the end of Germany. Yesterday evening when I was sitting on the old footstool by her bed and we were quite alone she said, 'Do you sometimes still think, child, of what it says in the old Bible?'

I rolled the sentence off my tongue like clockwork.

'And how will you one day carry out what it says to you?' asked Grandma, looking at me. After some consideration I said that I want to help all needy people, but animals too, because they so often suffer and through no fault of their own. Grandma thought this was a good resolution, and I had made a good start with my care for the sick infants and children; I had also tried to help the soldiers and I should carry on in this way. But I thought also to myself that when I get to Berlin I will fight against war and every evil that men commit against mankind; I don't yet know just how, but the way forward will appear in due course. If for example someone learns to sing so wonderfully that the listeners are totally gripped by it, they won't so easily be brought round to kill someone else. Or if a person learns to paint like the artist Käthe Kollwitz or the Spanish Goya, so that his heart beats in sympathy with someone, he will hesitate before going to war. I also have indeed Uncle Bruno's army boots and César van Glabeke's helmet. And you can write books. There are many ways of using the arts. They would have to be masterpieces of course. But there are teachers and schools for that. Dear God, just give me good, worthy teachers, so that I don't have to leave a school again.

By the way, I have never told what Grandma said to the school governors when they approached her about me. She simply said, 'A teacher must not besmirch a pupil's innocent soul.'

22nd October, 1918

Now Austro-Hungary is falling apart. The Czechs and the Slovaks have turned their backs on the government and made themselves independent. A new country has been founded – Czechoslovakia. It has declared its independence from Austria. What Emperor Karl I proclaimed about a new, strong Austria has burst like a bubble. Fräulein Ella Gumprecht said at once, 'What the young Emperor said is of no use to the people. I always did say that he has always been weak, has let the Left take him by the nose and lead him a pretty dance. Mark my works, Frau Golz, they will shoot him the same as the Archduke Franz Ferdinand in Sarajevo.'

'Or the Tsar and his family,' cried Frau Schönfeld. All the ladies who were sitting at Grandma's bedside drinking coffee were absolutely overcome with despair. They couldn't believe that the end of the war was suddenly so near and that everything was turning out so differently from what they had expected. I eyed Grandma, who had sat up in bed and said, 'I want to get up! Piete, where is my dressing-gown? Bring me my stockings too. Where are my slippers?'

I brought dressing-gown, stockings and slippers, and helped Grandma out of bed. She was filled with new energy. Frau Schönfeld was dumbfounded, but cried out, 'What are you doing, dear Frau Golz? Why do you want to rush around out of bed?'

Grandma announced that she had finsihed with being ill; she

had no more time to lie in bed when such a thing had happened to Austria. Everything was probably getting higgledy-piggledy now at the station. She probably had a vision of all the soldiers from the trains running around in hopeless confusion and beating up officers or God knows what, and in the midst of it her Red Cross ladies facing overturned soup-kettles and smashed crockery. Fräulein Gumprecht and Frau Schönfeld did their best to persuade her to get back into bed; but Grandma was like an old general who tries to hold his troops together even at the last moment. I could hardly stop myself laughing, so full of energy was she all of a sudden. From this you could plainly see how weak she had become from this long illness; she has certainly lost ten pounds and her voice has no strength in spite of all the excitement. But nothing could be done about it; she got Frau Schönfeld to dress her while I had to hang the bed-clothes over three chairs to air. Then she tottered into the dining-room, sat down on the sofa and drew up a plan of campaign for preparing everything at the Red Cross canteen on the station in case of a collapse of the fronts. She wanted in the first place to speak to the Station Commander about the hiding-place for provisions, a foodstuff depot, from which fresh supplies could be drawn in secret. In this way the troops could be catered for right to the end without the supplies being plundered.

I thought Grandma was magnificent, and promised to act as a courier between the soup-kitchen and the secret food-depot. It was almost a high-point of morale as at the beginning of the war, when we were all in our enthusiasm ready to die for Germany. Only this time our enthusiasm is directed towards the last survivors of the war; they at least ought to get home safe and sound from the jaws of hell. That is what I thought, Dear Diary, and so did Grandma. But Fräulein Gumprecht still thinks our troops will be victorious and that their strength must be kept up to the last. When this became clear to me from their conversation I suddenly felt as if a black cloud was descending on us. I had only one desire then – to get out! Out!

I told Grandma I wanted to go and see Gretel in the yard, put on my hat and coat and ran out of the house towards the goods station, Schwarzer Weg and Baggen, where everything was soaked with rain and my shoes stuck in the mud and squelched when I drew them out again. It was already evening and dark. I was so terribly lonely!

302

23rd October, 1918

This afternoon there was a ring at the door. When I opened it, I found Hans Androwski standing there. He was very excited and stammered, 'Excuse me coming like this – there is a revolution in Vienna!'

I asked where he got this news from and he said that some soldiers passing through had brought it and that the whole town was full of it.

'And what now?' I said. I felt very stupid.

'There is certain to be a Soviet government', Androwski declared. 'The Emperor will have to go, and the government too of course. Where is Willi? Is he not on leave?' 'He won't be on leave for another fortnight,' I said. I was glad to be able to turn the conversation on to Gil, for the news that revolution had broken out in our brother country brought me to a state of total confusion. The Austrians always seem to be so peaceful, although I am well aware that they have fought for their country just as fiercely as we have. And they began with 'Red' general strikes in January. So now they are bringing about a revolution before us although we have a Karl Liebknecht and a Rosa Luxembourg. And Androwski was still standing at the door. I was nervous about discussing politics with him; he is so much cleverer than I. Dear Diary, I tell you, I understand hardly anything about politics. I knew the constitution by heart as a silly young twelve-year-old, but I know nothing about revolution. I have grown accustomed to this filthy war. I know how people can descend to the level of a louse; but I don't know how they can descend to these levels in a revolution. If there is shooting in the Russian revolution I would rather not have anything to do with it. No more bloodshed, only peace! Perhaps they would do harm to Grandma because she cared for soldiers day and night at the station. It's just inconceivable what I would do if Grandma were to die. That would be worse than losing Schneidemühl. Perhaps it is only people that make a 'Homeland'? A completely new thought! But yet I love our fields so much too, the quiet lakes with reedy banks, the sandy footpaths, the many glistening little rivers that flow so quickly, the villages with their humble cottages, the meadow flowers, the grass – Our seasons, it is said, are different from those in West Germany; the spring is lovelier, the summer brighter, the autumn richer, the winter so long, dark and full of snow. Meanwhile I was still leaning on the doorpost and Androwski was still outside longing for his friend Willi. I too was longing for Gil, but I would rather have listened to him playing the piano than be philosophising with Androwski about the revolution. Nevertheless we eventually went to sit in Gil's room; I had cut some bread for Androwski and taken some coffee from the stove, and Androwski said that it was only through a revolution that the country would be at peace again, because great armaments concerns like Krupps would be put out of business and all occasion for war would fade away. He thought also that the great estates of the gentry would be divided among the small farmers.

'The Adlig Liebenthal Domain too?' I asked. I thought of dear Frau Kenzler, who had said to her workers, 'Vote Left!'

Androwski gave the names of all the aristocracy and of the many great landowners in the province of Posen. I thought of the titled officers I have known; most of them have given their lives. Then Androwski found nothing more to say because I didn't know what more to say either, but just sat stuffing myself with bread and butter and jam. It was fresh plum jam that Gretel had made for us. Then suddenly I couldn't bear the longing for Gretel any more. Androwski took his departure and I whistled our old whistle out of the window of the lav. Gretel flew out of the door of the rear flat like a shot from a gun, so I had to laugh; it was as if for weeks she had done nothing but wait for this whistle.

'What are you doing?' I shouted.

'I? Nothing! And you?'

'Also nothing. I have just been talking with Androwski about the revolution in Vienna, you know. But now I am doing nothing. It will soon be dark, too.'

'Yes. It will very soon be dark. Have you any heating?'

'Yes. Two briquettes. Have you?'

'We are using wood for heating. I collected some fir-cones with Mother. Will you come down?'

'No – not to-day. Perhaps to-morrow.'

'Well, good-night then,' said Gretel.

I think she was very disappointed. I was disappointed too with myself. Good night.

28th October, 1918

Strummed continually on 'El Bobo'. And practised ballet. You really need ballet-shoes. How else can you stand on your points?

But if I put on my ancient wooden clogs, I can stand on my points, even walk through the room. I can do the 'bridges' quite well. It is a pity that I have to wait two years for ballet lessons.

29th October, 1918

Now General Ludendorff too has resigned his post. I am no longer particularly interested in that, but as I am carrying on with the war diary to please Mummy, I must take note of it. Fräulein Gumprecht, who burst in to us with the news, cried, 'You could knock me down with a feather! What do you say, dear Frau Golz? I would never have thought it of Ludendorff, no, never! A General Groener has succeeded him. Do you know Groener?' Grandma said General Groener was unknown to her. I just shrugged my shoulders and made as if I was leaving the house; but I just heard Fräulein Gumprecht calling out 'It's the hinterland that's to blame. It's a true stab in the back! And a stab in the back for our victorious troops!'

I had an appointment with the doctor and wanted under all circumstances to be certified fit; that would actually mean 'fit for war service', but for me it would mean 'fit for service in the children's home'!

With the certificate of fitness in my coat pocket I trotted straight off to the Municipal Home for Children and Infants and announced my return. What joy there was! I put on my second best apron, washed my hands, and rushed in to the babies; there were some very distressing ones there. Among the bigger children my Annemieken laughed to see me, and poor little Trudy with the wretched little plaits, who always looked as if a puff of wind could blow her away, whimpered with joy. I immediately sat all the big ones on their potties. I carried Annemieken around on my arm and swung her through the air so that she wriggled and laughed still more. I am happy, Dear Diary, terribly happy.

30th october, 1918

Letter from Mummy:-

Dear Mamma & children, my dear ones! Never would I have thought that the revolution in Russia would ever bring good fortune to my house. Just imagine: I have some pupils. Two Russian Jews. They came with a stream of refugees from Russia

305

and are officiating ministers in synagogues. During the journey (by God knows what roundabout route) they heard of my singing method, and want to develop their voices more. One of them – dark, muscular and strong – is called Lexandrowitsch; his voice is a wonderful bass; the other, short, thin and red-haired, is a tenor. He has to have special training because his whole being has suffered through the stress of the flight. I asked a reasonable price for lessons and, what do you think, they agreed to pay it without any hesitation. Presumably they are supported by the Jewish community in Berlin. As everything in Berlin is at sixes and sevens and one's life is no longer assured I have at last given notice to the office. My precious ones, I am free – free!!! Mamma, could you possibly advance me something for a new enamel plate: 'Training in house-and-concert-singing. Margarete Kuhr-Golz, voice trainer'? That would be a big help to me. Now I only hope that things are going reasonably well for you, and that you, Willi – Gil, have not suffered through the prevailing unruliness among the soldiers (it's a scandal!). Hold high the German honour, which has been dragged through the mud by political passions. What times, children! Let us stand fast in love!

Yours, Grete Kuhr

Mummy nearly always signs her letter with her name. Sometimes I think she is so enlightened that she considers words like 'mother' and 'mamma' unsuitable. She's certainly far in advance of us. Grandma will send her the money for the new enamel plate, then Mummy can re-establish the singing school. We rejoice with her, although we know she will find it hard.

'Your mother doesn't believe in God,' said Grandma this evening, as we were knitting socks for Uncle Bruno under the lamp.

I looked at Grandma in amazement. 'How do you know that?' I said. It made me quite ill to hear that Mummy must be an atheist.

'I have known it for a long time. Your grandfather didn't believe in God either. And I don't think your brother believes in God any more.' I was thunderstruck. Never had it occurred to me that Gil could no longer believe in God.

'Androwski doesn't believe in God either,' I declared at once. 'The war, all this evil has caused Androwski to believe only in the human spirit.'

'Like your mother,' said Grandma with a sigh. 'As if the war

306

should not lead us back to faith! In suffering you find the way back to God.' That wasn't at all clear to me. Why exactly should we find our way back to God in suffering when God makes no response to all our misfortune? Does he really love us? Where are the soldiers? In mass graves, aren't they? And no reunion in the homeland, oh no; no reunion. Empty words, lies. How I hate all that! But I must not shock Grandma; I can only discuss things carefully with her. So I said, 'You say – suffering, I cannot imagine that people find their way back to God through suffering. How can that be, Grandma?'

'I will tell you the dream that I had the night before last,' said Grandma and stopped knitting but sat quietly looking in front of her. 'I saw my father, your great grandfather Haber. He was very, very tall in the dream and stood high above me. I thought how good it was that I could pour out my troubles to him; he has been dead so many years and I had no-one to whom I could talk. Everything came back into my mind, all my troubles, and I couldn't help crying. Because Father in the dream was so terribly tall I couldn't put my arms round him but fell at his feet; they were bare and like white light. I kept calling, "Father! Father!" Then suddenly it wasn't Father, but the Lord Jesus; he stretched out his arms to me and lifted me up. And all was well. Do you understand? All, all was well.'

I gazed at Grandma; her face was wet with tears. And yet she looked happy. For a while I didn't dare say anything. Then I said, 'Where do the soldiers go to, Grandma? Does grass grow out of them – or an apple tree as with Herr Ribbek at Ribbek in the Havelland?' That is a poem that we learned at school and that I particularly like. Grandma said that grass and trees might well grow out of the body for it decays in the earth, but the soul enters Paradise. But I can't think how that can be; I was just unhappy and probably became feverish again. I thought of my dead babies, who were just like wax, and of Lieutenant Waldecker. Then it was as if my heart was bursting; I really crumpled up. I absolutely cannot imagine how souls can come to God. For example, a whole army corps has been wiped out in a single day; it's all the same whether it's a German Army corps, or an English, French, American or Italian or whatever. How do all these come at the same time, from the place where they died, to God?

Grandma answered that every one has a guardian angel, who was his companion during his lifetime. After death the angel leads the soul to heaven. There are to be found all the loved ones who have gone on before and they rejoice.

I wanted to know whether all souls are admitted to God's presence, even those who have done evil in their lifetime, for that seemed to me unjust.

Grandma answered, 'Perhaps not immediately to God; a soul must purify itself before it can look upon God. It must not be in any way unclean.' I asked how then there could be room in heaven for so many dead. Every one has died since the creation of the world. Their souls must be crammed into Paradise like sardines in a tin. Grandma thought there were no boundaries on the other side; we exist in eternity and infinity. Could I picture eternity? I said no, and asked whether there were flowers there.

'As many as you want.'

'And trees too?'

'Trees too. Everything that we have loved – only it is made of other material. You have to read the Revelation of John; there he has described everything.'

'But that was a dream!'

'He saw it in the same way that I saw the Lord in a dream'.

'And animals as well, Grandma?'

'I believe, animals as well,' said Grandma. 'Why should God not take pity on the animals? After all, they are his creatures. Yes, animals as well.'

I was not convinced, but the idea that there would be grass, flowers, trees and animals in heaven pleased me, and I was delighted with the thought that angels led the dead into Paradise. I pictured to myself how they also rescue the horses that have been shot to pieces; they could not take them suddenly by the bridle, but must just say gently, 'Hey, old horse, up you get!' and then the horse trots off obediently behind the angel, getting stronger and more lively all the time, and suddenly ceases to feel his body, is able to rise from the earth and flies higher and higher right up to heaven or whatever you may call it. And the poor Red Cross dogs collect their scattered bones and fly off behind them. I soon dreamed a whole story. After picturing grand processions of fallen soldiers, horses, dogs and so forth, I said to Grandma, 'Do you really believe in all that you have said?'

Grandma answered that she was as sure of it as that I was sitting in front of her. There had been too many miracles and mysteries in her life for her to have any doubts. I should have no doubts either.

But I do doubt, although according to the Bible I am to be

'God's prophet'. Anyway, that is how Grandma has described it. Dear God, please understand that because of your everlasting silence I sometimes think that you live in cloud-cuckoo-land. You could for example send the Egyptian plagues over the blood-drenched earth as a punishment! If you were to punish terribly those who are responsible for the war, then they would perhaps live again according to your commandments. So it says in the Old Testament anyway; we learnt it at school. At least give me a sign, just speak to me one single time. But plainly, dear God, so that I clearly understand you.

2nd November, 1918

The sailors mutinied in Kiel on 28th October because they thought Admiral Scheer was going to have the German High Seas Fleet sunk with all hands off the coast of England as a matter of honour. The battleships had been ordered to sail for the English coast where, with American help, they would be decisively defeated. The sailors hadn't the slightest desire to be sacrificed in the last minutes in a futile sea-fight. They wanted home.

Emperor Wilhelm is said to have established himself at Supreme Headquarters. Many people say that it would preserve Germany's honour if he decided to die a hero's death like a soldier at the Front before he is taken prisoner. They say that every true captain must go down with his ship and it is now time for the Emperor to do so.

The war is as good as over, but fighting still goes on. One day the last soldier will be killed. Oh God, who will that be?

3rd November, 1918

On 31st October the Austro-Hungarian Prime Minister Tisza was murdered in Budapest. The monarchy has collapsed. And our brothers-in-arms, the Turks, have concluded an armistice with the Entente. Some people suspect that the Turks will now turn against us. In this chaos you really can't find your way round any more. Thank God that I can look after sick children; it is peaceful in the wards in spite of the crying and squawking of the little ones.

I long for Gil and his music. It snowed for the first time to-night as I was walking home from the Infants' Home. First a little, then the flakes fell thicker and thicker, and in the end it turned into a real blizzard. Then I saw Gretel walking in front of me; her coat was quite white with snow. I was so pleased that I ran after her, caught her up and took her arm. She gave a little cry of fright. We walked home together. When we said good-night on the stairs Gretel said, 'Please sing to me once more Willi's lullaby with the guitar; you know the one – "A tree is sleeping by the door –"'

I asked her to come straight up to us; she could have supper with us; then I would sing for her all of Gil's songs that I can play on 'El Bobo'. So she came back to me for the first time. With Grandma we ate jacket potatoes with sweet and sour apple sauce, sat near the open stove, and I played and sang all Gil's songs. The glow in the stove door sometimes sparkled like red stars. It was like old times. I was so happy.

4th November, 1918

I shall soon finish my war diary. It will be the last war diary that I write in my life, for never again must there be a war, never again. If only the armistice agreements could just be signed, for fighting keeps flaring up again. On the south Front the Italians have even seized Trieste and are advancing on Innsbruck. They encounter no real resistance any more; it is said that the Austro-Hungarian army is in complete disarray. The Hungarians in particular want no more fighting, but want to get back to wives and children and rebuild their country. They want no more truck with the Emperor Karl.

What would have happened now to Lieutenant Joan von Yellenic? Perhaps he would have been shot under martial law as a fighter-pilot and also because he is a count. Frau Kenzler said it was now all over with the nobility; counts and barons might as well write off their titles. A good thing that in our game we buried Lieutenant von Yellenic; it was a presentiment of the things that are now happening in reality. But Gretel can't forget our game and yesterday she asked me in front of the open stove, 'When can we play again?'

I said cautiously. 'I have to work, you know. That only leaves time for eating and sleeping.'

'Don't you do any more training?' she said, meaning ballet.

I answered that I do training every day according to a special system, so that I don't lose touch with the ballet school later on in Berlin. I told her also that I want to invent dances which illustrate stories like a picture-book, something like the posters of Käthe Kollwitz or the drawings of Heinrich Zille or, for that matter, like Dürer's woodcut 'The Knight, Death and the devil.' For this I also needed Uncle Bruno's army boots and César van Glabeke's dented helmet. I simply lacked a real field uniform, then I would already have the first costume.

'Then are you going to dance the "Dying Swan" like Pavlova?' 'No,' I said.

Gretel opened her eyes wide. I asked whether she would go for a walk in the snow with me to the prisoner's cemetery on the next free day. She agreed enthusiastically at once.

'We will break off fir twigs in the wood and make a wreath out of them,' I suggested. 'We will lay it on some grave. That is then our signal, "Cease fire".' 'Yes,' said Gretel. 'Then the war is over.'

8th November, 1918

Revolution everywhere. It has just been reported that the Supreme High Command wanted to use the front-line troops against the rebellious sailors, workers and citizens. But it came to nothing. The soldiers refused to fire. Many soldiers have gone over to the revolution. Fraternization has occurred all over the place, with kissing and embracing. Everyone shouts, 'No more war!' The Bavarian King Ludwig III has fled from his capital. The revolution is at its wildest in Münich. An older revolutionary named Dr Kurt Eisner, together with the new People's Council, has proclaimed the 'Bavarian People's State'. Bavaria is no longer a kingdom. Where can Emperor Wilhelm, the Empress, the Crown Prince and the whole family of princes and princesses be? Perhaps they are all dead already. I feel as if I am in a roundabout which is going round quite fast.

People stand shoulder to shoulder in front of the newspaper office as at the beginning of the war. The latest news is written in blue pencil on printing paper. People discuss the events and sometimes there are disputes. A boy was crying loudly; he had said something that didn't please a newspaper reader and the latter had landed him one. I was sorry for the boy because he was so upset. I suddenly thought of Gil and would have loved to run to the Flying Corps barracks, especially as fresh soldiers kept appearing, coming down the streets arm in arm, singing. A lieutenant who hurried across the Neue Markt was no longer saluted by them. When he shouted at them he almost risked a fight. The lieutenant went deathly pale and had to pick up his own cap which one of the soldiers had knocked off his head. A few people shouted in their turn at the soldiers and called them traitors to the Fatherland. I went home as fast as I could and, as I was heating up water for coffee, I almost felt like crying. I was glad when there was a ring at the door and Androwski stood there. It used not to be his way to come to us so often but this time he seemed driven to us. He was pale and, with a smile, asked after Gil.

I answered that Gil was at the barracks and took Androwski into the bedroom because there was the big tiled stove and that's where it was warmest. I had already set out supper for Grandma and myself on a serviette. Androwski dropped into a chair and said, 'The war is dead! Long live the war.'

I didn't understand him and stared at him.

He wiped his hair (which was quite damp) off his forehead and said, 'Well, it's quite true. The new war is already at our door.'

I asked why he thought that.

He answered that in the first place 'The high-ups' will nip the revolution in the bud and secondly the victorious powers would impose such harsh peace terms that sooner or later a new war would be inevitable.

'But we will prevent it!' I cried indignantly.

'Who? You?' he asked.

I said, yes – definitely – I would fight against any new war, although not with a gun because I am not a man, but with other weapons. He would soon see!

At this moment there was another ring and when, trembling with anger, I flung the door of the flat open, there stood Gil. His uniform was open over his shirt, the buttons had been torn off taking bits of cloth with them, the shoulder-strips had likewise been torn off, his collar was dangling half-way down, and he had neither sword-belt nor forage cap.

'Androwski!' I shouted.

Androwski ran to us, and when he saw Gil standing at the door looking so sheepish and dishevelled, he began to laugh.

'Oh boy! Poor Kuhr!' he cried. 'What do I behold! The remains of our glorious army. Come in, you specimen of German youth; our Pliny has just made some coffee. Get your strength up! You will need it!'

Gil came into the room. He was obviously horribly embarrassed although he didn't know whether to grin or stay serious.

Then he decided to grin.

But I!!!

It was immediately obvious to me that I needed this torn uniform for my 'dead soldier' dance. This very uniform! This would complete that most important dance costume – Steel helmet, army boots, battle-dress! I would paint 'blood' on my forehead and nose with rouge – also on my hands. I began to take the uniform off Gil, but he clung to it desperately.

'Are you crazy!' he cried laughing. 'What's come over you! Let go at once!' When I didn't do this, he turned to Androwski and said, 'This is the limit! What does she want with my uniform, Hans?' And turning to me again and holding the coat against his chest, said 'Stop it now, you stupid child! You are tearing it still more!' He suddenly cried angrily, 'Yes, now she has actually torn the sleeve off! God in Heaven, I've got to return the uniform. What's the matter with you!'

Androwski was soon lying on the ground laughing, while I broke out into loud crying and held on all the more firmly to the uniform. I had to have it at all costs before Gil surrendered it to an idiotic quartermaster. What was left of it, anyway? It was more or less worthless now. But to me it was worth something, even worth a lot; and it made me so horribly sad. And I cried even louder and I tore and tugged at it with all my strength.

'Ow, help, Androwski!' cried Gil, turning round half in anger, half laughing. 'The beast has bitten me! What do you say? When she was little, she once happened to bite me; grandfather was still alive then, and he clocked her one. Tell me, do you think she has gone mad?'

I had finally seized the uniform and he was licking the tooth-marks on his arm.

'Let her have her fun!' said Androwski, drying his tears of laughter.

But I held the uniform pressed tight against me with both arms, sobbing bitterly – the poor, poor, German field uniform. I ran out of the room into the kitchen and threw myself down with it onto the basket of potatoes that Herr Kenzler had sent to-day. Grandma arrived from her duty at the station and was frightened to death when she heard me crying loudly while the other two were still laughing in the bedroom. She said, 'Child, child, calm yourself!'

But what could I say to her?

313

12th November, 1918

This is the latest. The German troops are on the retreat. General Field-Marshall Paul von Hindenburg has already proposed to bring the remainder of the army in an orderly manner back to the Homeland. All railway trains must be kept ready for this, good supplies and horses for the cavalry squadrons and the Army Service Corps. Guns and weapons are to be brought in good condition to Berlin.

Androwski has only one description for this – 'A load of Prussian bullshit!' and declares that the weapons will have to be handed over immediately to General Foch.

I didn't like to ask whether we were now well and truly beaten. We have clearly perished from a surfeit of victories. And to what purpose, to what purpose? How can a child understand it?

But perhaps I am no longer a child. Do you know something, Dear Diary? It could be that God has for a long time been sending us the great punishment and we haven't realised it; the punishment is the war. Perhaps God expected us from the beginning to end the war and we haven't done it, but have moreover kept on singing 'Now thank we all our God' as on the first day of the war. If that is so, then we have just kept on sinning.

13th November, 1918

The Emperor has abdicated!

The following decree from Reich Chancellor Prince Max von Boden appears in the newspaper:–

'His Majesty the Emperor and King has decided to renounce the throne. The Reich Chancellor will remain in office until all matters connected with His Majesty's abdication, the renunciation of the throne by his Imperial and Royal Highness the Crown Prince of the German Empire and of Prussia, and the establishment of the Regency, have been settled.'

Prince Max von Boden went on to nominate the Member of Parliament Ebert as the new Reich Chancellor before a so-called general election for a German National Constituent Assembly.

I studied the decree for ages before I understood it. Then I asked Gil who was this M.P. Ebert. Gil explained that Friedrich Ebert was a representative of the Social Democratic Party. He thought that Prince Max von Boden was also a Social Democrat; in any case he was an opponent of Emperor Wilhelm and had himself brought about the latter's resignation.

Grandma, who had managed to get a horse-meat sausage from Johr the butcher, already knew all about it. Nevertheless she said wearily, 'Give me the news-sheet!', placed her glasses on her nose, and read the announcement just as long and closely as I had. Finally she gave a deep sigh but said nothing. I didn't say anything either. And again, when we were having supper with Frau Schönfeld, Agatha Otter and Fräulein Gumprecht, eating baked potatoes and slices of sausage, we didn't say a word about the abdication of the Emperor. Gil and I exchanged glances. Gil was wearing his old, grey-striped jacket again. He had been playing the piano all the afternoon. I had only heard the last song, 'Sleep, sleep, do nothing but sleep, no waking, no dreaming –'

I was late getting back from the Children's Home. Half the people there are ill with 'flu. They say that 'flu has flared up all over the town; some people have died already.

14th November, 1918

We read to-day that Emperor Wilhelm and the Crown Prince have fled to Holland in exile. Gil shrugged his shoulders and whistled scornfully. We don't know whether the Empress has gone with him. Grandma thinks she obviously would; no wife would abandon her husband in such a situation. Now my former Girls' High School will no longer be called the Empress Augusta Victoria School.[17]

In the town people pass each other by with downcast eyes as if they were ashamed. Soldiers walk about only without rank and unit markings and without weapons; most of them stroll arm in arm, singing new, rousing songs. When I was coming home from the Children's Home in the evening, some soldiers intercepted me in Bahnhofstrasse, formed a chain and wouldn't let me through. They said, laughing, 'come on now, little Miss; we're interested in your opinion. What have you to say about "Willem"?' (They meant Emperor Wilhelm). I recognised one of them as Sergeant Friedrich and implored him to let me pass. He immediately set me free and accompanied me chivalrously to the door of my house. When we were parting, he said, 'Remember me to my friend Kuhr. I wish him good luck in Berlin!'

'I wish you good luck too. Where will you be going now?'

He looked at me with sparkling eyes. 'Home. Have you read the terms of the Armistice?'

'No!' I cried in surprise. 'Are they bad?'

'Even worse!' He drew a crumpled sheet of newspaper from his coat pocket. 'Keep this document of shame. It will astound you. We shall bleed to death.'

'We have already done that,' I murmured.

'Now our children will be affected. Do you know, we are just soldiers; but even we have enough brains to see that it is a pig-headed stupid business that will be settled over our heads. Damn it! It is not yet over, Miss Piete.'

I then read it all under the lamp. The members of the German Armistice Commission travelled in army cars to Compiègne in France and were received by Marshall Foch. Compiègne! At school they will now stick a pin with a black flag in the name. Suddenly they will be interested in the map again. The war is over. The agreement has been signed by Secretary of State Matthias Erzberger and his colleagues on the German side and by Marshall Foch and his other commanders on the French side. By this fighting was stopped on all fronts. Now all the bells should ring. Now all the flags should fly.

But it is all quiet! A saucepan of potatoes is boiling in the kitchen. From the station there echoes the creaking, clanging and clanking of military trains. It is night already. It has been snowing again. Now they would have good grounds for singing: 'There we'll meet again'. The retreat of the troops to Berlin has begun.

Grandma says that fully-laden hospital trains are coming from East Prussia; they are transferring the wounded to Mid-Germany. The 'flu is said to have broken out there too.

Oh no – how it is snowing!

28th November, 1918

Yesterday I walked a little way into the Sandsee woods to cut some spruce and other greenery for an Advent wreath. The snow lay quite deep already; winter has come early. My footprints were the only tracks in the snow apart from those of hares. I stayed at the edge of the wood. It was all quiet. The twigs would only with difficulty come away; sometimes I had to help them with grandfather's old hedge-cutters. On one slope I found some blue berries on juniper bushes and quite yellow-red sand-thorn panicles. It was difficult to carry it all home. It took Gretel and me over an hour to make a wreath; I used nearly a whole ball of string. The garland looks lovely; the berries shine out of the greenery like jewels.

To-morrow we will take it to the prisoners' cemetery because it is my day off. Gretel asked if we wouldn't do better to take it to our 'heroes' cemetery'. But I said, 'No – the others have no one to bring them a wreath.'

29th November, 1918

Grandma grumbled a bit when she heard that we intended to go all the way to the prisoners' cemetery and said we would get our feet wet in the snow. I put my slippers carefully at the back of the warm stove and looked into the oven to make sure everything was alright. There stood the blue tin can of coffee; so we were well prepared.

It was not still snowing, but everything was white, and the air misty and grey, a typical last-but-one day of November. Gretel trudged alongside me; she looked pretty, though, in her old thin coat. I looked at her sideways and declared, 'Your cheeks are blue with cold.' I rubbed her face with my woollen gloves till it was warm and rosy again.

The way to the prisoners' cemetery had never seemed so far to us; it was never-ending. Our shoes were soon full of snow. I could no longer feel my toes for cold. I had hung the wreath over my left shoulder; it pricked me in the face whenever I stumbled. We hardly made any headway for we sank half-way up to our knees in snow. Although we had started out before three o'clock, it was already beginning to get dark. The sun hadn't once been visible all day. Gretel said that many of the pupils at her council school were ill with 'flu; also two teachers were away. The school is to be closed for fear of infection. Gretel said I must on no account get 'flu because I have become so thin and couldn't offer enough resistance to the illness. I laughed and answered that I would however resist it with my energy; besides, I had no time to be ill, for the sake of the poor little ones in the Infants' Home.

'And for my sake too,' said Gretel, falling full length in the snow. We laughed because at least thirty crows were so startled by Gretel's downfall that they streaked, croaking and grumbling, across the snow field. 'Shall we soon be there?' asked Gretel. 'We have been so long on the way. Do you know the right path in the snow?'

I pointed ahead; there was already the first of the barbed wire

317

that surrounded the graves. The low mounds were hardly recognisable under the mass of white; only the black wooden crosses stuck out a bit. And the trees suddenly appeared much smaller because the lower parts of their trunks were buried in the snow; everything looked uncannily different. When we reached the fence we were amazed. So many crosses! We hadn't been here for a long time; and now the prisoners' cemetery had suddenly become so big – enormous!

'Look,' said Gretel, 'they lie there so still!'

What can they all have died from? But in fact typhus and influenza had been around; there had been many cases of dysentery too, and some perhaps died from home-sickness.

'Or hunger!' whispered Gretel.

'Or hunger!' I agreed sadly.

'And now?' Gretel eyed the thick expanse of barbed wire.

'The gate will be open,' I said consolingly, but when we reached the gate it was fastened with an iron chain on which a padlock hung. And the gate itself was covered in barbed wire.

Gretel thought she would never get over it; she would wait for me at the gate. She probably placed all her hope in my gymnastic ability. I was glad that I would be alone when I laid the wreath; perhaps I would not be able to help crying. I was looking for a particular grave that we had once seen long years before; I haven't forgotten it. Terrible that I can't forget impressions. So I climbed over the gate in spite of the barbed wire. While doing this I grazed the skin on my legs, but I quickly dragged myself on to the wooden parapet and jumped down. 'Wasn't so bad!' I assured Gretel, involuntarily softening my voice, although there was no-one else in the vicinity. 'Give me the wreath. And wait here!'

'I'll wait,' she whispered.

So many dead –! It was really already dark, but I could still read the names of the dead, not only Russians as at the beginning of the war, but also French and English. There were even names in strange lettering, perhaps Mohammedan. How did they come to be in our Schneidemühl camp? But then there was also the Frenchman's grave that I was looking for.

The snow had piled up so high between the graves that I almost fell when I struck a mound that I hadn't noticed. I gradually began to fear that I would not find the grave again. How on earth was I to distinguish it from the other graves? They were all just alike. In death all are, so to speak, just like the others; for this reason it will be quite right for me to wear, in my dance of the Spectre of War, a Belgian steel helmet. I prayed, 'Dear God, help me to find the grave. It was here before; it must still be here to-day – it must be!'

And there I was, standing right in front of it! On the bar of the cross, almost buried in a snow-drift, looked out the old wreath with glass beads. It had by now gone quite rusty. When I touched it a few thin hair-like pieces of wire broke off into dust. I tried to clear some of the snow from the wreath, and now a few pale beads appeared; most of them had certainly fallen off long before. But the upper border of the white enamel plate with its black lettering was still as good as new. I looked round at Gretel and held up my hand as a sign that I had found the right place. I saw her nod and I laid our green fir wreath on the mound.

Then I scraped the gaunt beaded wreath clear with my hands. Now the old enamel plate was clean.

À toi mes pensées
et mes larmes,
tous les jours.

Postscript

Now that you have finished reading Piete's wartime diary let's see how she fared later on.

Piete's mother, as you know, wanted to train her to help with the singing school in Berlin, but Piete had her heart set on becoming a dancer. Ever since she had persuaded her Uncle Bruno to give her his old army boots and sword and the Belgian soldier's helmet which he had picked up on the battlefield of Verdun she had been determined to use these in an anti-war dance that she would herself devise. She did indeed achieve this and the dance was among those for which she had become well-known on the Berlin stage in 1933 when Hitler came to power. It is an interesting side-line that she illustrated this dance in a 1987 television interview, quoting the soldier's name which was found on the helmet, with the result that a Belgian who saw the programme traced someone of that name whose grandfather had been killed at Verdun, and put him in touch with Jo Mihaly (as she then was).

But we must return to 1918–19, when Piete was still working in the sick children's home in Schneidemühl. After some two years of heart-rending experiences there she joined her mother in Berlin in 1920 and had singing lessons with her, but unknown to her mother, and with the help of money earned as a typist, she continued with dancing-lessons.

When in 1923 her dancing-master invited her to join in a touring engagement, she broke the news to her mother with a dramatic demonstration of her prowess as a ballet dancer. Mother was so impressed that she raised no objection. The grandmother, that outstanding character in the diary, raised no objection either, but could not quite stomach the family name being associated with this not altogether respectable career and that is why Piete adopted the name 'Jo Mihaly' which she used throughout the rest of her life. This name was derived from Hungarian gipsies and had been applied to herself by Piete in childhood games.

So began a period of travelling in Germany and other countries, appearing in cabarets, music-halls and circuses. Living and travelling with circus folk had a great appeal for her, but when her much-loved mother died in 1924 she felt the need for a time of quiet reflection and took to roaming the highways and byways of Germany with her guitar, getting a night's lodging in a farmhouse or barn in return for music and singing or helping the farmer's wife, or just sleeping under the stars – a time she describes as the happiest of her life.

After a while she joined two of her companions from the touring ballet in an engagement with the 'Three-town Theatre', (covering three small towns in Silesia). Here they performed solo and group dances and Jo was able to develop her talent for producing her own expressionist dances.

But this was a time of great poverty and distress in Germany with massive unemployment and inflation running completely out of control, resulting in vast numbers of homeless people roaming the country and a great number of suicides. (Do you remember brother Willi's serious-minded friend Androwski, who keeps popping up in the diary? He was one who, I am told, sadly took his own life). Mihaly, as I shall now call her, still felt herself at one with the 'tramps and vagabonds' and became associated with a 'Brotherhood of Wayfarers' initiated by one Gregor Gog, of the Christian Socialist Movement. Gog produced a magazine to which Mihaly contributed articles and poems, thus beginning to fulfil her other childhood ambition of becoming a writer. One of her first major publications was a novel about a gipsy family, 'Michael Arpad and his Child'; this came under the Nazi's ban when Hitler came to power.

What with the continuing poverty and distress around her and the horrifying activities of the Brownshirts, as the Nazis were at first known, Mihaly became more and more politically involved with the left-wing. At a later stage she saw the Communist Party as the only effective opposition to the Nazis but for the present her support went only as far as the Revolutionary Trades Union Movement, and it was through an important trade union official that she gained entry into the theatrical world of Berlin where she met, and in 1927 married, a prominent avant-garde actor, Leonard Steckel, who was a Jew.

Mihaly was soon developing her expressionist dances to a high level, including dances with an anti-war message and against persecution of the Jews. By the time Hitler came to full power

321

on 30th Jan 1933 she had made quite a name for herself but was having to take a rest from dancing, for her daughter Anja was born on 3rd February that year. They were then living in a left-wing artists' colony known as the 'Red Block' and before February was out the Nazis made a vicious raid on these flats, described in some detail by Mihaly in her 1987 television interview. Many of the residents were taken off to prisons and concentration camps and it was fortunate for the Steckels that Leonard was out at a rehearsal and that Jo, although at home with little Anja, was undergoing a minor operation at the hands of two doctors and so was spared.

A few months later, while Leonard was away on a theatrical tour, Jo was visited by an S.S. officer who was also a writer of cultural reviews in a Nazi paper called 'The Young German'. In the previous year he had highly praised Mihaly's dances and he now came with the authority of the Ministry of Propaganda to ask if she would become a 'cultural dancer' for the Nazis. She asked if she would be allowed free expression, continuing her dances against war and the persecution of the Jews; the answer was of course 'no' and she politely declined the offer. The officer, before leaving, very courteously but most emphatically advised her to leave the country as soon as she could – if possible the next day. A telephone call to her husband brought him home that night, and next day they were on their way to Zürich.

At the very moment of departure Leonard received a telegram from Zürich offering him a long-hoped-for theatrical engagement. In spite of this, however, life in Zürich presented tremendous difficulties, especially for Mihaly who was not allowed to enter into gainful employment. Her promising career as a dancer was virtually nipped in the bud, and the loss of all that Berlin life held for her was traumatic. But soon she became involved in work for the benefit of other emigrants, such as organising cultural activities for the many who were confined to internment camps, as well as working for their physical well-being.

In the years 1934–1938 Mihaly had just a few opportunities to appear on the stage. One of her dances was called 'Flower in the backyard', portraying a flower that withered through lack of sunlight, and on one occasion this called forth high praise from a Swiss poet, Albin Zollinger:–

'I have never before seen any dance so poetical...
In another time such talent would have broken through

322

> triumphantly, but to-day murderers stand at the
> gate of our temple and a gifted person like
> Jo Mihaly is like the "Flower in the back yard"'

A performance near the end of 1934 led to her being asked to take on the directorship of the New Choir of Zürich, a young people's choir of speech and movement connected with the Zürich Workers' Cultural Movement. This was a gift to her, allowing her to exercise her talents in dancing, voice training and writing. A serious heart attack forced her to give this up in 1938. In the meantine, increasing difficulties with the Swiss authorities owing to the growing threat from Germany had led the Steckels to think of the possibility of emigrating to America and, with the object of earning money for the voyage, Mihaly in 1937 had begun writing a novel. This was completed in 1938 and published in 1939, under the title 'My brother's keeper' (re-published in 1971 under the title 'Wanted: Stefan Varesku'). This book was very well received, but the outbreak of war destroyed all hope of America.

War-time in Zürich brought further difficulties but gave Mihaly opportunities for service in many directions. Soon after the end of the war she travelled with some difficulty to Frankfurt-am-Main, where she took part in the re-establishment of a free Germany as a member of the Free German Cultural Society, becoming also a member of the Frankfurt City Council and of the regional assembly which sat in Wiesbaden in preparation for the first post-war Reichstag.

In 1946 she suffered another break-down in health and returned to Zürich where her husband and daughter had remained. Three years later she went to live in Ascona, on the shore of Lake Maggiore, where she continued to write and to organise social and cultural activities for many years, especially for German emigrants like herself.

Much of Mihaly's post-war work in Germany had been undertaken as a member of the Communist Party, when those with whom she worked were true democrats and advocates of freedom, but when this ceased to be the case she left the Party in disgust. Many of her co-workers suffered under the Stalinist purges.

In answer to the final question in her 1987 television interview she says her guiding principle, in politics as in all life, may be summed up in the one word – love. Ever the same Piete!

Translator's Notes

1 *Page 2* Black, white and red were the colours of the German Imperial flag, as distinct from the black and white of the Prussian flag.

2 *Page 10* These brothers attended their mother's funeral in 1924, but refused to have anything more to do with Piete when, as Jo Mihaly, she married the Jewish actor Leonard Steckel in 1927.

3 *Page 23* I know that Liège is not in the Flemish part of Belgium, but the temptation of a rhyme with Emmich was irresistible.

4 *Page 44* This is clearly a mistake for the 'Bowes Castle' – see photograph of the Karlsruhe with the captured 'Bowes Castle', reproduced with the consent of Cassell from 'The Kaiser's Pirates' by John Walter. The accompanying report in that book states that the English ship was spotted at 16.00 on 18th August, hove-to after a short chase, and was sunk at 19.35 after the crew had been transferred to another ship, the 'Patagonia'. The discrepancy in date is hardly surprising, for it is unlikely that news disclosing the location of the 'Karlsruhe' would be released immediately.

5 *Page 46* This appears to be a man's name – Jo-an— and is the origin of the stage-name and pen-name – Jo Mihaly – adopted by Piete in later life.

6 *Page 75* Paul Dreier is mentioned again on 21st December, 1914, as having lost both his eyes, and the family's wine business is mentioned on 22nd April, 1918. It appears, from a photograph of this shop, that Paul was later able to continue the business.

7 *Page 77* The truth appears to be that the total number of 'Karlsruhe's victims had reached 13 or 14 by 23rd October. 'Karlsruhe' herself was destroyed on 4th November by an explosion of which the cause is unknown. Her commander (Köhler) was thanked by his victims on at least one occasion

for his 'courteous and generous treatment'. (Information from John Walter's 'The Kaiser's Pirates'.)

8   *Page 78* From a letter sent to the Emden's captain by the captain of H.M.S. Sydney (quoted in John Walter's 'The Kaiser's Pirates') –

Sir, I have the honour to request that in the name of humanity you now surrender your ship to me. In order to show how much I appreciate your gallantry, I will recapitulate the position. (1) You are ashore, 3 funnels and 1 mast down and most guns disabled. (2) You cannot leave this island, and my ship is intact. In the event of your surrendering, in which I venture to remind you is no disgrace but rather your misfortune, I will endeavour to do all I can for your sick and wounded and take them to hospital. I have the honour to be, Sir, your obedient servant. *John C. Y. Glossop, Captain.*

9   *Page 95* Piete and Gretel were not the only ones to visit this cemetery and tend the 'enemy' graves. I have a copy of a letter written by Piete (Jo Mihaly) in 1966 to the author of an article in a magazine circulated among Schneidemühl emigrants which evidently described similar activities.

10 *Page 116* The poem containing these lines is *Harzreise im Winter*.

11 *Page 141* I have located Willi's grave in the vast Uhlsdorf cemetery in Hamburg and find that the stone next to his is inscribed 'Die Familie Voss!'. Any connection with his 'marble queen'? A photograph of one of his songs dedicated to Charlotte Voss is included in this book.

12 *Page 167* Uncle Bruno (Dr. Bruno-Golz) later became a highly respected author of books on philosophy and history. He also assembled a valuable collection of art treasures which he presented to the town of Schneidermühl in 1943. Since the Russian attack on Schneidemühl in 1945 the whereabouts of this collection is unknown but is the subject of investigation by an emigrant from Schneidemühl now living in Bielefeld.

13 *Page 188* Hans Androwski did in fact take his own life during the desperate early post-war years.

14 *Page 188* A photograph of the official notification of this award is included.

15 *Page 209* My translation of a printed copy of Löns's diary reads thus:–

25th Sept, 1914. At 6 o'clock (p.m.) with my battalion.
Everyone resting, smoking, singing, laughing, yet in two
hours we go into the front firing-line. Pale crescent moon
in the south, sun setting peacefully above silvery haze,
casting warm shadows over the countryside. Horse transport snaking darkly along the roads. In the north, our
people firing at aircraft with shrapnel. Whole sky bright
with golden yellow clouds and flashes of light. Pea soup
(tastes good again). Tea, the lieutenant adds some
burgundy. A happy feeling and off into the line.

[Added in a stranger's handwriting – 'He was never to
return, was killed 26.9 near Loire. Honour to his
memory!' O.M.]

16 *Page 249* On the point of going to press I have received from
the Schneidemühler Heimatkreis in Cuxhaven further information about Werner Waldecker which includes the
following family notice of his death:

Den Tod fürs Vaterland starb infolge Absturzes
am 1. Dezember mein lieber, guter Sohn, unser
treuer Bruder, Neffe und Vetter

Werner Waldecker

Leutnant d. Res. in einem Feld-Art.-Regt,
kommandiert zu einer Flieger-Ers.-Abtlg. i. Schneidemühl
Inhaber des Eisernen Kreuzes.

BIELEFELD, im Dezember 1917.

In tiefem Schmerz:

Frau Elisabeth Waldecker
geb. Marten

Margarete Waldecker
Erich Waldecker
Leutnant im Inf.-Rgt. 131.

---

17 *Page 315* The school was re-named 'The Helene Lange
School'. Helene Lange (1848–1930) was one of the most
active and successful campaigners for higher education for
women in Germany.